SPANISH
Verbs

Second Edition

Christopher Kendris

B.S., M.S., Columbia University
M.A., Ph.D., Northwestern University

Former Assistant Professor
Department of French and Spanish
State University of New York at Albany

ESTAR - 156
SER - 273

BARRON'S

BARRON'S EDUCATIONAL SERIES, INC.

To my wife, Yolanda,
my two sons, Alex and Ted,
my daughters-in-law Tina and Francesca,
and my four grandsons, Alexander Bryan,
Daniel Patrick Christopher, Matthew David,
and Andrew Dimitri

with love

© Copyright 2001 by Barron's Educational Series, Inc.
Prior edition © Copyright 1990 by
Barron's Educational Series, Inc.
Adapted from *301 Spanish Verbs,* © Copyright 1982
by Barron's Educational Series, Inc.

All inquiries should be addressed to:
Barron's Educational Series, Inc.
250 Wireless Boulevard
Hauppauge, New York 11788

http://www.barronseduc.com

Library of Congress Catalog Card No. 00-044442

International Standard Book No. 0-7641-1357-7

Library of Congress Cataloging-in-Publication Data

Kendris, Christopher.
    Spanish verbs / by Christopher Kendris.—2nd ed.
        p.   cm.
    Adapted from: 301 Spanish verbs fully conjugated
in all the tenses. © 1982.
Includes indexes.
    ISBN 0-7641-1357-7
    1. Spanish Language—Verb—Tables. I. Kendris,
Christopher. 301 Spanish verbs fully conjugated in
all the tenses. II. Title.
PC4271 .K43 2001
468.2'421—dc21   00-044442

PRINTED IN CHINA
17 16 15 14 13 12 11

Contents

About the Author

Christopher Kendris has taught French and Spanish at Northwestern University, at the College of the University of Chicago, at Rutgers University, at the State University of New York at Albany, and at Schenectady County Community College. For several years he also taught French and Spanish at Farmingdale High School, Farmingdale, New York, where he was chairman of the Department of Foreign Languages.

Dr. Kendris received his B.S. and M.S. degrees at Columbia University in the City of New York and his M.A. and Ph.D. degrees at Northwestern University in Evanston, Illinois. He also earned two certificates with *Mention très Honorable* at the École Supérieure de Préparation et de Perfectionnement des Professeurs de Français à l'Étranger, Faculté des Lettres, Université de Paris.

Dr. Kendris is the author of many modern language books and workbooks, all of which have been published by Barron's Educational Series, Inc. All his French and Spanish books are listed on-line on the Internet, for example, on *webmaster@barronseduc.com,* on *amazon.com,* and other popular web sites.

Abbreviations

adj.	adjetivo (adjective)	*part. pr.*	participio de presente, participio activo, gerundio (present participle)
ant.	anterior		
comp.	compuesto (compound, perfect)		
		pas.	pasado, pasivo (past, passive)
e.g.	for example	*perf.*	perfecto (perfect)
fut.	futuro (future)	*perf. ind.*	perfecto de indicativo (present perfect indicative)
i.e.	that is, that is to say		
imp.	imperfecto (imperfect)		
ind.	indicativo (indicative)	*perf. subj.*	perfecto de subjuntivo (present perfect or past subjunctive)
inf.	infinitivo (infinitive)		
p.	page		
part.	participio (participle)	*plpf.*	pluscuamperfecto (pluperfect)
part. pas.	participio de pasado, participio pasivo (past participle)		

Introduction

This pocket reference of over 300 commonly used Spanish verbs for students, businesspeople, and travelers provides fingertip access to correct verb forms. This new, second edition of *Spanish Verbs* includes improvements and additional new material. It also provides an important, new feature—color as an aid to learning. In the front section of this book, rules regarding the use of verbs are made clearer by color highlights. In the body of the book, color takes the mystery out of conjugation. In all, the reader will find that color makes the entire book easier to use. *Buena suerte, estudiantes.*

Verb conjugations are usually found scattered in Spanish grammar books and they are difficult to find quickly when needed. Verbs have always been a major problem for students no matter what system or approach the teacher uses. You will master Spanish verb forms if you study this book a few minutes every day, especially the pages before and after the alphabetical listing of the 301 verbs.

I compiled this book in order to help make your work easier and at the same time to teach you Spanish verb forms systematically. It is a useful book because it provides a quick and easy way to find the full conjugation of many Spanish verbs.

The verbs included here are arranged alphabetically by infinitive at the top of each page. The book contains many common verbs of high frequency, both reflexive and non-reflexive, which you need to know. It also contains many other frequently used verbs that are irregular in some way. On page 310 I give you an additional 1,000 Spanish verbs that are conjugated in the same way as model verbs. If the verb you have in mind is not given, consult the list that begins on page 310. My other book, *501 Spanish verbs fully conjugated in all the tenses,* fourth edition, contains two hundred additional verbs and new features.

The subject pronouns have been omitted from the conjugations in order to emphasize the verb forms. I give you the subject pronouns on page xl. Turn to that page now and become acquainted with them.

The first thing to do when you use this book is to become familiar with it from cover to cover—in particular, the front and back pages where you will find valuable and useful information to make your work easier and more enjoyable. Take a minute right now and turn to the table of contents at the beginning of this book as I guide you in the following way:

(a)   Beginning on page vii I show you how to form a present participle regularly in Spanish, and I give you examples. I also give you the common irregular present participles and the many uses of the present participle.

(b)   Beginning on page ix I show you how to form a past participle regularly in Spanish, and I give you examples. I also give you the common irregular past participles and the many uses of the past participle.

(c)   Beginning on page xi you will find the principal parts of some important Spanish verbs. This is useful because if you know these you are well on your way to mastering Spanish verb forms.

(d)   Beginning on page xiii I give you a sample English verb conjugation so that you can get an idea of the way a verb is expressed in the English tenses. Many people do not know one tense from another because they have never learned the use of verb tenses in a systematic and organized way—not even in English! How can you know, for example, that you need the conditional form of a verb in Spanish when you want to say *"I would go* to the movies if . . ."* or the pluperfect tense in Spanish if you want to say *"I had gone . . . ?"* The sample English verb conjugation with the names of the tenses and their numerical ranking will help you to distinguish one tense from another so that you will know what tense you need to express a verb in Spanish.

(e)   On page xiv I begin a summary of meanings and uses of Spanish verb tenses and moods as related to English verb tenses and moods. That section is very important and useful because I separate the seven simple tenses from the seven compound tenses. I give you the name of each tense in Spanish and English starting with the present indicative, which I call tense number one because it is the tense most frequently used. I assign a number to each tense name so that you can fix each one in your mind and associate the tense names and numbers in their logical order. I explain briefly what each tense is, when you use it, and I give examples using verbs in sentences in Spanish and English. At the end of each tense I show you how to form that tense for regular verbs.

(f)   Beginning on page xxxiii I explain the Imperative, which is a mood, not a tense, and I give numerous examples using it.

(g)   Beginning on page xxxvi I explain briefly the progressive forms of tenses, and I give examples. I also note the future subjunctive and the future perfect subjunctive. I explain how these two rarely used tenses are formed, and I give examples of what tenses are used in place of them in informal writing and in conversation.

(h)   Beginning on page xxxvii I give you a summary of all the fourteen tenses in Spanish with English equivalents, which I have divided into the seven simple tenses and the seven compound tenses. After referring to that summary frequently, you will soon know that tense number 1 is the present indicative, tense number 2 is the imperfect indicative, and so on. I also explain how each compound tense is based on each simple tense. Try to see these two divisions as two frames, two pictures, with the seven simple tenses in one frame and the seven compound tenses in another frame. Place them side by side in your mind, and you will see how tense number 8 is related to tense number 1, tense number 9 to tense number 2, and so on. If you study the numerical arrangement of each of the seven simple tenses and associate the tense number with the tense name, you will find it very easy to learn the names of the seven compound tenses, how they rank numerically according to use, how they are formed, and when they are used. Spend at least ten minutes every day studying these preliminary pages to help you understand better the fourteen tenses in Spanish.

Finally, in the back pages of this book there are useful indexes: an index of English-Spanish verbs, an index of common irregular Spanish verb forms identified by infinitive, and a list of over 1,000 Spanish verbs that are conjugated like model verbs among the 301.

I sincerely hope that this book will be of some help to you in learning and using Spanish verbs.

CHRISTOPHER KENDRIS
B.S., M.S., M.A., Ph.D.

Formation of the Present and Past Participles in Spanish

Formation of the present participle in Spanish

A present participle is a verb form which, in English, ends in *-ing;* for example, *singing, eating, receiving.* In Spanish, a present participle is regularly formed as follows:

drop the **ar** of an **-ar** ending verb, like **cantar,** and add **ando:** **cantando**/singing

drop the **er** of an **-er** ending verb, like **comer,** and add **-iendo:** **comiendo**/eating

drop the **ir** of an **-ir** ending verb, like **recibir,** and add **iendo:** **recibiendo**/receiving

In English, a gerund also ends in **-ing,** but there is a distinct difference in use between a gerund and a present participle in English. In brief, it is this: in English, when a present participle is used as a noun it is called a gerund; for example, *Reading is good.* As a present participle in English, it would be used as follows: *While reading,* the boy fell asleep.

In the first example *(Reading is good), reading* is a gerund because it is the subject of the verb *is.* In Spanish, however, we do not use the present participle form as a noun to serve as a subject; we use the infinitive form of the verb: *Leer es bueno.*

Common irregular present participles

INFINITIVE	PRESENT PARTICIPLE
caer to fall	**cayendo** falling
conseguir to attain, to achieve	**consiguiendo** attaining, achieving
construir to construct	**construyendo** constructing
corregir to correct	**corrigiendo** correcting
creer to believe	**creyendo** believing
decir to say, to tell	**diciendo** saying, telling
despedirse to say good-bye	**despidiéndose** saying good-bye
destruir to destroy	**destruyendo** destroying
divertirse to enjoy oneself	**divirtiéndose** enjoying oneself
dormir to sleep	**durmiendo** sleeping
huir to flee	**huyendo** fleeing
ir to go	**yendo** going
leer to read	**leyendo** reading
mentir to lie (tell a falsehood)	**mintiendo** lying
morir to die	**muriendo** dying
oír to hear	**oyendo** hearing
pedir to ask (for), to request	**pidiendo** asking (for), requesting
poder to be able	**pudiendo** being able
reír to laugh	**riendo** laughing
repetir to repeat	**repitiendo** repeating

seguir	to follow	**siguiendo**	following
sentir	to feel	**sintiendo**	feeling
servir	to serve	**sirviendo**	serving
traer	to bring	**trayendo**	bringing
venir	to come	**viniendo**	coming
vestir	to dress	**vistiendo**	dressing
vestirse	to dress oneself	**vistiéndose**	dressing oneself

Uses of the present participle

1. To form the progressive tenses: **The Progressive Present** is formed by using **estar** in the present tense plus the present participle of the main verb you are using. **The Progressive Past** is formed by using **estar** in the imperfect indicative plus the present participle of the main verb you are using. (See pages xxxi–xxxii for a complete description of the uses and formation of the progressive tenses.)

2. To express vividly an action that occurred (preterit + present participle): *El niño entró llorando en la casa*/The little boy came into the house crying.

3. To express the English use of *by* + present participle in Spanish, we use the gerund form, which has the same ending as a present participle explained above: *Trabajando, se gana dinero*/By working, one earns (a person earns) money; *Estudiando mucho, Pepe recibió buenas notas*/By studying hard, Joe received good grades.

   Note that no preposition is used in front of the present participle (the Spanish gerund) even though it is expressed in English as *by* + present participle.

   Note, too, that in Spanish we use **al** + inf. (not + present part.) to express *on* or *upon* + present part. in English: *Al entrar en la casa, el niño comenzó a llorar*/Upon entering the house, the little boy began to cry.

4. To form the Perfect Participle: **habiendo hablado**/having talked.

Formation of the past participle in Spanish

A past participle is a verb form which, in English, usually ends in *-ed*: for example, *worked, talked, arrived,* as in *I have worked, I have* *talked, I have arrived.* There are many irregular past participles in English; for example, *gone, sung,* as in *She has gone, We have sung.* In Spanish, a past participle is regularly formed as follows:

drop the **ar** of an **-ar** ending verb, like **cantar,** add **-ado:** **cantado**/sung

drop the **er** of an **-er** ending verb, like **comer,** add **-ido: comido**/eaten

drop the **ir** of an **-ir** ending verb, like **recibir,** add **-ido: recibido**/received

Common irregular past participles

INFINITIVE		PAST PARTICIPLE	
abrir	to open	**abierto**	opened
caer	to fall	**caído**	fallen
creer	to believe	**creído**	believed
cubrir	to cover	**cubierto**	covered
decir	to say, to tell	**dicho**	said, told
descubrir	to discover	**descubierto**	discovered
deshacer	to undo	**deshecho**	undone
devolver	to return (something)	**devuelto**	returned (something)
escribir	to write	**escrito**	written
hacer	to do, to make	**hecho**	done, made
imponer	to impose	**impuesto**	imposed
imprimir	to print	**impreso**	printed
ir	to go	**ido**	gone
leer	to read	**leído**	read
morir	to die	**muerto**	died
oír	to hear	**oído**	heard
poner	to put	**puesto**	put
rehacer	to redo, to remake	**rehecho**	redone, remade
reír	to laugh	**reído**	laughed
resolver	to resolve, to solve	**resuelto**	resolved, solved
romper	to break	**roto**	broken
traer	to bring	**traído**	brought
ver	to see	**visto**	seen
volver	to return	**vuelto**	returned

Uses of the past participle

1. To form the seven compound tenses

2. To form the Perfect Infinitive: *haber hablado*/to have spoken

3. To form the Perfect Participle: *habiendo hablado*/having spoken

4. To serve as an adjective, which must agree in gender and number with the noun it modifies: *El señor Molina es muy respetado*/Mr. Molina is very respected. *La señora González es muy conocida*/Mrs. González is very well known.

5. To express the result of an action with **estar** and sometimes with **quedar** or **quedarse:** *La puerta está abierta*/The door is open; *Las cartas están escritas*/The letters are written; *Los niños se quedaron asustados*/The children remained frightened.

6. To express the passive voice with **ser:** *La ventana fue abierta por el ladrón*/The window was opened by the robber.

Principal Parts of Some Important Spanish Verbs

INFINITIVE	PRESENT PARTICIPLE	PAST PARTICIPLE	PRESENT INDICATIVE	PRETERIT
abrir	abriendo	abierto	abro	abrí
andar	andando	andado	ando	anduve
caber	cabiendo	cabido	quepo	cupe
caer	cayendo	caído	caigo	caí
conseguir	consiguiendo	conseguido	consigo	conseguí
construir	construyendo	construido	construyo	construí
corregir	corrigiendo	corregido	corrijo	corregí
creer	creyendo	creído	creo	creí
cubrir	cubriendo	cubierto	cubro	cubrí
dar	dando	dado	doy	di
decir	diciendo	dicho	digo	dije
descubrir	descubriendo	descubierto	descubro	descubrí
deshacer	deshaciendo	deshecho	deshago	deshice
despedirse	despidiéndose	despedido	me despido	me despedí
destruir	destruyendo	destruido	destruyo	destruí

INFINITIVE	PRESENT PARTICIPLE	PAST PARTICIPLE	PRESENT INDICATIVE	PRETERIT
devolver	devolviendo	devuelto	devuelvo	devolví
divertirse	divirtiéndose	divertido	me divierto	me divertí
dormir	durmiendo	dormido	duermo	dormí
escribir	escribiendo	escrito	escribo	escribí
estar	estando	estado	estoy	estuve
haber	habiendo	habido	he	hube
hacer	haciendo	hecho	hago	hice
huir	huyendo	huido	huyo	huí
ir	yendo	ido	voy	fui
irse	yéndose	ido	me voy	me fui
leer	leyendo	leído	leo	leí
mentir	mintiendo	mentido	miento	mentí
morir	muriendo	muerto	muero	morí
oír	oyendo	oído	oigo	oí
oler	oliendo	olido	huelo	olí
pedir	pidiendo	pedido	pido	pedí
poder	pudiendo	podido	puedo	pude
poner	poniendo	puesto	pongo	puse
querer	queriendo	querido	quiero	quise
reír	riendo	reído	río	reí
repetir	repitiendo	repetido	repito	repetí
resolver	resolviendo	resuelto	resuelvo	resolví
romper	rompiendo	roto	rompo	rompí
saber	sabiendo	sabido	sé	supe
salir	saliendo	salido	salgo	salí
seguir	siguiendo	seguido	sigo	seguí
sentir	sintiendo	sentido	siento	sentí
ser	siendo	sido	soy	fui
servir	sirviendo	servido	sirvo	serví
tener	teniendo	tenido	tengo	tuve
traer	trayendo	traído	traigo	traje
venir	viniendo	venido	vengo	vine
ver	viendo	visto	veo	vi
vestir	vistiendo	vestido	visto	vestí
volver	volviendo	vuelto	vuelvo	volví

Sample English Verb Conjugation

INFINITIVE **to eat**
PRESENT PARTICIPLE eating   *PAST PARTICIPLE* eaten

Tense no.	The seven simple tenses
1 *Present Indicative*	I eat, you eat, he (she, it) eats; we eat, you eat, they eat
	or: I do eat, you do eat, he (she, it) does eat; we do eat, you do eat, they do eat
	or: I am eating, you are eating, he (she, it) is eating; we are eating, you are eating, they are eating
2 *Imperfect Indicative*	I was eating, you were eating, he (she, it) was eating; we were eating, you were eating, they were eating
	or: I ate, you ate, he (she, it) ate; we ate, you ate, they ate
	or: I used to eat, you used to eat, he (she, it) used to eat; we used to eat, you used to eat, they used to eat
3 *Preterit*	I ate, you ate, he (she, it) ate; we ate, you ate, they ate
	or: I did eat, you did eat, he (she, it) did eat; we did eat, you did eat, they did eat
4 *Future*	I shall eat, you will eat, he (she, it) will eat; we shall eat, you will eat, they will eat
5 *Conditional*	I would eat, you would eat, he (she, it) would eat; we would eat, you would eat, they would eat
6 *Present Subjunctive*	that I may eat, that you may eat, that he (she, it) may eat; that we may eat, that you may eat, that they may eat
7 *Imperfect or Past Subjunctive*	that I might eat, that you might eat, that he (she, it) might eat; that we might eat, that you might eat, that they might eat

. Summary of Meanings and Uses of Spanish Verb Tenses and Moods as Related to English Verb Tenses and Moods

A verb is where the action is! A verb is a word that expresses an action (like *go, eat, write*) or a state of being (like *think, believe, be*). Tense means time. Spanish and English verb tenses are divided into three main groups of time: past, present, and future. A verb tense shows if an action or state of being took place, is taking place, or will take place.

Spanish and English verbs are also used in four moods, or modes. (There is also the Infinitive Mood, but we are not concerned with that here.) Mood has to do with the *way* a person regards an action or a state that he expresses. For example, a person may merely make a statement or ask a question—this is the Indicative Mood, which we use most of the time in Spanish and English. A person may say that he *would do* something if something else were possible or that he *would have done* something if something else had been possible—this is the Conditional Mood. A person may use a verb *in such a way* that he indicates a wish, a fear, a regret, a joy, a request, a supposition, or something of this sort—this is the Subjunctive Mood. The Subjunctive Mood is used in Spanish much more than in English. Finally, a person may command someone to do something or demand that something be done—this is the Imperative Mood.

There are six tenses in English: Present, Past, Future, Present Perfect, Past Perfect, and Future Perfect. The first three are simple tenses. The other three are compound tenses and are based on the simple tenses. In Spanish, however, there are fourteen tenses, seven of which are simple and seven of which are compound. The seven compound tenses are based on the seven simple tenses. In Spanish and English a verb tense is simple if it consists of one verb form, e.g., *estudio.* A verb tense is compound if it consists of two parts—the auxiliary (or helping) verb plus the past participle, e.g., *he estudiado.* See the Summary of verb tenses and moods in Spanish with English equivalents on page xxxvii. I have numbered each tense name for easy reference and recognition.

In Spanish there is also another tense that is used to express an action in the present. It is called the Progressive Present. It is used only if an action is actually in progress at the present time; for example, *Estoy leyendo*/I am reading (right now). It is formed by using the Present Indicative of *estar* plus the present participle of the verb. There is still another tense in Spanish that is used to express an action that was taking place in the past. It is called the Progressive Past. It is used if an action was actually in progress at a certain moment in the past; for example, *Estaba leyendo cuando mi hermano entró*/I was reading when my brother came in. The Progressive Past is formed by using the Imperfect Indicative of *estar* plus the present participle of the verb.

In the pages that follow, the tenses and moods are given in Spanish and the equivalent name or names in English are given in parentheses. Although some of the names given in English are not considered to be tenses (for there are only six), they are given for the purpose of identification as they are related to the Spanish names. The comparison includes only the essential points you need to know about the meanings and uses of Spanish verb tenses and moods as related to English usage. I shall use examples to illustrate their meanings and uses. This is not intended to be a treatise in detail. It is merely a summary. I hope you find it helpful.

Tense no.	The seven compound tenses
8 *Present Perfect or Past Indefinite*	I have eaten, you have eaten, he (she, it) has eaten; we have eaten, you have eaten, they have eaten
9 *Pluperfect Indic. or Past Perfect*	I had eaten, you had eaten, he (she, it) had eaten; we had eaten, you had eaten, they had eaten
10 *Past Anterior or Preterit Perfect*	I had eaten, you had eaten, he (she, it) had eaten; we had eaten, you had eaten, they had eaten
11 *Future Perfect or Future Anterior*	I shall have eaten, you will have eaten, he (she, it) will have eaten; we shall have eaten, you will have eaten, they will have eaten
12 *Conditional Perfect*	I would have eaten, you would have eaten, he (she, it) would have eaten; we would have eaten, you would have eaten, they would have eaten
13 *Present Perfect or Past Subjunctive*	that I may have eaten, that you may have eaten, that he (she, it) may have eaten; that we may have eaten, that you may have eaten that they may have eaten

| **14** *Pluperfect or Past Perfect Subjunctive* | that I might have eaten, that you might have eaten, that he (she, it) might have eaten; that we might have eaten, that you might have eaten, that they might have eaten |
| *Imperative or Command* | — eat, let him (her) eat; let us eat, let them eat |

THE SEVEN SIMPLE TENSES

Tense No. 1   Presente de Indicativo
(Present Indicative)

This tense is used most of the time in Spanish and English. It indicates:

(a) An action or a state of being at the present time.

EXAMPLES:

1. **Hablo** español. *I speak* Spanish.
   I am speaking Spanish.
   I do speak Spanish.
2. **Creo en** Dios. *I believe* in God.

(b) Habitual action.

EXAMPLES:

Voy a la biblioteca todos los días.
I go to the library every day.
I do go to the library every day.

(c) A general truth, something that is permanently true.

EXAMPLES:

1. Seis menos dos **son** cuatro.
   Six minus two *are* four.
2. El ejercicio **hace** maestro al novicio.
   Practice *makes* perfect.

(d) Vividness when talking or writing about past events.

EXAMPLES:

El asesino **se pone** pálido. **Tiene** miedo. **Sale** de la casa y **corre** a lo largo del río. The murderer *turns* pale. *He is* afraid. *He goes out* of the house and *runs* along the river.

(e) A near future.

EXAMPLES:
1. Mi hermano **llega** mañana.
   My brother *arrives* tomorrow.
2. ¿**Escuchamos** un disco ahora?
   Shall we *listen* to a record now?

(f) An action or state of being that occurred in the past and *continues up to the present*. In Spanish this is an idiomatic use of the present tense of a verb with **hace,** which is also in the present.

EXAMPLES:
Hace tres horas que **miro** la televisión.
I have been watching television for three hours.

(g) The meaning of *almost* or *nearly* when used with **por poco.**

EXAMPLES:
Por poco me **matan.**
They almost *killed* me.

This tense is regularly formed as follows:
Drop the **-ar** ending of an infinitive, like **hablar,** and add the following endings: **o, as, a; amos, áis, an**
You then get: hablo, hablas, habla;
            hablamos, habláis, hablan

Drop the **-er** ending of an infinitive, like **beber,** and add the following endings: **o, es, e; emos, éis, en**
You then get: bebo, bebes, bebe;
            bebemos, bebéis, beben

Drop the **-ir** ending of an infinitive, like **recibir,** and add the following endings: **o, es, e; imos, ís, en**
You then get: recibo, recibes, recibe;
            recibimos, recibís, reciben

Tense No. 2   Imperfecto de Indicativo
             (Imperfect Indicative)

This is a past tense. Imperfect suggests incomplete. The imperfect tense expresses an action or a state of being that was continuous in the past and its completion is not indicated. This tense is used, therefore, to express:

(a) An action that was going on in the past at the same time as another action.

EXAMPLE:
Mi hermano **leía** y mi padre **hablaba.**
My brother *was reading* and my father *was talking.*

(b) An action that was going on in the past when another action occurred.

> EXAMPLE:
> Mi hermana **cantaba** cuando yo entré.
> My sister *was singing* when I came in.

(c) An action that a person did habitually in the past.

> EXAMPLE:
> 1. Cuando **estábamos** en Nueva York, **íbamos** al cine todos los sábados.
>   When *we were* in New York, *we went* to the movies every Saturday.
>   When *we were* in New York, *we used to go* to the movies every Saturday.
> 2. Cuando **vivíamos** en California, **íbamos** a la playa todos los días.
>   When *we used to live* in California, *we would go* to the beach every day.
>
> NOTE: In this last example, *we would go* looks like the conditional, but it is not. It is the imperfect tense in this sentence because habitual action in the past is expressed.

(d) A description of a mental, emotional, or physical condition in the past.

> EXAMPLES:
> 1. (mental condition)   **Quería** ir al cine.
>   I *wanted* to go to the movies.
>
> Common verbs in this use are **creer, desear, pensar, poder, preferir, querer, saber, sentir.**
> 2. (emotional condition)   **Estaba** contento de verlo.
>   I *was* happy to see him.
> 3. (physical condition)   Mi madre **era** hermosa cuando **era** pequeña.
>   My mother *was* beautiful when she *was* young.

(e) The time of day in the past.

> EXAMPLES:
> 1. ¿Qué hora **era?**
>   What time *was* it?
> 2. **Eran** las tres.
>   *It was* three o'clock.

(f) An action or state of being that occurred in the past and *lasted for a certain length of time* prior to another past action. In English it is usually translated as a pluperfect tense and is formed with *had been* plus the present participle of the verb you are using. It is like the special use of the presente de indicativo explained in the above section in paragraph (f), except that the action or state of being no longer exists at present. This is an idiomatic use of the imperfect tense of a verb with **hacía**, which is also in the imperfect.

EXAMPLE:

Hacía tres horas que **miraba** la televisión cuando mi hermano entró.
I had been watching television for three hours when my brother came in.

(g) An indirect quotation in the past.

EXAMPLE:

Present: Dice que **quiere** venir a mi casa.
               He says *he wants to come* to my house.

Past: Dijo que **quería** venir a mi casa.
               He said *he wanted* to come to my house.

This tense is regularly formed as follows:

Drop the -ar ending of an infinitive, like **hablar,** and add the following endings: aba, abas, aba; ábamos, abais, aban

You then get: hablaba, hablabas, hablaba;
                  hablábamos, hablabais, hablaban

The usual equivalent in English is: I was talking OR I used to talk OR I talked; you were talking OR you used to talk OR you talked, etc.

Drop the -er ending of an infinitive, like **beber,** or the -ir ending of an infinitive, like **recibir,** and add the following endings: ía, ías, ía; íamos, íais, ían

You then get: bebía, bebías, bebía;
                  bebíamos, bebíais, bebían
                  recibía, recibías, recibía;
                  recibíamos, recibíais, recibían

The usual equivalent in English is: I was drinking OR I used to drink OR I drank; you were drinking OR you used to drink OR you drank, etc.; I was receiving OR I used to receive OR I received; you were receiving OR you used to receive OR you received, etc.

Verbs irregular in the imperfect indicative:

ir/to go   iba, ibas, iba; (I was going, I used to go, etc.)
             íbamos, ibais, iban

ser/to be   era, eras, era; (I was, I used to be, etc.)
             éramos, erais, eran

ver/to see   veía, veías, veía; (I was seeing, I used to see, etc.)
             veíamos, veíais, veían

Tense No. 3   Pretérito
(Preterit)

This tense expresses an action that was completed at some time in the past.

EXAMPLES:

1. Mi padre **llegó** ayer.
   My father *arrived* yesterday.
   My father *did arrive* yesterday.
2. María **fue** a la iglesia esta mañana.
   Mary *went* to church this morning.
   Mary *did go* to church this morning.
3. ¿Qué **pasó?**
   What *happened?*
   What *did happen?*
4. **Tomé** el desayuno a las siete.
   I *had* breakfast at seven o'clock.
   I *did have* breakfast at seven o'clock.
5. **Salí** de casa, **tomé** el autobús y **llegué** a la escuela a las ocho.
   I *left* the house, I *took* the bus and I *arrived* at school at eight o'clock.

In Spanish, some verbs that express a mental state have a different meaning when used in the preterit.

EXAMPLES:

1. La **conocí** la semana pasada en el baile.
   I *met* her last week at the dance.
   (**Conocer,** which means *to know* or *be acquainted with,* means *met,* that is, introduced to for the first time, in the preterit.)
2. **Pude** hacerlo.
   I *succeeded* in doing it.
   (**Poder,** which means *to be able,* means *succeeded* in the preterit.)
3. **No pude** hacerlo.
   I *failed* to do it.
   (**Poder,** when used in the negative in the preterit, means *failed* or *did not succeed.*)
4. **Quise** llamarle.
   I *tried* to call you.
   (**Querer,** which means *to wish* or *want,* means *tried* in the preterit.)
5. **No quise** hacerlo.
   I *refused* to do it.
   (**Querer,** when used in the negative in the preterit, means *refused.*)
6. **Supe** la verdad.
   I *found out* the truth.
   (**Saber,** which means *to know,* means *found out* in the preterit.)

7. **Tuve** una carta de mi amigo Roberto.

   I received a letter from my friend Robert.

   (**Tener,** which means *to have,* means *received* in the preterit.)

This tense is regularly formed as follows:

Drop the -ar ending of an infinitive, like **hablar,** and add the following endings: **é, aste, ó; amos, asteis, aron**

You then get: **hablé, hablaste, habló;**
               hablamos, hablasteis, hablaron

The usual equivalent in English is: I talked OR I did talk; you talked OR you did talk, etc. OR I spoke OR I did speak; you spoke OR you did speak, etc.

Drop the **-er** ending of an infinitive, like **beber,** or the **-ir** ending of an infinitive, like **recibir,** and add the following endings: **í, iste, ió; imos, isteis, ieron**

You then get: **bebí, bebiste, bebió;**
               bebimos, bebisteis, bebieron
               recibí, recibiste, recibió;
               recibimos, recibisteis, recibieron

The usual equivalent in English is: I drank OR I did drink; you drank OR you did drink, etc.; I received OR I did receive, etc.

Tense No. 4   **Futuro**
              (Future)

In Spanish and English, the future tense is used to express an action or a state of being that will take place at some time in the future.

EXAMPLES:

1. Lo **haré.**

   I shall do it.

   I will do it.

2. **Iremos** al campo la semana que viene.

   We shall go to the country next week.

   We will go to the country next week.

Also, in Spanish the future tense is used to indicate:

(a) Conjecture regarding the present.

EXAMPLES:

1. ¿Qué hora **será?**

   I wonder what time it is.

2. ¿Quién **será** a la puerta?

   Who *can that be* at the door?

   I wonder who is at the door.

(b) Probability regarding the present.

EXAMPLES:

1. **Serán** las cinco.
   It is probably five o'clock.
   It must be five o'clock.
2. **Tendrá** muchos amigos.
   He probably has many friends.
   He must have many friends.
3. María **estará** enferma.
   Mary *is probably* sick.
   Mary *must be* sick.

(c) An indirect quotation.

EXAMPLE:

María dice que **vendrá** mañana.
Mary says that she *will come* tomorrow.

Finally, remember that the future is never used in Spanish after *si* when *si* means *if*.

This tense is regularly formed as follows:

Add the following endings to the whole infinitive: **é, ás, á; emos, éis, án**

Note that these Future endings happen to be the endings of **haber** in the present indicative: **he, has ha; hemos, habéis, han.** Also note the accent marks on the Future endings, except for **emos.**

You then get: **hablaré, hablarás, hablará;**
hablaremos, hablaréis, hablarán
beberé, beberás, beberá;
beberemos, beberéis, beberán
recibiré, recibirás, recibirá;
recibiremos, recibiréis, recibirán

Tense No. 5   **Potencial Simple**
(Conditional)

The conditional is used in Spanish and in English to express:

(a) An action that you *would do* if something else were possible.

EXAMPLE:

Iría a España si tuviera dinero.
I would go to Spain if I had money.

(b) A conditional desire. This is a conditional of courtesy.

EXAMPLE:

Me **gustaría** tomar una limonada.
I would like (I should like) to have a lemonade . . . (if you are willing to let me have it.)

(c) An indirect quotation.

EXAMPLES:

1. María **dijo** que **vendría** mañana.

   Mary *said* that she *would come* tomorrow.

2. María **decía** que **vendría** mañana.

   Mary *was saying* that she *would come* tomorrow.

3. María **había dicho** que **vendría** mañana.

   Mary *had said* that she *would come* tomorrow.

(d) Conjecture regarding the past.

EXAMPLE:

¿Quién **sería**?

I wonder who that was.

(e) Probability regarding the past.

EXAMPLE:

Serían las cinco cuando salieron.

It was probably five o'clock when they went out.

This tense is regularly formed as follows:

Add the following endings to the whole infinitive:

ía, ías, ía; íamos, íais, ían

> Note that these conditional endings are the same endings of the
> imperfect indicative for **-er** and **-ir** verbs.

You then get: hablar**ía**, hablar**ías**, hablar**ía**;
hablar**íamos**, hablar**íais**, hablar**ían**

beber**ía**, beber**ías**, beber**ía**;
beber**íamos**, beber**íais**, beber**ían**

recibir**ía**, recibir**ías**, recibir**ía**;
recibir**íamos**, recibir**íais**, recibir**ían**

The usual translation in English is: I would talk, you would talk, etc.; I
would drink, you would drink, etc.; I would receive, you would receive,
etc.

Tense No. 6   **Presente de Subjuntivo**
              (Present Subjunctive)

The subjunctive mood is used in Spanish much more than in English. In
Spanish the present subjunctive is used:

(a) To express a command in the **usted** or **ustedes** form, either in the
affirmative or negative.

EXAMPLES:

1. **Siéntese** Vd. *Sit down.*

2. **No se siente** Vd. *Don't sit down.*

3. **Cierren** Vds. la puerta. *Close* the door.

4. **No cierren** Vds. la puerta. *Don't close* the door.

5. **Dígame** Vd. la verdad. *Tell me* the truth.

(b) To express a negative command in the familiar form **(tú).**

EXAMPLES:

1. **No te sientes.** *Don't sit down.*

2. **No entres.** *Don't come in.*

3. **No duermas.** *Don't sleep.*

4. **No lo hagas.** *Don't do it.*

(c) To express a negative command in the second plural **(vosotros).**

EXAMPLES:

1. **No os sentéis.** *Don't sit down.*

2. **No entréis.** *Don't come in.*

3. **No durmáis.** *Don't sleep.*

4. **No lo hagáis.** *Don't do it.*

(d) To express a command in the first person plural, either in the affirmative or negative **(nosotros).**

EXAMPLES:

1. **Sentémonos.** *Let's sit down.*

2. **No entremos.** *Let's not go in.*

See also **Imperativo** (Imperative) farther on.

(e) After a verb that expresses some kind of wish, insistence, preference, suggestion, or request.

EXAMPLES:

1. *Quiero* que María lo **haga.**
   I want Mary to do it.
   NOTE: In this example, English uses the infinitive form, *to do.* In Spanish, however, a new clause is needed introduced by *que* because there is a new subject, María. The present subjunctive of *hacer* is used (haga) because the main verb is *Quiero,* which indicates a wish. If there were no change in subject, Spanish would use the infinitive form, as we do in English, for example, *Quiero hacerlo*/I want to do it.

2. *Insisto* en que María lo **haga.**
   I insist that Mary *do* it.

3. *Prefiero* que María lo **haga.**
   I prefer that Mary *do* it.

4. *Pido* que María lo **haga.**
   I ask that Mary *do* it.

NOTE: In examples 2, 3, and 4 here, English also uses the subjunctive form *do.* Not so in example no. 1, however.

(f) After a verb that expresses doubt, fear, joy, hope, sorrow, or some other emotion. Notice in the following examples, however, that the subjunctive is not used in English.

EXAMPLES:
1. *Dudo* que María lo **haga.**
   I doubt that Mary *is doing* it.
   I doubt that Mary *will do* it.
2. *No creo* que María **venga.**
   I don't believe (I doubt) that Mary *is coming.*
   I don't believe (I doubt) that Mary *will come.*
3. *Temo* que María **esté** enferma.
   I fear that Mary *is* ill.
4. *Me alegro* de que **venga** María.
   I'm glad that Mary *is coming.*
   I'm glad that Mary *will come.*
5. *Espero* que María no **esté** enferma.
   I hope that Mary *is* not ill.

(g) After certain impersonal expressions that show necessity, doubt, regret, importance, urgency, or possibility. Notice, however, that the subjunctive is not used in English in some of the following examples.
EXAMPLES:
1. *Es necesario que* María lo **haga.**
   It is necessary for Mary to do it.
   It is necessary that Mary *do* it.
2. *No es cierto que* María **venga.**
   It is doubtful (not certain) that Mary *is coming.*
   It is doubtful (not certain) that Mary *will come.*
3. *Es lástima que* María **no venga.**
   It's too bad (a pity) that Mary *isn't coming.*
4. *Es importante que* María **venga.**
   It is important for Mary to come.
   It is important that Mary *come.*
5. *Es preciso que* María **venga.**
   It is necessary for Mary to come.
   It is necessary that Mary *come.*
6. *Es urgente que* María **venga.**
   It is urgent for Mary to come.
   It is urgent that Mary *come.*

(h) After certain conjunctions of time, such as, **antes (de) que, cuando, en cuanto, después (de) que, hasta que, mientras,** and the like. The subjunctive form of the verb is used when introduced by any of these time conjunctions if the time referred to is either indefinite or is expected to take place in the future. However, if the action was completed in the past, the indicative mood is used.

EXAMPLES:

1. Le hablaré a María cuando **venga.**

   I shall talk to Mary when she *comes.*

2. Vámonos antes (de) que **llueva.**

   Let's go before *it rains.*

3. En cuanto la **vea** yo, le hablaré.

   As soon as *I see her,* I shall talk to her.

4. Me quedo aquí hasta que **vuelva.**

   I'm staying here until *he returns.*

NOTE: In the above examples, the subjunctive is not used in English.

(i) After certain conjunctions that express a condition, negation, purpose, such as, **a menos que, con tal que, para que, a fin de que, sin que, en caso (de) que,** and the like. Notice, however, that the subjunctive is not used in English in the following examples.

   EXAMPLES:

   1. Démelo con tal que **sea** bueno.

      Give it to me provided that *it is* good.

   2. Me voy a menos que **venga.**

      I'm leaving unless *he comes.*

(j) After certain adverbs, such as, **acaso, quizá,** and **tal vez.**

   EXAMPLE:

   Acaso **venga** mañana.

   Perhaps *he will come* tomorrow.

   Perhaps *he is coming* tomorrow.

(k) After **aunque** if the action has not yet occurred.

   EXAMPLE:

   Aunque María **venga** esta noche, no me quedo.

   Although Mary *may come* tonight, I'm not staying.

   Although Mary *is coming* tonight, I'm not staying.

(l) In an adjectival clause if the antecedent is something or someone that is indefinite, negative, vague, or nonexistent.

   EXAMPLES:

   1. Busco un libro que **sea** interesante.

      I'm looking for a book that *is* interesting.

      NOTE: In this example, *que* (which is the relative pronoun) refers to *un libro* (which is the antecedent). Since *un libro* is indefinite, the verb in the following clause must be in the subjunctive *(sea).* Notice, however, that the subjunctive is not used in English.

2. ¿Hay alguien aquí que **hable** francés?

   Is there anyone here who *speaks* French?

   NOTE: In this example, *que* (which is the relative pronoun) refers to *alguien* (which is the antecedent). Since *alguien* is indefinite and somewhat vague—we do not know who this anyone might be—the verb in the following clause must be in the subjunctive *(hable)*. Notice, however, that the subjunctive is not used in English.

3. No hay nadie que **pueda** hacerlo.

   There is no one who *can* do it.

   NOTE: In this example, *que* (which is the relative pronoun) refers to *nadie* (which is the antecedent). Since *nadie* is nonexistent, the verb in the following clause must be in the subjunctive *(pueda)*. Notice, however, that the subjunctive is not used in English.

(m) After **por más que** or **por mucho que**.

   EXAMPLES:

   1. **Por más que hable usted,** no quiero escuchar.

      No matter how much you talk, I don't want to listen.

   2. **Por mucho que se alegre,** no me importa.

      No matter how glad he is, I don't care.

(n) After the expression **ojalá (que),** which expresses a great desire. This interjection means *would to God!* or *may God grant!* . . . It is derived from the Arabic, *ya Allah!* (Oh, God!)

   EXAMPLE:

   ¡Ojalá que vengan mañana!

   Would to God that they come tomorrow!

   May God grant that they come tomorrow!

   How I wish that they would come tomorrow!

   If only they would come tomorrow!

Finally, remember that the present subjunctive is never used in Spanish after *si* when *si* means *if.*

The present subjunctive of regular verbs and many irregular verbs is normally formed as follows:

Go to the present indicative, 1st pers. sing., of the verb you have in mind, drop the ending **o,** and

   for an **-ar** ending type, add: **e, es, e; emos, éis, en**

   for an **-er** or **-ir** ending type, add: **a, as, a; amos, áis, an**

As you can see, the characteristic vowel in the present subjunctive endings for an **-ar** type verb is **e** in the six persons.

As you can see, the characteristic vowel in the present subjunctive endings for an **-er** or **-ir** type verb is **a** in the six persons.

Since the present subjunctive of some irregular verbs is not normally formed as stated above *(e.g.,* **dar, dormir, haber, ir, secar, sentir, ser, tocar)**, you must look up the verb you have in mind in the alphabetical listing in this book.

Tense No. 7 Imperfecto de Subjuntivo
             (Imperfect Subjunctive)

This past tense is used for the same reasons as the presente de subjuntivo—that is, after certain verbs, conjunctions, impersonal expressions, etc., which were explained and illustrated above in tense no. 6. The main difference between these two tenses is the time of the action.

If the verb in the main clause is in the present indicative or future or present perfect indicative or imperative, the *present subjunctive* or the *present perfect subjunctive* is used in the dependent clause—provided, of course, that there is some element that requires the use of the subjunctive.

However, if the verb in the main clause is in the imperfect indicative, preterit, conditional, or pluperfect indicative, the *imperfect subjunctive* (this tense) or *pluperfect subjunctive* is ordinarily used in the dependent clause—provided, of course, that there is some element that requires the use of the subjunctive.

> EXAMPLES:
> 1. *Insistí* en que María lo **hiciera**.
>   I insisted that Mary *do* it.
> 2. Se lo *explicaba* a María **para que lo comprendiera**.
>   I was explaining it to Mary *so that she might understand it.*

Note that the imperfect subjunctive is used after **como si** to express a condition contrary to fact.

> EXAMPLE:
> Me habla como si **fuera** un niño.
> He speaks to me as if *I were* a child.

> NOTE: In this last example, the subjunctive is used in English also for the same reason.

Finally, note that **quisiera** (the imperfect subjunctive of **querer**) can be used to express politely a wish or desire, as in *I should like:* **Quisiera hablar ahora**/I should like to speak now.

The imperfect subjunctive is regularly formed as follows:

For all verbs, drop the **ron** ending of the 3rd pers. pl. of the preterit and add the following endings:

ra, ras, ra;	OR	se, ses, se;
ramos, rais, ran		semos, seis, sen

The only accent mark on the forms of the imperfect subjunctive is on the 1st pers. pl. form (**nosotros**) and it is placed on the vowel which is right in front of the ending **ramos** or **semos.**

THE SEVEN COMPOUND TENSES

Tense No. 8 Perfecto de Indicativo
          (Present Perfect Indicative)

This is the first of the seven compound tenses that follow here. This tense expresses an action that took place at no definite time in the past. It is also called the past indefinite. It is a compound tense because it is formed with the present indicative of **haber** (the auxiliary or helping verb) plus the past participle of your main verb. Note the translation into English in the examples that follow. Then compare this tense with the **perfecto de subjuntivo,** which is tense no. 13. For the seven simple tenses of **haber** (which you need to know to form these seven compound tenses), see **haber** listed alphabetically among the 301 verbs in this book.
   EXAMPLES:
   1. (Yo) **he hablado.**
      I have spoken.
   2. (Tú) no **has venido** a verme.
      You have not come to see me.
   3. Elena **ha ganado** el premio.
      Helen *has won* the prize.

Tense No. 9 Pluscuamperfecto de Indicativo
          (Pluperfect *or* Past Perfect Indicative)

This is the second of the compound tenses. In Spanish and English, this past tense is used to express an action that happened in the past *before* another past action. Since it is used in relation to another past action, the other past action is ordinarily expressed in the preterit. However, it is not always necessary to have the other past action expressed, as in example 2 on the following page.

In English, this tense is formed with the past tense of *to have* (had) plus the past participle of your main verb. In Spanish, this tense is formed with the imperfect indicative of **haber** plus the past participle of the verb you have in mind. Note the translation into English in the examples that follow. Then compare this tense with the **pluscuamperfecto de subjuntivo**, which is tense no. 14. For the seven simple tenses of **haber** (which you need to know to form these seven compound tenses), see **haber** listed alphabetically among the 301 verbs in this book.

EXAMPLES:

1. Cuando **llegué a casa, mi hermano había salido.**
   When I *arrived* home, my brother *had gone out.*
   NOTE: *First,* my brother went out; *then,* I arrived home. Both actions happened in the past. The action that occurred in the past *before* the other past action is in the pluperfect, and in this example, it is *my brother had gone out* (**mi hermano había salido).**
   NOTE also that **llegué** *(I arrived)* is in the preterit because it is an action that happened in the past and it was completed.

2. Juan lo **había perdido** en la calle.
   John *had lost* it in the street.
   NOTE: In this example, the pluperfect indicative is used even though no other past action is expressed. It is assumed that John *had lost* something *before* some other past action.

Tense No. 10   Pretérito Anterior *or* Pretérito Perfecto
              (Past Anterior *or* Preterit Perfect)

This is the third of the compound tenses. This past tense is compound because it is formed with the preterit of **haber** plus the past participle of the verb you are using. It is translated into English like the pluperfect indicative, which is tense no. 9. This tense is not used much in spoken Spanish. Ordinarily, the pluperfect indicative is used in spoken Spanish (and sometimes even the simple preterit) in place of the past anterior.

This tense is ordinarily used in formal writing, such as history and literature. It is normally used after certain conjunctions of time, e.g., **después que, cuando, apenas, luego que, en cuanto.**

EXAMPLE:

Después que **hubo hablado,** salió.
After *he had spoken,* he left.

Tense No. 11 Futuro Perfecto
(Future Perfect or Future Anterior)

This is the fourth of the compound tenses. This compound tense is formed with the future of **haber** plus the past participle of the verb you have in mind. In Spanish and in English, this tense is used to express an action that will happen in the future *before* another future action. In English, this tense is formed by using *shall have* or *will have* plus the past participle of the verb you have in mind.

EXAMPLE:

María llegará mañana y **habré terminado** mi trabajo.
Mary will arrive tomorrow and *I shall have finished* my work.

NOTE: *First,* I shall finish my work; *then,* Mary will arrive. The action that will occur in the future *before* the other future action is in the **Futuro perfecto,** and in this example it is (yo) **habré terminado mi trabajo.**

Also, in Spanish the future perfect is used to indicate conjecture or probability regarding recent past time.

EXAMPLES:

1. María **se habrá acostado.**
   Mary *has probably gone to bed.*
   Mary *must have gone to bed.*
2. José **habrá llegado.**
   Joseph *has probably arrived.*
   Joseph *must have arrived.*

Tense No. 12 Potencial Compuesto
(Conditional Perfect)

This is the fifth of the compound tenses. It is formed with the conditional of **haber** plus the past participle of your main verb. It is used in Spanish and English to express an action that you *would have done* if something else had been possible; that is, you would have done something *on condition* that something else had been possible.

In English it is formed by using *would have* plus the past participle of the verb you have in mind. Observe the difference between the following example and the one given for the use of the potencial simple.

EXAMPLE:

Habría ido a España si hubiera tenido dinero.
I would have gone to Spain if I had had money.

Also, in Spanish the conditional perfect is used to indicate probability or conjecture in the past.

EXAMPLES:
1. **Habrían sido** las cinco cuando salieron.
   It must have been five o'clock when they went out.
   (Compare this with the example given for the simple conditional.)
2. ¿Quién **habría sido**?
   Who *could that have been?* (*or* I wonder *who that could have been.*)
   (Compare this with the example given for the simple conditional.)

Tense No. 13 Perfecto de Subjuntivo
(Present Perfect *or* Past Subjunctive)

This is the sixth of the compound tenses. It is formed by using the present subjunctive of **haber** as the helping verb plus the past participle of the verb you have in mind.

If the verb in the main clause is in the present indicative, future, or present perfect tense, the present subjunctive is used *or* this tense is used in the dependent clause—provided, of course, that there is some element that requires the use of the subjunctive.

The present subjunctive is used if the action is not past. However, if the action is past, this tense (present perfect subjunctive) is used, as in the examples given below.

EXAMPLES:
1. María duda que yo le **haya hablado** al profesor.
   Mary doubts that *I have spoken* to the professor.
2. Siento que tú no **hayas venido** a verme.
   I am sorry that you *have not come* to see me.
3. Me alegro de que Elena **haya ganado** el premio.
   I am glad that Helen *has won* the prize.

In these three examples, the auxiliary verb **haber** is used in the present subjunctive because the main verb in the clause that precedes is one that requires the subjunctive mood of the verb in the dependent clause.

Tense No. 14 Pluscuamperfecto de Subjuntivo
(Pluperfect *or* Past Perfect Subjunctive)

This is the seventh of the compound tenses. It is formed by using the imperfect subjunctive of **haber** as the helping verb plus the past participle of your main verb.

The translation of this tense into English is often like the pluperfect indicative.

If the verb in the main clause is in a past tense, this tense is used in the dependent clause—provided, of course, that there is some element that requires the use of the subjunctive.

EXAMPLES:
1. Sentí mucho que **no hubiera venido** María.
   I was very sorry that Mary *had not come.*
2. Me alegraba de que **hubiera venido** María.
   I was glad that Mary *had come.*
3. No creía que María **hubiera llegado.**
   I did not believe that Mary *had arrived.*

So much for the seven simple tenses and the seven compound tenses. Now, let's look at the Imperative Mood.

Imperativo
(Imperative *or* Command)

The imperative mood is used in Spanish and in English to express a command. We saw earlier that the subjunctive mood is used to express commands in the **Ud.** and **Uds.** forms, in addition to other uses of the subjunctive mood.

Here are other points you ought to know about the imperative.

(a) An indirect command or deep desire expressed in the third pers. sing. or pl. is in the subjunctive. Notice the use of *Let* or *May* in the English translations. **Que** introduces this kind of command.
   EXAMPLES:
1. ¡Que lo **haga** Jorge!   4. ¡Que **entre** Roberto!
   Let George do it!   *Let* Robert enter!
2. ¡Que Dios se lo **pague!**   5. ¡Que **salgan!**
   May God reward you!   *Let* them leave!
3. ¡Que **vengan** pronto!   6. ¡Que **entren** las muchachas!
   Let them come quickly!   *Let* the girls come in!

(b) In some indirect commands, **que** is omitted. Here, too, the subjunctive is used.
   EXAMPLE:
   ¡Viva el presidente!
   Long live the president!

(c) The verb form of the affirmative sing. familiar (**tú**) is the same as the 3rd pers. sing. of the present indicative when expressing a command.
   EXAMPLES:
1. ¡**Entra** pronto!   2. ¡**Sigue** leyendo!
   Come in quickly!   *Keep on* reading!
                                    Continue reading!

(d) There are some exceptions, however, to (c) above. The following verb forms are irregular in the affirmative sing. imperative (**tú** form only).

di (decir)	**sal** (salir)	**val** (valer)
haz (hacer)	**sé** (ser)	**ve** (ir)
he (haber)	**ten** (tener)	**ven** (venir)
pon (poner)		

(e) In the affirmative command, 1st per. pl., instead of using the present subjunctive hortatory command, **vamos a** *(Let's* or *Let us)* + **inf.** may be used.

EXAMPLES:

1. **Vamos a** comer/Let's eat.
   or: **Comamos** (1st pers. pl., present subj., hortatory command)
2. **Vamos a** cantar/Let's sing.
   or: **Cantemos** (1st pers. pl., present subj., hortatory command)

(f) In the affirmative command, 1st pers. pl., **vamos** may be used to mean
Let's go: **Vamos** al cine/Let's go to the movies.

(g) However, if in the negative *(Let's not go),* the present subjunctive of **ir** must be used: **No vayamos** al cine/Let's not go to the movies.

(h) Note that **vámonos** (1st pers. pl. of **irse,** imperative) means *Let's go,*
or
Let's go away, or *Let's leave.* See (m) below.

(i) Also note that **no nos vayamos** (1st pers. pl. of **irse,** present subjunctive) means *Let's not go,* or *Let's not go away,* or *Let's not leave.*

(j) The imperative in the affirmative familiar plural (**vosotros, vosotras**) is formed by dropping the final **r** of the inf. and adding **d.**

EXAMPLES:

1. **¡Hablad!**/Speak!   3. **¡Id!**/Go!
2. **¡Comed!**/Eat!   4. **¡Venid!**/Come!

(k) When forming the affirmative familiar plural (**vosotros, vosotras**) imperative of a reflexive verb, the final **d** on the inf. must be dropped before the reflexive pronoun **os** is added, and both elements are joined to make one word.

EXAMPLES:

1. **¡Levantaos!**/Get up!   2. **¡Sentaos!**/Sit down!

(l) Referring to (k) above, when the final **d** is dropped in a reflexive verb ending in **-ir,** an accent mark must be written on the **i.**

EXAMPLES:

1. **¡Vestíos!**/Get dressed!   2. **¡Divertíos!**/Have a good time!

(m) When forming the 1st pers. pl. affirmative imperative of a reflexive verb, the final **s** must drop before the reflexive pronoun **os** is added, and both elements are joined to make one word. This requires an accent mark on the vowel of the syllable that was stressed before **os** was added.

EXAMPLE:

Vamos + nos changes to: **¡Vámonos!**/*Let's go!* or *Let's go away!* or *Let's leave!* See (h) above.

(n) All negative imperatives in the familiar 2nd pers. sing. (**tú**) and plural (**vosotros, vosotras**) are expressed in the present subjunctive.

EXAMPLES:

1. **¡No corras (tú)!**/Don't run!
2. **¡No corráis (vosotros** or **vosotras!**)/Don't run!
3. **¡No vengas (tú)!**/Don't come!
4. **¡No vengáis (vosotros** or **vosotras!**)/Don't come!

(o) Object pronouns (direct, indirect, or reflexive) with an imperative verb form in the **affirmative** are attached to the verb form.

EXAMPLES:

1. **¡Hágalo (Ud.)!**/Do it!
2. **¡Díganoslo (Ud.)!**/Tell it to us!
3. **¡Dímelo (tú)!**/Tell it to me!
4. **¡Levántate (tú)!**/Get up!
5. **¡Siéntese (Ud.)!**/Sit down!
6. **¡Hacedlo (vosotros, vosotras)!**/Do it!
7. **¡Démelo (Ud.)!**/Give it to me!

(p) Object pronouns (direct, indirect, or reflexive) with an imperative verb form in the **negative** are placed in front of the verb form. Compare the following examples with those given in (o) above:

EXAMPLES:

1. **¡No lo haga (Ud.)!**/Don't do it!
2. **¡No nos lo diga (Ud.)!**/Don't tell it to us!
3. **¡No me lo digas (tú)!**/Don't tell it to me!
4. **¡No te levantes (tú)!**/Don't get up!
5. **¡No se siente (Ud.)!**/Don't sit down!
6. **¡No lo hagáis (vosotros, vosotras)!**/Don't do it!
7. **¡No me lo dé (Ud.)!**/Don't give it to me!

(q) Note that in some Latin American countries the 2nd pers. pl. familiar (**vosotros, vosotras**) forms are avoided. In place of them, the 3rd pers. pl. **Uds.** forms are customarily used.

The Progressive forms of tenses: a note

(1) In Spanish, there are also progressive forms of tenses. They are the Progressive Present and the Progressive Past.

(2) The **Progressive Present** is formed by using *estar* in the present tense plus the present participle of your main verb; e.g., *Estoy hablando*/I am talking, i.e., I am (in the act of) talking (right now).

(3) The **Progressive Past** is formed by using *estar* in the imperfect indicative plus the present participle of your main verb; e.g., *Estaba hablando*/I was talking, i.e., I was (in the act of) talking (right then).

(4) The progressive forms are generally used when you want to emphasize or intensify an action; if you don't want to do that, then just use the simple present or simple imperfect; e.g., say *Hablo*, not *Estoy hablando;* or *Hablaba*, not *Estaba hablando*.

(5) Sometimes *ir* is used instead of *estar* to form the progressive tenses; e.g., *Va hablando*/He (she) keeps right on talking, *Iba hablando*/He (she) kept right on talking. Note that they do not have the exact same meaning as *Está hablando* and *Estaba hablando*. See (2) and (3) above.

(6) Also, at times *andar, continuar, seguir,* and *venir* are used as helping verbs in the present or imperfect indicative tenses plus the present participle to express the progressive forms: *Los muchachos andaban cantando*/The boys were walking along singing; *La maestra seguía leyendo a la clase*/The teacher kept right on reading to the class.

The Future Subjunctive and the Future Perfect Subjunctive: a note

The future subjunctive and the future perfect subjunctive exist in Spanish, but they are rarely used. Nowadays, instead of using the future subjunctive, one uses the present subjunctive or the present indicative. Instead of using the future perfect subjunctive, one uses the future perfect indicative or the present perfect subjunctive. However, if you are curious to know how to form the future subjunctive and the future perfect subjunctive in Spanish, the following is offered:

(1) To form the future subjunctive, take the third person plural of the preterit of any Spanish verb and change the ending **-ron** to **re, res, re; remos, reis, ren.** An accent mark is needed as shown below on the first person plural form to preserve the stress.

EXAMPLES:

amar	amare, amares, amare;
	amáremos, amareis, amaren

comer	comiere, comieres, comiere;
	comiéremos, comiereis, comieren
dar	diere, dieres, diere;
	diéremos, diereis, dieren
haber	hubiere, hubieres, hubiere;
	hubiéremos, hubiereis, hubieren
hablar	hablare, hablares, hablare;
	habláremos, hablareis, hablaren
ir *or* ser	fuere, fueres, fuere;
	fuéremos, fuereis, fueren

(2) Let's look at the forms of **amar** above to see what the English translation is of this tense:

(que) yo amare, (that) I love . . .
(que) tú amares, (that) you love . . .
(que) Vd. (él, ella) amare, (that) you (he, she) love . . .
(que) nosotros (-tras) amáremos, (that) we love . . .
(que) vosotros (-tras) amareis, (that) you love . . .
(que) Vds. (ellos ellas) amaren, (that) you (they) love . . .

(3) To form the future perfect subjunctive, use the future subjunctive form of **haber** (shown above) as your auxiliary plus the past participle of the verb you have in mind.

EXAMPLES:

(que) hubiere amado, hubieres amado, hubiere amado;
(que) hubiéremos amado, hubiereis amado, hubieren amado

English translation: (that) I have *or* I shall have loved, (that) you have *or* will have loved, etc.

Summary of verb tenses and moods in Spanish with English equivalents

	Los siete tiempos simples		Los siete tiempos compuestos	
	The seven simple tenses		*The seven compound tenses*	
Tense No.	Tense Name		Tense No.	Tense Name
1	**Presente de indicativo** *Present indicative*		8	**Perfecto de indicativo** *Present perfect indicative*
2	**Imperfecto de indicativo** *Imperfect indicative*		9	**Pluscuamperfecto de indicativo** *Pluperfect or Past perfect indicative*

3	**Pretérito**	10	**Pretérito anterior (Pret. perfecto)**
	Preterit		*Past anterior or Preterit perfect*
4	**Futuro**	11	**Futuro perfecto**
	Future		*Future perfect or Future anterior*
5	**Potencial simple**	12	**Potencial compuesto**
	Conditional		*Conditional perfect*
6	**Presente de subjuntivo**	13	**Perfecto de subjuntivo**
	Present subjunctive		*Present perfect or Past subjunctive*
7	**Imperfecto de subjuntivo**	14	**Pluscuamperfecto de subjuntivo**
	Imperfect subjunctive		*Pluperfect or Past perfect subjunctive*

The imperative is not a tense; it is a mood.

In Spanish, there are 7 simple tenses and 7 compound tenses. A simple tense means that the verb form consists of one word. A compound tense means that the verb form consists of two words (the auxiliary verb and the past participle). The auxiliary verb is also called a helping verb and in Spanish, as you know, it is any of the 7 simple tenses of **haber** *(to have)*.

Each compound tense is based on each simple tense. The 14 tenses given on the previous page are arranged in the following logical order:

Tense number 8 is based on Tense number 1; in other words, you form the **Perfecto de indicativo** by using the auxiliary **haber** in the **Presente de indicativo** plus the past participle of the verb you are dealing with.

Tense number 9 is based on Tense number 2; in other words, you form the **Pluscuamperfecto de indicativo** by using the auxiliary **haber** in the **Imperfecto de indicativo** plus the past participle of the verb you are dealing with.

Tense number 10 is based on Tense number 3; in other words, you form the **Pretérito anterior** by using the auxiliary **haber** in the **Pretérito** plus the past participle of the verb you are dealing with.

Tense number 11 is based on Tense number 4; in other words, you form the **Futuro perfecto** by using the auxiliary **haber** in the **Futuro** plus the past participle of the verb you are dealing with.

Tense number 12 is based on Tense number 5; in other words, you form the **Potencial compuesto** by using the auxiliary **haber** in the **Potencial simple** plus the past participle of the verb you are dealing with.

Tense number 13 is based on Tense number 6; in other words, you form the **Perfecto de subjuntivo** by using the auxiliary **haber** in the **Presente de subjuntivo** plus the past participle of the verb you are dealing with.

Tense number 14 is based on Tense number 7; in other words, you form the **Pluscuamperfecto de subjuntivo** by using the auxiliary **haber** in the **Imperfecto de subjuntivo** plus the past participle of the verb you are dealing with.

What does all the above mean? This: If you ever expect to know or even recognize the meaning of any of the 7 compound tenses, you certainly have to know **haber** in the 7 simple tenses. If you do not, you cannot form the 7 compound tenses. This is one perfect example to illustrate that learning Spanish verb forms is a cumulative experience. Look up **haber** where it is listed alphabetically among the 301 verbs in this book and study the seven simple tenses.

An Easy Way to Form the Seven Compound Tenses in Spanish

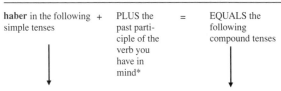

haber in the following + simple tenses	PLUS the past participle of the verb you have in mind*	=	EQUALS the following compound tenses

1. Presente de indicativo
2. Imperfecto de indicativo
3. Pretérito
4. Futuro
5. Potencial simple
6. Presente de subjuntivo
7. Imperfecto de subjuntivo

8. Perfecto de indicativo
9. Pluscuamperfecto de indicativo
10. Pretérito anterior *(Pret. Perfecto)*
11. Futuro perfecto
12. Potencial compuesto
13. Perfecto de subjuntivo
14. Pluscuamperfecto de subjuntivo

*To know how to form a past participle, see p. ix.

Subject Pronouns

(a) The subject pronouns for all verb forms on the following pages have been omitted in order to emphasize the verb forms, which is what this book is all about.

(b) The subject pronouns that have been omitted are as follows:

singular	*plural*
yo	**nosotros (nosotras)**
tú	**vosotros (vosotras)**
Ud. (él, ella)	**Uds. (ellos, ellas)**

The Spanish Alphabet and the New System of Alphabetizing

The Association of Spanish Language Academies met in Madrid for its 10th Annual Congress on April 27, 1994 and voted to eliminate **CH** and **LL** as separate letters of the Spanish alphabet.

Words beginning with **CH** will be listed alphabetically under the letter **C**. Words beginning with **LL** will be listed alphabetically under the letter **L**. The two separate letters historically have had separate headings in dictionaries and alphabetized word lists. Spanish words that contain the letter **ñ** are now alphabetized accordingly with words that do not contain the tilde over the **n**. For example, the Spanish system of alphabetizing used to place the word **andar** before **añadir** because the **ñ** would fall in after all words containing **n**. According to the new system, **añadir** is placed before **andar** because alphabetizing is now done letter by letter. The same applies to words containing **rr.**

The move was taken to simplify dictionaries, to make Spanish more compatible with English, and to aid translation and computer standardization. The vote was 17 in favor, 1 opposed, and 3 abstentions. Ecuador voted "no" and Panama, Nicaragua, and Uruguay abstained. The source of this information is on page 16, International Section, of *The New York Times* newspaper, Sunday edition, May 1, 1994.

Subject Pronouns

singular	*plural*
yo	**nosotros (nosotras)**
tú	**vosotros (vosotras)**
Ud. (él, ella)	**Uds. (ellos, ellas)**

The Seven Simple Tenses		The Seven Compound Tenses	
Singular	Plural	Singular	Plural
1 presente de indicativo		8 perfecto de indicativo	
abro	abrimos	he abierto	hemos abierto
abres	abrís	has abierto	habéis abierto
abre	abren	ha abierto	han abierto
2 imperfecto de indicativo		9 pluscuamperfecto de indicativo	
abría	abríamos	había abierto	habíamos abierto
abrías	abríais	habías abierto	habíais abierto
abría	abrían	había abierto	habían abierto
3 pretérito		10 pretérito anterior	
abrí	abrimos	hube abierto	hubimos abierto
abriste	abristeis	hubiste abierto	hubisteis abierto
abrió	abrieron	hubo abierto	hubieron abierto
4 futuro		11 futuro perfecto	
abriré	abriremos	habré abierto	habremos abierto
abrirás	abriréis	habrás abierto	habréis abierto
abrirá	abrirán	habrá abierto	habrán abierto
5 potencial simple		12 potencial compuesto	
abriría	abriríamos	habría abierto	habríamos abierto
abrirías	abriríais	habrías abierto	habríais abierto
abriría	abrirían	habría abierto	habrían abierto
6 presente de subjuntivo		13 perfecto de subjuntivo	
abra	abramos	haya abierto	hayamos abierto
abras	abráis	hayas abierto	hayáis abierto
abra	abran	haya abierto	hayan abierto
7 imperfecto de subjuntivo		14 pluscuamperfecto de subjuntivo	
abriera	abriéramos	hubiera abierto	hubiéramos abierto
abrieras	abrierais	hubieras abierto	hubierais abierto
abriera	abrieran	hubiera abierto	hubieran abierto
OR		OR	
abriese	abriésemos	hubiese abierto	hubiésemos abierto
abrieses	abrieseis	hubieses abierto	hubieseis abierto
abriese	abriesen	hubiese abierto	hubiesen abierto

imperativo	
—	abramos
abre; no abras	abrid; no abráis
abra	abran

Words and expressions related to this verb

un abrimiento opening   **La puerta está abierta.**   The door is open.
abrir paso to make way   **Los libros están abiertos.**   The books are open.

1

to absolve, to acquit

The Seven Simple Tenses		The Seven Compound Tenses	
Singular	Plural	Singular	Plural
1 presente de indicativo		8 perfecto de indicativo	
absuelvo	absolvemos	he absuelto	hemos absuelto
absuelves	absolvéis	has absuelto	habéis absuelto
absuelve	absuelven	ha absuelto	han absuelto
2 imperfecto de indicativo		9 pluscuamperfecto de indicativo	
absolvía	absolvíamos	había absuelto	habíamos absuelto
absolvías	absolvíais	habías absuelto	habíais absuelto
absolvía	absolvían	había absuelto	habían absuelto
3 pretérito		10 pretérito anterior	
absolví	absolvimos	hube absuelto	hubimos absuelto
absolviste	absolvisteis	hubiste absuelto	hubisteis absuelto
absolvió	absolvieron	hubo absuelto	hubieron absuelto
4 futuro		11 futuro perfecto	
absolveré	absolveremos	habré absuelto	habremos absuelto
absolverás	absolveréis	habrás absuelto	habréis absuelto
absolverá	absolverán	habrá absuelto	habrán absuelto
5 potencial simple		12 potencial compuesto	
absolvería	absolveríamos	habría absuelto	habríamos absuelto
absolverías	absolveríais	habrías absuelto	habríais absuelto
absolvería	absolverían	habría absuelto	habrían absuelto
6 presente de subjuntivo		13 perfecto de subjuntivo	
absuelva	absolvamos	haya absuelto	hayamos absuelto
absuelvas	absolváis	hayas absuelto	hayáis absuelto
absuelva	absuelvan	haya absuelto	hayan absuelto
7 imperfecto de subjuntivo		14 pluscuamperfecto de subjuntivo	
absolviera	absolviéramos	hubiera absuelto	hubiéramos absuelto
absolvieras	absolvierais	hubieras absuelto	hubierais absuelto
absolviera	absolvieran	hubiera absuelto	hubieran absuelto
OR		OR	
absolviese	absolviésemos	hubiese absuelto	hubiésemos absuelto
absolvieses	absolvieseis	hubieses absuelto	hubieseis absuelto
absolviese	absolviesen	hubiese absuelto	hubiesen absuelto

imperativo	
—	absolvamos
absuelve; no absuelvas	absolved; no absolváis
absuelva	absuelvan

Words related to this verb
la absolución absolution, acquittal, pardon
absolutamente absolutely
absoluto, absoluta absolute, unconditional

2

abstenerse

to abstain

The Seven Simple Tenses		The Seven Compound Tenses	
Singular	Plural	Singular	Plural
1 presente de indicativo		**8 perfecto de indicativo**	
me abstengo	nos abstenemos	me he	nos hemos
te abstienes	os abstenéis	te has	os habéis + abstenido
se abstiene	se abstienen	se ha	se han
2 imperfecto de indicativo		**9 pluscuamperfecto de indicativo**	
me abstenía	nos absteníamos	me había	nos habíamos
te abstenías	os absteníais	te habías	os habíais + abstenido
se abstenía	se abstenían	se había	se habían
3 pretérito		**10 pretérito anterior**	
me abstuve	nos abstuvimos	me hube	nos hubimos
te abstuviste	os abstuvisteis	te hubiste	os hubisteis + abstenido
se abstuvo	se abstuvieron	se hubo	se hubieron
4 futuro		**11 futuro perfecto**	
me abstendré	nos abstendremos	me habré	nos habremos
te abstendrás	os abstendréis	te habrás	os habréis + abstenido
se abstendrá	se abstendrán	se habrá	se habrán
5 potencial simple		**12 potencial compuesto**	
me abstendría	nos abstendríamos	me habría	nos habríamos
te abstendrías	os abstendríais	te habrías	os habríais + abstenido
se abstendría	se abstendrían	se habría	se habrían
6 presente de subjuntivo		**13 perfecto de subjuntivo**	
me abstenga	nos abstengamos	me haya	nos hayamos
te abstengas	os abstengáis	te hayas	os hayáis + abstenido
se abstenga	se abstengan	se haya	se hayan
7 imperfecto de subjuntivo		**14 pluscuamperfecto de subjuntivo**	
me abstuviera	nos abstuviéramos	me hubiera	nos hubiéramos
te abstuvieras	os abstuvierais	te hubieras	os hubierais + abstenido
se abstuviera	se abstuvieran	se hubiera	se hubieran
OR		OR	
me abstuviese	nos abstuviésemos	me hubiese	nos hubiésemos
te abstuvieses	os abstuvieseis	te hubieses	os hubieseis + abstenido
se abstuviese	se abstuviesen	se hubiese	se hubiesen

imperativo	
—	abstengámonos
abstente; no te abstengas	absteneos; no os abstengáis
absténgase	absténganse

Words related to this verb

la abstención   abstention, forbearance
abstenerse de   to abstain from, to refrain from
la abstinencia   abstinence, fasting

aburrir   Gerundio **aburriendo**   Part. pas. **aburrido**

to annoy, to bore, to vex

The Seven Simple Tenses		The Seven Compound Tenses	
Singular	Plural	Singular	Plural
1 presente de indicativo		**8 perfecto de indicativo**	
aburro	aburrimos	he aburrido	hemos aburrido
aburres	aburrís	has aburrido	habéis aburrido
aburre	aburren	ha aburrido	han aburrido
2 imperfecto de indicativo		**9 pluscuamperfecto de indicativo**	
aburría	aburríamos	había aburrido	habíamos aburrido
aburrías	aburríais	habías aburrido	habíais aburrido
aburría	aburrían	había aburrido	habían aburrido
3 pretérito		**10 pretérito anterior**	
aburrí	aburrimos	hube aburrido	hubimos aburrido
aburriste	aburristeis	hubiste aburrido	hubisteis aburrido
aburrió	aburrieron	hubo aburrido	hubieron aburrido
4 futuro		**11 futuro perfecto**	
aburriré	aburriremos	habré aburrido	habremos aburrido
aburrirás	aburriréis	habrás aburrido	habréis aburrido
aburrirá	aburrirán	habrá aburrido	habrán aburrido
5 potencial simple		**12 potencial compuesto**	
aburriría	aburriríamos	habría aburrido	habríamos aburrido
aburrirías	aburriríais	habrías aburrido	habríais aburrido
aburriría	aburrirían	habría aburrido	habrían aburrido
6 presente de subjuntivo		**13 perfecto de subjuntivo**	
aburra	aburramos	haya aburrido	hayamos aburrido
aburras	aburráis	hayas aburrido	hayáis aburrido
aburra	aburran	haya aburrido	hayan aburrido
7 imperfecto de subjuntivo		**14 pluscuamperfecto de subjuntivo**	
aburriera	aburriéramos	hubiera aburrido	hubiéramos aburrido
aburrieras	aburrierais	hubieras aburrido	hubierais aburrido
aburriera	aburrieran	hubiera aburrido	hubieran aburrido
OR		OR	
aburriese	aburriésemos	hubiese aburrido	hubiésemos aburrido
aburrieses	aburrieseis	hubieses aburrido	hubieseis aburrido
aburriese	aburriesen	hubiese aburrido	hubiesen aburrido

	imperativo
—	aburramos
aburre; no aburras	aburrid; no aburráis
aburra	aburran

Sentences using this verb and words related to it

El profesor de español cree que Pedro está aburrido, que María está aburrida, que todos los alumnos en la clase están aburridos.

un aburrimiento   annoyance, weariness

un aburridor, una aburridora   boring person

See also **aburrirse.**

to be bored, to grow tired, to grow weary

The Seven Simple Tenses		The Seven Compound Tenses	
Singular	Plural	Singular	Plural

1   presente de indicativo

		8 perfecto de indicativo	
me aburro	nos aburrimos	me he aburrido	nos hemos aburrido
te aburres	os aburrís	te has aburrido	os habéis aburrido
se aburre	se aburren	se ha aburrido	se han aburrido

2   imperfecto de indicativo

		9 pluscuamperfecto de indicativo	
me aburría	nos aburríamos	me había aburrido	nos habíamos aburrido
te aburrías	os aburríais	te habías aburrido	os habíais aburrido
se aburría	se aburrían	se había aburrido	se habían aburrido

3   pretérito

		10 pretérito anterior	
me aburrí	nos aburrimos	me hube aburrido	nos hubimos aburrido
te aburriste	os aburristeis	te hubiste aburrido	os hubisteis aburrido
se aburrió	se aburrieron	se hubo aburrido	se hubieron aburrido

4   futuro

		11 futuro perfecto	
me aburriré	nos aburriremos	me habré aburrido	nos habremos aburrido
te aburrirás	os aburriréis	te habrás aburrido	os habréis aburrido
se aburrirá	se aburrirán	se habrá aburrido	se habrán aburrido

5   potencial simple

		12 potencial compuesto	
me aburriría	nos aburriríamos	me habría aburrido	nos habríamos aburrido
te aburrirías	os aburriríais	te habrías aburrido	os habríais aburrido
se aburriría	se aburrirían	se habría aburrido	se habrían aburrido

6   presente de subjuntivo

		13 perfecto de subjuntivo	
me aburra	nos aburramos	me haya aburrido	nos hayamos aburrido
te aburras	os aburráis	te hayas aburrido	os hayáis aburrido
se aburra	se aburran	se haya aburrido	se hayan aburrido

7   imperfecto de subjuntivo

		14 pluscuamperfecto de subjuntivo	
me aburriera	nos aburriéramos	me hubiera aburrido	nos hubiéramos aburrido
te aburrieras	os aburrierais	te hubieras aburrido	os hubierais aburrido
se aburriera	se aburrieran	se hubiera aburrido	se hubieran aburrido
OR		OR	
me aburriese	nos aburriésemos	me hubiese aburrido	nos hubiésemos aburrido
te aburrieses	os aburrieseis	te hubieses aburrido	os hubieseis aburrido
se aburriese	se aburriesen	se hubiese aburrido	se hubiesen aburrido

imperativo

—	aburrámonos
abúrrete; no te aburras	aburríos; no os aburráis
abúrrase	abúrranse

Sentences using this verb and words related to it
**El profesor de español se aburre en la clase de español porque hace treinta años
que enseña la lengua en la misma escuela.**
un aburrimiento   annoyance, weariness
aburridamente   tediously
See also **aburrir**.

acabar	Gerundio **acabando**	Part. pas. **acabado**

to finish, to end, to complete

The Seven Simple Tenses		The Seven Compound Tenses	
Singular	Plural	Singular	Plural
1 presente de indicativo		**8 perfecto de indicativo**	
acabo	acabamos	he acabado	hemos acabado
acabas	acabáis	has acabado	habéis acabado
acaba	acaban	ha acabado	han acabado
2 imperfecto de indicativo		**9 pluscuamperfecto de indicativo**	
acababa	acabábamos	había acabado	habíamos acabado
acababas	acababais	habías acabado	habíais acabado
acababa	acababan	había acabado	habían acabado
3 pretérito		**10 pretérito anterior**	
acabé	acabamos	hube acabado	hubimos acabado
acabaste	acabasteis	hubiste acabado	hubisteis acabado
acabó	acabaron	hubo acabado	hubieron acabado
4 futuro		**11 futuro perfecto**	
acabaré	acabaremos	habré acabado	habremos acabado
acabarás	acabaréis	habrás acabado	habréis acabado
acabará	acabarán	habrá acabado	habrán acabado
5 potencial simple		**12 potencial compuesto**	
acabaría	acabaríamos	habría acabado	habríamos acabado
acabarías	acabaríais	habrías acabado	habríais acabado
acabaría	acabarían	habría acabado	habrían acabado
6 presente de subjuntivo		**13 perfecto de subjuntivo**	
acabe	acabemos	haya acabado	hayamos acabado
acabes	acabéis	hayas acabado	hayáis acabado
acabe	acaben	haya acabado	hayan acabado
7 imperfecto de subjuntivo		**14 pluscuamperfecto de subjuntivo**	
acabara	acabáramos	hubiera acabado	hubiéramos acabado
acabaras	acabarais	hubieras acabado	hubierais acabado
acabara	acabaran	hubiera acabado	hubieran acabado
OR		OR	
acabase	acabásemos	hubiese acabado	hubiésemos acabado
acabases	acabaseis	hubieses acabado	hubieseis acabado
acabase	acabasen	hubiese acabado	hubiesen acabado

imperativo	
—	acabemos
acaba; no acabes	acabad; no acabéis
acabe	acaben

Sentences using this verb and words related to it
Yo acabo de leer la lección de español, Miguel acaba de escribir una composición,
y los otros alumnos acaban de hablar en español.

el acabamiento completion	se acabó It's all over. It's finished.
acabar de + inf. to have just + past part.	acabar en to result in
acabar por to end by	acabar bien to terminate successfully

to accept

The Seven Simple Tenses		The Seven Compound Tenses	
Singular	Plural	Singular	Plural
1 presente de indicativo		8 perfecto de indicativo	
acepto	aceptamos	he aceptado	hemos aceptado
aceptas	aceptáis	has aceptado	habéis aceptado
acepta	aceptan	ha aceptado	han aceptado
2 imperfecto de indicativo		9 pluscuamperfecto de indicativo	
aceptaba	aceptábamos	había aceptado	habíamos aceptado
aceptabas	aceptabais	habías aceptado	habíais aceptado
aceptaba	aceptaban	había aceptado	habían aceptado
3 pretérito		10 pretérito anterior	
acepté	aceptamos	hube aceptado	hubimos aceptado
aceptaste	aceptasteis	hubiste aceptado	hubisteis aceptado
aceptó	aceptaron	hubo aceptado	hubieron aceptado
4 futuro		11 futuro perfecto	
aceptaré	aceptaremos	habré aceptado	habremos aceptado
aceptarás	aceptaréis	habrás aceptado	habréis aceptado
aceptará	aceptarán	habrá aceptado	habrán aceptado
5 potencial simple		12 potencial compuesto	
aceptaría	aceptaríamos	habría aceptado	habríamos aceptado
aceptarías	aceptaríais	habrías aceptado	habríais aceptado
aceptaría	aceptarían	habría aceptado	habrían aceptado
6 presente de subjuntivo		13 perfecto de subjuntivo	
acepte	aceptemos	haya aceptado	hayamos aceptado
aceptes	aceptéis	hayas aceptado	hayáis aceptado
acepte	acepten	haya aceptado	hayan aceptado
7 imperfecto de subjuntivo		14 pluscuamperfecto de subjuntivo	
aceptara	aceptáramos	hubiera aceptado	hubiéramos aceptado
aceptaras	aceptarais	hubieras aceptado	hubierais aceptado
aceptara	aceptaran	hubiera aceptado	hubieran aceptado
OR		OR	
aceptase	aceptásemos	hubiese aceptado	hubiésemos aceptado
aceptases	aceptaseis	hubieses aceptado	hubieseis aceptado
aceptase	aceptasen	hubiese aceptado	hubiesen aceptado

imperativo

—	aceptemos
acepta; no aceptes	aceptad; no aceptéis
acepte	acepten

Words and expressions related to this verb

aceptable acceptable
el aceptador, la aceptadora acceptor
el aceptante, la aceptante accepter
la aceptación acceptance, acceptation

aceptar + inf. to agree + inf.
aceptar empleo to take a job
acepto, acepta acceptable

7

to bring near, to place near

The Seven Simple Tenses		The Seven Compound Tenses	
Singular	Plural	Singular	Plural
1 presente de indicativo		8 perfecto de indicativo	
acerco	acercamos	he acercado	hemos acercado
acercas	acercáis	has acercado	habéis acercado
acerca	acercan	ha acercado	han acercado
2 imperfecto de indicativo		9 pluscuamperfecto de indicativo	
acercaba	acercábamos	había acercado	habíamos acercado
acercabas	acercabais	habías acercado	habíais acercado
acercaba	acercaban	había acercado	habían acercado
3 pretérito		10 pretérito anterior	
acerqué	acercamos	hube acercado	hubimos acercado
acercaste	acercasteis	hubiste acercado	hubisteis acercado
acercó	acercaron	hubo acercado	hubieron acercado
4 futuro		11 futuro perfecto	
acercaré	acercaremos	habré acercado	habremos acercado
acercarás	acercaréis	habrás acercado	habréis acercado
acercará	acercarán	habrá acercado	habrán acercado
5 potencial simple		12 potencial compuesto	
acercaría	acercaríamos	habría acercado	habríamos acercado
acercarías	acercaríais	habrías acercado	habríais acercado
acercaría	acercarían	habría acercado	habrían acercado
6 presente de subjuntivo		13 perfecto de subjuntivo	
acerque	acerquemos	haya acercado	hayamos acercado
acerques	acerquéis	hayas acercado	hayáis acercado
acerque	acerquen	haya acercado	hayan acercado
7 imperfecto de subjuntivo		14 pluscuamperfecto de subjuntivo	
acercara	acercáramos	hubiera acercado	hubiéramos acercado
acercaras	acercarais	hubieras acercado	hubierais acercado
acercara	acercaran	hubiera acercado	hubieran acercado
OR		OR	
acercase	acercásemos	hubiese acercado	hubiésemos acercado
acercases	acercaseis	hubieses acercado	hubieseis acercado
acercase	acercasen	hubiese acercado	hubiesen acercado

imperativo	
—	acerquemos
acerca; no acerques	acercad; no acerquéis
acerque	acerquen

Words and expressions related to this verb

acerca de   about, regarding, with regard to
el acercamiento   approaching, approximation
cerca de   near
de cerca   close at hand, closely
See also **acercarse.**

acerca de esto   hereof
la cerca   fence, hedge
el cercado   fenced in area

8

to approach, to draw near

The Seven Simple Tenses		The Seven Compound Tenses	
Singular	Plural	Singular	Plural

1   presente de indicativo

me acerco	nos acercamos	
te acercas	os acercáis	
se acerca	se acercan	

8   perfecto de indicativo

me he acercado	nos hemos acercado
te has acercado	os habéis acercado
se ha acercado	se han acercado

2   imperfecto de indicativo

me acercaba	nos acercábamos
te acercabas	os acercabais
se acercaba	se acercaban

9   pluscuamperfecto de indicativo

me había acercado	nos habíamos acercado
te habías acercado	os habíais acercado
se había acercado	se habían acercado

3   pretérito

me acerqué	nos acercamos
te acercaste	os acercasteis
se acercó	se acercaron

10   pretérito anterior

me hube acercado	nos hubimos acercado
te hubiste acercado	os hubisteis acercado
se hubo acercado	se hubieron acercado

4   futuro

me acercaré	nos acercaremos
te acercarás	os acercaréis
se acercará	se acercarán

11   futuro perfecto

me habré acercado	nos habremos acercado
te habrás acercado	os habréis acercado
se habrá acercado	se habrán acercado

5   potencial simple

me acercaría	nos acercaríamos
te acercarías	os acercaríais
se acercaría	se acercarían

12   potencial compuesto

me habría acercado	nos habríamos acercado
te habrías acercado	os habríais acercado
se habría acercado	se habrían acercado

6   presente de subjuntivo

me acerque	nos acerquemos
te acerques	os acerquéis
se acerque	se acerquen

13   perfecto de subjuntivo

me haya acercado	nos hayamos acercado
te hayas acercado	os hayáis acercado
se haya acercado	se hayan acercado

7   imperfecto de subjuntivo

me acercara	nos acercáramos
te acercaras	os acercarais
se acercara	se acercaran
OR	
me acercase	nos acercásemos
te acercases	os acercaseis
se acercase	se acercasen

14   pluscuamperfecto de subjuntivo

me hubiera acercado	nos hubiéramos acercado
te hubieras acercado	os hubierais acercado
se hubiera acercado	se hubieran acercado
OR	
me hubiese acercado	nos hubiésemos acercado
te hubieses acercado	os hubieseis acercado
se hubiese acercado	se hubiesen acercado

imperativo

—	acerquémonos
acércate; no te acerques	acercaos; no os acerquéis
acérquese	acérquense

Words and expressions related to this verb

acerca de   about, regarding, with regard to
el acercamiento   approaching, approximation
cerca de   near
de cerca   close at hand, closely
See also **acercar.**

la cercadura   fence
cercano, cercana   near
cercar   to enclose, fence in
las cercanías   neighborhood

to hit the mark, to hit upon, to do (something) right, to succeed in

The Seven Simple Tenses		The Seven Compound Tenses	
Singular	Plural	Singular	Plural
1 presente de indicativo		**8 perfecto de indicativo**	
acierto	acertamos	he acertado	hemos acertado
aciertas	acertáis	has acertado	habéis acertado
acierta	aciertan	ha acertado	han acertado
2 imperfecto de indicativo		**9 pluscuamperfecto de indicativo**	
acertaba	acertábamos	había acertado	habíamos acertado
acertabas	acertabais	habías acertado	habíais acertado
acertaba	acertaban	había acertado	habían acertado
3 pretérito		**10 pretérito anterior**	
acerté	acertamos	hube acertado	hubimos acertado
acertaste	acertasteis	hubiste acertado	hubisteis acertado
acertó	acertaron	hubo acertado	hubieron acertado
4 futuro		**11 futuro perfecto**	
acertaré	acertaremos	habré acertado	habremos acertado
acertarás	acertaréis	habrás acertado	habréis acertado
acertará	acertarán	habrá acertado	habrán acertado
5 potencial simple		**12 potencial compuesto**	
acertaría	acertaríamos	habría acertado	habríamos acertado
acertarías	acertaríais	habrías acertado	habríais acertado
acertaría	acertarían	habría acertado	habrían acertado
6 presente de subjuntivo		**13 perfecto de subjuntivo**	
acierte	acertemos	haya acertado	hayamos acertado
aciertes	acertéis	hayas acertado	hayáis acertado
acierte	acierten	haya acertado	hayan acertado
7 imperfecto de subjuntivo		**14 pluscuamperfecto de subjuntivo**	
acertara	acertáramos	hubiera acertado	hubiéramos acertado
acertaras	acertarais	hubieras acertado	hubierais acertado
acertara	acertaran	hubiera acertado	hubieran acertado
OR		OR	
acertase	acertásemos	hubiese acertado	hubiésemos acertado
acertases	acertaseis	hubieses acertado	hubieseis acertado
acertase	acertasen	hubiese acertado	hubiesen acertado

imperativo	
—	acertemos
acierta; no aciertes	acertad; no acertéis
acierte	acierten

Words and expressions related to this verb

acertado, acertada proper, fit
el acertador, la acertadora good guesser
acertar a to happen
acertar con to come across, to find

acertamiento tact, ability
el acertajo riddle
acertadamente opportunely
ciertamente certainly

Gerundio acompañando   Part. pas. acompañado   **acompañar**

to accompany, to escort, to go with, to keep company

The Seven Simple Tenses		The Seven Compound Tenses	
Singular	Plural	Singular	Plural
1 presente de indicativo		8 perfecto de indicativo	
acompaño	**acompañamos**	**he acompañado**	**hemos acompañado**
acompañas	**acompañáis**	**has acompañado**	**habéis acompañado**
acompaña	**acompañan**	**ha acompañado**	**han acompañado**
2 imperfecto de indicativo		9 pluscuamperfecto de indicativo	
acompañaba	**acompañábamos**	**había acompañado**	**habíamos acompañado**
acompañabas	**acompañabais**	**habías acompañado**	**habíais acompañado**
acompañaba	**acompañaban**	**había acompañado**	**habían acompañado**
3 pretérito		10 pretérito anterior	
acompañé	**acompañamos**	**hube acompañado**	**hubimos acompañado**
acompañaste	**acompañasteis**	**hubiste acompañado**	**hubisteis acompañado**
acompañó	**acompañaron**	**hubo acompañado**	**hubieron acompañado**
4 futuro		11 futuro perfecto	
acompañaré	**acompañaremos**	**habré acompañado**	**habremos acompañado**
acompañarás	**acompañaréis**	**habrás acompañado**	**habréis acompañado**
acompañará	**acompañarán**	**habrá acompañado**	**habrán acompañado**
5 potencial simple		12 potencial compuesto	
acompañaría	**acompañaríamos**	**habría acompañado**	**habríamos acompañado**
acompañarías	**acompañaríais**	**habrías acompañado**	**habríais acompañado**
acompañaría	**acompañarían**	**habría acompañado**	**habrían acompañado**
6 presente de subjuntivo		13 perfecto de subjuntivo	
acompañe	**acompañemos**	**haya acompañado**	**hayamos acompañado**
acompañes	**acompañéis**	**hayas acompañado**	**hayáis acompañado**
acompañe	**acompañen**	**haya acompañado**	**hayan acompañado**
7 imperfecto de subjuntivo		14 pluscuamperfecto de subjuntivo	
acompañara	**acompañáramos**	**hubiera acompañado**	**hubiéramos acompañado**
acompañaras	**acompañarais**	**hubieras acompañado**	**hubierais acompañado**
acompañara	**acompañaran**	**hubiera acompañado**	**hubieran acompañado**
OR		OR	
acompañase	**acompañásemos**	**hubiese acompañado**	**hubiésemos acompañado**
acompañases	**acompañaseis**	**hubieses acompañado**	**hubieseis acompañado**
acompañase	**acompañasen**	**hubiese acompañado**	**hubiesen acompañado**

imperativo

—	**acompañemos**
acompaña; no acompañes	**acompañad; no acompañéis**
acompañe	**acompañen**

Words and expressions related to this verb
el acompañador, la acompañadora   companion, chaperon, accompanist
el acompañamiento   accompaniment, attendance
el acompañado, la acompañada   assistant
un compañero, una compañera   friend, mate, companion;
   compañero de cuarto   roommate; compañero de juego   playmate

to advise, to counsel

The Seven Simple Tenses		The Seven Compound Tenses	
Singular	Plural	Singular	Plural
1 presente de indicativo		**8 perfecto de indicativo**	
aconsejo	aconsejamos	he aconsejado	hemos aconsejado
aconsejas	aconsejáis	has aconsejado	habéis aconsejado
aconseja	aconsejan	ha aconsejado	han aconsejado
2 imperfecto de indicativo		**9 pluscuamperfecto de indicativo**	
aconsejaba	aconsejábamos	había aconsejado	habíamos aconsejado
aconsejabas	aconsejabais	habías aconsejado	habíais aconsejado
aconsejaba	aconsejaban	había aconsejado	habian aconsejado
3 pretérito		**10 pretérito anterior**	
aconsejé	aconsejamos	hube aconsejado	hubimos aconsejado
aconsejaste	aconsejasteis	hubiste aconsejado	hubisteis aconsejado
aconsejó	aconsejaron	hubo aconsejado	hubieron aconsejado
4 futuro		**11 futuro perfecto**	
aconsejaré	aconsejaremos	habré aconsejado	habremos aconsejado
aconsejarás	aconsejaréis	habrás aconsejado	habréis aconsejado
aconsejará	aconsejarán	habrá aconsejado	habrán aconsejado
5 potencial simple		**12 potencial compuesto**	
aconsejaría	aconsejaríamos	habría aconsejado	habríamos aconsejado
aconsejarías	aconsejaríais	habrías aconsejado	habríais aconsejado
aconsejaría	aconsejarían	habría aconsejado	habrían aconsejado
6 presente de subjuntivo		**13 perfecto de subjuntivo**	
aconseje	aconsejemos	haya aconsejado	hayamos aconsejado
aconsejes	aconsejéis	hayas aconsejado	hayáis aconsejado
aconseje	aconsejen	haya aconsejado	hayan aconsejado
7 imperfecto de subjuntivo		**14 pluscuamperfecto de subjuntivo**	
aconsejara	aconsejáramos	hubiera aconsejado	hubiéramos aconsejado
aconsejaras	aconsejarais	hubieras aconsejado	hubierais aconsejado
aconsejara	aconsejaran	hubiera aconsejado	hubieran aconsejado
OR		OR	
aconsejase	aconsejásemos	hubiese aconsejado	hubiésemos aconsejado
aconsejases	aconsejaseis	hubieses aconsejado	hubieseis aconsejado
aconsejase	aconsejasen	hubiese aconsejado	hubiesen aconsejado

imperativo	
—	aconsejemos
aconseja; no aconsejes	aconsejad; aconsejéis
aconseje	aconsejen

Words and expressions related to this verb
el aconsejador, la aconsejadora   adviser, counselor
aconsejar con   to consult
el consejo   advice, counsel
El tiempo da buen consejo.   Time will tell.

Gerundio **acordando**   Part. pas. **acordado**   **acordar**

to agree (upon)

The Seven Simple Tenses		The Seven Compound Tenses	
Singular	Plural	Singular	Plural
1 presente de indicativo		**8 perfecto de indicativo**	
acuerdo	acordamos	he acordado	hemos acordado
acuerdas	acordáis	has acordado	habéis acordado
acuerda	acuerdan	ha acordado	han acordado
2 imperfecto de indicativo		**9 pluscuamperfecto de indicativo**	
acordaba	acordábamos	había acordado	habíamos acordado
acordabas	acordabais	habías acordado	habíais acordado
acordaba	acordaban	había acordado	habían acordado
3 pretérito		**10 pretérito anterior**	
acordé	acordamos	hube acordado	hubimos acordado
acordaste	acordasteis	hubiste acordado	hubisteis acordado
acordó	acordaron	hubo acordado	hubieron acordado
4 futuro		**11 futuro perfecto**	
acordaré	acordaremos	habré acordado	habremos acordado
acordarás	acordaréis	habrás acordado	habréis acordado
acordará	acordarán	habrá acordado	habrán acordado
5 potencial simple		**12 potencial compuesto**	
acordaría	acordaríamos	habría acordado	habríamos acordado
acordarías	acordaríais	habrías acordado	habríais acordado
acordaría	acordarían	habría acordado	habrían acordado
6 presente de subjuntivo		**13 perfecto de subjuntivo**	
acuerde	acordemos	haya acordado	hayamos acordado
acuerdes	acordéis	hayas acordado	hayáis acordado
acuerde	acuerden	haya acordado	hayan acordado
7 imperfecto de subjuntivo		**14 pluscuamperfecto de subjuntivo**	
acordara	acordáramos	hubiera acordado	hubiéramos acordado
acordaras	acordarais	hubieras acordado	hubierais acordado
acordara	acordaran	hubiera acordado	hubieran acordado
OR		OR	
acordase	acordásemos	hubiese acordado	hubiésemos acordado
acordases	acordaseis	hubieses acordado	hubieseis acordado
acordase	acordasen	hubiese acordado	hubiesen acordado

imperativo

—	acordemos
acuerda; no acuerdes	acordad; no acordéis
acuerde	acuerden

Words and expressions related to this verb
la acordada decision, resolution
acordadamente jointly, by common consent
un acuerdo agreement
de acuerdo in agreement
See also **acordarse.**

desacordar to put out of tune
desacordante discordant
desacordado, desacordada
    out of tune (music)

13

to remember

The Seven Simple Tenses		The Seven Compound Tenses	
Singular	Plural	Singular	Plural

1 presente de indicativo

		8 perfecto de indicativo	
me acuerdo	nos acordamos	me he acordado	nos hemos acordado
te acuerdas	os acordáis	te has acordado	os habéis acordado
se acuerda	se acuerdan	se ha acordado	se han acordado

2 imperfecto de indicativo

		9 pluscuamperfecto de indicativo	
me acordaba	nos acordábamos	me había acordado	nos habíamos acordado
te acordabas	os acordabais	te habías acordado	os habíais acordado
se acordaba	se acordaban	se había acordado	se habían acordado

3 pretérito

		10 pretérito anterior	
me acordé	nos acordamos	me hube acordado	nos hubimos acordado
te acordaste	os acordasteis	te hubiste acordado	os hubisteis acordado
se acordó	se acordaron	se hubo acordado	se hubieron acordado

4 futuro

		11 futuro perfecto	
me acordaré	nos acordaremos	me habré acordado	nos habremos acordado
te acordarás	os acordaréis	te habrás acordado	os habréis acordado
se acordará	se acordarán	se habrá acordado	se habrán acordado

5 potencial simple

		12 potencial compuesto	
me acordaría	nos acordaríamos	me habría acordado	nos habríamos acordado
te acordarías	os acordaríais	te habrías acordado	os habríais acordado
se acordaría	se acordarían	se habría acordado	se habrían acordado

6 presente de subjuntivo

		13 perfecto de subjuntivo	
me acuerde	nos acordemos	me haya acordado	nos hayamos acordado
te acuerdes	os acordéis	te hayas acordado	os hayáis acordado
se acuerde	se acuerden	se haya acordado	se hayan acordado

7 imperfecto de subjuntivo

		14 pluscuamperfecto de subjuntivo	
me acordara	nos acordáramos	me hubiera acordado	nos hubiéramos acordado
te acordaras	os acordarais	te hubieras acordado	os hubierais acordado
se acordara	se acordaran	se hubiera acordado	se hubieran acordado
OR		OR	
me acordase	nos acordásemos	me hubiese acordado	nos hubiésemos acordado
te acordases	os acordaseis	te hubieses acordado	os hubieseis acordado
se acordase	se acordasen	se hubiese acordado	se hubiesen acordado

imperativo	
—	acordémonos
acuérdate; no te acuerdes	acordaos; no os acordéis
acuérdese	acuérdense

Words and expressions related to this verb
si mal no me acuerdo   if I remember correctly, if my memory does not fail me

un acuerdo agreement	de común acuerdo unanimously, by mutual
de acuerdo in agreement	agreement
See also acordar.	desacordarse to become forgetful

to go to bed, to lie down

The Seven Simple Tenses		The Seven Compound Tenses	
Singular	Plural	Singular	Plural

1   presente de indicativo

		8 perfecto de indicativo	
me acuesto	nos acostamos	me he acostado	nos hemos acostado
te acuestas	os acostáis	te has acostado	os habéis acostado
se acuesta	se acuestan	se ha acostado	se han acostado

2   imperfecto de indicativo

		9 pluscuamperfecto de indicativo	
me acostaba	nos acostábamos	me había acostado	nos habíamos acostado
te acostabas	os acostabais	te habías acostado	os habíais acostado
se acostaba	se acostaban	se había acostado	se habían acostado

3   pretérito

		10 pretérito anterior	
me acosté	nos acostamos	me hube acostado	nos hubimos acostado
te acostaste	os acostasteis	te hubiste acostado	os hubisteis acostado
se acostó	se acostaron	se hubo acostado	se hubieron acostado

4   futuro

		11 futuro perfecto	
me acostaré	nos acostaremos	me habré acostado	nos habremos acostado
te acostarás	os acostaréis	te habrás acostado	os habréis acostado
se acostará	se acostarán	se habrá acostado	se habrán acostado

5   potencial simple

		12 potencial compuesto	
me acostaría	nos acostaríamos	me habría acostado	nos habríamos acostado
te acostarías	os acostaríais	te habrías acostado	os habríais acostado
se acostaría	se acostarían	se habría acostado	se habrían acostado

6   presente de subjuntivo

		13 perfecto de subjuntivo	
me acueste	nos acostemos	me haya acostado	nos hayamos acostado
te acuestes	os acostéis	te hayas acostado	os hayáis acostado
se acueste	se acuesten	se haya acostado	se hayan acostado

7   imperfecto de subjuntivo

		14 pluscuamperfecto de subjuntivo	
me acostara	nos acostáramos	me hubiera acostado	nos hubiéramos acostado
te acostaras	os acostarais	te hubieras acostado	os hubierais acostado
se acostara	se acostaran	se hubiera acostado	se hubieran acostado
OR		OR	
me acostase	nos acostásemos	me hubiese acostado	nos hubiésemos acostado
te acostases	os acostaseis	te hubieses acostado	os hubieseis acostado
se acostase	se acostasen	se hubiese acostado	se hubiesen acostado

imperativo

—	acostémonos; no nos acostemos
acuéstate; no te acuestes	acostaos; no os acostéis
acuéstese; no se acueste	acuéstense; no se acuesten

Sentences using this verb and words and expressions related to it

Todas las noches me acuesto a las diez, mi hermanito se acuesta a las ocho, y mis padres se acuestan a las once.

acostado, acostada in bed, lying down	acostarse con las gallinas to go to bed
acostar to put to bed	very early

acostumbrar   Gerundio **acostumbrando**   Part. pas. **acostumbrado**

to be accustomed, to be in the habit of

The Seven Simple Tenses		The Seven Compound Tenses	
Singular	Plural	Singular	Plural

1   presente de indicativo

Singular	Plural
acostumbro	acostumbramos
acostumbras	acostumbráis
acostumbra	acostumbran

8   perfecto de indicativo

Singular	Plural	
he	hemos	
has	habéis	+ acostumbrado
ha	han	

2   imperfecto de indicativo

Singular	Plural
acostumbraba	acostumbrábamos
acostumbrabas	acostumbrabais
acostumbraba	acostumbraban

9   pluscuamperfecto de indicativo

Singular	Plural	
había	habíamos	
habías	habíais	+ acostumbrado
había	habían	

3   pretérito

Singular	Plural
acostumbré	acostumbramos
acostumbraste	acostumbrasteis
acostumbró	acostumbraron

10   pretérito anterior

Singular	Plural	
hube	hubimos	
hubiste	hubisteis	+ acostumbrado
hubo	hubieron	

4   futuro

Singular	Plural
acostumbraré	acostumbraremos
acostumbrarás	acostumbraréis
acostumbrará	acostumbrarán

11   futuro perfecto

Singular	Plural	
habré	habremos	
habrás	habréis	+ acostumbrado
habrá	habrán	

5   potencial simple

Singular	Plural
acostumbraría	acostumbraríamos
acostumbrarías	acostumbraríais
acostumbraría	acostumbrarían

12   potencial compuesto

Singular	Plural	
habría	habríamos	
habrías	habríais	+ acostumbrado
habría	habrían	

6   presente de subjuntivo

Singular	Plural
acostumbre	acostumbremos
acostumbres	acostumbréis
acostumbre	acostumbren

13   perfecto de subjuntivo

Singular	Plural	
haya	hayamos	
hayas	hayáis	+ acostumbrado
haya	hayan	

7   imperfecto de subjuntivo

Singular	Plural
acostumbrara	acostumbráramos
acostumbraras	acostumbrarais
acostumbrara	acostumbraran
OR	
acostumbrase	acostumbrásemos
acostumbrases	acostumbraseis
acostumbrase	acostumbrasen

14   pluscuamperfecto de subjuntivo

Singular	Plural	
hubiera	hubiéramos	
hubieras	hubierais	+ acostumbrado
hubiera	hubieran	
OR		
hubiese	hubiésemos	
hubieses	hubieseis	+ acostumbrado
hubiese	hubiesen	

imperativo

—	acostumbremos
acostumbra; no acostumbres	acostumbrad; no acostumbréis
acostumbre	acostumbren

Words and expressions related to this verb

acostumbradamente customarily	de costumbre customary, usual
la costumbre custom, habit	tener por costumbre to be in the habit of

to accuse

The Seven Simple Tenses		The Seven Compound Tenses	
Singular	Plural	Singular	Plural
1 presente de indicativo		**8 perfecto de indicativo**	
acuso	acusamos	he acusado	hemos acusado
acusas	acusáis	has acusado	habéis acusado
acusa	acusan	ha acusado	han acusado
2 imperfecto de indicativo		**9 pluscuamperfecto de indicativo**	
acusaba	acusábamos	había acusado	habíamos acusado
acusabas	acusabais	habías acusado	habíais acusado
acusaba	acusaban	había acusado	habían acusado
3 pretérito		**10 pretérito anterior**	
acusé	acusamos	hube acusado	hubimos acusado
acusaste	acusasteis	hubiste acusado	hubisteis acusado
acusó	acusaron	hubo acusado	hubieron acusado
4 futuro		**11 futuro perfecto**	
acusaré	acusaremos	habré acusado	habremos acusado
acusarás	acusaréis	habrás acusado	habréis acusado
acusará	acusarán	habrá acusado	habrán acusado
5 potencial simple		**12 potencial compuesto**	
acusaría	acusaríamos	habría acusado	habríamos acusado
acusarías	acusaríais	habrías acusado	habríais acusado
acusaría	acusarían	habría acusado	habrían acusado
6 presente de subjuntivo		**13 perfecto de subjuntivo**	
acuse	acusemos	haya acusado	hayamos acusado
acuses	acuséis	hayas acusado	hayáis acusado
acuse	acusen	haya acusado	hayan acusado
7 imperfecto de subjuntivo		**14 pluscuamperfecto de subjuntivo**	
acusara	acusáramos	hubiera acusado	hubiéramos acusado
acusaras	acusarais	hubieras acusado	hubierais acusado
acusara	acusaran	hubiera acusado	hubieran acusado
OR		OR	
acusase	acusásemos	hubiese acusado	hubiésemos acusado
acusases	acusaseis	hubieses acusado	hubieseis acusado
acusase	acusasen	hubiese acusado	hubiesen acusado

imperativo

—	acusemos
acusa; no acuses	acusad; no acuséis
acuse	acusen

Words related to this verb

el acusado, la acusada defendant, accused
la acusación accusation   **acusar recibo** to acknowledge receipt
el acusador, la acusadora accuser

17

admirar	Gerundio **admirando**	Part. pas. **admirado**

to admire

The Seven Simple Tenses		The Seven Compound Tenses	
Singular	Plural	Singular	Plural

1 presente de indicativo		8 perfecto de indicativo	
admiro	**admiramos**	he admirado	hemos admirado
admiras	**admiráis**	has admirado	habéis admirado
admira	**admiran**	ha admirado	han admirado

2 imperfecto de indicativo		9 pluscuamperfecto de indicativo	
admiraba	**admirábamos**	había admirado	habíamos admirado
admirabas	**admirabais**	habías admirado	habíais admirado
admiraba	**admiraban**	había admirado	habían admirado

3 pretérito		10 pretérito anterior	
admiré	**admiramos**	hube admirado	hubimos admirado
admiraste	**admirasteis**	hubiste admirado	hubisteis admirado
admiró	**admiraron**	hubo admirado	hubieron admirado

4 futuro		11 futuro perfecto	
admiraré	**admiraremos**	habré admirado	habremos admirado
admirarás	**admiraréis**	habrás admirado	habréis admirado
admirará	**admirarán**	habrá admirado	habrán admirado

5 potencial simple		12 potencial compuesto	
admiraría	**admiraríamos**	habría admirado	habríamos admirado
admirarías	**admiraríais**	habrías admirado	habríais admirado
admiraría	**admirarían**	habría admirado	habrían admirado

6 presente de subjuntivo		13 perfecto de subjuntivo	
admire	**admiremos**	haya admirado	hayamos admirado
admires	**admiréis**	hayas admirado	hayáis admirado
admire	**admiren**	haya admirado	hayan admirado

7 imperfecto de subjuntivo		14 pluscuamperfecto de subjuntivo	
admirara	**admiráramos**	hubiera admirado	hubiéramos admirado
admiraras	**admirarais**	hubieras admirado	hubierais admirado
admirara	**admiraran**	hubiera admirado	hubieran admirado
OR		OR	
admirase	**admirásemos**	hubiese admirado	hubiésemos admirado
admirases	**admiraseis**	hubieses admirado	hubieseis admirado
admirase	**admirasen**	hubiese admirado	hubiesen admirado

imperativo		
—		**admiremos**
	admira; no admires	**admirad; no admiréis**
	admire	**admiren**

Words related to this verb
el admirador, la admiradora admirer
la admiración admiration

admirable admirable
admirablemente admirably

to admit, to grant, to permit

The Seven Simple Tenses		The Seven Compound Tenses	
Singular	Plural	Singular	Plural
1 presente de indicativo		8 perfecto de indicativo	
admito	**admitimos**	**he admitido**	**hemos admitido**
admites	**admitís**	**has admitido**	**habéis admitido**
admite	**admiten**	**ha admitido**	**han admitido**
2 imperfecto de indicativo		9 pluscuamperfecto de indicativo	
admitía	**admitíamos**	**había admitido**	**habíamos admitido**
admitías	**admitíais**	**habías admitido**	**habíais admitido**
admitía	**admitían**	**había admitido**	**habían admitido**
3 pretérito		10 pretérito anterior	
admití	**admitimos**	**hube admitido**	**hubimos admitido**
admitiste	**admitisteis**	**hubiste admitido**	**hubisteis admitido**
admitió	**admitieron**	**hubo admitido**	**hubieron admitido**
4 futuro		11 futuro perfecto	
admitiré	**admitiremos**	**habré admitido**	**habremos admitido**
admitirás	**admitiréis**	**habrás admitido**	**habréis admitido**
admitirá	**admitirán**	**habrá admitido**	**habrán admitido**
5 potencial simple		12 potencial compuesto	
admitiría	**admitiríamos**	**habría admitido**	**habríamos admitido**
admitirías	**admitiríais**	**habrías admitido**	**habríais admitido**
admitiría	**admitirían**	**habría admitido**	**habrían admitido**
6 presente de subjuntivo		13 perfecto de subjuntivo	
admita	**admitamos**	**haya admitido**	**hayamos admitido**
admitas	**admitáis**	**hayas admitido**	**hayáis admitido**
admita	**admitan**	**haya admitido**	**hayan admitido**
7 imperfecto de subjuntivo		14 pluscuamperfecto de subjuntivo	
admitiera	**admitiéramos**	**hubiera admitido**	**hubiéramos admitido**
admitieras	**admitierais**	**hubieras admitido**	**hubierais admitido**
admitiera	**admitieran**	**hubiera admitido**	**hubieran admitido**
OR		OR	
admitiese	**admitiésemos**	**hubiese admitido**	**hubiésemos admitido**
admitieses	**admitieseis**	**hubieses admitido**	**hubieseis admitido**
admitiese	**admitiesen**	**hubiese admitido**	**hubiesen admitido**

imperativo

—	**admitamos**
admite; no admitas	**admitid; no admitáis**
admita	**admitan**

Words related to this verb
la admisión   acceptance, admission   admitido, admitida   admitted
admisible   admissible   un examen de admisión   entrance exam

19

to adore, to worship

The Seven Simple Tenses		The Seven Compound Tenses	
Singular	Plural	Singular	Plural
1 presente de indicativo		8 perfecto de indicativo	
adoro	adoramos	he adorado	hemos adorado
adoras	adoráis	has adorado	habéis adorado
adora	adoran	ha adorado	han adorado
2 imperfecto de indicativo		9 pluscuamperfecto de indicativo	
adoraba	adorábamos	había adorado	habíamos adorado
adorabas	adorabais	habías adorado	habíais adorado
adoraba	adoraban	había adorado	habían adorado
3 pretérito		10 pretérito anterior	
adoré	adoramos	hube adorado	hubimos adorado
adoraste	adorasteis	hubiste adorado	hubisteis adorado
adoró	adoraron	hubo adorado	hubieron adorado
4 futuro		11 futuro perfecto	
adoraré	adoraremos	habré adorado	habremos adorado
adorarás	adoraréis	habrás adorado	habréis adorado
adorará	adorarán	habrá adorado	habrán adorado
5 potencial simple		12 potencial compuesto	
adoraría	adoraríamos	habría adorado	habríamos adorado
adorarías	adoraríais	habrías adorado	habríais adorado
adoraría	adorarían	habría adorado	habrían adorado
6 presente de subjuntivo		13 perfecto de subjuntivo	
adore	adoremos	haya adorado	hayamos adorado
adores	adoréis	hayas adorado	hayáis adorado
adore	adoren	haya adorado	hayan adorado
7 imperfecto de subjuntivo		14 pluscuamperfecto de subjuntivo	
adorara	adoráramos	hubiera adorado	hubiéramos adorado
adoraras	adorarais	hubieras adorado	hubierais adorado
adorara	adoraran	hubiera adorado	hubieran adorado
OR		OR	
adorase	adorásemos	hubiese adorado	hubiésemos adorado
adorases	adoraseis	hubieses adorado	hubieseis adorado
adorase	adorasen	hubiese adorado	hubiesen adorado

	imperativo	
—	adoremos	
adora; no adores	adorad; no adoréis	
adore	adoren	

Words related to this verb
el adorador, la adoradora adorer, worshipper
adorable adorable   **adorado, adorada** adored
la adoración adoration   **adorablemente** adorably, adoringly

to acquire, to get, to obtain

The Seven Simple Tenses		The Seven Compound Tenses	
Singular	Plural	Singular	Plural
1 presente de indicativo		**8 perfecto de indicativo**	
adquiero	**adquirimos**	**he adquirido**	**hemos adquirido**
adquieres	**adquirís**	**has adquirido**	**habéis adquirido**
adquiere	**adquieren**	**ha adquirido**	**han adquirido**
2 imperfecto de indicativo		**9 pluscuamperfecto de indicativo**	
adquiría	**adquiríamos**	**había adquirido**	**habíamos adquirido**
adquirías	**adquiríais**	**habías adquirido**	**habíais adquirido**
adquiría	**adquirían**	**había adquirido**	**habían adquirido**
3 pretérito		**10 pretérito anterior**	
adquirí	**adquirimos**	**hube adquirido**	**hubimos adquirido**
adquiriste	**adquiristeis**	**hubiste adquirido**	**hubisteis adquirido**
adquirió	**adquirieron**	**hubo adquirido**	**hubieron adquirido**
4 futuro		**11 futuro perfecto**	
adquiriré	**adquiriremos**	**habré adquirido**	**habremos adquirido**
adquirirás	**adquiriréis**	**habrás adquirido**	**habréis adquirido**
adquirirá	**adquirirán**	**habrá adquirido**	**habrán adquirido**
5 potencial simple		**12 potencial compuesto**	
adquiriría	**adquiriríamos**	**habría adquirido**	**habríamos adquirido**
adquirirías	**adquiriríais**	**habrías adquirido**	**habríais adquirido**
adquiriría	**adquirirían**	**habría adquirido**	**habrían adquirido**
6 presente de subjuntivo		**13 perfecto de subjuntivo**	
adquiera	**adquiramos**	**haya adquirido**	**hayamos adquirido**
adquieras	**adquiráis**	**hayas adquirido**	**hayáis adquirido**
adquiera	**adquieran**	**haya adquirido**	**hayan adquirido**
7 imperfecto de subjuntivo		**14 pluscuamperfecto de subjuntivo**	
adquiriera	**adquiriéramos**	**hubiera adquirido**	**hubiéramos adquirido**
adquirieras	**adquirierais**	**hubieras adquirido**	**hubierais adquirido**
adquiriera	**adquirieran**	**hubiera adquirido**	**hubieran adquirido**
OR		OR	
adquiriese	**adquiriésemos**	**hubiese adquirido**	**hubiésemos adquirido**
adquirieses	**adquirieseis**	**hubieses adquirido**	**hubieseis adquirido**
adquiriese	**adquiriesen**	**hubiese adquirido**	**hubiesen adquirido**

imperativo	
—	**adquiramos**
adquiere; no adquieras	**adquirid; no adquiráis**
adquiera	**adquieran**

Words related to this verb

el adquirido, la adquiridora   acquirer
el (la) adquirente, el (la) adquiriente   acquirer
la adquisición   acquisition, attainment   **adquirir un derecho**   to acquire a right

to advise, to give notice, to give warning, to take notice of, to warn

The Seven Simple Tenses		The Seven Compound Tenses	
Singular	Plural	Singular	Plural
1 presente de indicativo		8 perfecto de indicativo	
advierto	advertimos	he advertido	hemos advertido
adviertes	advertís	has advertido	habéis advertido
advierte	advierten	ha advertido	han advertido
2 imperfecto de indicativo		9 pluscuamperfecto de indicativo	
advertía	advertíamos	había advertido	habíamos advertido
advertías	advertíais	habías advertido	habíais advertido
advertía	advertían	había advertido	habían advertido
3 pretérito		10 pretérito anterior	
advertí	advertimos	hube advertido	hubimos advertido
advertiste	advertisteis	hubiste advertido	hubisteis advertido
advirtió	advirtieron	hubo advertido	hubieron advertido
4 futuro		11 futuro perfecto	
advertiré	advertiremos	habré advertido	habremos advertido
advertirás	advertiréis	habrás advertido	habréis advertido
advertirá	advertirán	habrá advertido	habrán advertido
5 potencial simple		12 potencial compuesto	
advertiría	advertiríamos	habría advertido	habríamos advertido
advertirías	advertiríais	habrías advertido	habríais advertido
advertiría	advertirían	habría advertido	habrían advertido
6 presente de subjuntivo		13 perfecto de subjuntivo	
advierta	advirtamos	haya advertido	hayamos advertido
adviertas	advirtáis	hayas advertido	hayáis advertido
advierta	adviertan	haya advertido	hayan advertido
7 imperfecto de subjuntivo		14 pluscuamperfecto de subjuntivo	
advirtiera	advirtiéramos	hubiera advertido	hubiéramos advertido
advirtieras	advirtierais	hubieras advertido	hubierais advertido
advirtiera	advirtieran	hubiera advertido	hubieran advertido
OR		OR	
advirtiese	advirtiésemos	hubiese advertido	hubiésemos advertido
advirtieses	advirtieseis	hubieses advertido	hubieseis advertido
advirtiese	advirtiesen	hubiese advertido	hubiesen advertido

imperativo	
—	advirtamos
advierte; no adviertas	advertid; no advirtáis
advierta	adviertan

Words related to this verb
advertido, advertida skillful, clever, advised
la advertencia warning, notice, foreword
advertidamente advisedly   advertir en to notice, to take into account

afeitarse

to shave oneself

The Seven Simple Tenses		The Seven Compound Tenses	
Singular	Plural	Singular	Plural
1 presente de indicativo		8 perfecto de indicativo	
me afeito	nos afeitamos	me he afeitado	nos hemos afeitado
te afeitas	os afeitáis	te has afeitado	os habéis afeitado
se afeita	se afeitan	se ha afeitado	se han afeitado
2 imperfecto de indicativo		9 pluscuamperfecto de indicativo	
me afeitaba	nos afeitábamos	me había afeitado	nos habíamos afeitado
te afeitabas	os afeitabais	te habías afeitado	os habíais afeitado
se afeitaba	se afeitaban	se había afeitado	se habían afeitado
3 pretérito		10 pretérito anterior	
me afeité	nos afeitamos	me hube afeitado	nos hubimos afeitado
te afeitaste	os afeitasteis	te hubiste afeitado	os hubisteis afeitado
se afeitó	se afeitaron	se hubo afeitado	se hubieron afeitado
4 futuro		11 futuro perfecto	
me afeitaré	nos afeitaremos	me habré afeitado	nos habremos afeitado
te afeitarás	os afeitaréis	te habrás afeitado	os habréis afeitado
se afeitará	se afeitarán	se habrá afeitado	se habrán afeitado
5 potencial simple		12 potencial compuesto	
me afeitaría	nos afeitaríamos	me habría afeitado	nos habríamos afeitado
te afeitarías	os afeitaríais	te habrías afeitado	os habríais afeitado
se afeitaría	se afeitarían	se habría afeitado	se habrían afeitado
6 presente de subjuntivo		13 perfecto de subjuntivo	
me afeite	nos afeitemos	me haya afeitado	nos hayamos afeitado
te afeites	os afeitéis	te hayas afeitado	os hayáis afeitado
se afeite	se afeiten	se haya afeitado	se hayan afeitado
7 imperfecto de subjuntivo		14 pluscuamperfecto de subjuntivo	
me afeitara	nos afeitáramos	me hubiera afeitado	nos hubiéramos afeitado
te afeitaras	os afeitarais	te hubieras afeitado	os hubierais afeitado
se afeitara	se afeitaran	se hubiera afeitado	se hubieran afeitado
OR		OR	
me afeitase	nos afeitásemos	me hubiese afeitado	nos hubiésemos afeitado
te afeitases	os afeitaseis	te hubieses afeitado	os hubieseis afeitado
se afeitase	se afeitasen	se hubiese afeitado	se hubiesen afeitado

	imperativo	
—		afeitémonos
aféitate; no te afeites		afeitaos; no os afeitéis
aféitese		aféitense

Words related to this verb

afeitar   to shave
una afeitada   a shave
el afeite   cosmetic, makeup

el jabón para afeitarse   shaving soap
el paño de afeitar   shaving cloth
la brocha de afeitar   shaving brush

agradar Gerundio **agradando** Part. pas. **agradado**

to please, to be pleasing

The Seven Simple Tenses		The Seven Compound Tenses	
Singular	Plural	Singular	Plural
1 presente de indicativo		8 perfecto de indicativo	
agrado	agradamos	he agradado	hemos agradado
agradas	agradáis	has agradado	habéis agradado
agrada	agradan	ha agradado	han agradado
2 imperfecto de indicativo		9 pluscuamperfecto de indicativo	
agradaba	agradábamos	había agradado	habíamos agradado
agradabas	agradabais	habías agradado	habíais agradado
agradaba	agradaban	había agradado	habían agradado
3 pretérito		10 pretérito anterior	
agradé	agradamos	hube agradado	hubimos agradado
agradaste	agradasteis	hubiste agradado	hubisteis agradado
agradó	agradaron	hubo agradado	hubieron agradado
4 futuro		11 futuro perfecto	
agradaré	agradaremos	habré agradado	habremos agradado
agradarás	agradaréis	habrás agradado	habréis agradado
agradará	agradarán	habrá agradado	habrán agradado
5 potencial simple		12 potencial compuesto	
agradaría	agradaríamos	habría agradado	habríamos agradado
agradarías	agradaríais	habrías agradado	habríais agradado
agradaría	agradarían	habría agradado	habrían agradado
6 presente de subjuntivo		13 perfecto de subjuntivo	
agrade	agrademos	haya agradado	hayamos agradado
agrades	agradéis	hayas agradado	hayáis agradado
agrade	agraden	haya agradado	hayan agradado
7 imperfecto de subjuntivo		14 pluscuamperfecto de subjuntivo	
agradara	agradáramos	hubiera agradado	hubiéramos agradado
agradaras	agradarais	hubieras agradado	hubierais agradado
agradara	agradaran	hubiera agradado	hubieran agradado
OR		OR	
agradase	agradásemos	hubiese agradado	hubiésemos agradado
agradases	agradaseis	hubieses agradado	hubieseis agradado
agradase	agradasen	hubiese agradado	hubiesen agradado

imperativo	
—	agrademos
agrada; no agrades	agradad; no agradéis
agrade	agraden

Words and expressions related to this verb
agradable pleasing, pleasant, agreeable
agradablemente agreeably, pleasantly

el agrado pleasure, liking
Es de mi agrado. It's to my liking.

Gerundio **agradeciendo** Part. pas. **agradecido**   **agradecer**

to thank, to be thankful for

The Seven Simple Tenses		The Seven Compound Tenses	
Singular	Plural	Singular	Plural
1 presente de indicativo		**8 perfecto de indicativo**	
agradezco	agradecemos	he agradecido	hemos agradecido
agradeces	agradecéis	has agradecido	habéis agradecido
agradece	agradecen	ha agradecido	han agradecido
2 imperfecto de indicativo		**9 pluscuamperfecto de indicativo**	
agradecía	agradecíamos	había agradecido	habíamos agradecido
agraceías	agradecíais	habías agradecido	habíais agradecido
agradecía	agradecían	había agradecido	habían agradecido
3 pretérito		**10 pretérito anterior**	
agradecí	agradecimos	hube agradecido	hubimos agradecido
agradeciste	agradecisteis	hubiste agradecido	hubisteis agradecido
agradeció	agradecieron	hubo agradecido	hubieron agradecido
4 futuro		**11 futuro perfecto**	
agradeceré	agradeceremos	habré agradecido	habremos agradecido
agradecerás	agradeceréis	habrás agradecido	habréis agradecido
agradecerá	agradecerán	habrá agradecido	habrán agradecido
5 potencial simple		**12 potencial compuesto**	
agradecería	agradeceríamos	habría agradecido	habríamos agradecido
agradecerías	agradeceríais	habrías agradecido	habríais agradecido
agradecería	agradecerían	habría agradecido	habrían agradecido
6 presente de subjuntivo		**13 perfecto de subjuntivo**	
agradezca	agradezcamos	haya agradecido	hayamos agradecido
agradezcas	agradezcáis	hayas agradecido	hayáis agradecido
agradezca	agradezcan	haya agradecido	hayan agradecido
7 imperfecto de subjuntivo		**14 pluscuamperfecto de subjuntivo**	
agradeciera	agradeciéramos	hubiera agradecido	hubiéramos agradecido
agradecieras	agradecierais	hubieras agradecido	hubierais agradecido
agradeciera	agradecieran	hubiera agradecido	hubieran agradecido
OR		OR	
agradeciese	agradeciésemos	hubiese agradecido	hubiésemos agradecido
agradecieses	agradecieseis	hubieses agradecido	hubieseis agradecido
agradeciese	agradeciesen	hubiese agradecido	hubiesen agradecido

imperativo	
—	agradezcamos
agradece; no agradezcas	agradeced; no agradezcáis
agradezca	agradezcan

Words and expressions related to this verb
agradecido, agradecida thankful, grateful
el agradecimiento gratitude, gratefulness
desagradecer to be ungrateful
desagradecidamente ungratefully

to expect, to wait for

The Seven Simple Tenses		The Seven Compound Tenses	
Singular	Plural	Singular	Plural
1 presente de indicativo		8 perfecto de indicativo	
aguardo	aguardamos	he aguardado	hemos aguardado
aguardas	aguardáis	has aguardado	habéis aguardado
aguarda	aguardan	ha aguardado	han aguardado
2 imperfecto de indicativo		9 pluscuamperfecto de indicativo	
aguardaba	aguardábamos	había aguardado	habíamos aguardado
aguardabas	aguardabais	habías aguardado	habíais aguardado
aguardaba	aguardaban	había aguardado	habían aguardado
3 pretérito		10 pretérito anterior	
aguardé	aguardamos	hube aguardado	hubimos aguardado
aguardaste	aguardasteis	hubiste aguardado	hubisteis aguardado
aguardó	aguardaron	hubo aguardado	hubieron aguardado
4 futuro		11 futuro perfecto	
aguardaré	aguardaremos	habré aguardado	habremos aguardado
aguardarás	aguardaréis	habrás aguardado	habréis aguardado
aguardará	aguardarán	habrá aguardado	habrán aguardado
5 potencial simple		12 potencial compuesto	
aguardaría	aguardaríamos	habría aguardado	habríamos aguardado
aguardarías	aguardaríais	habrías aguardado	habríais aguardado
aguardaría	aguardarían	habría aguardado	habrían aguardado
6 presente de subjuntivo		13 perfecto de subjuntivo	
aguarde	aguardemos	haya aguardado	hayamos aguardado
aguardes	aguardéis	hayas aguardado	hayáis aguardado
aguarde	aguarden	haya aguardado	hayan aguardado
7 imperfecto de subjuntivo		14 pluscuamperfecto de subjuntivo	
aguardara	aguardáramos	hubiera aguardado	hubiéramos aguardado
aguardaras	aguardarais	hubieras aguardado	hubierais aguardado
aguardara	aguardaran	hubiera aguardado	hubieran aguardado
OR		OR	
aguardase	aguardásemos	hubiese aguardado	hubiésemos aguardado
aguardases	aguardaseis	hubieses aguardado	hubieseis aguardado
aguardase	aguardasen	hubiese aguardado	hubiesen aguardado

	imperativo	
—	aguardemos	
aguarda; no aguardes	aguardad; no aguardéis	
aguarde	aguarden	

Words and expressions related to this verb
la aguardada   expecting, waiting
guardar   to guard, to watch (over)

guardar silencio   to keep silent
¡Dios guarde al Rey!   God save the King!

to reach, to overtake

The Seven Simple Tenses		The Seven Compound Tenses	
Singular	Plural	Singular	Plural
1 presente de indicativo		8 perfecto de indicativo	
alcanzo	alcanzamos	he alcanzado	hemos alcanzado
alcanzas	alcanzáis	has alcanzado	habéis alcanzado
alcanza	alcanzan	ha alcanzado	han alcanzado
2 imperfecto de indicativo		9 pluscuamperfecto de indicativo	
alcanzaba	alcanzábamos	había alcanzado	habíamos alcanzado
alcanzabas	alcanzabais	habías alcanzado	habíais alcanzado
alcanzaba	alcanzaban	había alcanzado	habían alcanzado
3 pretérito		10 pretérito anterior	
alcancé	alcanzamos	hube alcanzado	hubimos alcanzado
alcanzaste	alcanzasteis	hubiste alcanzado	hubisteis alcanzado
alcanzó	alcanzaron	hubo alcanzado	hubieron alcanzado
4 futuro		11 futuro perfecto	
alcanzaré	alcanzaremos	habré alcanzado	habremos alcanzado
alcanzarás	alcanzaréis	habrás alcanzado	habréis alcanzado
alcanzará	alcanzarán	habrá alcanzado	habrán alcanzado
5 potencial simple		12 potencial compuesto	
alcanzaría	alcanzaríamos	habría alcanzado	habríamos alcanzado
alcanzarías	alcanzaríais	habrías alcanzado	habríais alcanzado
alcanzaría	alcanzarían	habría alcanzado	habrían alcanzado
6 presente de subjuntivo		13 perfecto de subjuntivo	
alcance	alcancemos	haya alcanzado	hayamos alcanzado
alcances	alcancéis	hayas alcanzado	hayáis alcanzado
alcance	alcancen	haya alcanzado	hayan alcanzado
7 imperfecto de subjuntivo		14 pluscuamperfecto de subjuntivo	
alcanzara	alcanzáramos	hubiera alcanzado	hubiéramos alcanzado
alcanzaras	alcanzarais	hubieras alcanzado	hubierais alcanzado
alcanzara	alcanzaran	hubiera alcanzado	hubieran alcanzado
OR		OR	
alcanzase	alcanzásemos	hubiese alcanzado	hubiésemos alcanzado
alcanzases	alcanzaseis	hubieses alcanzado	hubieseis alcanzado
alcanzase	alcanzasen	hubiese alcanzado	hubiesen alcanzado

imperativo	
—	alcancemos
alcanza; no alcances	alcanzad; no alcancéis
alcance	alcancen

Words and expressions related to this verb
el alcance overtaking, reach
al alcance de within reach of
dar alcance a to overtake

alcanzar a + inf. to manage to + inf.
alcanzar una cuota to fill a quota
alcanzar el tren to catch the train

27

alegrarse Gerundio **alegrándose** Part. pas. **alegrado**

to be glad, to rejoice

The Seven Simple Tenses		The Seven Compound Tenses	
Singular	Plural	Singular	Plural
1 presente de indicativo		8 perfecto de indicativo	
me alegro	nos alegramos	me he alegrado	nos hemos alegrado
te alegras	os alegráis	te has alegrado	os habéis alegrado
se alegra	se alegran	se ha alegrado	se han alegrado
2 imperfecto de indicativo		9 pluscuamperfecto de indicativo	
me alegraba	nos alegrábamos	me había alegrado	nos habíamos alegrado
te alegrabas	os alegrabais	te habías alegrado	os habíais alegrado
se alegraba	se alegraban	se había alegrado	se habían alegrado
3 pretérito		10 pretérito anterior	
me alegré	nos alegramos	me hube alegrado	nos hubimos alegrado
te alegraste	os alegrasteis	te hubiste alegrado	os hubisteis alegrado
se alegró	se alegraron	se hubo alegrado	se hubieron alegrado
4 futuro		11 futuro perfecto	
me alegraré	nos alegraremos	me habré alegrado	nos habremos alegrado
te alegrarás	os alegraréis	te habrás alegrado	os habréis alegrado
se alegrará	se alegrarán	se habrá alegrado	se habrán alegrado
5 potencial simple		12 potencial compuesto	
me alegraría	nos alegraríamos	me habría alegrado	nos habríamos alegrado
te alegrarías	os alegraríais	te habrías alegrado	os habríais alegrado
se alegraría	se alegrarían	se habría alegrado	se habrían alegrado
6 presente de subjuntivo		13 perfecto de subjuntivo	
me alegre	nos alegremos	me haya alegrado	nos hayamos alegrado
te alegres	os alegréis	te hayas alegrado	os hayáis alegrado
se alegre	se alegren	se haya alegrado	se hayan alegrado
7 imperfecto de subjuntivo		14 pluscuamperfecto de subjuntivo	
me alegrara	nos alegráramos	me hubiera alegrado	nos hubiéramos alegrado
te alegraras	os alegrarais	te hubieras alegrado	os hubierais alegrado
se alegrara	se alegraran	se hubiera alegrado	se hubieran alegrado
OR		OR	
me alegrase	nos alegrásemos	me hubiese alegrado	nos hubiésemos alegrado
te alegrases	os alegraseis	te hubieses alegrado	os hubieseis alegrado
se alegrase	se alegrasen	se hubiese alegrado	se hubiesen alegrado

	imperativo	
—		alegrémonos
alégrate; no te alegres		alegraos; no os alegréis
alégrese		alégrense

Words related to this verb
la alegría joy, rejoicing, mirth   **alegremente** gladly, cheerfully
alegro allegro   **alegre** happy, joyful, merry

to lunch, to have lunch

The Seven Simple Tenses		The Seven Compound Tenses	
Singular	Plural	Singular	Plural
1 presente de indicativo		8 perfecto de indicativo	
almuerzo	almorzamos	he almorzado	hemos almorzado
almuerzas	almorzáis	has almorzado	habéis almorzado
almuerza	almuerzan	ha almorzado	han almorzado
2 imperfecto de indicativo		9 pluscuamperfecto de indicativo	
almorzaba	almorzábamos	había almorzado	habíamos almorzado
almorzabas	almorzabais	habías almorzado	habíais almorzado
almorzaba	almorzaban	había almorzado	habían almorzado
3 pretérito		10 pretérito anterior	
almorcé	almorzamos	hube almorzado	hubimos almorzado
almorzaste	almorzasteis	hubiste almorzado	hubisteis almorzado
almorzó	almorzaron	hubo almorzado	hubieron almorzado
4 futuro		11 futuro perfecto	
almorzaré	almorzaremos	habré almorzado	habremos almorzado
almorzarás	almorzaréis	habrás almorzado	habréis almorzado
almorzará	almorzarán	habrá almorzado	habrán almorzado
5 potencial simple		12 potencial compuesto	
almorzaría	almorzaríamos	habría almorzado	habríamos almorzado
almorzarías	almorzaríais	habrías almorzado	habríais almorzado
almorzaría	almorzarían	habría almorzado	habrían almorzado
6 presente de subjuntivo		13 perfecto de subjuntivo	
almuerce	almorcemos	haya almorzado	hayamos almorzado
almuerces	almorcéis	hayas almorzado	hayáis almorzado
almuerce	almuercen	haya almorzado	hayan almorzado
7 imperfecto de subjuntivo		14 pluscuamperfecto de subjuntivo	
almorzara	almorzáramos	hubiera almorzado	hubiéramos almorzado
almorzaras	almorzarais	hubieras almorzado	hubierais almorzado
almorzara	almorzaran	hubiera almorzado	hubieran almorzado
OR		OR	
almorzase	almorzásemos	hubiese almorzado	hubiésemos almorzado
almorzases	almorzaseis	hubieses almorzado	hubieseis almorzado
almorzase	almorzasen	hubiese almorzado	hubiesen almorzado

imperativo	
—	almorcemos
almuerza; no almuerces	almorzad; no almorcéis
almuerce	almuercen

Sentences using this verb and words related to it

Todos los días tomo el desayuno en casa, tomo el almuerzo en la escuela con mis amigos, y ceno con mi familia a las ocho.

el desayuno breakfast	**le cena** dinner, supper
el almuerzo lunch	**cenar** to have dinner, supper

alzar
Gerundio **alzando** Part. pas. **alzado**

to heave, to lift, to pick up, to raise (prices)

The Seven Simple Tenses		The Seven Compound Tenses	
Singular	Plural	Singular	Plural
1 presente de indicativo		8 perfecto de indicativo	
alzo	alzamos	he alzado	hemos alzado
alzas	alzáis	has alzado	habéis alzado
alza	alzan	ha alzado	han alzado
2 imperfecto de indicativo		9 pluscuamperfecto de indicativo	
alzaba	alzábamos	había alzado	habíamos alzado
alzabas	alzabais	habías alzado	habíais alzado
alzaba	alzaban	había alzado	habían alzado
3 pretérito		10 pretérito anterior	
alcé	alzamos	hube alzado	hubimos alzado
alzaste	alzasteis	hubiste alzado	hubisteis alzado
alzó	alzaron	hubo alzado	hubieron alzado
4 futuro		11 futuro perfecto	
alzaré	alzaremos	habré alzado	habremos alzado
alzarás	alzaréis	habrás alzado	habréis alzado
alzará	alzarán	habrá alzado	habrán alzado
5 potencial simple		12 potencial compuesto	
alzaría	alzaríamos	habría alzado	habríamos alzado
alzarías	alzaríais	habrías alzado	habríais alzado
alzaría	alzarían	habría alzado	habrían alzado
6 presente de subjuntivo		13 perfecto de subjuntivo	
alce	alcemos	haya alzado	hayamos alzado
alces	alcéis	hayas alzado	hayáis alzado
alce	alcen	haya alzado	hayan alzado
7 imperfecto de subjuntivo		14 pluscuamperfecto de subjuntivo	
alzara	alzáramos	hubiera alzado	hubiéramos alzado
alzaras	alzarais	hubieras alzado	hubierais alzado
alzara	alzaran	hubiera alzado	hubieran alzado
OR		OR	
alzase	alzásemos	hubiese alzado	hubiésemos alzado
alzases	alzaseis	hubieses alzado	hubieseis alzado
alzase	alzasen	hubiese alzado	hubiesen alzado

imperativo	
—	alcemos
alza; no alces	alzad; no alcéis
alce	alcen

Words and expressions related to this verb
alzar velas to set the sails
alzar con to run off with, to steal
la alzadura elevation
el alzamiento raising, lifting

to love

The Seven Simple Tenses		The Seven Compound Tenses	
Singular	Plural	Singular	Plural
1 presente de indicativo		8 perfecto de indicativo	
amo	amamos	he amado	hemos amado
amas	amáis	has amado	habéis amado
ama	aman	ha amado	han amado
2 imperfecto de indicativo		9 pluscuamperfecto de indicativo	
amaba	amábamos	había amado	habíamos amado
amabas	amabais	habías amado	habíais amado
amaba	amaban	había amado	habían amado
3 pretérito		10 pretérito anterior	
amé	amamos	hube amado	hubimos amado
amaste	amasteis	hubiste amado	hubisteis amado
amó	amaron	hubo amado	hubieron amado
4 futuro		11 futuro perfecto	
amaré	amaremos	habré amado	habremos amado
amarás	amaréis	habrás amado	habréis amado
amará	amarán	habrá amado	habrán amado
5 potencial simple		12 potencial compuesto	
amaría	amaríamos	habría amado	habríamos amado
amarías	amaríais	habrías amado	habríais amado
amaría	amarían	habría amado	habrían amado
6 presente de subjuntivo		13 perfecto de subjuntivo	
ame	amemos	haya amado	hayamos amado
ames	améis	hayas amado	hayáis amado
ame	amen	haya amado	hayan amado
7 imperfecto de subjuntivo		14 pluscuamperfecto de subjuntivo	
amara	amáramos	hubiera amado	hubiéramos amado
amaras	amarais	hubieras amado	hubierais amado
amara	amaran	hubiera amado	hubieran amado
OR		OR	
amase	amásemos	hubiese amado	hubiésemos amado
amases	amaseis	hubieses amado	hubieseis amado
amase	amasen	hubiese amado	hubiesen amado

	imperativo	
—		amemos
	ama; no ames	amad; no améis
	ame	amen

Words related to this verb
la amabilidad   amiability, kindness   **amablemente**   amiably, kindly
amable   amiable, kind, affable   **el amor**   love

añadir   Gerundio **añadiendo**   Part. pas. **añadido**

to add

The Seven Simple Tenses		The Seven Compound Tenses	
Singular	Plural	Singular	Plural
1 presente de indicativo		8 perfecto de indicativo	
añado	añadimos	he añadido	hemos añadido
añades	añadís	has añadido	habéis añadido
añade	añaden	ha añadido	han añadido
2 imperfecto de indicativo		9 pluscuamperfecto de indicativo	
añadía	añadíamos	había añadido	habíamos añadido
añadías	añadíais	habías añadido	habíais añadido
añadía	añadían	había añadido	habían añadido
3 pretérito		10 pretérito anterior	
añadí	añadimos	hube añadido	hubimos añadido
añadiste	añadisteis	hubiste añadido	hubisteis añadido
añadió	añadieron	hubo añadido	hubieron añadido
4 futuro		11 futuro perfecto	
añadiré	añadiremos	habré añadido	habremos añadido
añadirás	añadiréis	habrás añadido	habréis añadido
añadirá	añadirán	habrá añadido	habrán añadido
5 potencial simple		12 potencial compuesto	
añadiría	añadiríamos	habría añadido	habríamos añadido
añadirías	añadiríais	habrías añadido	habríais añadido
añadiría	añadirían	habría añadido	habrían añadido
6 presente de subjuntivo		13 perfecto de subjuntivo	
añada	añadamos	haya añadido	hayamos añadido
añadas	añadáis	hayas añadido	hayáis añadido
añada	añadan	haya añadido	hayan añadido
7 imperfecto de subjuntivo		14 pluscuamperfecto de subjuntivo	
añadiera	añadiéramos	hubiera añadido	hubiéramos añadido
añadieras	añadierais	hubieras añadido	hubierais añadido
añadiera	añadieran	hubiera añadido	hubieran añadido
OR		OR	
añadiese	añadiésemos	hubiese añadido	hubiésemos añadido
añadieses	añadieseis	hubieses añadido	hubieseis añadido
añadiese	añadiesen	hubiese añadido	hubiesen añadido

imperativo	
—	añadamos
añade; no añadas	añadid; no añadáis
añada	añadan

Words and expressions related to this verb

la añadidura increase, addition   **el añadimiento** addition
por añadidura in addition   **añadido, añadida** added, additional

to walk

The Seven Simple Tenses		The Seven Compound Tenses	
Singular	Plural	Singular	Plural
1 presente de indicativo		8 perfecto de indicativo	
ando	andamos	he andado	hemos andado
andas	andáis	has andado	habéis andado
anda	andan	ha andado	han andado
2 imperfecto de indicativo		9 pluscuamperfecto de indicativo	
andaba	andábamos	había andado	habíamos andado
andabas	andabais	habías andado	habíais andado
andaba	andaban	había andado	habían andado
3 pretérito		10 pretérito anterior	
anduve	anduvimos	hube andado	hubimos andado
anduviste	anduvisteis	hubiste andado	hubisteis andado
anduvo	anduvieron	hubo andado	hubieron andado
4 futuro		11 futuro perfecto	
andaré	andaremos	habré andado	habremos andado
andarás	andaréis	habrás andado	habréis andado
andará	andarán	habrá andado	habrán andado
5 potencial simple		12 potencial compuesto	
andaría	andaríamos	habría andado	habríamos andado
andarías	andaríais	habrías andado	habríais andado
andaría	andarían	habría andado	habrían andado
6 presente de subjuntivo		13 perfecto de subjuntivo	
ande	andemos	haya andado	hayamos andado
andes	andéis	hayas andado	hayáis andado
ande	anden	haya andado	hayan andado
7 imperfecto de subjuntivo		14 pluscuamperfecto de subjuntivo	
anduviera	anduviéramos	hubiera andado	hubiéramos andado
anduvieras	anduvierais	hubieras andado	hubierais andado
anduviera	anduvieran	hubiera andado	hubieran andado
OR		OR	
anduviese	anduviésemos	hubiese andado	hubiésemos andado
anduvieses	anduvieseis	hubieses andado	hubieseis andado
anduviese	anduviesen	hubiese andado	hubiesen andado

imperativo	
—	andemos
anda; no andes	andad; no andéis
ande	anden

Words and expressions related to this verb
buena andanza   good fortune
mala andanza   bad fortune

a todo andar   at full speed
a largo andar   in the long run

33

aparecer	Gerundio **apareciendo**	Part. pas. **aparecido**

to appear, to show up

The Seven Simple Tenses		The Seven Compound Tenses	
Singular	Plural	Singular	Plural
1 presente de indicativo		8 perfecto de indicativo	
aparezco	**aparecemos**	**he aparecido**	**hemos aparecido**
apareces	**aparecéis**	**has aparecido**	**habéis aparecido**
aparece	**aparecen**	**ha aparecido**	**han aparecido**
2 imperfecto de indicativo		9 pluscuamperfecto de indicativo	
aparecía	**aparecíamos**	**había aparecido**	**habíamos aparecido**
aparecías	**aparecíais**	**habías aparecido**	**habíais aparecido**
aparecía	**aparecían**	**había aparecido**	**habían aparecido**
3 pretérito		10 pretérito anterior	
aparecí	**aparecimos**	**hube aparecido**	**hubimos aparecido**
apareciste	**aparecisteis**	**hubiste aparecido**	**hubisteis aparecido**
apareció	**aparecieron**	**hubo aparecido**	**hubieron aparecido**
4 futuro		11 futuro perfecto	
apareceré	**apareceremos**	**habré aparecido**	**habremos aparecido**
aparecerás	**apareceréis**	**habrás aparecido**	**habréis aparecido**
aparecerá	**aparecerán**	**habrá aparecido**	**habrán aparecido**
5 potencial simple		12 potencial compuesto	
aparecería	**apareceríamos**	**habría aparecido**	**habríamos aparecido**
aparecerías	**apareceríais**	**habrías aparecido**	**habríais aparecido**
aparecería	**aparecerían**	**habría aparecido**	**habrían aparecido**
6 presente de subjuntivo		13 perfecto de subjuntivo	
aparezca	**aparezcamos**	**haya aparecido**	**hayamos aparecido**
aparezcas	**aparezcáis**	**hayas aparecido**	**hayáis aparecido**
aparezca	**aparezcan**	**haya aparecido**	**hayan aparecido**
7 imperfecto de subjuntivo		14 pluscuamperfecto de subjuntivo	
apareciera	**apareciéramos**	**hubiera aparecido**	**hubiéramos aparecido**
aparecieras	**aparecierais**	**hubieras aparecido**	**hubierais aparecido**
apareciera	**aparecieran**	**hubiera aparecido**	**hubieran aparecido**
OR		OR	
apareciese	**apareciésemos**	**hubiese aparecido**	**hubiésemos aparecido**
aparecieses	**aparecieseis**	**hubieses aparecido**	**hubieseis aparecido**
apareciese	**apareciesen**	**hubiese aparecido**	**hubiesen aparecido**

imperativo	
—	**aparezcamos**
aparece; no aparezcas	**apareced; no aparezcáis**
aparezca	**aparezcan**

Words and expressions related to this verb

una aparición apparition, appearance
parecer to seem, to appear
parecerse a to look alike

aparecerse en casa to arrive home unexpectedly
aparecerse a alguno to see a ghost

to applaud

The Seven Simple Tenses		The Seven Compound Tenses	
Singular	Plural	Singular	Plural
1 presente de indicativo		**8 perfecto de indicativo**	
aplaudo	aplaudimos	he aplaudido	hemos aplaudido
aplaudes	aplaudís	has aplaudido	habéis aplaudido
aplaude	aplauden	ha aplaudido	han aplaudido
2 imperfecto de indicativo		**9 pluscuamperfecto de indicativo**	
aplaudía	aplaudíamos	había aplaudido	habíamos aplaudido
aplaudías	aplaudíais	habías aplaudido	habíais aplaudido
aplaudía	aplaudían	había aplaudido	habían aplaudido
3 pretérito		**10 pretérito anterior**	
aplaudí	aplaudimos	hube aplaudido	hubimos aplaudido
aplaudiste	aplaudisteis	hubiste aplaudido	hubisteis aplaudido
aplaudió	aplaudieron	hubo aplaudido	hubieron aplaudido
4 futuro		**11 futuro perfecto**	
aplaudiré	aplaudiremos	habré aplaudido	habremos aplaudido
aplaudirás	aplaudiréis	habrás aplaudido	habréis aplaudido
aplaudirá	aplaudirán	habrá aplaudido	habrán aplaudido
5 potencial simple		**12 potencial compuesto**	
aplaudiría	aplaudiríamos	habría aplaudido	habríamos aplaudido
aplaudirías	aplaudiríais	habrías aplaudido	habríais aplaudido
aplaudiría	aplaudirían	habría aplaudido	habrían aplaudido
6 presente de subjuntivo		**13 perfecto de subjuntivo**	
aplauda	aplaudamos	haya aplaudido	hayamos aplaudido
aplaudas	aplaudáis	hayas aplaudido	hayáis aplaudido
aplauda	aplaudan	haya aplaudido	hayan aplaudido
7 imperfecto de subjuntivo		**14 pluscuamperfecto de subjuntivo**	
aplaudiera	aplaudiéramos	hubiera aplaudido	hubiéramos aplaudido
aplaudieras	aplaudierais	hubieras aplaudido	hubierais aplaudido
aplaudiera	aplaudieran	hubiera aplaudido	hubieran aplaudido
OR		OR	
aplaudiese	aplaudiésemos	hubiese aplaudido	hubiésemos aplaudido
aplaudieses	aplaudieseis	hubieses aplaudido	hubieseis aplaudido
aplaudiese	aplaudiesen	hubiese aplaudido	hubiesen aplaudido

imperativo	
—	aplaudamos
aplaude; no aplaudas	aplaudid; no aplaudáis
aplauda	aplaudan

Words related to this verb
el aplauso applause, praise
el aplaudidor, la aplaudidora   applauder

35

apoderarse   Gerundio **apoderándose**   Part. pas. **apoderado**

to take power, to take possession

The Seven Simple Tenses		The Seven Compound Tenses	
Singular	Plural	Singular	Plural

1 presente de indicativo		8 perfecto de indicativo		
me apodero	nos apoderamos	me he	nos hemos	
te apoderas	os apoderáis	te has	os habéis	+ apoderado
se apodera	se apoderan	se ha	se han	

2 imperfecto de indicativo		9 pluscuamperfecto de indicativo		
me apoderaba	nos apoderábamos	me había	nos habíamos	
te apoderabas	os apoderabais	te habías	os habíais	+ apoderado
se apoderaba	se apoderaban	se había	se habían	

3 pretérito		10 pretérito anterior		
me apoderé	nos apoderamos	me hube	nos hubimos	
te apoderaste	os apoderasteis	te hubiste	os hubisteis	+ apoderado
se apoderó	se apoderaron	se hubo	se hubieron	

4 futuro		11 futuro perfecto		
me apoderaré	nos apoderaremos	me habré	nos habremos	
te apoderarás	os apoderaréis	te habrás	os habréis	+ apoderado
se apoderará	se apoderarán	se habrá	se habrán	

5 potencial simple		12 potencial compuesto		
me apoderaría	nos apoderaríamos	me habría	nos habríamos	
te apoderarías	os apoderaríais	te habrías	os habríais	+ apoderado
se apoderaría	se apoderarían	se habría	se habrían	

6 presente de subjuntivo		13 perfecto de subjuntivo		
me apodere	nos apoderemos	me haya	nos hayamos	
te apoderes	os apoderéis	te hayas	os hayáis	+ apoderado
se apodere	se apoderen	se haya	se hayan	

7 imperfecto de subjuntivo		14 pluscuamperfecto de subjuntivo		
me apoderara	nos apoderáramos	me hubiera	nos hubiéramos	
te apoderaras	os apoderarais	te hubieras	os hubierais	+ apoderado
se apoderara	se apoderaran	se hubiera	se hubieran	
OR		OR		
me apoderase	nos apoderásemos	me hubiese	nos hubiésemos	
te apoderases	os apoderaseis	te hubieses	os hubieseis	+ apoderado
se apoderase	se apoderasen	se hubiese	se hubiesen	

imperativo	
—	apoderémonos
apodérate; no te apoderes	apoderaos; no os apoderéis
apodérese	apodérense

Words and expressions related to this verb

poder to be able   **apoderarse de algo** to take possession of something
el poder power   **apoderado, apoderada** empowered
el apoderado proxy

to learn

The Seven Simple Tenses		The Seven Compound Tenses	
Singular	Plural	Singular	Plural
1 presente de indicativo		8 perfecto de indicativo	
aprendo	aprendemos	he aprendido	hemos aprendido
aprendes	aprendéis	has aprendido	habéis aprendido
aprende	aprenden	ha aprendido	han aprendido
2 imperfecto de indicativo		9 pluscuamperfecto de indicativo	
aprendía	aprendíamos	había aprendido	habíamos aprendido
aprendías	aprendíais	habías aprendido	habíais aprendido
aprendía	aprendían	había aprendido	habían aprendido
3 pretérito		10 pretérito anterior	
aprendí	aprendimos	hube aprendido	hubimos aprendido
aprendiste	aprendisteis	hubiste aprendido	hubisteis aprendido
aprendió	aprendieron	hubo aprendido	hubieron aprendido
4 futuro		11 futuro perfecto	
aprenderé	aprenderemos	habré aprendido	habremos aprendido
aprenderás	aprenderéis	habrás aprendido	habréis aprendido
aprenderá	aprenderán	habrá aprendido	habrán aprendido
5 potencial simple		12 potencial compuesto	
aprendería	aprenderíamos	habría aprendido	habríamos aprendido
aprenderías	aprenderíais	habrías aprendido	habríais aprendido
aprendería	aprenderían	habría aprendido	habrían aprendido
6 presente de subjuntivo		13 perfecto de subjuntivo	
aprenda	aprendamos	haya aprendido	hayamos aprendido
aprendas	aprendáis	hayas aprendido	hayáis aprendido
aprenda	aprendan	haya aprendido	hayan aprendido
7 imperfecto de subjuntivo		14 pluscuamperfecto de subjuntivo	
aprendiera	aprendiéramos	hubiera aprendido	hubiéramos aprendido
aprendieras	aprendierais	hubieras aprendido	hubierais aprendido
aprendiera	aprendieran	hubiera aprendido	hubieran aprendido
OR		OR	
aprendiese	aprendiésemos	hubiese aprendido	hubiésemos aprendido
aprendieses	aprendieseis	hubieses aprendido	hubieseis aprendido
aprendiese	aprendiesen	hubiese aprendido	hubiesen aprendido

	imperativo	
—	aprendamos	
aprende; no aprendas	aprended; no aprendáis	
aprenda	aprendan	

Sentences using this verb and words and expressions related to it

Aprendo mucho en la escuela. En la clase de español aprendemos a hablar, a leer, y a escribir en español.

el aprendedor, la aprendedora learner		**aprender a + inf.** to learn + inf.	
el aprendizaje apprenticeship		**aprender de memoria** to memorize	

to hasten, to hurry, to rush

The Seven Simple Tenses		The Seven Compound Tenses	
Singular	Plural	Singular	Plural
1 presente de indicativo		8 perfecto de indicativo	
me apresuro	nos apresuramos	me he	nos hemos
te apresuras	os apresuráis	te has	os habéis + apresurado
se apresura	se apresuran	se ha	se han
2 imperfecto de indicativo		9 pluscuamperfecto de indicativo	
me apresuraba	nos apresurábamos	me había	nos habíamos
te apresurabas	os apresurabais	te habías	os habíais + apresurado
se apresuraba	se apresuraban	se había	se habían
3 pretérito		10 pretérito anterior	
me apresuré	nos apresuramos	me hube	nos hubimos
te apresuraste	os apresurasteis	te hubiste	os hubisteis + apresurado
se apresuró	se apresuraron	se hubo	se hubieron
4 futuro		11 futuro perfecto	
me apresuraré	nos apresuraremos	me habré	nos habremos
te apresurarás	os apresuraréis	te habrás	os habréis + apresurado
se apresurará	se apresurarán	se habrá	se habrán
5 potencial simple		12 potencial compuesto	
me apresuraría	nos apresuraríamos	me habría	nos habríamos
te apresurarías	os apresuraríais	te habrías	os habríais + apresurado
se apresuraría	se apresurarían	se habría	se habrían
6 presente de subjuntivo		13 perfecto de subjuntivo	
me apresure	nos apresuremos	me haya	nos hayamos
te apresures	os apresuréis	te hayas	os hayáis + apresurado
se apresure	se apresuren	se haya	se hayan
7 imperfecto de subjuntivo		14 pluscuamperfecto de subjuntivo	
me apresurara	nos apresuráramos	me hubiera	nos hubiéramos
te apresuraras	os apresurarais	te hubieras	os hubierais + apresurado
se apresurara	se apresuraran	se hubiera	se hubieran
OR		OR	
me apresurase	nos apresurásemos	me hubiese	nos hubiésemos
te apresurases	os apresuraseis	te hubieses	os hubieseis + apresurado
se apresurase	se apresurasen	se hubiese	se hubiesen

imperativo

—	apresurémonos
apresúrate; no te apresures	apresuraos; no os apresuréis
apresúrese	apresúrense

Words and expressions related to this verb
la apresuración haste
apresurado, apresurada hasty, quick
apresuradamente hastily
la prisa haste

el apresuramiento hastiness
apresurar to accelerate
apresurarse a + inf. to hurry + inf.
tener prisa to be in a hurry

Gerundio **aprovechándose**   Part. pas. **aprovechado**   **aprovecharse**

to take advantage, to avail oneself

The Seven Simple Tenses		The Seven Compound Tenses	
Singular	Plural	Singular	Plural

1 presente de indicativo

me aprovecho	nos aprovechamos		
te aprovechas	os aprovecháis		
se aprovecha	se aprovechan		

8 perfecto de indicativo

me he	nos hemos	
te has	os habéis	+ aprovechado
se ha	se han	

2 imperfecto de indicativo

me aprovechaba	nos aprovechábamos
te aprovechabas	os aprovechabais
se aprovechaba	se aprovechaban

9 pluscuamperfecto de indicativo

me había	nos habíamos	
te habías	os habíais	+ aprovechado
se había	se habían	

3 pretérito

me aproveché	nos aprovechamos
te aprovechaste	os aprovechasteis
se aprovechó	se aprovecharon

10 pretérito anterior

me hube	nos hubimos	
te hubiste	os hubisteis	+ aprovechado
se hubo	se hubieron	

4 futuro

me aprovecharé	nos aprovecharemos
te aprovecharás	os aprovecharéis
se aprovechará	se aprovecharán

11 futuro perfecto

me habré	nos habremos	
te habrás	os habréis	+ aprovechado
se habrá	se habrán	

5 potencial simple

me aprovecharía	nos aprovecharíamos
te aprovecharías	os aprovecharíais
se aprovecharía	se aprovecharían

12 potencial compuesto

me habría	nos habríamos	
te habrías	os habríais	+ aprovechado
se habría	se habrían	

6 presente de subjuntivo

me aproveche	nos aprovechemos
te aproveches	os aprovechéis
se aproveche	se aprovechen

13 perfecto de subjuntivo

me haya	nos hayamos	
te hayas	os hayáis	+ aprovechado
se haya	se hayan	

7 imperfecto de subjuntivo

me aprovechara	nos aprovecháramos
te aprovecharas	os aprovecharais
se aprovechara	se aprovecharan
OR	
me aprovechase	nos aprovechásemos
te aprovechases	os aprovechaseis
se aprovechase	se aprovechasen

14 pluscuamperfecto de subjuntivo

me hubiera	nos hubiéramos	
te hubieras	os hubierais	+ aprovechado
se hubiera	se hubieran	
OR		
me hubiese	nos hubiésemos	
te hubieses	os hubieseis	+ aprovechado
se hubiese	se hubiesen	

imperativo

—	aprovechémonos
aprovéchate; no te aproveches	aprovechaos; no os aprovechéis
aprovéchese	aprovéchense

Words and expressions related to this verb

aprovechado, aprovechada economical
aprovechable available, profitable
aprovechamiento use, utilization
aprovecharse de to take advantage of

aprovechar to make use of
aprovechar la ocasión to take the opportunity

arrojar

Gerundio **arrojando**   Part. pas. **arrojado**

to fling, to hurl, to throw

The Seven Simple Tenses		The Seven Compound Tenses	
Singular	Plural	Singular	Plural
1 presente de indicativo		**8 perfecto de indicativo**	
arrojo	arrojamos	he arrojado	hemos arrojado
arrojas	arrojáis	has arrojado	habéis arrojado
arroja	arrojan	ha arrojado	han arrojado
2 imperfecto de indicativo		**9 pluscuamperfecto de indicativo**	
arrojaba	arrojábamos	había arrojado	habíamos arrojado
arrojabas	arrojabais	habías arrojado	habíais arrojado
arrojaba	arrojaban	había arrojado	habían arrojado
3 pretérito		**10 pretérito anterior**	
arrojé	arrojamos	hube arrojado	hubimos arrojado
arrojaste	arrojasteis	hubiste arrojado	hubisteis arrojado
arrojó	arrojaron	hubo arrojado	hubieron arrojado
4 futuro		**11 futuro perfecto**	
arrojaré	arrojaremos	habré arrojado	habremos arrojado
arrojarás	arrojaréis	habrás arrojado	habréis arrojado
arrojará	arrojarán	habrá arrojado	habrán arrojado
5 potencial simple		**12 potencial compuesto**	
arrojaría	arrojaríamos	habría arrojado	habríamos arrojado
arrojarías	arrojaríais	habrías arrojado	habríais arrojado
arrojaría	arrojarían	habría arrojado	habrían arrojado
6 presente de subjuntivo		**13 perfecto de subjuntivo**	
arroje	arrojemos	haya arrojado	hayamos arrojado
arrojes	arrojéis	hayas arrojado	hayáis arrojado
arroje	arrojen	haya arrojado	hayan arrojado
7 imperfecto de subjuntivo		**14 pluscuamperfecto de subjuntivo**	
arrojara	arrojáramos	hubiera arrojado	hubiéramos arrojado
arrojaras	arrojarais	hubieras arrojado	hubierais arrojado
arrojara	arrojaran	hubiera arrojado	hubieran arrojado
OR		OR	
arrojase	arrojásemos	hubiese arrojado	hubiésemos arrojado
arrojases	arrojaseis	hubieses arrojado	hubieseis arrojado
arrojase	arrojasen	hubiese arrojado	hubiesen arrojado

	imperativo	
—	arrojemos	
arroja; no arrojes	arrojad; no arrojéis	
arroje	arrojen	

Words and expressions related to this verb

el arrojador, la arrojadora thrower
arrojado, arrojada fearless
el arrojo fearlessness

arrojar la esponja to throw in the towel (sponge)
el arrojallamas flame thrower

to assure, to affirm, to assert, to insure

The Seven Simple Tenses		The Seven Compound Tenses	
Singular	Plural	Singular	Plural
1 presente de indicativo		8 perfecto de indicativo	
aseguro	aseguramos	he asegurado	hemos asegurado
aseguras	aseguráis	has asegurado	habéis asegurado
asegura	aseguran	ha asegurado	han asegurado
2 imperfecto de indicativo		9 pluscuamperfecto de indicativo	
aseguraba	asegurábamos	había asegurado	habíamos asegurado
asegurabas	asegurabais	habías asegurado	habíais asegurado
aseguraba	aseguraban	había asegurado	habían asegurado
3 pretérito		10 pretérito anterior	
aseguré	aseguramos	hube asegurado	hubimos asegurado
aseguraste	asegurasteis	hubiste asegurado	hubisteis asegurado
aseguró	aseguraron	hubo asegurado	hubieron asegurado
4 futuro		11 futuro perfecto	
aseguraré	aseguraremos	habré asegurado	habremos asegurado
asegurarás	aseguraréis	habrás asegurado	habréis asegurado
asegurará	asegurarán	habrá asegurado	habrán asegurado
5 potencial simple		12 potencial compuesto	
aseguraría	aseguraríamos	habría asegurado	habríamos asegurado
asegurarías	aseguraríais	habrías asegurado	habríais asegurado
aseguraría	asegurarían	habría asegurado	habrían asegurado
6 presente de subjuntivo		13 perfecto de subjuntivo	
asegure	aseguremos	haya asegurado	hayamos asegurado
asegures	aseguréis	hayas asegurado	hayáis asegurado
asegure	aseguren	haya asegurado	hayan asegurado
7 imperfecto de subjuntivo		14 pluscuamperfecto de subjuntivo	
asegurara	aseguráramos	hubiera asegurado	hubiéramos asegurado
aseguraras	asegurarais	hubieras asegurado	hubierais asegurado
asegurara	aseguraran	hubiera asegurado	hubieran asegurado
OR		OR	
asegurase	asegurásemos	hubiese asegurado	hubiésemos asegurado
asegurases	aseguraseis	hubieses asegurado	hubieseis asegurado
asegurase	asegurasen	hubiese asegurado	hubiesen asegurado

imperativo		
—		aseguremos
	asegura; no asegures	asegurad; no aseguréis
	asegure	aseguren

Words and expressions related to this verb

la aseguración insurance	**¡Ya puede usted asegurarlo!** You
asegurable insurable	can be sure of it!
el asegurado, la asegurada insured person	**tener por seguro** for sure
la seguridad security, surety	**de seguro** surely
seguramente surely, securely	

asir	Gerundio **asiendo**	Part. pas. **asido**

to seize, to grasp

The Seven Simple Tenses		The Seven Compound Tenses	
Singular	Plural	Singular	Plural
1 presente de indicativo		8 perfecto de indicativo	
asgo	asimos	he asido	hemos asido
ases	asís	has asido	habéis asido
ase	asen	ha asido	han asido
2 imperfecto de indicativo		9 pluscuamperfecto de indicativo	
asía	asíamos	había asido	habíamos asido
asías	asíais	habías asido	habíais asido
asía	asían	había asido	habían asido
3 pretérito		10 pretérito anterior	
así	asimos	hube asido	hubimos asido
asiste	asisteis	hubiste asido	hubisteis asido
asió	asieron	hubo asido	hubieron asido
4 futuro		11 futuro perfecto	
asiré	asiremos	habré asido	habremos asido
asirás	asiréis	habrás asido	habréis asido
asirá	asirán	habrá asido	habrán asido
5 potencial simple		12 potencial compuesto	
asiría	asiríamos	habría asido	habríamos asido
asirías	asiríais	habrías asido	habríais asido
asiría	asirían	habría asido	habrían asido
6 presente de subjuntivo		13 perfecto de subjuntivo	
asga	asgamos	haya asido	hayamos asido
asgas	asgáis	hayas asido	hayáis asido
asga	asgan	haya asido	hayan asido
7 imperfecto de subjuntivo		14 pluscuamperfecto de subjuntivo	
asiera	asiéramos	hubiera asido	hubiéramos asido
asieras	asierais	hubieras asido	hubierais asido
asiera	asieran	hubiera asido	hubieran asido
OR		OR	
asiese	asiésemos	hubiese asido	hubiésemos asido
asieses	asieseis	hubieses asido	hubieseis asido
asiese	asiesen	hubiese asido	hubiesen asido

imperativo	
—	asgamos
ase; no asgas	asid; no asgáis
asga	asgan

Words and expressions related to this verb
asir de los cabellos   to grab by the hair
asirse a (or de)   to take hold of, to seize, grab
asirse con   to grapple with   asidos del brazo   arm in arm

Gerundio **asistiendo**   Part. pas. **asistido**   **asistir**

to attend, to assist, to be present

The Seven Simple Tenses		The Seven Compound Tenses	
Singular	Plural	Singular	Plural
1 presente de indicativo		8 perfecto de indicativo	
asisto	asistimos	he asistido	hemos asistido
asistes	asistís	has asistido	habéis asistido
asiste	asisten	ha asistido	han asistido
2 imperfecto de indicativo		9 pluscuamperfecto de indicativo	
asistía	asistíamos	había asistido	habíamos asistido
asistías	asistíais	habías asistido	habíais asistido
asistía	asistían	había asistido	habían asistido
3 pretérito		10 pretérito anterior	
asistí	asistimos	hube asistido	hubimos asistido
asististe	asististeis	hubiste asistido	hubisteis asistido
asistió	asistieron	hubo asistido	hubieron asistido
4 futuro		11 futuro perfecto	
asistiré	asistiremos	habré asistido	habremos asistido
asistirás	asistiréis	habrás asistido	habréis asistido
asistirá	asistirán	habrá asistido	habrán asistido
5 potencial simple		12 potencial compuesto	
asistiría	asistiríamos	habría asistido	habríamos asistido
asistirías	asistiríais	habrías asistido	habríais asistido
asistiría	asistirían	habría asistido	habrían asistido
6 presente de subjuntivo		13 perfecto de subjuntivo	
asista	asistamos	haya asistido	hayamos asistido
asistas	asistáis	hayas asistido	hayáis asistido
asista	asistan	haya asistido	hayan asistido
7 imperfecto de subjuntivo		14 pluscuamperfecto de subjuntivo	
asistiera	asistiéramos	hubiera asistido	hubiéramos asistido
asistieras	asistierais	hubieras asistido	hubierais asistido
asistiera	asistieran	hubiera asistido	hubieran asistido
OR		OR	
asistiese	asistiésemos	hubiese asistido	hubiésemos asistido
asistieses	asistieseis	hubieses asistido	hubieseis asistido
asistiese	asistiesen	hubiese asistido	hubiesen asistido

	imperativo	
—	asistamos	
asiste; no asistas	asistid; no asistáis	
asista	asistan	

Words and expressions related to this verb

asistir a to attend, to be present at
la asistencia attendance, presence
el asistimiento assistance

la asistencia social social welfare
la asistencia técnica technical assistance

to frighten, to scare

The Seven Simple Tenses		The Seven Compound Tenses	
Singular	Plural	Singular	Plural
1 presente de indicativo		**8 perfecto de indicativo**	
asusto	asustamos	he asustado	hemos asustado
asustas	asustáis	has asustado	habéis asustado
asusta	asustan	ha asustado	han asustado
2 imperfecto de indicativo		**9 pluscuamperfecto de indicativo**	
asustaba	asustábamos	había asustado	habíamos asustado
asustabas	asustabais	habías asustado	habíais asustado
asustaba	asustaban	había asustado	habían asustado
3 pretérito		**10 pretérito anterior**	
asusté	asustamos	hube asustado	hubimos asustado
asustaste	asustasteis	hubiste asustado	hubisteis asustado
asustó	asustaron	hubo asustado	hubieron asustado
4 futuro		**11 futuro perfecto**	
asustaré	asustaremos	habré asustado	habremos asustado
asustarás	asustaréis	habrás asustado	habréis asustado
asustará	asustarán	habrá asustado	habrán asustado
5 potencial simple		**12 potencial compuesto**	
asustaría	asustaríamos	habría asustado	habríamos asustado
asustarías	asustaríais	habrías asustado	habríais asustado
asustaría	asustarían	habría asustado	habrían asustado
6 presente de subjuntivo		**13 perfecto de subjuntivo**	
asuste	asustemos	haya asustado	hayamos asustado
asustes	asustéis	hayas asustado	hayáis asustado
asuste	asusten	haya asustado	hayan asustado
7 imperfecto de subjuntivo		**14 pluscuamperfecto de subjuntivo**	
asustara	asustáramos	hubiera asustado	hubiéramos asustado
asustaras	asustarais	hubieras asustado	hubierais asustado
asustara	asustaran	hubiera asustado	hubieran asustado
OR		OR	
asustase	asustásemos	hubiese asustado	hubiésemos asustado
asustases	asustaseis	hubieses asustado	hubieseis asustado
asustase	asustasen	hubiese asustado	hubiesen asustado

imperativo	
—	asustemos
asusta; no asustes	asustad; no asustéis
asuste	asusten

Words related to this verb
asustado, asustada   frightened, scared
asustadizo, asustadiza   easily frightened

Gerundio **asustándose**   Part. pas. **asustado**   **asustarse**

to be frightened, to be scared

The Seven Simple Tenses		The Seven Compound Tenses	
Singular	Plural	Singular	Plural

1 presente de indicativo

me asusto	nos asustamos
te asustas	os asustáis
se asusta	se asustan

8 perfecto de indicativo

me he asustado	nos hemos asustado
te has asustado	os habéis asustado
se ha asustado	se han asustado

2 imperfecto de indicativo

me asustaba	nos asustábamos
te asustabas	os asustabais
se asustaba	se asustaban

9 pluscuamperfecto de indicativo

me había asustado	nos habíamos asustado
te habías asustado	os habíais asustado
se había asustado	se habían asustado

3 pretérito

me asusté	nos asustamos
te asustaste	os asustasteis
se asustó	se asustaron

10 pretérito anterior

me hube asustado	nos hubimos asustado
te hubiste asustado	os hubisteis asustado
se hubo asustado	se hubieron asustado

4 futuro

me asustaré	nos asustaremos
te asustarás	os asustaréis
se asustará	se asustarán

11 futuro perfecto

me habré asustado	nos habremos asustado
te habrás asustado	os habréis asustado
se habrá asustado	se habrán asustado

5 potencial simple

me asustaría	nos asustaríamos
te asustarías	os asustaríais
se asustaría	se asustarían

12 potencial compuesto

me habría asustado	nos habríamos asustado
te habrías asustado	os habríais asustado
se habría asustado	se habrían asustado

6 presente de subjuntivo

me asuste	nos asustemos
te asustes	os asustéis
se asuste	se asusten

13 perfecto de subjuntivo

me haya asustado	nos hayamos asustado
te hayas asustado	os hayáis asustado
se haya asustado	se hayan asustado

7 imperfecto de subjuntivo

me asustara	nos asustáramos
te asustaras	os asustarais
se asustara	se asustaran
OR	
me asustase	nos asustásemos
te asustases	os asustaseis
se asustase	se asustasen

14 pluscuamperfecto de subjuntivo

me hubiera asustado	nos hubiéramos asustado
te hubieras asustado	os hubierais asustado
se hubiera asustado	se hubieran asustado
OR	
me hubiese asustado	nos hubiésemos asustado
te hubieses asustado	os hubieseis asustado
se hubiese asustado	se hubiesen asustado

imperativo

—	asustémonos
asústate; no te asustes	asustaos; no os asustéis
asústese	asústense

Words and expressions related to this verb
asustado, asustada frightened, scared
asustadizo, asustadiza easily frightened
asustador, asustadora frightening

asustar to frighten, to scare
asustarse de + inf. to be afraid + inf.

to attack

The Seven Simple Tenses		The Seven Compound Tenses	
Singular	Plural	Singular	Plural
1 presente de indicativo		8 perfecto de indicativo	
ataco	atacamos	he atacado	hemos atacado
atacas	atacáis	has atacado	habéis atacado
ataca	atacan	ha atacado	han atacado
2 imperfecto de indicativo		9 pluscuamperfecto de indicativo	
atacaba	atacábamos	había atacado	habíamos atacado
atacabas	atacabais	habías atacado	habíais atacado
atacaba	atacaban	había atacado	habían atacado
3 pretérito		10 pretérito anterior	
ataqué	atacamos	hube atacado	hubimos atacado
atacaste	atacasteis	hubiste atacado	hubisteis atacado
atacó	atacaron	hubo atacado	hubieron atacado
4 futuro		11 futuro perfecto	
atacaré	atacaremos	habré atacado	habremos atacado
atacarás	atacaréis	habrás atacado	habréis atacado
atacará	atacarán	habrá atacado	habrán atacado
5 potencial simple		12 potencial compuesto	
atacaría	atacaríamos	habría atacado	habríamos atacado
atacarías	atacaríais	habrías atacado	habríais atacado
atacaría	atacarían	habría atacado	habrían atacado
6 presente de subjuntivo		13 perfecto de subjuntivo	
ataque	ataquemos	haya atacado	hayamos atacado
ataques	ataquéis	hayas atacado	hayáis atacado
ataque	ataquen	haya atacado	hayan atacado
7 imperfecto de subjuntivo		14 pluscuamperfecto de subjuntivo	
atacara	atacáramos	hubiera atacado	hubiéramos atacado
atacaras	atacarais	hubieras atacado	hubierais atacado
atacara	atacaran	hubiera atacado	hubieran atacado
OR		OR	
atacase	atacásemos	hubiese atacado	hubiésemos atacado
atacases	atacaseis	hubieses atacado	hubieseis atacado
atacase	atacasen	hubiese atacado	hubiesen atacado

imperativo	
—	ataquemos
ataca; no ataques	atacad; no ataquéis
ataque	ataquen

Words related to this verb
el ataque attack
atacado, atacada attacked

el, la atacante attacker
el atacador, la atacadora aggressor

to cross, to go through, to run through

The Seven Simple Tenses		The Seven Compound Tenses	
Singular	Plural	Singular	Plural
1 presente de indicativo		8 perfecto de indicativo	
atravieso	atravesamos	he atravesado	hemos atravesado
atraviesas	atravesáis	has atravesado	habéis atravesado
atraviesa	atraviesan	ha atravesado	han atravesado
2 imperfecto de indicativo		9 pluscuamperfecto de indicativo	
atravesaba	atravesábamos	había atravesado	habíamos atravesado
atravesabas	atravesabais	habías atravesado	habíais atravesado
atravesaba	atravesaban	había atravesado	habían atravesado
3 pretérito		10 pretérito anterior	
atravesé	atravesamos	hube atravesado	hubimos atravesado
atravesaste	atravesasteis	hubiste atravesado	hubisteis atravesado
atravesó	atravesaron	hubo atravesado	hubieron atravesado
4 futuro		11 futuro perfecto	
atravesaré	atravesaremos	habré atravesado	habremos atravesado
atravesarás	atravesaréis	habrás atravesado	habréis atravesado
atravesará	atravesarán	habrá atravesado	habrán atravesado
5 potencial simple		12 potencial compuesto	
atravesaría	atravesaríamos	habría atravesado	habríamos atravesado
atravesarías	atravesaríais	habrías atravesado	habríais atravesado
atravesaría	atravesarían	habría atravesado	habrían atravesado
6 presente de subjuntivo		13 perfecto de subjuntivo	
atraviese	atravesemos	haya atravesado	hayamos atravesado
atravieses	atraveséis	hayas atravesado	hayáis atravesado
atraviese	atraviesen	haya atravesado	hayan atravesado
7 imperfecto de subjuntivo		14 pluscuamperfecto de subjuntivo	
atravesara	atravesáramos	hubiera atravesado	hubiéramos atravesado
atravesaras	atravesarais	hubieras atravesado	hubierais atravesado
atravesara	atravesaran	hubiera atravesado	hubieran atravesado
OR		OR	
atravesase	atravesásemos	hubiese atravesado	hubiésemos atravesado
atravesases	atravesaseis	hubieses atravesado	hubieseis atravesado
atravesase	atravesasen	hubiese atravesado	hubiesen atravesado

imperativo	
—	atravesemos
atraviesa; no atravieses	atravesad; no atraveséis
atraviese	atraviesen

Words and expressions related to this verb
atravesar con   to meet
travesar   to cross
mirar de través   to look out of the corner of one's eye
la travesía   crossing (sea)

atreverse Gerundio **atreviéndose** Part. pas. **atrevido**

to dare, to venture

The Seven Simple Tenses		The Seven Compound Tenses	
Singular	Plural	Singular	Plural
1 presente de indicativo		**8 perfecto de indicativo**	
me atrevo	nos atrevemos	me he atrevido	nos hemos atrevido
te atreves	os atrevéis	te has atrevido	os habéis atrevido
se atreve	se atreven	se ha atrevido	se han atrevido
2 imperfecto de indicativo		**9 pluscuamperfecto de indicativo**	
me atrevía	nos atrevíamos	me había atrevido	nos habíamos atrevido
te atrevías	os atrevíais	te habías atrevido	os habíais atrevido
se atrevía	se atrevían	se había atrevido	se habían atrevido
3 pretérito		**10 pretérito anterior**	
me atreví	nos atrevimos	me hube atrevido	nos hubimos atrevido
te atreviste	os atrevisteis	te hubiste atrevido	os hubisteis atrevido
se atrevió	se atrevieron	se hubo atrevido	se hubieron atrevido
4 futuro		**11 futuro perfecto**	
me atreveré	nos atreveremos	me habré atrevido	nos habremos atrevido
te atreverás	os atreveréis	te habrás atrevido	os habréis atrevido
se atreverá	se atreverán	se habrá atrevido	se habrán atrevido
5 potencial simple		**12 potencial compuesto**	
me atrevería	nos atreveríamos	me habría atrevido	nos habríamos atrevido
te atreverías	os atreveríais	te habrías atrevido	os habríais atrevido
se atrevería	se atreverían	se habría atrevido	se habrían atrevido
6 presente de subjuntivo		**13 perfecto de subjuntivo**	
me atreva	nos atrevamos	me haya atrevido	nos hayamos atrevido
te atrevas	os atreváis	te hayas atrevido	os hayáis atrevido
se atreva	se atrevan	se haya atrevido	se hayan atrevido
7 imperfecto de subjuntivo		**14 pluscuamperfecto de subjuntivo**	
me atreviera	nos atreviéramos	me hubiera atrevido	nos hubiéramos atrevido
te atrevieras	os atrevierais	te hubieras atrevido	os hubierais atrevido
se atreviera	se atrevieran	se hubiera atrevido	se hubieran atrevido
OR		OR	
me atreviese	nos atreviésemos	me hubiese atrevido	nos hubiésemos atrevido
te atrevieses	os atrevieseis	te hubieses atrevido	os hubieseis atrevido
se atreviese	se atreviesen	se hubiese atrevido	se hubiesen atrevido

imperativo	
—	atrevámonos
atrévete; no te atrevas	atreveos; no os atreváis
atrévase	atrévanse

Words related to this verb
atrevido, atrevida daring, bold
el atrevimiento audacity, boldness
atrevidamente boldly, daringly

Gerundio **avanzando**   Part. pas. **avanzado**

avanzar

to advance

The Seven Simple Tenses		The Seven Compound Tenses	
Singular	Plural	Singular	Plural
1 presente de indicativo		**8 perfecto de indicativo**	
avanzo	avanzamos	he avanzado	hemos avanzado
avanzas	avanzáis	has avanzado	habéis avanzado
avanza	avanzan	ha avanzado	han avanzado
2 imperfecto de indicativo		**9 pluscuamperfecto de indicativo**	
avanzaba	avanzábamos	había avanzado	habíamos avanzado
avanzabas	avanzabais	habías avanzado	habíais avanzado
avanzaba	avanzaban	había avanzado	habían avanzado
3 pretérito		**10 pretérito anterior**	
avancé	avanzamos	hube avanzado	hubimos avanzado
avanzaste	avanzasteis	hubiste avanzado	hubisteis avanzado
avanzó	avanzaron	hubo avanzado	hubieron avanzado
4 futuro		**11 futuro perfecto**	
avanzaré	avanzaremos	habré avanzado	habremos avanzado
avanzarás	avanzaréis	habrás avanzado	habréis avanzado
avanzará	avanzarán	habrá avanzado	habrán avanzado
5 potencial simple		**12 potencial compuesto**	
avanzaría	avanzaríamos	habría avanzado	habríamos avanzado
avanzarías	avanzaríais	habrías avanzado	habríais avanzado
avanzaría	avanzarían	habría avanzado	habrían avanzado
6 presente de subjuntivo		**13 perfecto de subjuntivo**	
avance	avancemos	haya avanzado	hayamos avanzado
avances	avancéis	hayas avanzado	hayáis avanzado
avance	avancen	haya avanzado	hayan avanzado
7 imperfecto de subjuntivo		**14 pluscuamperfecto de subjuntivo**	
avanzara	avanzáramos	hubiera avanzado	hubiéramos avanzado
avanzaras	avanzarais	hubieras avanzado	hubierais avanzado
avanzara	avanzaran	hubiera avanzado	hubieran avanzado
OR		OR	
avanzase	avanzásemos	hubiese avanzado	hubiésemos avanzado
avanzases	avanzaseis	hubieses avanzado	hubieseis avanzado
avanzase	avanzasen	hubiese avanzado	hubiesen avanzado

imperativo	
—	avancemos
avanza; no avances	avanzad; no avancéis
avance	avancen

Words and expressions related to this verb
avanzado, avanzada   advanced; **edad avanzada**   advanced in years
la avanzada   advance guard
avante   forward, ahead
salir avante   to succeed

to find out, to inquire, to investigate

The Seven Simple Tenses		The Seven Compound Tenses	
Singular	Plural	Singular	Plural
1 presente de indicativo		8 perfecto de indicativo	
averiguo	averiguamos	he averiguado	hemos averiguado
averiguas	averiguáis	has averiguado	habéis averiguado
averigua	averiguan	ha averiguado	han averiguado
2 imperfecto de indicativo		9 pluscuamperfecto de indicativo	
averiguaba	averiguábamos	había averiguado	habíamos averiguado
averiguabas	averiguabais	habías averiguado	habíais averiguado
averiguaba	averiguaban	había averiguado	habían averiguado
3 pretérito		10 pretérito anterior	
averigüé	averiguamos	hube averiguado	hubimos averiguado
averiguaste	averiguasteis	hubiste averiguado	hubisteis averiguado
averiguó	averiguaron	hubo averiguado	hubieron averiguado
4 futuro		11 futuro perfecto	
averiguaré	averiguaremos	habré averiguado	habremos averiguado
averiguarás	averiguaréis	habrás averiguado	habréis averiguado
averiguará	averiguarán	habrá averiguado	habrán averiguado
5 potencial simple		12 potencial compuesto	
averiguaría	averiguaríamos	habría averiguado	habríamos averiguado
averiguarías	averiguaríais	habrías averiguado	habríais averiguado
averiguaría	averiguarían	habría averiguado	habrían averiguado
6 presente de subjuntivo		13 perfecto de subjuntivo	
averigüe	averigüemos	haya averiguado	hayamos averiguado
averigües	averigüéis	hayas averiguado	hayáis averiguado
averigüe	averigüen	haya averiguado	hayan averiguado
7 imperfecto de subjuntivo		14 pluscuamperfecto de subjuntivo	
averiguara	averiguáramos	hubiera averiguado	hubiéramos averiguado
averiguaras	averiguarais	hubieras averiguado	hubierais averiguado
averiguara	averiguaran	hubiera averiguado	hubieran averiguado
OR		OR	
averiguase	averiguásemos	hubiese averiguado	hubiésemos averiguado
averiguases	averiguaseis	hubieses averiguado	hubieseis averiguado
averiguase	averiguasen	hubiese averiguado	hubiesen averiguado

	imperativo
—	averigüemos
averigua; no averigües	averiguad; no averigüéis
averigüe	averigüen

Words related to this verb
el averiguador, la averiguadora   investigator
la averiguación   inquiry, investigation
averiguable   investigable
averiguadamente   surely, certainly

to help, to aid, to assist

The Seven Simple Tenses		The Seven Compound Tenses	
Singular	Plural	Singular	Plural
1 presente de indicativo		**8 perfecto de indicativo**	
ayudo	ayudamos	he ayudado	hemos ayudado
ayudas	ayudáis	has ayudado	habéis ayudado
ayuda	ayudan	ha ayudado	han ayudado
2 imperfecto de indicativo		**9 pluscuamperfecto de indicativo**	
ayudaba	ayudábamos	había ayudado	habíamos ayudado
ayudabas	ayudabais	habías ayudado	habíais ayudado
ayudaba	ayudaban	había ayudado	habían ayudado
3 pretérito		**10 pretérito anterior**	
ayudé	ayudamos	hube ayudado	hubimos ayudado
ayudaste	ayudasteis	hubiste ayudado	hubisteis ayudado
ayudó	ayudaron	hubo ayudado	hubieron ayudado
4 futuro		**11 futuro perfecto**	
ayudaré	ayudaremos	habré ayudado	habremos ayudado
ayudarás	ayudaréis	habrás ayudado	habréis ayudado
ayudará	ayudarán	habrá ayudado	habrán ayudado
5 potencial simple		**12 potencial compuesto**	
ayudaría	ayudaríamos	habría ayudado	habríamos ayudado
ayudarías	ayudaríais	habrías ayudado	habríais ayudado
ayudaría	ayudarían	habría ayudado	habrían ayudado
6 presente de subjuntivo		**13 perfecto de subjuntivo**	
ayude	ayudemos	haya ayudado	hayamos ayudado
ayudes	ayudéis	hayas ayudado	hayáis ayudado
ayude	ayuden	haya ayudado	hayan ayudado
7 imperfecto de subjuntivo		**14 pluscuamperfecto de subjuntivo**	
ayudara	ayudáramos	hubiera ayudado	hubiéramos ayudado
ayudaras	ayudarais	hubieras ayudado	hubierais ayudado
ayudara	ayudaran	hubiera ayudado	hubieran ayudado
OR		OR	
ayudase	ayudásemos	hubiese ayudado	hubiésemos ayudado
ayudases	ayudaseis	hubieses ayudado	hubieseis ayudado
ayudase	ayudasen	hubiese ayudado	hubiesen ayudado

imperativo	
—	ayudemos
ayuda; no ayudes	ayudad; no ayudéis
ayude	ayuden

Words and expressions related to this verb
la ayuda   aid, assistance, help
ayuda de cámara   valet
un ayudador, una ayudadora   helper
ayudante   assistant

51

bailar Gerundio **bailando** Part. pas. **bailado**

to dance

The Seven Simple Tenses		The Seven Compound Tenses	
Singular	Plural	Singular	Plural

1 presente de indicativo
bailo	**bailamos**		
bailas	**bailáis**		
baila	**bailan**		

8 perfecto de indicativo
he bailado	hemos bailado		
has bailado	habéis bailado		
ha bailado	han bailado		

2 imperfecto de indicativo
bailaba	**bailábamos**
bailabas	**bailabais**
bailaba	**bailaban**

9 pluscuamperfecto de indicativo
había bailado	habíamos bailado
habías bailado	habíais bailado
había bailado	habían bailado

3 pretérito
bailé	**bailamos**
bailaste	**bailasteis**
bailó	**bailaron**

10 pretérito anterior
hube bailado	hubimos bailado
hubiste bailado	hubisteis bailado
hubo bailado	hubieron bailado

4 futuro
bailaré	**bailaremos**
bailarás	**bailaréis**
bailará	**bailarán**

11 futuro perfecto
habré bailado	habremos bailado
habrás bailado	habréis bailado
habrá bailado	habrán bailado

5 potencial simple
bailaría	**bailaríamos**
bailarías	**bailaríais**
bailaría	**bailarían**

12 potencial compuesto
habría bailado	habríamos bailado
habrías bailado	habríais bailado
habría bailado	habrían bailado

6 presente de subjuntivo
baile	**bailemos**
bailes	**bailéis**
baile	**bailen**

13 perfecto de subjuntivo
haya bailado	hayamos bailado
hayas bailado	hayáis bailado
haya bailado	hayan bailado

7 imperfecto de subjuntivo
bailara	**bailáramos**
bailaras	**bailarais**
bailara	**bailaran**
OR	
bailase	**bailásemos**
bailases	**bailaseis**
bailase	**bailasen**

14 pluscuamperfecto de subjuntivo
hubiera bailado	hubiéramos bailado
hubieras bailado	hubierais bailado
hubiera bailado	hubieran bailado
OR	
hubiese bailado	hubiésemos bailado
hubieses bailado	hubieseis bailado
hubiese bailado	hubiesen bailado

imperativo
—	bailemos
baila; no bailes	bailad; no bailéis
baile	bailen

Sentence using this verb and words related to it
Cuando el gato va a sus devociones, bailan los ratones.
When the cat is away, the mice will play.
un baile dance
un bailarín, una bailarina dancer
un bailador, una bailadora dancer

52

to lower, to let down, to come down, to go down, to descend

The Seven Simple Tenses		The Seven Compound Tenses	
Singular	Plural	Singular	Plural
1 presente de indicativo		**8 perfecto de indicativo**	
bajo	bajamos	he bajado	hemos bajado
bajas	bajáis	has bajado	habéis bajado
baja	bajan	ha bajado	han bajado
2 imperfecto de indicativo		**9 pluscuamperfecto de indicativo**	
bajaba	bajábamos	había bajado	habíamos bajado
bajabas	bajabais	habías bajado	habíais bajado
bajaba	bajaban	había bajado	habían bajado
3 pretérito		**10 pretérito anterior**	
bajé	bajamos	hube bajado	hubimos bajado
bajaste	bajasteis	hubiste bajado	hubisteis bajado
bajó	bajaron	hubo bajado	hubieron bajado
4 futuro		**11 futuro perfecto**	
bajaré	bajaremos	habré bajado	habremos bajado
bajarás	bajaréis	habrás bajado	habréis bajado
bajará	bajarán	habrá bajado	habrán bajado
5 potencial simple		**12 potencial compuesto**	
bajaría	bajaríamos	habría bajado	habríamos bajado
bajarías	bajaríais	habrías bajado	habríais bajado
bajaría	bajarían	habría bajado	habrían bajado
6 presente de subjuntivo		**13 perfecto de subjuntivo**	
baje	bajemos	haya bajado	hayamos bajado
bajes	bajéis	hayas bajado	hayáis bajado
baje	bajen	haya bajado	hayan bajado
7 imperfecto de subjuntivo		**14 pluscuamperfecto de subjuntivo**	
bajara	bajáramos	hubiera bajado	hubiéramos bajado
bajaras	bajarais	hubieras bajado	hubierais bajado
bajara	bajaran	hubiera bajado	hubieran bajado
OR		OR	
bajase	bajásemos	hubiese bajado	hubiésemos bajado
bajases	bajaseis	hubieses bajado	hubieseis bajado
bajase	bajasen	hubiese bajado	hubiesen bajado

imperativo	
—	bajemos
baja; no bajes	bajad; no bajéis
baje	bajen

Words and expressions related to this verb

la baja reduction (fall) in prices	**rebajar** to reduce
la bajada descent	**bajar de** to get off
bajamente basely	**bajar de valor** to decline in value
en voz baja in a low voice	**el piso baja** ground floor
bajo down, below	**una rebaja** rebate, discount

bañarse Gerundio **bañándose** Part. pas. **bañado**

to bathe oneself, to take a bath

The Seven Simple Tenses		The Seven Compound Tenses	
Singular	Plural	Singular	Plural
1 presente de indicativo		8 perfecto de indicativo	
me baño	nos bañamos	me he bañado	nos hemos bañado
te bañas	os bañáis	te has bañado	os habéis bañado
se baña	se bañan	se ha bañado	se han bañado
2 imperfecto de indicativo		9 pluscuamperfecto de indicativo	
me bañaba	nos bañábamos	me había bañado	nos habíamos bañado
te bañabas	os bañabais	te habías bañado	os habíais bañado
se bañaba	se bañaban	se había bañado	se habían bañado
3 pretérito		10 pretérito anterior	
me bañé	nos bañamos	me hube bañado	nos hubimos bañado
te bañaste	os bañasteis	te hubiste bañado	os hubisteis bañado
se bañó	se bañaron	se hubo bañado	se hubieron bañado
4 futuro		11 futuro perfecto	
me bañaré	nos bañaremos	me habré bañado	nos habremos bañado
te bañarás	os bañaréis	te habrás bañado	os habréis bañado
se bañará	se bañarán	se habrá bañado	se habrán bañado
5 potencial simple		12 potencial compuesto	
me bañaría	nos bañaríamos	me habría bañado	nos habríamos bañado
te bañarías	os bañaríais	te habrías bañado	os habríais bañado
se bañaría	se bañarían	se habría bañado	se habrían bañado
6 presente de subjuntivo		13 perfecto de subjuntivo	
me bañe	nos bañemos	me haya bañado	nos hayamos bañado
te bañes	os bañéis	te hayas bañado	os hayáis bañado
se bañe	se bañen	se haya bañado	se hayan bañado
7 imperfecto de subjuntivo		14 pluscuamperfecto de subjuntivo	
me bañara	nos bañáramos	me hubiera bañado	nos hubiéramos bañado
te bañaras	os bañarais	te hubieras bañado	os hubierais bañado
se bañara	se bañaran	se hubiera bañado	se hubieran bañado
OR		OR	
me bañase	nos bañásemos	me hubiese bañado	nos hubiésemos bañado
te bañases	os bañaseis	te hubieses bañado	os hubieseis bañado
se bañase	se bañasen	se hubiese bañado	se hubiesen bañado

	imperativo	
—		bañémonos
báñate; no te bañes		bañaos; no os bañéis
báñese		báñense

Words and expressions related to this verb

una bañera, una bañadera bathtub
un bañador, una bañadora bather
un baño bath, bathing
un baño de vapor steam bath

bañar to bathe
bañar un papel de lágrimas to write a
  mournful letter
bañar a la luz to light up, to illuminate

Gerundio **bastando**	Part. pas. **bastado**	**bastar**

to be enough, to be sufficient, to suffice

The Seven Simple Tenses		The Seven Compound Tenses	
Singular	Plural	Singular	Plural
1 presente de indicativo		8 perfecto de indicativo	
basta	**bastan**	**ha bastado**	**han bastado**
2 imperfecto de indicativo		9 pluscuamperfecto de indicativo	
bastaba	**bastaban**	**había bastado**	**habían bastado**
3 pretérito		10 pretérito anterior	
bastó	**bastaron**	**hubo bastado**	**hubieron bastado**
4 futuro		11 futuro perfecto	
bastará	**bastarán**	**habrá bastado**	**habrán bastado**
5 potencial simple		12 potencial compuesto	
bastaría	**bastarían**	**habría bastado**	**habrían bastado**
6 presente de subjuntivo		13 perfecto de subjuntivo	
que baste	**que basten**	**haya bastado**	**hayan bastado**
7 imperfecto de subjuntivo		14 pluscuamperfecto de subjuntivo	
que bastara	**que bastaran**	**hubiera bastado**	**hubieran bastado**
OR		OR	
que bastase	**que bastasen**	**hubiese bastado**	**hubiesen bastado**

imperativo
¡Que baste!   ¡Que basten!

Common expression related to this verb
¡Basta! Enough! That will do!
This is an impersonal verb and it is used mainly in the third person singular and plural.
It is a regular **ar** verb and can be conjugated in all the persons.

bautizar

Gerundio **bautizando**   Part. pas. **bautizado**

to baptize, to christen

The Seven Simple Tenses		The Seven Compound Tenses	
Singular	Plural	Singular	Plural
1 presente de indicativo		**8 perfecto de indicativo**	
bautizo	bautizamos	he bautizado	hemos bautizado
bautizas	bautizáis	has bautizado	habéis bautizado
bautiza	bautizan	ha bautizado	han bautizado
2 imperfecto de indicativo		**9 pluscuamperfecto de indicativo**	
bautizaba	bautizábamos	había bautizado	habíamos bautizado
bautizabas	bautizabais	habías bautizado	habíais bautizado
bautizaba	bautizaban	había bautizado	habían bautizado
3 pretérito		**10 pretérito anterior**	
bauticé	bautizamos	hube bautizado	hubimos bautizado
bautizaste	bautizasteis	hubiste bautizado	hubisteis bautizado
bautizó	bautizaron	hubo bautizado	hubieron bautizado
4 futuro		**11 futuro perfecto**	
bautizaré	bautizaremos	habré bautizado	habremos bautizado
bautizarás	bautizaréis	habrás bautizado	habréis bautizado
bautizará	bautizarán	habrá bautizado	habrán bautizado
5 potencial simple		**12 potencial compuesto**	
bautizaría	bautizaríamos	habría bautizado	habríamos bautizado
bautizarías	bautizaríais	habrías bautizado	habríais bautizado
bautizaría	bautizarían	habría bautizado	habrían bautizado
6 presente de subjuntivo		**13 perfecto de subjuntivo**	
bautice	bauticemos	haya bautizado	hayamos bautizado
bautices	bauticéis	hayas bautizado	hayáis bautizado
bautice	bauticen	haya bautizado	hayan bautizado
7 imperfecto de subjuntivo		**14 pluscuamperfecto de subjuntivo**	
bautizara	bautizáramos	hubiera bautizado	hubiéramos bautizado
bautizaras	bautizarais	hubieras bautizado	hubierais bautizado
bautizara	bautizaran	hubiera bautizado	hubieran bautizado
OR		OR	
bautizase	bautizásemos	hubiese bautizado	hubiésemos bautizado
bautizases	bautizaseis	hubieses bautizado	hubieseis bautizado
bautizase	bautizasen	hubiese bautizado	hubiesen bautizado

	imperativo
—	bauticemos
bautiza; no bautices	bautizad; no bauticéis
bautice	bauticen

Words related to this verb
el bautisterio baptistery
el bautismo baptism, christening
bautismal baptismal

Gerundio **bebiendo**   Part. pas. **bebido**   **beber**

The Seven Simple Tenses		The Seven Compound Tenses	
Singular	Plural	Singular	Plural
1 presente de indicativo		8 perfecto de indicativo	
bebo	bebemos	he bebido	hemos bebido
bebes	bebéis	has bebido	habéis bebido
bebe	beben	ha bebido	han bebido
2 imperfecto de indicativo		9 pluscuamperfecto de indicativo	
bebía	bebíamos	había bebido	habíamos bebido
bebías	bebíais	habías bebido	habíais bebido
bebía	bebían	había bebido	habían bebido
3 pretérito		10 pretérito anterior	
bebí	bebimos	hube bebido	hubimos bebido
bebiste	bebisteis	hubiste bebido	hubisteis bebido
bebió	bebieron	hubo bebido	hubieron bebido
4 futuro		11 futuro perfecto	
beberé	beberemos	habré bebido	habremos bebido
beberás	beberéis	habrás bebido	habréis bebido
beberá	beberán	habrá bebido	habrán bebido
5 potencial simple		12 potencial compuesto	
bebería	beberíamos	habría bebido	habríamos bebido
beberías	beberíais	habrías bebido	habríais bebido
bebería	beberían	habría bebido	habrían bebido
6 presente de subjuntivo		13 perfecto de subjuntivo	
beba	bebamos	haya bebido	hayamos bebido
bebas	bebáis	hayas bebido	hayáis bebido
beba	beban	haya bebido	hayan bebido
7 imperfecto de subjuntivo		14 pluscuamperfecto de subjuntivo	
bebiera	bebiéramos	hubiera bebido	hubiéramos bebido
bebieras	bebierais	hubieras bebido	hubierais bebido
bebiera	bebieran	hubiera bebido	hubieran bebido
OR		OR	
bebiese	bebiésemos	hubiese bebido	hubiésemos bebido
bebieses	bebieseis	hubieses bebido	hubieseis bebido
bebiese	bebiesen	hubiese bebido	hubiesen bebido

imperativo	
—	bebamos
bebe; no bebas	bebed; no bebáis
beba	beban

Words and expressions related to this verb
una bebida drink, beverage
beber en to drink from
beber a la salud to drink to health

beber como una cuba to drink like a fish
querer beber la sangre a otro to hate
    somebody bitterly

bendecir

Gerundio **bendiciendo**   Part. pas. **bendecido**

to bless, to consecrate

The Seven Simple Tenses		The Seven Compound Tenses	
Singular	Plural	Singular	Plural
1 presente de indicativo		8 perfecto de indicativo	
bendigo	bendecimos	he bendecido	hemos bendecido
bendices	bendecís	has bendecido	habéis bendecido
bendice	bendicen	ha bendecido	han bendecido
2 imperfecto de indicativo		9 pluscuamperfecto de indicativo	
bendecía	bendecíamos	había bendecido	habíamos bendecido
bendecías	bendecíais	habías bendecido	habíais bendecido
bendecía	bendecían	había bendecido	habían bendecido
3 pretérito		10 pretérito anterior	
bendije	bendijimos	hube bendecido	hubimos bendecido
bendijiste	bendijisteis	hubiste bendecido	hubisteis bendecido
bendijo	bendijeron	hubo bendecido	hubieron bendecido
4 futuro		11 futuro perfecto	
bendeciré	bendeciremos	habré bendecido	habremos bendecido
bendecirás	bendeciréis	habrás bendecido	habréis bendecido
bendecirá	bendecirán	habrá bendecido	habrán bendecido
5 potencial simple		12 potencial compuesto	
bendeciría	bendeciríamos	habría bendecido	habríamos bendecido
bendecirías	bendeciríais	habrías bendecido	habríais bendecido
bendeciría	bendecirían	habría bendecido	habrían bendecido
6 presente de subjuntivo		13 perfecto de subjuntivo	
bendiga	bendigamos	haya bendecido	hayamos bendecido
bendigas	bendigáis	hayas bendecido	hayáis bendecido
bendiga	bendigan	haya bendecido	hayan bendecido
7 imperfecto de subjuntivo		14 pluscuamperfecto de subjuntivo	
bendijera	bendijéramos	hubiera bendecido	hubiéramos bendecido
bendijeras	bendijerais	hubieras bendecido	hubierais bendecido
bendijera	bendijeran	hubiera bendecido	hubieran bendecido
OR		OR	
bendijese	bendijésemos	hubiese bendecido	hubiésemos bendecido
bendijeses	bendijeseis	hubieses bendecido	hubieseis bendecido
bendijese	bendijesen	hubiese bendecido	hubiesen bendecido

	imperativo	
—	bendigamos
bendice; no bendigas	bendecid; no bendigáis
bendiga	bendigan

Words and expressions related to this verb
la bendición benediction, blessing
las bendiciones nupciales marriage ceremony
un bendecidor, una bendecidora blesser

Gerundio **borrando**   Part. pas. **borrado**   **borrar**

to erase, to cross out

The Seven Simple Tenses		The Seven Compound Tenses	
Singular	Plural	Singular	Plural
1 presente de indicativo		8 perfecto de indicativo	
borro	borramos	he borrado	hemos borrado
borras	borráis	has borrado	habéis borrado
borra	borran	ha borrado	han borrado
2 imperfecto de indicativo		9 pluscuamperfecto de indicativo	
borraba	borrábamos	había borrado	habíamos borrado
borrabas	borrabais	habías borrado	habíais borrado
borraba	borraban	había borrado	habían borrado
3 pretérito		10 pretérito anterior	
borré	borramos	hube borrado	hubimos borrado
borraste	borrasteis	hubiste borrado	hubisteis borrado
borró	borraron	hubo borrado	hubieron borrado
4 futuro		11 futuro perfecto	
borraré	borraremos	habré borrado	habremos borrado
borrarás	borraréis	habrás borrado	habréis borrado
borrará	borrarán	habrá borrado	habrán borrado
5 potencial simple		12 potencial compuesto	
borraría	borraríamos	habría borrado	habríamos borrado
borrarías	borraríais	habrías borrado	habríais borrado
borraría	borrarían	habría borrado	habrían borrado
6 presente de subjuntivo		13 perfecto de subjuntivo	
borre	borremos	haya borrado	hayamos borrado
borres	borréis	hayas borrado	hayáis borrado
borre	borren	haya borrado	hayan borrado
7 imperfecto de subjuntivo		14 pluscuamperfecto de subjuntivo	
borrara	borráramos	hubiera borrado	hubiéramos borrado
borraras	borrarais	hubieras borrado	hubierais borrado
borrara	borraran	hubiera borrado	hubieran borrado
OR		OR	
borrase	borrásemos	hubiese borrado	hubiésemos borrado
borrases	borraseis	hubieses borrado	hubieseis borrado
borrase	borrasen	hubiese borrado	hubiesen borrado

	imperativo	
—	borremos	
borra; no borres	borrad; no borréis	
borre	borren	

Words and expressions related to this verb

la goma de borrar   rubber eraser
la borradura   erasure
el borrador   eraser (chalk)

desborrar   to burl
emborrar   to pad, to stuff, to wad; to gulp down food

| bullir | Gerundio **bullendo** | Part. pas. **bullido** |

to boil, to bustle, to hustle, to stir

The Seven Simple Tenses		The Seven Compound Tenses	
Singular	Plural	Singular	Plural
1 presente de indicativo		8 perfecto de indicativo	
bullo	bullimos	he bullido	hemos bullido
bulles	bullís	has bullido	habéis bullido
bulle	bullen	ha bullido	han bullido
2 imperfecto de indicativo		9 pluscuamperfecto de indicativo	
bullía	bullíamos	había bullido	habíamos bullido
bullías	bullíais	habías bullido	habíais bullido
bullía	bullían	había bullido	habían bullido
3 pretérito		10 pretérito anterior	
bullí	bullimos	hube bullido	hubimos bullido
bulliste	bullisteis	hubiste bullido	hubisteis bullido
bulló	bulleron	hubo bullido	hubieron bullido
4 futuro		11 futuro perfecto	
bulliré	bulliremos	habré bullido	habremos bullido
bullirás	bulliréis	habrás bullido	habréis bullido
bullirá	bullirán	habrá bullido	habrán bullido
5 potencial simple		12 potencial compuesto	
bulliría	bulliríamos	habría bullido	habríamos bullido
bullirías	bulliríais	habrías bullido	habríais bullido
bulliría	bullirían	habría bullido	habrían bullido
6 presente de subjuntivo		13 perfecto de subjuntivo	
bulla	bullamos	haya bullido	hayamos bullido
bullas	bulláis	hayas bullido	hayáis bullido
bulla	bullan	haya bullido	hayan bullido
7 imperfecto de subjuntivo		14 pluscuamperfecto de subjuntivo	
bullera	bulléramos	hubiera bullido	hubiéramos bullido
bulleras	bullerais	hubieras bullido	hubierais bullido
bullera	bulleran	hubiera bullido	hubieran bullido
OR		OR	
bullese	bullésemos	hubiese bullido	hubiésemos bullido
bulleses	bulleseis	hubieses bullido	hubieseis bullido
bullese	bullesen	hubiese bullido	hubiesen bullido

	imperativo
—	bullamos
bulle; no bullas	bullid; no bulláis
bulla	bullan

Words related to this verb
un, una bullebulle busybody
el bullicio noise, bustle
bulliciosamente noisily

bullente bubbling
la bulla bustle, noise, mob
un bullaje noisy crowd

Gerundio **burlándose**   Part. pas. **burlado**   **burlarse**

to make fun of, to poke fun at, to ridicule

The Seven Simple Tenses		The Seven Compound Tenses	
Singular	Plural	Singular	Plural
1 presente de indicativo		8 perfecto de indicativo	
me burlo	nos burlamos	me he burlado	nos hemos burlado
te burlas	os burláis	te has burlado	os habéis burlado
se burla	se burlan	se ha burlado	se han burlado
2 imperfecto de indicativo		9 pluscuamperfecto de indicativo	
me burlaba	nos burlábamos	me había burlado	nos habíamos burlado
te burlabas	os burlabais	te habías burlado	os habíais burlado
se burlaba	se burlaban	se había burlado	se habían burlado
3 pretérito		10 pretérito anterior	
me burlé	nos burlamos	me hube burlado	nos hubimos burlado
te burlaste	os burlasteis	te hubiste burlado	os hubisteis burlado
se burló	se burlaron	se hubo burlado	se hubieron burlado
4 futuro		11 futuro perfecto	
me burlaré	nos burlaremos	me habré burlado	nos habremos burlado
te burlarás	os burlaréis	te habrás burlado	os habréis burlado
se burlará	se burlarán	se habrá burlado	se habrán burlado
5 potencial simple		12 potencial compuesto	
me burlaría	nos burlaríamos	me habría burlado	nos habríamos burlado
te burlarías	os burlaríais	te habrías burlado	os habríais burlado
se burlaría	se burlarían	se habría burlado	se habrían burlado
6 presente de subjuntivo		13 perfecto de subjuntivo	
me burle	nos burlemos	me haya burlado	nos hayamos burlado
te burles	os burléis	te hayas burlado	os hayáis burlado
se burle	se burlen	se haya burlado	se hayan burlado
7 imperfecto de subjuntivo		14 pluscuamperfecto de subjuntivo	
me burlara	nos burláramos	me hubiera burlado	nos hubiéramos burlado
te burlaras	os burlarais	te hubieras burlado	os hubierais burlado
se burlara	se burlaran	se hubiera burlado	se hubieran burlado
OR		OR	
me burlase	nos burlásemos	me hubiese burlado	nos hubiésemos burlado
te burlases	os burlaseis	te hubieses burlado	os hubieseis burlado
se burlase	se burlasen	se hubiese burlado	se hubiesen burlado

imperativo	
—	burlémonos
búrlate; no te burles	burlaos; no os burléis
búrlese	búrlense

Words and expressions related to this verb

el burlador, la burladora   practical joker,
   jester, wag
burlescamente   comically
la burleta   joke, little trick
la burlería   mockery

burlesco, burlesca   burlesque
burlarse de alguien   to make
   fun of someone
burlar a alguien   to deceive
   someone

buscar Gerundio **buscando** Part. pas. **buscado**

to look for, to seek

The Seven Simple Tenses		The Seven Compound Tenses	
Singular	Plural	Singular	Plural
1 presente de indicativo		8 perfecto de indicativo	
busco	buscamos	he buscado	hemos buscado
buscas	buscáis	has buscado	habéis buscado
busca	buscan	ha buscado	han buscado
2 imperfecto de indicativo		9 pluscuamperfecto de indicativo	
buscaba	buscábamos	había buscado	habíamos buscado
buscabas	buscabais	habías buscado	habíais buscado
buscaba	buscaban	había buscado	habían buscado
3 pretérito		10 pretérito anterior	
busqué	buscamos	hube buscado	hubimos buscado
buscaste	buscasteis	hubiste buscado	hubisteis buscado
buscó	buscaron	hubo buscado	hubieron buscado
4 futuro		11 futuro perfecto	
buscaré	buscaremos	habré buscado	habremos buscado
buscarás	buscaréis	habrás buscado	habréis buscado
buscará	buscarán	habrá buscado	habrán buscado
5 potencial simple		12 potencial compuesto	
buscaría	buscaríamos	habría buscado	habríamos buscado
buscarías	buscaríais	habrías buscado	habríais buscado
buscaría	buscarían	habría buscado	habrían buscado
6 presente de subjuntivo		13 perfecto de subjuntivo	
busque	busquemos	haya buscado	hayamos buscado
busques	busquéis	hayas buscado	hayáis buscado
busque	busquen	haya buscado	hayan buscado
7 imperfecto de subjuntivo		14 pluscuamperfecto de subjuntivo	
buscara	buscáramos	hubiera buscado	hubiéramos buscado
buscaras	buscarais	hubieras buscado	hubierais buscado
buscara	buscaran	hubiera buscado	hubieran buscado
OR		OR	
buscase	buscásemos	hubiese buscado	hubiésemos buscado
buscases	buscaseis	hubieses buscado	hubieseis buscado
buscase	buscasen	hubiese buscado	hubiesen buscado

imperativo	
—	busquemos
busca; no busques	buscad; no busquéis
busque	busquen

Sentences using this verb and words related to it
¿Qué busca Ud.? What are you looking for?
Busco mis libros. I'm looking for my books.
la busca, la buscada research, search

la búsqueda search
rebuscar to search into
el rebuscamiento searching

62

Gerundio **cabiendo**   Part. pas. **cabido**   **caber**

to be contained, to fit into

The Seven Simple Tenses		The Seven Compound Tenses	
Singular	Plural	Singular	Plural
1 presente de indicativo		8 perfecto de indicativo	
quepo	**cabemos**	**he cabido**	**hemos cabido**
cabes	**cabéis**	**has cabido**	**habéis cabido**
cabe	**caben**	**ha cabido**	**han cabido**
2 imperfecto de indicativo		9 pluscuamperfecto de indicativo	
cabía	**cabíamos**	**había cabido**	**habíamos cabido**
cabías	**cabíais**	**habías cabido**	**habíais cabido**
cabía	**cabían**	**había cabido**	**habían cabido**
3 pretérito		10 pretérito anterior	
cupe	**cupimos**	**hube cabido**	**hubimos cabido**
cupiste	**cupisteis**	**hubiste cabido**	**hubisteis cabido**
cupo	**cupieron**	**hubo cabido**	**hubieron cabido**
4 futuro		11 futuro perfecto	
cabré	**cabremos**	**habré cabido**	**habremos cabido**
cabrás	**cabréis**	**habrás cabido**	**habréis cabido**
cabrá	**cabrán**	**habrá cabido**	**habrán cabido**
5 potencial simple		12 potencial compuesto	
cabría	**cabríamos**	**habría cabido**	**habríamos cabido**
cabrías	**cabríais**	**habrías cabido**	**habríais cabido**
cabría	**cabrían**	**habría cabido**	**habrían cabido**
6 presente de subjuntivo		13 perfecto de subjuntivo	
quepa	**quepamos**	**haya cabido**	**hayamos cabido**
quepas	**quepáis**	**hayas cabido**	**hayáis cabido**
quepa	**quepan**	**haya cabido**	**hayan cabido**
7 imperfecto de subjuntivo		14 pluscuamperfecto de subjuntivo	
cupiera	**cupiéramos**	**hubiera cabido**	**hubiéramos cabido**
cupieras	**cupierais**	**hubieras cabido**	**hubierais cabido**
cupiera	**cupieran**	**hubiera cabido**	**hubieran cabido**
OR		OR	
cupiese	**cupiésemos**	**hubiese cabido**	**hubiésemos cabido**
cupieses	**cupieseis**	**hubieses cabido**	**hubieseis cabido**
cupiese	**cupiesen**	**hubiese cabido**	**hubiesen cabido**

imperativo

—	**quepamos**
cabe; no quepas	**cabed; no quepáis**
quepa	**quepan**

Common idiomatic expressions using this verb
Pablo no cabe en sí.   Paul has a swelled head.
No quepo aquí.   I don't have enough room here.
No cabe duda de que . . .   There is no doubt that . . .

caer   Gerundio **cayendo**   Part. pas. **caído**

to fall

The Seven Simple Tenses		The Seven Compound Tenses	
Singular	Plural	Singular	Plural
1 presente de indicativo		**8 perfecto de indicativo**	
caigo	caemos	he caído	hemos caído
caes	caéis	has caído	habéis caído
cae	caen	ha caído	han caído
2 imperfecto de indicativo		**9 pluscuamperfecto de indicativo**	
caía	caíamos	había caído	habíamos caído
caías	caíais	habías caído	habíais caído
caía	caían	había caído	habían caído
3 pretérito		**10 pretérito anterior**	
caí	caímos	hube caído	hubimos caído
caíste	caísteis	hubiste caído	hubisteis caído
cayó	cayeron	hubo caído	hubieron caído
4 futuro		**11 futuro perfecto**	
caeré	caeremos	habré caído	habremos caído
caerás	caeréis	habrás caído	habréis caído
caerá	caerán	habrá caído	habrán caído
5 potencial simple		**12 potencial compuesto**	
caería	caeríamos	habría caído	habríamos caído
caerías	caeríais	habrías caído	habríais caído
caería	caerían	habría caído	habrían caído
6 presente de subjuntivo		**13 perfecto de subjuntivo**	
caiga	caigamos	haya caído	hayamos caído
caigas	caigáis	hayas caído	hayáis caído
caiga	caigan	haya caído	hayan caído
7 imperfecto de subjuntivo		**14 pluscuamperfecto de subjuntivo**	
cayera	cayéramos	hubiera caído	hubiéramos caído
cayeras	cayerais	hubieras caído	hubierais caído
cayera	cayeran	hubiera caído	hubieran caído
OR		OR	
cayese	cayésemos	hubiese caído	hubiésemos caído
cayeses	cayeseis	hubieses caído	hubieseis caído
cayese	cayesen	hubiese caído	hubiesen caído

imperativo	
—	caigamos
cae; no caigas	caed; no caigáis
caiga	caigan

Words and expressions related to this verb

la caída the fall	**caer enfermo (enferma)** to fall sick
a la caída del sol at sunset	**decaer** to decay, decline
a la caída de la tarde at the end of the	**recaer** to relapse, fall back
afternoon	**dejar caer** to drop

Gerundio **callándose**   Part. pas. **callado**   **callarse**

to be silent, to keep quiet

The Seven Simple Tenses		The Seven Compound Tenses	
Singular	Plural	Singular	Plural
1 presente de indicativo		8 perfecto de indicativo	
me callo	nos callamos	me he callado	nos hemos callado
te callas	os calláis	te has callado	os habéis callado
se calla	se callan	se ha callado	se han callado
2 imperfecto de indicativo		9 pluscuamperfecto de indicativo	
me callaba	nos callábamos	me había callado	nos habíamos callado
te callabas	os callabais	te habías callado	os habíais callado
se callaba	se callaban	se había callado	se habían callado
3 pretérito		10 pretérito anterior	
me callé	nos callamos	me hube callado	nos hubimos callado
te callaste	os callasteis	te hubiste callado	os hubisteis callado
se calló	se callaron	se hubo callado	se hubieron callado
4 futuro		11 futuro perfecto	
me callaré	nos callaremos	me habré callado	nos habremos callado
te callarás	os callaréis	te habrás callado	os habréis callado
se callará	se callarán	se habrá callado	se habrán callado
5 potencial simple		12 potencial compuesto	
me callaría	nos callaríamos	me habría callado	nos habríamos callado
te callarías	os callaríais	te habrías callado	os habríais callado
se callaría	se callarían	se habría callado	se habrían callado
6 presente de subjuntivo		13 perfecto de subjuntivo	
me calle	nos callemos	me haya callado	nos hayamos callado
te calles	os calléis	te hayas callado	os hayáis callado
se calle	se callen	se haya callado	se hayan callado
7 imperfecto de subjuntivo		14 pluscuamperfecto de subjuntivo	
me callara	nos calláramos	me hubiera callado	nos hubiéramos callado
te callaras	os callarais	te hubieras callado	os hubierais callado
se callara	se callaran	se hubiera callado	se hubieran callado
OR		OR	
me callase	nos callásemos	me hubiese callado	nos hubiésemos callado
te callases	os callaseis	te hubieses callado	os hubieseis callado
se callase	se callasen	se hubiese callado	se hubiesen callado

imperativo	
—	callémonos
cállate; no te calles	callaos; no os calléis
cállese	cállense

Common idomatic expressions using this verb
Quien calla, otorga.   Silence means consent.
¡Cállese Ud.!   Keep quiet!
callar la boca   to hold one's tongue
callarse la boca   to shut up

cambiar	Gerundio **cambiando**	Part. pas. **cambiado**

to change

The Seven Simple Tenses		The Seven Compound Tenses	
Singular	Plural	Singular	Plural
1 presente de indicativo		8 perfecto de indicativo	
cambio	cambiamos	he cambiado	hemos cambiado
cambias	cambiáis	has cambiado	habéis cambiado
cambia	cambian	ha cambiado	han cambiado
2 imperfecto de indicativo		9 pluscuamperfecto de indicativo	
cambiaba	cambiábamos	había cambiado	habíamos cambiado
cambiabas	cambiabais	habías cambiado	habíais cambiado
cambiaba	cambiaban	había cambiado	habían cambiado
3 pretérito		10 pretérito anterior	
cambié	cambiamos	hube cambiado	hubimos cambiado
cambiaste	cambiasteis	hubiste cambiado	hubisteis cambiado
cambió	cambiaron	hubo cambiado	hubieron cambiado
4 futuro		11 futuro perfecto	
cambiaré	cambiaremos	habré cambiado	habremos cambiado
cambiarás	cambiaréis	habrás cambiado	habréis cambiado
cambiará	cambiarán	habrá cambiado	habrán cambiado
5 potencial simple		12 potencial compuesto	
cambiaría	cambiaríamos	habría cambiado	habríamos cambiado
cambiarías	cambiaríais	habrías cambiado	habríais cambiado
cambiaría	cambiarían	habría cambiado	habrían cambiado
6 presente de subjuntivo		13 perfecto de subjuntivo	
cambie	cambiemos	haya cambiado	hayamos cambiado
cambies	cambiéis	hayas cambiado	hayáis cambiado
cambie	cambien	haya cambiado	hayan cambiado
7 imperfecto de subjuntivo		14 pluscuamperfecto de subjuntivo	
cambiara	cambiáramos	hubiera cambiado	hubiéramos cambiado
cambiaras	cambiarais	hubieras cambiado	hubierais cambiado
cambiara	cambiaran	hubiera cambiado	hubieran cambiado
OR		OR	
cambiase	cambiásemos	hubiese cambiado	hubiésemos cambiado
cambiases	cambiaseis	hubieses cambiado	hubieseis cambiado
cambiase	cambiasen	hubiese cambiado	hubiesen cambiado

	imperativo	
—	cambiemos	
cambia; no cambies	cambiad; no cambiéis	
cambie	cambien	

Common idiomatic expressions using this verb
cambiar de traje   to change one's clothing
cambiar de opinión   to change one's mind
el cambio   exchange
cambio minuto   small change

to walk, to move along

The Seven Simple Tenses		The Seven Compound Tenses	
Singular	Plural	Singular	Plural
1 presente de indicativo		8 perfecto de indicativo	
camino	caminamos	he caminado	hemos caminado
caminas	camináis	has caminado	habéis caminado
camina	caminan	ha caminado	han caminado
2 imperfecto de indicativo		9 pluscuamperfecto de indicativo	
caminaba	caminábamos	había caminado	habíamos caminado
caminabas	caminabais	habías caminado	habíais caminado
caminaba	caminaban	había caminado	habían caminado
3 pretérito		10 pretérito anterior	
caminé	caminamos	hube caminado	hubimos caminado
caminaste	caminasteis	hubiste caminado	hubisteis caminado
caminó	caminaron	hubo caminado	hubieron caminado
4 futuro		11 futuro perfecto	
caminaré	caminaremos	habré caminado	habremos caminado
caminarás	caminaréis	habrás caminado	habréis caminado
caminará	caminarán	habrá caminado	habrán caminado
5 potencial simple		12 potencial compuesto	
caminaría	caminaríamos	habría caminado	habríamos caminado
caminarías	caminaríais	habrías caminado	habríais caminado
caminaría	caminarían	habría caminado	habrían caminado
6 presente de subjuntivo		13 perfecto de subjuntivo	
camine	caminemos	haya caminado	hayamos caminado
camines	caminéis	hayas caminado	hayáis caminado
camine	caminen	haya caminado	hayan caminado
7 imperfecto de subjuntivo		14 pluscuamperfecto de subjuntivo	
caminara	camináramos	hubiera caminado	hubiéramos caminado
caminaras	caminarais	hubieras caminado	hubierais caminado
caminara	caminaran	hubiera caminado	hubieran caminado
OR		OR	
caminase	caminásemos	hubiese caminado	hubiésemos caminado
caminases	caminaseis	hubieses caminado	hubieseis caminado
caminase	caminasen	hubiese caminado	hubiesen caminado

imperativo	
—	caminemos
camina; no camines	caminad; no caminéis
camine	caminen

Words and expressions related to this verb
el camino   road, highway
el camino de hierro   railroad
en camino de   on the way to
una caminata   a long walk

cansar   Gerundio **cansando**   Part. pas. **cansado**

to fatigue, to tire, to weary

The Seven Simple Tenses		The Seven Compound Tenses	
Singular	Plural	Singular	Plural
1 presente de indicativo		8 perfecto de indicativo	
canso	cansamos	he cansado	hemos cansado
cansas	cansáis	has cansado	habéis cansado
cansa	cansan	ha cansado	han cansado
2 imperfecto de indicativo		9 pluscuamperfecto de indicativo	
cansaba	cansábamos	había cansado	habíamos cansado
cansabas	cansabais	habías cansado	habíais cansado
cansaba	cansaban	había cansado	habían cansado
3 pretérito		10 pretérito anterior	
cansé	cansamos	hube cansado	hubimos cansado
cansaste	cansasteis	hubiste cansado	hubisteis cansado
cansó	cansaron	hubo cansado	hubieron cansado
4 futuro		11 futuro perfecto	
cansaré	cansaremos	habré cansado	habremos cansado
cansarás	cansaréis	habrás cansado	habréis cansado
cansará	cansarán	habrá cansado	habrán cansado
5 potencial simple		12 potencial compuesto	
cansaría	cansaríamos	habría cansado	habríamos cansado
cansarías	cansaríais	habrías cansado	habríais cansado
cansaría	cansarían	habría cansado	habrían cansado
6 presente de subjuntivo		13 perfecto de subjuntivo	
canse	cansemos	haya cansado	hayamos cansado
canses	canséis	hayas cansado	hayáis cansado
canse	cansen	haya cansado	hayan cansado
7 imperfecto de subjuntivo		14 pluscuamperfecto de subjuntivo	
cansara	cansáramos	hubiera cansado	hubiéramos cansado
cansaras	cansarais	hubieras cansado	hubierais cansado
cansara	cansaran	hubiera cansado	hubieran cansado
OR		OR	
cansase	cansásemos	hubiese cansado	hubiésemos cansado
cansases	cansaseis	hubieses cansado	hubieseis cansado
cansase	cansasen	hubiese cansado	hubiesen cansado

	imperativo	
—	cansemos
cansa; no canses	cansad; no canséis
canse	cansen

Sentences using this verb and words related to it
María está cansada, Pedro está cansado y yo estoy cansado.
    Nosotros estamos cansados.

la cansera fatigue	**el descanso** rest, relief
el cansancio fatigue, weariness	**el descansadero** resting place

Gerundio **cansándose**   Part. pas. **cansado**   **cansarse**

to become tired, to become weary, to get tired

The Seven Simple Tenses		The Seven Compound Tenses	
Singular	Plural	Singular	Plural
1 presente de indicativo		8 perfecto de indicativo	
me canso	nos cansamos	me he cansado	nos hemos cansado
te cansas	os cansáis	te has cansado	os habéis cansado
se cansa	se cansan	se ha cansado	se han cansado
2 imperfecto de indicativo		9 pluscuamperfecto de indicativo	
me cansaba	nos cansábamos	me había cansado	nos habíamos cansado
te cansabas	os cansabais	te habías cansado	os habíais cansado
se cansaba	se cansaban	se había cansado	se habían cansado
3 pretérito		10 pretérito anterior	
me cansé	nos cansamos	me hube cansado	nos hubimos cansado
te cansaste	os cansasteis	te hubiste cansado	os hubisteis cansado
se cansó	se cansaron	se hubo cansado	se hubieron cansado
4 futuro		11 futuro perfecto	
me cansaré	nos cansaremos	me habré cansado	nos habremos cansado
te cansarás	os cansaréis	te habrás cansado	os habréis cansado
se cansará	se cansarán	se habrá cansado	se habrán cansado
5 potencial simple		12 potencial compuesto	
me cansaría	nos cansaríamos	me habría cansado	nos habríamos cansado
te cansarías	os cansaríais	te habrías cansado	os habríais cansado
se cansaría	se cansarían	se habría cansado	se habrían cansado
6 presente de subjuntivo		13 perfecto de subjuntivo	
me canse	nos cansemos	me haya cansado	nos hayamos cansado
te canses	os canséis	te hayas cansado	os hayáis cansado
se canse	se cansen	se haya cansado	se hayan cansado
7 imperfecto de subjuntivo		14 pluscuamperfecto de subjuntivo	
me cansara	nos cansáramos	me hubiera cansado	nos hubiéramos cansado
te cansaras	os cansarais	te hubieras cansado	os hubierais cansado
se cansara	se cansaran	se hubiera cansado	se hubieran cansado
OR		OR	
me cansase	nos cansásemos	me hubiese cansado	nos hubiésemos cansado
te cansases	os cansaseis	te hubieses cansado	os hubieseis cansado
se cansase	se cansasen	se hubiese cansado	se hubiesen cansado

	imperativo	
—		cansémonos
	cánsate; no te canses	cansaos; no os canséis
	cánsese	cánsense

Sentences using this verb and words and expressions related to it
María se cansa, Pedro se cansa y yo me canso. Nosotros nos cansamos.

la cansera fatigue	cansarse de esperar to get tired of waiting
el cansancio fatigue, weariness	cansado, cansada tired, exhausted
cansar to fatigue, to tire, to weary	

cantar   Gerundio **cantando**   Part. pas. **cantado**

to sing

The Seven Simple Tenses		The Seven Compound Tenses	
Singular	Plural	Singular	Plural

1 presente de indicativo		8 perfecto de indicativo	
canto	cantamos	he cantado	hemos cantado
cantas	cantáis	has cantado	habéis cantado
canta	cantan	ha cantado	han cantado

2 imperfecto de indicativo		9 pluscuamperfecto de indicativo	
cantaba	cantábamos	había cantado	habíamos cantado
cantabas	cantabais	habías cantado	habíais cantado
cantaba	cantaban	había cantado	habían cantado

3 pretérito		10 pretérito anterior	
canté	cantamos	hube cantado	hubimos cantado
cantaste	cantasteis	hubiste cantado	hubisteis cantado
cantó	cantaron	hubo cantado	hubieron cantado

4 futuro		11 futuro perfecto	
cantaré	cantaremos	habré cantado	habremos cantado
cantarás	cantaréis	habrás cantado	habréis cantado
cantará	cantarán	habrá cantado	habrán cantado

5 potencial simple		12 potencial compuesto	
cantaría	cantaríamos	habría cantado	habríamos cantado
cantarías	cantaríais	habrías cantado	habríais cantado
cantaría	cantarían	habría cantado	habrían cantado

6 presente de subjuntivo		13 perfecto de subjuntivo	
cante	cantemos	haya cantado	hayamos cantado
cantes	cantéis	hayas cantado	hayáis cantado
cante	canten	haya cantado	hayan cantado

7 imperfecto de subjuntivo		14 pluscuamperfecto de subjuntivo	
cantara	cantáramos	hubiera cantado	hubiéramos cantado
cantaras	cantarais	hubieras cantado	hubierais cantado
cantara	cantaran	hubiera cantado	hubieran cantado
OR		OR	
cantase	cantásemos	hubiese cantado	hubiésemos cantado
cantases	cantaseis	hubieses cantado	hubieseis cantado
cantase	cantasen	hubiese cantado	hubiesen cantado

imperativo	
—	cantemos
canta; no cantes	cantad; no cantéis
cante	canten

Sentence using this verb and words related to it
Quien canta su mal espanta.   When you sing you drive away your grief.

una canción song	**una cantatriz** woman singer
una cantata cantata (music)	**cantor, cantora, cantante** singer
encantar to enchant	**encantado, encantada** enchanted

to load, to burden

The Seven Simple Tenses		The Seven Compound Tenses	
Singular	Plural	Singular	Plural
1 presente de indicativo		8 perfecto de indicativo	
cargo	cargamos	he cargado	hemos cargado
cargas	cargáis	has cargado	habéis cargado
carga	cargan	ha cargado	han cargado
2 imperfecto de indicativo		9 pluscuamperfecto de indicativo	
cargaba	cargábamos	había cargado	habíamos cargado
cargabas	cargabais	habías cargado	habíais cargado
cargaba	cargaban	había cargado	habían cargado
3 pretérito		10 pretérito anterior	
cargué	cargamos	hube cargado	hubimos cargado
cargaste	cargasteis	hubiste cargado	hubisteis cargado
cargó	cargaron	hubo cargado	hubieron cargado
4 futuro		11 futuro perfecto	
cargaré	cargaremos	habré cargado	habremos cargado
cargarás	cargaréis	habrás cargado	habréis cargado
cargará	cargarán	habrá cargado	habrán cargado
5 potencial simple		12 potencial compuesto	
cargaría	cargaríamos	habría cargado	habríamos cargado
cargarías	cargaríais	habrías cargado	habríais cargado
cargaría	cargarían	habría cargado	habrían cargado
6 presente de subjuntivo		13 perfecto de subjuntivo	
cargue	carguemos	haya cargado	hayamos cargado
cargues	carguéis	hayas cargado	hayáis cargado
cargue	carguen	haya cargado	hayan cargado
7 imperfecto de subjuntivo		14 pluscuamperfecto de subjuntivo	
cargara	cargáramos	hubiera cargado	hubiéramos cargado
cargaras	cargarais	hubieras cargado	hubierais cargado
cargara	cargaran	hubiera cargado	hubieran cargado
OR		OR	
cargase	cargásemos	hubiese cargado	hubiésemos cargado
cargases	cargaseis	hubieses cargado	hubieseis cargado
cargase	cargasen	hubiese cargado	hubiesen cargado

imperativo	
—	carguemos
carga; no cargues	cargad; no carguéis
cargue	carguen

Words and expressions related to this verb
cargoso, cargosa burdensome
la cargazón cargo
una cargazón de cabeza heaviness of the head
el cargamento shipment
el cargador shipper

71

casarse   Gerundio **casándose**   Part. pas. **casado**

to get married, to marry

The Seven Simple Tenses		The Seven Compound Tenses	
Singular	Plural	Singular	Plural
1 presente de indicativo		8 perfecto de indicativo	
me caso	nos casamos	me he casado	nos hemos casado
te casas	os casáis	te has casado	os habéis casado
se casa	se casan	se ha casado	se han casado
2 imperfecto de indicativo		9 pluscuamperfecto de indicativo	
me casaba	nos casábamos	me había casado	nos habíamos casado
te casabas	os casabais	te habías casado	os habíais casado
se casaba	se casaban	se había casado	se habían casado
3 pretérito		10 pretérito anterior	
me casé	nos casamos	me hube casado	nos hubimos casado
te casaste	os casasteis	te hubiste casado	os hubisteis casado
se casó	se casaron	se hubo casado	se hubieron casado
4 futuro		11 futuro perfecto	
me casaré	nos casaremos	me habré casado	nos habremos casado
te casarás	os casaréis	te habrás casado	os habréis casado
se casará	se casarán	se habrá casado	se habrán casado
5 potencial simple		12 potencial compuesto	
me casaría	nos casaríamos	me habría casado	nos habríamos casado
te casarías	os casaríais	te habrías casado	os habríais casado
se casaría	se casarían	se habría casado	se habrían casado
6 presente de subjuntivo		13 perfecto de subjuntivo	
me case	nos casemos	me haya casado	nos hayamos casado
te cases	os caséis	te hayas casado	os hayáis casado
se case	se casen	se haya casado	se hayan casado
7 imperfecto de subjuntivo		14 pluscuamperfecto de subjuntivo	
me casara	nos casáramos	me hubiera casado	nos hubiéramos casado
te casaras	os casarais	te hubieras casado	os hubierais casado
se casara	se casaran	se hubiera casado	se hubieran casado
OR		OR	
me casase	nos casásemos	me hubiese casado	nos hubiésemos casado
te casases	os casaseis	te hubieses casado	os hubieseis casado
se casase	se casasen	se hubiese casado	se hubiesen casado

	imperativo
—	casémonos
cásate; no te cases	casaos; no os caséis
cásese	cásense

Words and expressions related to this verb
Antes que te cases, mira lo que haces.   Look before you leap.
casarse con alguien   to marry someone
los recién casados   newlyweds

Gerundio **celebrando**   Part. pas. **celebrado**   **celebrar**

to celebrate

The Seven Simple Tenses		The Seven Compound Tenses	
Singular	Plural	Singular	Plural
1 presente de indicativo		8 perfecto de indicativo	
celebro	celebramos	he celebrado	hemos celebrado
celebras	celebráis	has celebrado	habéis celebrado
celebra	celebran	ha celebrado	han celebrado
2 imperfecto de indicativo		9 pluscuamperfecto de indicativo	
celebraba	celebrábamos	había celebrado	habíamos celebrado
celebrabas	celebrabais	habías celebrado	habíais celebrado
celebraba	celebraban	había celebrado	habían celebrado
3 pretérito		10 pretérito anterior	
celebré	celebramos	hube celebrado	hubimos celebrado
celebraste	celebrasteis	hubiste celebrado	hubisteis celebrado
celebró	celebraron	hubo celebrado	hubieron celebrado
4 futuro		11 futuro perfecto	
celebraré	celebraremos	habré celebrado	habremos celebrado
celebrarás	celebraréis	habrás celebrado	habréis celebrado
celebrará	celebrarán	habrá celebrado	habrán celebrado
5 potencial simple		12 potencial compuesto	
celebraría	celebraríamos	habría celebrado	habríamos celebrado
celebrarías	celebraríais	habrías celebrado	habríais celebrado
celebraría	celebrarían	habría celebrado	habrían celebrado
6 presente de subjuntivo		13 perfecto de subjuntivo	
celebre	celebremos	haya celebrado	hayamos celebrado
celebres	celebréis	hayas celebrado	hayáis celebrado
celebre	celebren	haya celebrado	hayan celebrado
7 imperfecto de subjuntivo		14 pluscuamperfecto de subjuntivo	
celebrara	celebráramos	hubiera celebrado	hubiéramos celebrado
celebraras	celebrarais	hubieras celebrado	hubierais celebrado
celebrara	celebraran	hubiera celebrado	hubieran celebrado
OR		OR	
celebrase	celebrásemos	hubiese celebrado	hubiésemos celebrado
celebrases	celebraseis	hubieses celebrado	hubieseis celebrado
celebrase	celebrasen	hubiese celebrado	hubiesen celebrado

imperativo	
—	celebremos
celebra; no celebres	celebrad; no celebréis
celebre	celebren

Words related to this verb
célebre   famous, celebrated, renowned
la celebridad   fame, celebrity
la celebración   celebration

73

cenar   Gerundio **cenando**   Part. pas. **cenado**

to have supper, to eat supper

The Seven Simple Tenses		The Seven Compound Tenses	
Singular	Plural	Singular	Plural
1 presente de indicativo		8 perfecto de indicativo	
ceno	cenamos	he cenado	hemos cenado
cenas	cenáis	has cenado	habéis cenado
cena	cenan	ha cenado	han cenado
2 imperfecto de indicativo		9 pluscuamperfecto de indicativo	
cenaba	cenábamos	había cenado	habíamos cenado
cenabas	cenabais	habías cenado	habíais cenado
cenaba	cenaban	había cenado	habían cenado
3 pretérito		10 pretérito anterior	
cené	cenamos	hube cenado	hubimos cenado
cenaste	cenasteis	hubiste cenado	hubisteis cenado
cenó	cenaron	hubo cenado	hubieron cenado
4 futuro		11 futuro perfecto	
cenaré	cenaremos	habré cenado	habremos cenado
cenarás	cenaréis	habrás cenado	habréis cenado
cenará	cenarán	habrá cenado	habrán cenado
5 potencial simple		12 potencial compuesto	
cenaría	cenaríamos	habría cenado	habríamos cenado
cenarías	cenaríais	habrías cenado	habríais cenado
cenaría	cenarían	habría cenado	habrían cenado
6 presente de subjuntivo		13 perfecto de subjuntivo	
cene	cenemos	haya cenado	hayamos cenado
cenes	cenéis	hayas cenado	hayáis cenado
cene	cenen	haya cenado	hayan cenado
7 imperfecto de subjuntivo		14 pluscuamperfecto de subjuntivo	
cenara	cenáramos	hubiera cenado	hubiéramos cenado
cenaras	cenarais	hubieras cenado	hubierais cenado
cenara	cenaran	hubiera cenado	hubieran cenado
OR		OR	
cenase	cenásemos	hubiese cenado	hubiésemos cenado
cenases	cenaseis	hubieses cenado	hubieseis cenado
cenase	cenasen	hubiese cenado	hubiesen cenado

imperativo	
—	cenemos
cena; no cenes	cenad; no cenéis
cene	cenen

Sentences using this verb and words related to it
—Carlos, ¿A qué hora cenas?
—Ceno a las ocho con mi familia en casa.
la cena supper (dinner)   **la hora de cenar** dinnertime, suppertime
La Cena *(The Last Supper,* fresco by Leonardo da Vinci)

to close

The Seven Simple Tenses		The Seven Compound Tenses	
Singular	Plural	Singular	Plural
1 presente de indicativo		8 perfecto de indicativo	
cierro	**cerramos**	**he cerrado**	**hemos cerrado**
cierras	**cerráis**	**has cerrado**	**habéis cerrado**
cierra	**cierran**	**ha cerrado**	**han cerrado**
2 imperfecto de indicativo		9 pluscuamperfecto de indicativo	
cerraba	**cerrábamos**	**había cerrado**	**habíamos cerrado**
cerrabas	**cerrabais**	**habías cerrado**	**habíais cerrado**
cerraba	**cerraban**	**había cerrado**	**habían cerrado**
3 pretérito		10 pretérito anterior	
cerré	**cerramos**	**hube cerrado**	**hubimos cerrado**
cerraste	**cerrasteis**	**hubiste cerrado**	**hubisteis cerrado**
cerró	**cerraron**	**hubo cerrado**	**hubieron cerrado**
4 futuro		11 futuro perfecto	
cerraré	**cerraremos**	**habré cerrado**	**habremos cerrado**
cerrarás	**cerraréis**	**habrás cerrado**	**habréis cerrado**
cerrará	**cerrarán**	**habrá cerrado**	**habrán cerrado**
5 potencial simple		12 potencial compuesto	
cerraría	**cerraríamos**	**habría cerrado**	**habríamos cerrado**
cerrarías	**cerraríais**	**habrías cerrado**	**habríais cerrado**
cerraría	**cerrarían**	**habría cerrado**	**habrían cerrado**
6 presente de subjuntivo		13 perfecto de subjuntivo	
cierre	**cerremos**	**haya cerrado**	**hayamos cerrado**
cierres	**cerréis**	**hayas cerrado**	**hayáis cerrado**
cierre	**cierren**	**haya cerrado**	**hayan cerrado**
7 imperfecto de subjuntivo		14 pluscuamperfecto de subjuntivo	
cerrara	**cerráramos**	**hubiera cerrado**	**hubiéramos cerrado**
cerraras	**cerrarais**	**hubieras cerrado**	**hubierais cerrado**
cerrara	**cerraran**	**hubiera cerrado**	**hubieran cerrado**
OR		OR	
cerrase	**cerrásemos**	**hubiese cerrado**	**hubiésemos cerrado**
cerrases	**cerraseis**	**hubieses cerrado**	**hubieseis cerrado**
cerrase	**cerrasen**	**hubiese cerrado**	**hubiesen cerrado**

imperativo		
—		**cerremos**
	cierra; no cierres	**cerrad; no cerréis**
	cierre	**cierren**

Common idiomatic expressions using this verb

cerrar los ojos to close one's eyes
cerrar los oídos to turn a deaf ear
cerrar la boca to shut up, to keep silent
la cerradura lock
La puerta está cerrada. The door is closed.

Las ventanas están cerradas.
  The windows are closed.
encerrar to lock up, to confine
encerrarse to live in seclusion, to
  retire

certificar   Gerundio **certificando**   Part. pas. **certificado**

to certify, to register (a letter), to attest

The Seven Simple Tenses		The Seven Compound Tenses	
Singular	Plural	Singular	Plural
1 presente de indicativo		8 perfecto de indicativo	
certifico	**certificamos**	**he certificado**	**hemos certificado**
certificas	**certificáis**	**has certificado**	**habéis certificado**
certifica	**certifican**	**ha certificado**	**han certificado**
2 imperfecto de indicativo		9 pluscuamperfecto de indicativo	
certificaba	**certificábamos**	**había certificado**	**habíamos certificado**
certificabas	**certificabais**	**habías certificado**	**habíais certificado**
certificaba	**certificaban**	**había certificado**	**habían certificado**
3 pretérito		10 pretérito anterior	
certifiqué	**certificamos**	**hube certificado**	**hubimos certificado**
certificaste	**certificasteis**	**hubiste certificado**	**hubisteis certificado**
certificó	**certificaron**	**hubo certificado**	**hubieron certificado**
4 futuro		11 futuro perfecto	
certificaré	**certificaremos**	**habré certificado**	**habremos certificado**
certificarás	**certificaréis**	**habrás certificado**	**habréis certificado**
certificará	**certificarán**	**habrá certificado**	**habrán certificado**
5 potencial simple		12 potencial compuesto	
certificaría	**certificaríamos**	**habría certificado**	**habríamos certificado**
certificarías	**certificaríais**	**habrías certificado**	**habríais certificado**
certificaría	**certificarían**	**habría certificado**	**habrían certificado**
6 presente de subjuntivo		13 perfecto de subjuntivo	
certifique	**certifiquemos**	**haya certificado**	**hayamos certificado**
certifiques	**certifiquéis**	**hayas certificado**	**hayáis certificado**
certifique	**certifiquen**	**haya certificado**	**hayan certificado**
7 imperfecto de subjuntivo		14 pluscuamperfecto de subjuntivo	
certificara	**certificáramos**	**hubiera certificado**	**hubiéramos certificado**
certificaras	**certificarais**	**hubieras certificado**	**hubierais certificado**
certificara	**certificaran**	**hubiera certificado**	**hubieran certificado**
OR		OR	
certificase	**certificásemos**	**hubiese certificado**	**hubiésemos certificado**
certificases	**certificaseis**	**hubieses certificado**	**hubieseis certificado**
certificase	**certificasen**	**hubiese certificado**	**hubiesen certificado**

imperativo	
—	**certifiquemos**
certifica; no certifiques	**certificad; no certifiquéis**
certifique	**certifiquen**

Words related to this verb
la certificación certificate, certification
certificador, certificadora certifier
la certidumbre certainty

la certeza certainty
la certinidad assurance, certainty
la certitude certitude

76

to cook, to bake

The Seven Simple Tenses		The Seven Compound Tenses	
Singular	Plural	Singular	Plural
1 presente de indicativo		8 perfecto de indicativo	
cuezo	cocemos	he cocido	hemos cocido
cueces	cocéis	has cocido	habéis cocido
cuece	cuecen	ha cocido	han cocido
2 imperfecto de indicativo		9 pluscuamperfecto de indicativo	
cocía	cocíamos	había cocido	habíamos cocido
cocías	cocíais	habías cocido	habíais cocido
cocía	cocían	había cocido	habían cocido
3 pretérito		10 pretérito anterior	
cocí	cocimos	hube cocido	hubimos cocido
cociste	cocisteis	hubiste cocido	hubisteis cocido
coció	cocieron	hubo cocido	hubieron cocido
4 futuro		11 futuro perfecto	
coceré	coceremos	habré cocido	habremos cocido
cocerás	coceréis	habrás cocido	habréis cocido
cocerá	cocerán	habrá cocido	habrán cocido
5 potencial simple		12 potencial compuesto	
cocería	coceríamos	habría cocido	habríamos cocido
cocerías	coceríais	habrías cocido	habríais cocido
cocería	cocerían	habría cocido	habrían cocido
6 presente de subjuntivo		13 perfecto de subjuntivo	
cueza	cozamos	haya cocido	hayamos cocido
cuezas	cozáis	hayas cocido	hayáis cocido
cueza	cuezan	haya cocido	hayan cocido
7 imperfecto de subjuntivo		14 pluscuamperfecto de subjuntivo	
cociera	cociéramos	hubiera cocido	hubiéramos cocido
cocieras	cocierais	hubieras cocido	hubierais cocido
cociera	cocieran	hubiera cocido	hubieran cocido
OR		OR	
cociese	cociésemos	hubiese cocido	hubiésemos cocido
cocieses	cocieseis	hubieses cocido	hubieseis cocido
cociese	cociesen	hubiese cocido	hubiesen cocido

imperativo		
—	cozamos	
cuece; no cuezas	coced; no cozáis	
cueza	cuezan	

Words related to this verb
la cocina   kitchen
el cocinero, la cocinera   cook, chef
el cocimiento   cooking
el cocido   plate of boiled meat and vegetables

to seize, to take, to grasp, to grab, to catch

The Seven Simple Tenses		The Seven Compound Tenses	
Singular	Plural	Singular	Plural
1 presente de indicativo		8 perfecto de indicativo	
cojo	cogemos	he cogido	hemos cogido
coges	cogéis	has cogido	habéis cogido
coge	cogen	ha cogido	han cogido
2 imperfecto de indicativo		9 pluscuamperfecto de indicativo	
cogía	cogíamos	había cogido	habíamos cogido
cogías	cogíais	habías cogido	habíais cogido
cogía	cogían	había cogido	habían cogido
3 pretérito		10 pretérito anterior	
cogí	cogimos	hube cogido	hubimos cogido
cogiste	cogisteis	hubiste cogido	hubisteis cogido
cogió	cogieron	hubo cogido	hubieron cogido
4 futuro		11 futuro perfecto	
cogeré	cogeremos	habré cogido	habremos cogido
cogerás	cogeréis	habrás cogido	habréis cogido
cogerá	cogerán	habrá cogido	habrán cogido
5 potencial simple		12 potencial compuesto	
cogería	cogeríamos	habría cogido	habríamos cogido
cogerías	cogeríais	habrías cogido	habríais cogido
cogería	cogerían	habría cogido	habrían cogido
6 presente de subjuntivo		13 perfecto de subjuntivo	
coja	cojamos	haya cogido	hayamos cogido
cojas	cojáis	hayas cogido	hayáis cogido
coja	cojan	haya cogido	hayan cogido
7 imperfecto de subjuntivo		14 pluscuamperfecto de subjuntivo	
cogiera	cogiéramos	hubiera cogido	hubiéramos cogido
cogieras	cogierais	hubieras cogido	hubierais cogido
cogiera	cogieran	hubiera cogido	hubieran cogido
OR		OR	
cogiese	cogiésemos	hubiese cogido	hubiésemos cogido
cogieses	cogieseis	hubieses cogido	hubieseis cogido
cogiese	cogiesen	hubiese cogido	hubiesen cogido

imperativo	
—	cojamos
coge; no cojas	coged; no cojáis
coja	cojan

Words related to this verb

la cogida gathering of fruits, a catch	**recoger** to pick (up), to gather
el cogedor collector, dust pan	**acoger** to greet, to receive, to welcome
escoger to choose, to select	**encoger** to shorten, to shrink
coger catarro (o resfriado) to catch cold	**descoger** to expand, to extend

Gerundio **coligiendo**   Part. pas. **colegido**   **colegir**

The Seven Simple Tenses		The Seven Compound Tenses	
Singular	Plural	Singular	Plural
1 presente de indicativo		8 perfecto de indicativo	
colijo	colegimos	he colegido	hemos colegido
coliges	colegís	has colegido	habéis colegido
colige	coligen	ha colegido	han colegido
2 imperfecto de indicativo		9 pluscuamperfecto de indicativo	
colegía	colegíamos	había colegido	habíamos colegido
colegías	colegíais	habías colegido	habíais colegido
colegía	colegían	había colegido	habían colegido
3 pretérito		10 pretérito anterior	
colegí	colegimos	hube colegido	hubimos colegido
colegiste	colegisteis	hubiste colegido	hubisteis colegido
coligió	coligieron	hubo colegido	hubieron colegido
4 futuro		11 futuro perfecto	
colegiré	colegiremos	habré colegido	habremos colegido
colegirás	colegiréis	habrás colegido	habréis colegido
colegirá	colegirán	habrá colegido	habrán colegido
5 potencial simple		12 potencial compuesto	
colegiría	colegiríamos	habría colegido	habríamos colegido
colegirías	colegiríais	habrías colegido	habríais colegido
colegiría	colegirían	habría colegido	habrían colegido
6 presente de subjuntivo		13 perfecto de subjuntivo	
colija	colijamos	haya colegido	hayamos colegido
colijas	colijáis	hayas colegido	hayáis colegido
colija	colijan	haya colegido	hayan colegido
7 imperfecto de subjuntivo		14 pluscuamperfecto de subjuntivo	
coligiera	coligiéramos	hubiera colegido	hubiéramos colegido
coligieras	coligierais	hubieras colegido	hubierais colegido
coligiera	coligieran	hubiera colegido	hubieran colegido
OR		OR	
coligiese	coligiésemos	hubiese colegido	hubiésemos colegido
coligieses	coligieseis	hubieses colegido	hubieseis colegido
coligiese	coligiesen	hubiese colegido	hubiesen colegido

	imperativo
—	colijamos
colige; no colijas	colegid; no colijáis
colija	colijan

Words related to this verb
el colegio   college, school
la colección   collection

colectivo, colectiva   collective
el colegio electoral   electoral college

colgar   Gerundio **colgando**   Part. pas. **colgado**

to hang (up)

The Seven Simple Tenses		The Seven Compound Tenses	
Singular	Plural	Singular	Plural
1 presente de indicativo		8 perfecto de indicativo	
cuelgo	colgamos	he colgado	hemos colgado
cuelgas	colgáis	has colgado	habéis colgado
cuelga	cuelgan	ha colgado	han colgado
2 imperfecto de indicativo		9 pluscuamperfecto de indicativo	
colgaba	colgábamos	había colgado	habíamos colgado
colgabas	colgabais	habías colgado	habíais colgado
colgaba	colgaban	había colgado	habían colgado
3 pretérito		10 pretérito anterior	
colgué	colgamos	hube colgado	hubimos colgado
colgaste	colgasteis	hubiste colgado	hubisteis colgado
colgó	colgaron	hubo colgado	hubieron colgado
4 futuro		11 futuro perfecto	
colgaré	colgaremos	habré colgado	habremos colgado
colgarás	colgaréis	habrás colgado	habréis colgado
colgará	colgarán	habrá colgado	habrán colgado
5 potencial simple		12 potencial compuesto	
colgaría	colgaríamos	habría colgado	habríamos colgado
colgarías	colgaríais	habrías colgado	habríais colgado
colgaría	colgarían	habría colgado	habrían colgado
6 presente de subjuntivo		13 perfecto de subjuntivo	
cuelgue	colguemos	haya colgado	hayamos colgado
cuelgues	colguéis	hayas colgado	hayáis colgado
cuelgue	cuelguen	haya colgado	hayan colgado
7 imperfecto de subjuntivo		14 pluscuamperfecto de subjuntivo	
colgara	colgáramos	hubiera colgado	hubiéramos colgado
colgaras	colgarais	hubieras colgado	hubierais colgado
colgara	colgaran	hubiera colgado	hubieran colgado
OR		OR	
colgase	colgásemos	hubiese colgado	hubiésemos colgado
colgases	colgaseis	hubieses colgado	hubieseis colgado
colgase	colgasen	hubiese colgado	hubiesen colgado

imperativo	
—	colguemos
cuelga; no cuelgues	colgad; no colguéis
cuelgue	cuelguen

Words related to this verb
el colgadero   hanger, hook on which to hang things
dejar colgado (colgada)   to be left disappointed
la colgadura   drapery, tapestry

Gerundio **colocando**   Part. pas. **colocado**   **colocar**

to put, to place

The Seven Simple Tenses		The Seven Compound Tenses	
Singular	Plural	Singular	Plural
1 presente de indicativo		**8 perfecto de indicativo**	
coloco	colocamos	he colocado	hemos colocado
colocas	colocáis	has colocado	habéis colocado
coloca	colocan	ha colocado	han colocado
2 imperfecto de indicativo		**9 pluscuamperfecto de indicativo**	
colocaba	colocábamos	había colocado	habíamos colocado
colocabas	colocabais	habías colocado	habíais colocado
colocaba	colocaban	había colocado	habían colocado
3 pretérito		**10 pretérito anterior**	
coloqué	colocamos	hube colocado	hubimos colocado
colocaste	colocasteis	hubiste colocado	hubisteis colocado
colocó	colocaron	hubo colocado	hubieron colocado
4 futuro		**11 futuro perfecto**	
colocaré	colocaremos	habré colocado	habremos colocado
colocarás	colocaréis	habrás colocado	habréis colocado
colocará	colocarán	habrá colocado	habrán colocado
5 potencial simple		**12 potencial compuesto**	
colocaría	colocaríamos	habría colocado	habríamos colocado
colocarías	colocaríais	habrías colocado	habríais colocado
colocaría	colocarían	habría colocado	habrían colocado
6 presente de subjuntivo		**13 perfecto de subjuntivo**	
coloque	coloquemos	haya colocado	hayamos colocado
coloques	coloquéis	hayas colocado	hayáis colocado
coloque	coloquen	haya colocado	hayan colocado
7 imperfecto de subjuntivo		**14 pluscuamperfecto de subjuntivo**	
colocara	colocáramos	hubiera colocado	hubiéramos colocado
colocaras	colocarais	hubieras colocado	hubierais colocado
colocara	colocaran	hubiera colocado	hubieran colocado
OR		OR	
colocase	colocásemos	hubiese colocado	hubiésemos colocado
colocases	colocaseis	hubieses colocado	hubieseis colocado
colocase	colocasen	hubiese colocado	hubiesen colocado

imperativo	
—	coloquemos
coloca; no coloques	colocad; no coloquéis
coloque	coloquen

Words and expressions related to this verb
la colocación   job, employment, position
colocar dinero   to invest money
colocar un pedido   to place an order
la agencia de colocación   job placement agency

to begin, to start, to commence

The Seven Simple Tenses		The Seven Compound Tenses	
Singular	Plural	Singular	Plural
1 presente de indicativo		8 perfecto de indicativo	
comienzo	comenzamos	he comenzado	hemos comenzado
comienzas	comenzáis	has comenzado	habéis comenzado
comienza	comienzan	ha comenzado	han comenzado
2 imperfecto de indicativo		9 pluscuamperfecto de indicativo	
comenzaba	comenzábamos	había comenzado	habíamos comenzado
comenzabas	comenzabais	habías comenzado	habíais comenzado
comenzaba	comenzaban	había comenzado	habían comenzado
3 pretérito		10 pretérito anterior	
comencé	comenzamos	hube comenzado	hubimos comenzado
comenzaste	comenzasteis	hubiste comenzado	hubisteis comenzado
comenzó	comenzaron	hubo comenzado	hubieron comenzado
4 futuro		11 futuro perfecto	
comenzaré	comenzaremos	habré comenzado	habremos comenzado
comenzarás	comenzaréis	habrás comenzado	habréis comenzado
comenzará	comenzarán	habrá comenzado	habrán comenzado
5 potencial simple		12 potencial compuesto	
comenzaría	comenzaríamos	habría comenzado	habríamos comenzado
comenzarías	comenzaríais	habrías comenzado	habríais comenzado
comenzaría	comenzarían	habría comenzado	habrían comenzado
6 presente de subjuntivo		13 perfecto de subjuntivo	
comience	comencemos	haya comenzado	hayamos comenzado
comiences	comencéis	hayas comenzado	hayáis comenzado
comience	comiencen	haya comenzado	hayan comenzado
7 imperfecto de subjuntivo		14 pluscuamperfecto de subjuntivo	
comenzara	comenzáramos	hubiera comenzado	hubiéramos comenzado
comenzaras	comenzarais	hubieras comenzado	hubierais comenzado
comenzara	comenzaran	hubiera comenzado	hubieran comenzado
OR		OR	
comenzase	comenzásemos	hubiese comenzado	hubiésemos comenzado
comenzases	comenzaseis	hubieses comenzado	hubieseis comenzado
comenzase	comenzasen	hubiese comenzado	hubiesen comenzado

imperativo	
—	comencemos
comienza; no comiences	comenzad; no comencéis
comience	comiencen

Words and expressions related to this verb

—¿Qué tiempo hace?
—Comienza a llover.
el comienzo beginning
comenzante beginner

El comenzante comenzó al comienzo.
The beginner began at the beginning.
comenzar a + inf. to begin + inf.
comenzar por + inf. to begin by + pres. part.

to eat

The Seven Simple Tenses		The Seven Compound Tenses	
Singular	Plural	Singular	Plural

1 presente de indicativo		8 perfecto de indicativo	
como	**comemos**	**he comido**	**hemos comido**
comes	**coméis**	**has comido**	**habéis comido**
come	**comen**	**ha comido**	**han comido**

2 imperfecto de indicativo		9 pluscuamperfecto de indicativo	
comía	**comíamos**	**había comido**	**habíamos comido**
comías	**comíais**	**habías comido**	**habíais comido**
comía	**comían**	**había comido**	**habían comido**

3 pretérito		10 pretérito anterior	
comí	**comimos**	**hube comido**	**hubimos comido**
comiste	**comisteis**	**hubiste comido**	**hubisteis comido**
comió	**comieron**	**hubo comido**	**hubieron comido**

4 futuro		11 futuro perfecto	
comeré	**comeremos**	**habré comido**	**habremos comido**
comerás	**comeréis**	**habrás comido**	**habréis comido**
comerá	**comerán**	**habrá comido**	**habrán comido**

5 potencial simple		12 potencial compuesto	
comería	**comeríamos**	**habría comido**	**habríamos comido**
comerías	**comeríais**	**habrías comido**	**habríais comido**
comería	**comerían**	**habría comido**	**habrían comido**

6 presente de subjuntivo		13 perfecto de subjuntivo	
coma	**comamos**	**haya comido**	**hayamos comido**
comas	**comáis**	**hayas comido**	**hayáis comido**
coma	**coman**	**haya comido**	**hayan comido**

7 imperfecto de subjuntivo		14 pluscuamperfecto de subjuntivo	
comiera	**comiéramos**	**hubiera comido**	**hubiéramos comido**
comieras	**comierais**	**hubieras comido**	**hubierais comido**
comiera	**comieran**	**hubiera comido**	**hubieran comido**
OR		OR	
comiese	**comiésemos**	**hubiese comido**	**hubiésemos comido**
comieses	**comieseis**	**hubieses comido**	**hubieseis comido**
comiese	**comiesen**	**hubiese comido**	**hubiesen comido**

imperativo	
—	**comamos**
come; no comas	**comed; no comáis**
coma	**coman**

Words and expressions related to this verb

ganar de comer to earn a living	**comerse** to eat up
la comida meal	**el comer** food
la comidilla light meal	**comer con gana** to eat heartily
comer fuera de casa to eat out; dine out	**comer de todo** to eat everything

83

componer   Gerundio **componiendo**   Part. pas. **compuesto**

to compose

The Seven Simple Tenses		The Seven Compound Tenses	
Singular	Plural	Singular	Plural
1 presente de indicativo		8 perfecto de indicativo	
compongo	componemos	he compuesto	hemos compuesto
compones	componéis	has compuesto	habéis compuesto
compone	componen	ha compuesto	han compuesto
2 imperfecto de indicativo		9 pluscuamperfecto de indicativo	
componía	componíamos	había compuesto	habíamos compuesto
componías	componíais	habías compuesto	habíais compuesto
componía	componían	había compuesto	habían compuesto
3 pretérito		10 pretérito anterior	
compuse	compusimos	hube compuesto	hubimos compuesto
compusiste	compusisteis	hubiste compuesto	hubisteis compuesto
compuso	compusieron	hubo compuesto	hubieron compuesto
4 futuro		11 futuro perfecto	
compondré	compondremos	habré compuesto	habremos compuesto
compondrás	compondréis	habrás compuesto	habréis compuesto
compondrá	compondrán	habrá compuesto	habrán compuesto
5 potencial simple		12 potencial compuesto	
compondría	compondríamos	habría compuesto	habríamos compuesto
compondrías	compondríais	habrías compuesto	habríais compuesto
compondría	compondrían	habría compuesto	habrían compuesto
6 presente de subjuntivo		13 perfecto de subjuntivo	
compongo	compongamos	haya compuesto	hayamos compuesto
compongas	compongáis	hayas compuesto	hayáis compuesto
componga	compongan	haya compuesto	hayan compuesto
7 imperfecto de subjuntivo		14 pluscuamperfecto de subjuntivo	
compusiera	compusiéramos	hubiera compuesto	hubiéramos compuesto
compusieras	compusierais	hubieras compuesto	hubierais compuesto
compusiera	compusieran	hubiera compuesto	hubieran compuesto
OR		OR	
compusiese	compusiésemos	hubiese compuesto	hubiésemos compuesto
compusieses	compusieseis	hubieses compuesto	hubieseis compuesto
compusiese	compusiesen	hubiese compuesto	hubiesen compuesto

	imperativo	
—	compongamos	
compón; no compongas	componed; no compongáis	
componga	compongan	

Words related to this verb

el compuesto compound, mixture
compuestamente neatly, orderly
deponer to depose
imponer to impose

la composición composition
el compositor, la compositora composer (music)
exponer to expose, to exhibit
indisponer to indispose

84

| Gerundio **comprando** | Part. pas. **comprado** | **comprar** |

to buy, to purchase

The Seven Simple Tenses		The Seven Compound Tenses	
Singular	Plural	Singular	Plural
1 presente de indicativo		**8 perfecto de indicativo**	
compro	compramos	he comprado	hemos comprado
compras	compráis	has comprado	habéis comprado
compra	compran	ha comprado	han comprado
2 imperfecto de indicativo		**9 pluscuamperfecto de indicativo**	
compraba	comprábamos	había comprado	habíamos comprado
comprabas	comprabais	habías comprado	habíais comprado
compraba	compraban	había comprado	habían comprado
3 pretérito		**10 pretérito anterior**	
compré	compramos	hube comprado	hubimos comprado
compraste	comprasteis	hubiste comprado	hubisteis comprado
compró	compraron	hubo comprado	hubieron comprado
4 futuro		**11 futuro perfecto**	
compraré	compraremos	habré comprado	habremos comprado
comprarás	compraréis	habrás comprado	habréis comprado
comprará	comprarán	habrá comprado	habrán comprado
5 potencial simple		**12 potencial compuesto**	
compraría	compraríamos	habría comprado	habríamos comprado
comprarías	compraríais	habrías comprado	habríais comprado
compraría	comprarían	habría comprado	habrían comprado
6 presente de subjuntivo		**13 perfecto de subjuntivo**	
compre	compremos	haya comprado	hayamos comprado
compres	compréis	hayas comprado	hayáis comprado
compre	compren	haya comprado	hayan comprado
7 imperfecto de subjuntivo		**14 pluscuamperfecto de subjuntivo**	
comprara	compráramos	hubiera comprado	hubiéramos comprado
compraras	comprarais	hubieras comprado	hubierais comprado
comprara	compraran	hubiera comprado	hubieran comprado
OR		OR	
comprase	comprásemos	hubiese comprado	hubiésemos comprado
comprases	compraseis	hubieses comprado	hubieseis comprado
comprase	comprasen	hubiese comprado	hubiesen comprado

	imperativo	
—	compremos	
compra; no compres	comprad; no compréis	
compre	compren	

Words and expressions related to this verb

comprador, compradora, comprante buyer
la compra purchase
comprable purchasable
ir de compras to go shopping

comprar fiado, comprar a crédito
    to buy on credit
comprar con rebaja to buy at a
    discount

85

comprender   Gerundio **comprendiendo**   Part. pas. **comprendido**

to understand

The Seven Simple Tenses		The Seven Compound Tenses	
Singular	Plural	Singular	Plural
1 presente de indicativo		8 perfecto de indicativo	
comprendo	**comprendemos**	**he**	**hemos**
comprendes	**comprendéis**	**has**	**habéis** + comprendido
comprende	**comprenden**	**ha**	**han**
2 imperfecto de indicativo		9 pluscuamperfecto de indicativo	
comprendía	**comprendíamos**	**había**	**habíamos**
comprendías	**comprendíais**	**habías**	**habíais** + comprendido
comprendía	**comprendían**	**había**	**habían**
3 pretérito		10 pretérito anterior	
comprendí	**comprendimos**	**hube**	**hubimos**
comprendiste	**comprendisteis**	**hubiste**	**hubisteis** + comprendido
comprendió	**comprendieron**	**hubo**	**hubieron**
4 futuro		11 futuro perfecto	
comprenderé	**comprenderemos**	**habré**	**habremos**
comprenderás	**comprenderéis**	**habrás**	**habréis** + comprendido
comprenderá	**comprenderán**	**habrá**	**habrán**
5 potencial simple		12 potencial compuesto	
comprendería	**comprenderíamos**	**habría**	**habríamos**
comprenderías	**comprenderíais**	**habrías**	**habríais** + comprendido
comprendería	**comprenderían**	**habría**	**habrían**
6 presente de subjuntivo		13 perfecto de subjuntivo	
comprenda	**comprendamos**	**haya**	**hayamos**
comprendas	**comprendáis**	**hayas**	**hayáis** + comprendido
comprenda	**comprendan**	**haya**	**hayan**
7 imperfecto de subjuntivo		14 pluscuamperfecto de subjuntivo	
comprendiera	**comprendiéramos**	**hubiera**	**hubiéramos**
comprendieras	**comprendierais**	**hubieras**	**hubierais** + comprendido
comprendiera	**comprendieran**	**hubiera**	**hubieran**
OR		OR	
comprendiese	**comprendiésemos**	**hubiese**	**hubiésemos**
comprendieses	**comprendieseis**	**hubieses**	**hubieseis** + comprendido
comprendiese	**comprendiesen**	**hubiese**	**hubiesen**

imperativo	
—	**comprendamos**
comprende; no comprendas	**comprended; no comprendáis**
comprenda	**comprendan**

Words related to this verb
la comprensión   comprehension, understanding
la comprensibilidad   comprehensibility, intelligibility
comprensivo, comprensiva   comprehensive
comprensible   comprehensible, understandable

Gerundio **conduciendo** Part. pas. **conducido** **conducir**

to lead, to conduct, to drive

The Seven Simple Tenses		The Seven Compound Tenses	
Singular	Plural	Singular	Plural
1 presente de indicativo		8 perfecto de indicativo	
conduzco	**conducimos**	**he conducido**	**hemos conducido**
conduces	**conducís**	**has conducido**	**habéis conducido**
conduce	**conducen**	**ha conducido**	**han conducido**
2 imperfecto de indicativo		9 pluscuamperfecto de indicativo	
conducía	**conducíamos**	**había conducido**	**habíamos conducido**
conducías	**conducíais**	**habías conducido**	**habíais conducido**
conducía	**conducían**	**había conducido**	**habían conducido**
3 pretérito		10 pretérito anterior	
conduje	**condujimos**	**hube conducido**	**hubimos conducido**
condujiste	**condujisteis**	**hubiste conducido**	**hubisteis conducido**
condujo	**condujeron**	**hubo conducido**	**hubieron conducido**
4 futuro		11 futuro perfecto	
conduciré	**conduciremos**	**habré conducido**	**habremos conducido**
conducirás	**conduciréis**	**habrás conducido**	**habréis conducido**
conducirá	**conducirán**	**habrá conducido**	**habrán conducido**
5 potencial simple		12 potencial compuesto	
conduciría	**conduciríamos**	**habría conducido**	**habríamos conducido**
conducirías	**conduciríais**	**habrías conducido**	**habríais conducido**
conduciría	**conducirían**	**habría conducido**	**habrían conducido**
6 presente de subjuntivo		13 perfecto de subjuntivo	
conduzca	**conduzcamos**	**haya conducido**	**hayamos conducido**
conduzcas	**conduzcáis**	**hayas conducido**	**hayáis conducido**
conduzca	**conduzcan**	**haya conducido**	**hayan conducido**
7 imperfecto de subjuntivo		14 pluscuamperfecto de subjuntivo	
condujera	**condujéramos**	**hubiera conducido**	**hubiéramos conducido**
condujeras	**condujerais**	**hubieras conducido**	**hubierais conducido**
condujera	**condujeran**	**hubiera conducido**	**hubieran conducido**
OR		OR	
condujese	**condujésemos**	**hubiese conducido**	**hubiésemos conducido**
condujeses	**condujeseis**	**hubieses conducido**	**hubieseis conducido**
condujese	**condujesen**	**hubiese conducido**	**hubiesen conducido**

imperativo	
—	**conduzcamos**
conduce; no conduzcas	**conducid; no conduzcáis**
conduzca	**conduzcan**

Words related to this verb

conductor, conductora conductor, director
el conducto conduit, duct
la conducta conduct, behavior
conducente conducive

87

confesar   Gerundio **confesando**   Part. pas. **confesado**

to confess

The Seven Simple Tenses		The Seven Compound Tenses	
Singular	Plural	Singular	Plural
1 presente de indicativo		8 perfecto de indicativo	
confieso	confesamos	he confesado	hemos confesado
confiesas	confesáis	has confesado	habéis confesado
confiesa	confiesan	ha confesado	han confesado
2 imperfecto de indicativo		9 pluscuamperfecto de indicativo	
confesaba	confesábamos	había confesado	habíamos confesado
confesabas	confesabais	habías confesado	habíais confesado
confesaba	confesaban	había confesado	habían confesado
3 pretérito		10 pretérito anterior	
confesé	confesamos	hube confesado	hubimos confesado
confesaste	confesasteis	hubiste confesado	hubisteis confesado
confesó	confesaron	hubo confesado	hubieron confesado
4 futuro		11 futuro perfecto	
confesaré	confesaremos	habré confesado	habremos confesado
confesarás	confesaréis	habrás confesado	habréis confesado
confesará	confesarán	habrá confesado	habrán confesado
5 potencial simple		12 potencial compuesto	
confesaría	confesaríamos	habría confesado	habríamos confesado
confesarías	confesaríais	habrías confesado	habríais confesado
confesaría	confesarían	habría confesado	habrían confesado
6 presente de subjuntivo		13 perfecto de subjuntivo	
confiese	confesemos	haya confesado	hayamos confesado
confieses	confeséis	hayas confesado	hayáis confesado
confiese	confiesen	haya confesado	hayan confesado
7 imperfecto de subjuntivo		14 pluscuamperfecto de subjuntivo	
confesara	confesáramos	hubiera confesado	hubiéramos confesado
confesaras	confesarais	hubieras confesado	hubierais confesado
confesara	confesaran	hubiera confesado	hubieran confesado
OR		OR	
confesase	confesásemos	hubiese confesado	hubiésemos confesado
confesases	confesaseis	hubieses confesado	hubieseis confesado
confesase	confesasen	hubiese confesado	hubiesen confesado

	imperativo
—	confesemos
confiesa; no confieses	confesad; no confeséis
confiese	confiesen

Words and expressions related to this verb

la confesión confession
el confesionario confession box
el confesor confessor

confesar de plano to confess openly
un, una confesante confessor

Gerundio **conociendo**   Part. pas. **conocido**   **conocer**

to know, to be acquainted with

The Seven Simple Tenses		The Seven Compound Tenses	
Singular	Plural	Singular	Plural
1 presente de indicativo		8 perfecto de indicativo	
conozco	**conocemos**	**he conocido**	**hemos conocido**
conoces	**conocéis**	**has conocido**	**habéis conocido**
conoce	**conocen**	**ha conocido**	**han conocido**
2 imperfecto de indicativo		9 pluscuamperfecto de indicativo	
conocía	**conocíamos**	**había conocido**	**habíamos conocido**
conocías	**conocíais**	**habías conocido**	**habíais conocido**
conocía	**conocían**	**había conocido**	**habían conocido**
3 pretérito		10 pretérito anterior	
conocí	**conocimos**	**hube conocido**	**hubimos conocido**
conociste	**conocisteis**	**hubiste conocido**	**hubisteis conocido**
conoció	**conocieron**	**hubo conocido**	**hubieron conocido**
4 futuro		11 futuro perfecto	
conoceré	**conoceremos**	**habré conocido**	**habremos conocido**
conocerás	**conoceréis**	**habrás conocido**	**habréis conocido**
conocerá	**conocerán**	**habrá conocido**	**habrán conocido**
5 potencial simple		12 potencial compuesto	
conocería	**conoceríamos**	**habría conocido**	**habríamos conocido**
conocerías	**conoceríais**	**habrías conocido**	**habríais conocido**
conocería	**conocerían**	**habría conocido**	**habrían conocido**
6 presente de subjuntivo		13 perfecto de subjuntivo	
conozca	**conozcamos**	**haya conocido**	**hayamos conocido**
conozcas	**conozcáis**	**hayas conocido**	**hayáis conocido**
conozca	**conozcan**	**haya conocido**	**hayan conocido**
7 imperfecto de subjuntivo		14 pluscuamperfecto de subjuntivo	
conociera	**conociéramos**	**hubiera conocido**	**hubiéramos conocido**
conocieras	**conocierais**	**hubieras conocido**	**hubierais conocido**
conociera	**conocieran**	**hubiera conocido**	**hubieran conocido**
OR		OR	
conociese	**conociésemos**	**hubiese conocido**	**hubiésemos conocido**
conocieses	**conocieseis**	**hubieses conocido**	**hubieseis conocido**
conociese	**conociesen**	**hubiese conocido**	**hubiesen conocido**

imperativo	
—	**conozcamos**
conoce; no conozcas	**conoced; no conozcáis**
conozca	**conozcan**

Sentences using this verb and words related to it

—¿**Conoce Ud. a esa mujer?**
—Sí, la conozco.
un conocido, una conocida   an acquaintance
poner en conocimiento de   to inform (about)

el conocimiento   knowledge
reconocer   to recognize, to admit
desconocer   to be ignorant of

89

conseguir	Gerundio **consiguiendo**	Part. pas. **conseguido**

to attain, to get, to obtain

The Seven Simple Tenses		The Seven Compound Tenses	
Singular	Plural	Singular	Plural
1 presente de indicativo		8 perfecto de indicativo	
consigo	conseguimos	he conseguido	hemos conseguido
consigues	conseguís	has conseguido	habéis conseguido
consigue	consiguen	ha conseguido	han conseguido
2 imperfecto de indicativo		9 pluscuamperfecto de indicativo	
conseguía	conseguíamos	había conseguido	habíamos conseguido
conseguías	conseguíais	habías conseguido	habíais conseguido
conseguía	conseguían	había conseguido	habían conseguido
3 pretérito		10 pretérito anterior	
conseguí	conseguimos	hube conseguido	hubimos conseguido
conseguiste	conseguisteis	hubiste conseguido	hubisteis conseguido
consiguió	consiguieron	hubo conseguido	hubieron conseguido
4 futuro		11 futuro perfecto	
conseguiré	conseguiremos	habré conseguido	habremos conseguido
conseguirás	conseguiréis	habrás conseguido	habréis conseguido
conseguirá	conseguirán	habrá conseguido	habrán conseguido
5 potencial simple		12 potencial compuesto	
conseguiría	conseguiríamos	habría conseguido	habríamos conseguido
conseguirías	conseguiríais	habrías conseguido	habríais conseguido
conseguiría	conseguirían	habría conseguido	habrían conseguido
6 presente de subjuntivo		13 perfecto de subjuntivo	
consiga	consigamos	haya conseguido	hayamos conseguido
consigas	consigáis	hayas conseguido	hayáis conseguido
consiga	consigan	haya conseguido	hayan conseguido
7 imperfecto de subjuntivo		14 pluscuamperfecto de subjuntivo	
consiguiera	consiguiéramos	hubiera conseguido	hubiéramos conseguido
consiguieras	consiguierais	hubieras conseguido	hubierais conseguido
consiguiera	consiguieran	hubiera conseguido	hubieran conseguido
OR		OR	
consiguiese	consiguiésemos	hubiese conseguido	hubiésemos conseguido
consiguieses	consiguieseis	hubieses conseguido	hubieseis conseguido
consiguiese	consiguiesen	hubiese conseguido	hubiesen conseguido

imperativo	
—	consigamos
consigue; no consigas	conseguid; no consigáis
consiga	consigan

Words related to this verb
el conseguimiento attainment
el consiguiente consequence
See also **seguir**.

consiguientemente consequently
de consiguiente, por consiguiente consequently

Gerundio **constituyendo** Part. pas. **constituido**   **constituir**

to constitute, to make up

The Seven Simple Tenses		The Seven Compound Tenses	
Singular	Plural	Singular	Plural
1 presente de indicativo		8 perfecto de indicativo	
constituyo	constituimos	he constituido	hemos constituido
constituyes	constituís	has constituido	habéis constituido
constituye	constituyen	ha constituido	han constituido
2 imperfecto de indicativo		9 pluscuamperfecto de indicativo	
constituía	constituíamos	había constituido	habíamos constituido
constituías	constituíais	habías constituido	habíais constituido
constituía	constituían	había constituido	habían constituido
3 pretérito		10 pretérito anterior	
constituí	constituimos	hube constituido	hubimos constituido
constituiste	constituisteis	hubiste constituido	hubisteis constituido
constituyó	constituyeron	hubo constituido	hubieron constituido
4 futuro		11 futuro perfecto	
constituiré	constituiremos	habré constituido	habremos constituido
constituirás	constituiréis	habrás constituido	habréis constituido
constituirá	constituirán	habrá constituido	habrán constituido
5 potencial simple		12 potencial compuesto	
constituiría	constituiríamos	habría constituido	habríamos constituido
constituirías	constituiríais	habrías constituido	habríais constituido
constituiría	constituirían	habría constituido	habrían constituido
6 presente de subjuntivo		13 perfecto de subjuntivo	
constituya	constituyamos	haya constituido	hayamos constituido
constituyas	constituyáis	hayas constituido	hayáis constituido
constituya	constituyan	haya constituido	hayan constituido
7 imperfecto de subjuntivo		14 pluscuamperfecto de subjuntivo	
constituyera	constituyéramos	hubiera constituido	hubiéramos constituido
constituyeras	constituyerais	hubieras constituido	hubierais constituido
constituyera	constituyeran	hubiera constituido	hubieran constituido
OR		OR	
constituyese	constituyésemos	hubiese constituido	hubiésemos constituido
constituyeses	constituyeseis	hubieses constituido	hubieseis constituido
constituyese	constituyesen	hubiese constituido	hubiesen constituido

imperativo	
—	constituyamos
constituye; no constituyas	constituid; no constituyáis
constituya	constituyan

Words related to this verb

constitutivo, constitutiva constitutive, essential

la constitución constitution

el constitucionalismo constitutionalism

constituyente constituent

instituir to institute, to instruct, to teach

restituir to restore, to give back

construir   Gerundio **construyendo**   Part. pas. **construido**

to construct, to build

The Seven Simple Tenses		The Seven Compound Tenses	
Singular	Plural	Singular	Plural
1 presente de indicativo		8 perfecto de indicativo	
construyo	**construimos**	**he construido**	**hemos construido**
construyes	**construís**	**has construido**	**habéis construido**
construye	**construyen**	**ha construido**	**han construido**
2 imperfecto de indicativo		9 pluscuamperfecto de indicativo	
construía	**construíamos**	**había construido**	**habíamos construido**
construías	**construíais**	**habías construido**	**habíais construido**
construía	**construían**	**había construido**	**habían construido**
3 pretérito		10 pretérito anterior	
construí	**construimos**	**hube construido**	**hubimos construido**
construiste	**construisteis**	**hubiste construido**	**hubisteis construido**
construyó	**construyeron**	**hubo construido**	**hubieron construido**
4 futuro		11 futuro perfecto	
construiré	**construiremos**	**habré construido**	**habremos construido**
construirás	**construiréis**	**habrás construido**	**habréis construido**
construirá	**construirán**	**habrá construido**	**habrán construido**
5 potencial simple		12 potencial compuesto	
construiría	**construiríamos**	**habría construido**	**habríamos construido**
construirías	**construiríais**	**habrías construido**	**habríais construido**
construiría	**construirían**	**habría construido**	**habrían construido**
6 presente de subjuntivo		13 perfecto de subjuntivo	
construya	**construyamos**	**haya construido**	**hayamos construido**
construyas	**construyáis**	**hayas construido**	**hayáis construido**
construya	**construyan**	**haya construido**	**hayan construido**
7 imperfecto de subjuntivo		14 pluscuamperfecto de subjuntivo	
construyera	**construyéramos**	**hubiera construido**	**hubiéramos construido**
construyeras	**construyerais**	**hubieras construido**	**hubierais construido**
construyera	**construyeran**	**hubiera construido**	**hubieran construido**
OR		OR	
construyese	**construyésemos**	**hubiese construido**	**hubiésemos construido**
construyeses	**construyeseis**	**hubieses construido**	**hubieseis construido**
construyese	**construyesen**	**hubiese construido**	**hubiesen construido**

imperativo	
—	**construyamos**
construye; no construyas	**construid; no construyáis**
construya	**construyan**

Words related to this verb
la construcción construction
constructor, constructora builder
la construcción de buques shipbuilding

reconstruir to reconstruct
construible constructible

Gerundio **contando**   Part. pas. **contado**   **contar**

to count, to relate, to tell

The Seven Simple Tenses		The Seven Compound Tenses	
Singular	Plural	Singular	Plural
1 presente de indicativo		**8 perfecto de indicativo**	
cuento	**contamos**	**he contado**	**hemos contado**
cuentas	**contáis**	**has contado**	**habéis contado**
cuenta	**cuentan**	**ha contado**	**han contado**
2 imperfecto de indicativo		**9 pluscuamperfecto de indicativo**	
contaba	**contábamos**	**había contado**	**habíamos contado**
contabas	**contabais**	**habías contado**	**habíais contado**
contaba	**contaban**	**había contado**	**habían contado**
3 pretérito		**10 pretérito anterior**	
conté	**contamos**	**hube contado**	**hubimos contado**
contaste	**contasteis**	**hubiste contado**	**hubisteis contado**
contó	**contaron**	**hubo contado**	**hubieron contado**
4 futuro		**11 futuro perfecto**	
contaré	**contaremos**	**habré contado**	**habremos contado**
contarás	**contaréis**	**habrás contado**	**habréis contado**
contará	**contarán**	**habrá contado**	**habrán contado**
5 potencial simple		**12 potencial compuesto**	
contaría	**contaríamos**	**habría contado**	**habríamos contado**
contarías	**contaríais**	**habrías contado**	**habríais contado**
contaría	**contarían**	**habría contado**	**habrían contado**
6 presente de subjuntivo		**13 perfecto de subjuntivo**	
cuente	**contemos**	**haya contado**	**hayamos contado**
cuentes	**contéis**	**hayas contado**	**hayáis contado**
cuente	**cuenten**	**haya contado**	**hayan contado**
7 imperfecto de subjuntivo		**14 pluscuamperfecto de subjuntivo**	
contara	**contáramos**	**hubiera contado**	**hubiéramos contado**
contaras	**contarais**	**hubieras contado**	**hubierais contado**
contara	**contaran**	**hubiera contado**	**hubieran contado**
OR		OR	
contase	**contásemos**	**hubiese contado**	**hubiésemos contado**
contases	**contaseis**	**hubieses contado**	**hubieseis contado**
contase	**contasen**	**hubiese contado**	**hubiesen contado**

imperative	
—	**contemos**
cuenta; no cuentes	**contad; no contéis**
cuente	**cuenten**

Words and expressions related to this verb

un cuento   story, tale
estar en el cuento   to be informed
contar con   to depend on, to count on, to rely on

recontar   to recount
descontar   to discount, to deduct

93

contestar   Gerundio **contestando**   Part. pas. **contestado**

to answer, to reply

The Seven Simple Tenses		The Seven Compound Tenses	
Singular	Plural	Singular	Plural
1 presente de indicativo		8 perfecto de indicativo	
contesto	contestamos	he contestado	hemos contestado
contestas	contestáis	has contestado	habéis contestado
contesta	contestan	ha contestado	han contestado
2 imperfecto de indicativo		9 pluscuamperfecto de indicativo	
contestaba	contestábamos	había contestado	habíamos contestado
contestabas	contestabais	habías contestado	habíais contestado
contestaba	contestaban	había contestado	habían contestado
3 pretérito		10 pretérito anterior	
contesté	contestamos	hube contestado	hubimos contestado
contestaste	contestasteis	hubiste contestado	hubisteis contestado
contestó	contestaron	hubo contestado	hubieron contestado
4 futuro		11 futuro perfecto	
contestaré	contestaremos	habré contestado	habremos contestado
contestarás	contestaréis	habrás contestado	habréis contestado
contestará	contestarán	habrá contestado	habrán contestado
5 potencial simple		12 potencial compuesto	
contestaría	contestaríamos	habría contestado	habríamos contestado
contestarías	contestaríais	habrías contestado	habríais contestado
contestaría	contestarían	habría contestado	habrían contestado
6 presente de subjuntivo		13 perfecto de subjuntivo	
conteste	contestemos	haya contestado	hayamos contestado
contestes	contestéis	hayas contestado	hayáis contestado
conteste	contesten	haya contestado	hayan contestado
7 imperfecto de subjuntivo		14 pluscuamperfecto de subjuntivo	
contestara	contestáramos	hubiera contestado	hubiéramos contestado
contestaras	contestarais	hubieras contestado	hubierais contestado
contestara	contestaran	hubiera contestado	hubieran contestado
OR		OR	
contestase	contestásemos	hubiese contestado	hubiésemos contestado
contestases	contestaseis	hubieses contestado	hubieseis contestado
contestase	contestasen	hubiese contestado	hubiesen contestado

	imperativo	
—	contestemos	
contesta; no contestes	contestad; no contestéis	
conteste	contesten	

Words related to this verb
la contestación   answer, reply   **protestar**   to protest
contestable   contestable

Gerundio **continuando**   Part. pas. **continuado**   **continuar**

The Seven Simple Tenses		The Seven Compound Tenses	
Singular	Plural	Singular	Plural
1 presente de indicativo		8 perfecto de indicativo	
continúo	continuamos	he continuado	hemos continuado
continúas	continuáis	has continuado	habéis continuado
continúa	continúan	ha continuado	han continuado
2 imperfecto de indicativo		9 pluscuamperfecto de indicativo	
continuaba	continuábamos	había continuado	habíamos continuado
continuabas	continuabais	habías continuado	habíais continuado
continuaba	continuaban	había continuado	habían continuado
3 pretérito		10 pretérito anterior	
continué	continuamos	hube continuado	hubimos continuado
continuaste	continuasteis	hubiste continuado	hubisteis continuado
continuó	continuaron	hubo continuado	hubieron continuado
4 futuro		11 futuro perfecto	
continuaré	continuaremos	habré continuado	habremos continuado
continuarás	continuaréis	habrás continuado	habréis continuado
continuará	continuarán	habrá continuado	habrán continuado
5 potencial simple		12 potencial compuesto	
continuaría	continuaríamos	habría continuado	habríamos continuado
continuarías	continuaríais	habrías continuado	habríais continuado
continuaría	continuarían	habría continuado	habrían continuado
6 presente de subjuntivo		13 perfecto de subjuntivo	
continúe	continuemos	haya continuado	hayamos continuado
continúes	continuéis	hayas continuado	hayáis continuado
continúe	continúen	haya continuado	hayan continuado
7 imperfecto de subjuntivo		14 pluscuamperfecto de subjuntivo	
continuara	continuáramos	hubiera continuado	hubiéramos continuado
continuaras	continuarais	hubieras continuado	hubierais continuado
continuara	continuaran	hubiera continuado	hubieran continuado
OR		OR	
continuase	continuásemos	hubiese continuado	hubiésemos continuado
continusases	continuaseis	hubieses continuado	hubieseis continuado
continuase	continuasen	hubiese continuado	hubiesen continuado

	imperativo	
—	continuemos	
continúa; no continúes	continuad; no continuéis	
continúe	continúen	

Words and expressions related to this verb

la continuación	continuation	**descontinuar** to discontinue
continuamente	continually	**la descontinuación** discontinuation
a continuación	to be continued,	**continuadamente** continually
next, immediately after, below		

contradecir   Gerundio **contradiciendo** Part. pas. **contradicho**

to contradict

The Seven Simple Tenses		The Seven Compound Tenses	
Singular	Plural	Singular	Plural
1 presente de indicativo		**8 perfecto de indicativo**	
contradigo	contradecimos	he contradicho	hemos contradicho
contradices	contradecís	has contradicho	habéis contradicho
contradice	contradicen	ha contradicho	han contradicho
2 imperfecto de indicativo		**9 pluscuamperfecto de indicativo**	
contradecía	contradecíamos	había contradicho	habíamos contradicho
contradecías	contredecíais	habías contradicho	habíais contradicho
contradecía	contradecían	había contradicho	habían contradicho
3 pretérito		**10 pretérito anterior**	
contradije	contradijimos	hube contradicho	hubimos contradicho
contradijiste	contradijisteis	hubiste contradicho	hubisteis contradicho
contradijo	contradijeron	hubo contradicho	hubieron contradicho
4 futuro		**11 futuro perfecto**	
contradiré	contradiremos	habré contradicho	habremos contradicho
contradirás	contradiréis	habrás contradicho	habréis contradicho
contradirá	contradirán	habrá contradicho	habrán contradicho
5 potencial simple		**12 potencial compuesto**	
contradiría	contradiríamos	habría contradicho	habríamos contradicho
contradirías	contradiríais	habrías contradicho	habríais contradicho
contradiría	contradirían	habría contradicho	habrían contradicho
6 presente de subjuntivo		**13 perfecto de subjuntivo**	
contradiga	contradigamos	haya contradicho	hayamos contradicho
contradigas	contradigáis	hayas contradicho	hayáis contradicho
contradiga	contradigan	haya contradicho	hayan contradicho
7 imperfecto de subjuntivo		**14 pluscuamperfecto de subjuntivo**	
contradijera	contradijéramos	hubiera contradicho	hubiéramos contradicho
contradijeras	contradijerais	hubieras contradicho	hubierais contradicho
contradijera	contradijeran	hubiera contradicho	hubieran contradicho
OR		OR	
contradijese	contradijésemos	hubiese contradicho	hubiésemos contradicho
contradijeses	contradijeseis	hubieses contradicho	hubieseis contradicho
contradijese	contradijesen	hubiese contradicho	hubiesen contradicho

imperativo	
—	congradigamos
contradí; no contradigas	contradecid; contradigáis
contradiga	contradigan

Words related to this verb
contradictorio, contradictoria contradictory
contradictor, contradictora contradictor
la **contradicción** contradiction
contradictoriamente contradictorily

to contribute

The Seven Simple Tenses		The Seven Compound Tenses	
Singular	Plural	Singular	Plural
1 presente de indicativo		**8 perfecto de indicativo**	
contribuyo	**contribuimos**	**he contribuido**	**hemos contribuido**
contribuyes	**contribuís**	**has contribuido**	**habéis contribuido**
contribuye	**contribuyen**	**ha contribuido**	**han contribuido**
2 imperfecto de indicativo		**9 pluscuamperfecto de indicativo**	
contribuía	**contribuíamos**	**había contribuido**	**habíamos contribuido**
contribuías	**contribuíais**	**habías contribuido**	**habíais contribuido**
contribuía	**contribuían**	**había contribuido**	**habían contribuido**
3 pretérito		**10 pretérito anterior**	
contribuí	**contribuimos**	**hube contribuido**	**hubimos contribuido**
contribuiste	**contribuisteis**	**hubiste contribuido**	**hubisteis contribuido**
contribuyó	**contribuyeron**	**hubo contribuido**	**hubieron contribuido**
4 futuro		**11 futuro perfecto**	
contribuiré	**contribuiremos**	**habré contribuido**	**habremos contribuido**
contribuirás	**contribuiréis**	**habrás contribuido**	**habréis contribuido**
contribuirá	**contribuirán**	**habrá contribuido**	**habrán contribuido**
5 potencial simple		**12 potencial compuesto**	
contribuiría	**contribuiríamos**	**habría contribuido**	**habríamos contribuido**
contribuirías	**contribuiríais**	**habrías contribuido**	**habríais contribuido**
contribuiría	**contribuirían**	**habría contribuido**	**habrían contribuido**
6 presente de subjuntivo		**13 perfecto de subjuntivo**	
contribuya	**contribuyamos**	**haya contribuido**	**hayamos contribuido**
contribuyas	**contribuyáis**	**hayas contribuido**	**hayáis contribuido**
contribuya	**contribuyan**	**haya contribuido**	**hayan contribuido**
7 imperfecto de subjuntivo		**14 pluscuamperfecto de subjuntivo**	
contribuyera	**contribuyéramos**	**hubiera contribuido**	**hubiéramos contribuido**
contribuyeras	**contribuyerais**	**hubieras contribuido**	**hubierais contribuido**
contribuyera	**contribuyeran**	**hubiera contribuido**	**hubieran contribuido**
OR		OR	
contribuyese	**contribuyésemos**	**hubiese contribuido**	**hubiésemos contribuido**
contribuyeses	**contribuyeseis**	**hubieses contribuido**	**hubieseis contribuido**
contribuyese	**contribuyesen**	**hubiese contribuido**	**hubiesen contribuido**

imperativo	
—	**contribuyamos**
contribuye; no contribuyas	**contribuid; no contribuyáis**
contribuya	**contribuyan**

Words related to this verb
contribuidor, contribuidora contributor
la contribución contribution
contributario, contribuyente taxpayer

corregir	Gerundio **corrigiendo**	Part. pas. **corregido**

to correct

The Seven Simple Tenses		The Seven Compound Tenses	
Singular	Plural	Singular	Plural
1 presente de indicativo		**8 perfecto de indicativo**	
corrijo	corregimos	he corregido	hemos corregido
corriges	corregís	has corregido	habéis corregido
corrige	corrigen	ha corregido	han corregido
2 imperfecto de indicativo		**9 pluscuamperfecto de indicativo**	
corregía	corregíamos	había corregido	habíamos corregido
corregías	corregíais	habías corregido	habíais corregido
corregía	corregían	había corregido	habían corregido
3 pretérito		**10 pretérito anterior**	
corregí	corregimos	hube corregido	hubimos corregido
corregiste	corregisteis	hubiste corregido	hubisteis corregido
corrigió	corrigieron	hubo corregido	hubieron corregido
4 futuro		**11 futuro perfecto**	
corregiré	corregiremos	habré corregido	habremos corregido
corregirás	corregiréis	habrás corregido	habréis corregido
corregirá	corregirán	habrá corregido	habrán corregido
5 potencial simple		**12 potencial compuesto**	
corregiría	corregiríamos	habría corregido	habríamos corregido
corregirías	corregiríais	habrías corregido	habríais corregido
corregiría	corregirían	habría corregido	habrían corregido
6 presente de subjuntivo		**13 perfecto de subjuntivo**	
corrija	corrijamos	haya corregido	hayamos corregido
corrijas	corrijáis	hayas corregido	hayáis corregido
corrija	corrijan	haya corregido	hayan corregido
7 imperfecto de subjuntivo		**14 pluscuamperfecto de subjuntivo**	
corrigiera	corrigiéramos	hubiera corregido	hubiéramos corregido
corrigieras	corrigierais	hubieras corregido	hubierais corregido
corrigiera	corrigieran	hubiera corregido	hubieran corregido
OR		OR	
corrigiese	corrigiésemos	hubiese corregido	hubiésemos corregido
corrigieses	corrigieseis	hubieses corregido	hubieseis corregido
corrigiese	corrigiesen	hubiese corregido	hubiesen corregido

imperativo	
—	corrijamos
corrige; no corrijas	corregid; no corrijáis
corrija	corrijan

Words related to this verb

corregir pruebas to read proofs	**correcto, correcta** correct
corregible corrigible	**correctamente** correctly
incorregible incorrigible	**correccional** correctional
la corrección correction	**el correccionalismo** reformatory

Gerundio **corriendo**   Part. pas. **corrido**   **correr**

to run, to race, to flow

The Seven Simple Tenses		The Seven Compound Tenses	
Singular	Plural	Singular	Plural
1 presente de indicativo		8 perfecto de indicativo	
corro	corremos	he corrido	hemos corrido
corres	corréis	has corrido	habéis corrido
corre	corren	ha corrido	han corrido
2 imperfecto de indicativo		9 pluscuamperfecto de indicativo	
corría	corríamos	había corrido	habíamos corrido
corrías	corríais	habías corrido	habíais corrido
corría	corrían	había corrido	habían corrido
3 pretérito		10 pretérito anterior	
corrí	corrimos	hube corrido	hubimos corrido
corriste	corristeis	hubiste corrido	hubisteis corrido
corrió	corrieron	hubo corrido	hubieron corrido
4 futuro		11 futuro perfecto	
correré	correremos	habré corrido	habremos corrido
correrás	correréis	habrás corrido	habréis corrido
correrá	correrán	habrá corrido	habrán corrido
5 potencial simple		12 potencial compuesto	
correría	correríamos	habría corrido	habríamos corrido
correrías	correríais	habrías corrido	habríais corrido
correría	correrían	habría corrido	habrían corrido
6 presente de subjuntivo		13 perfecto de subjuntivo	
corra	corramos	haya corrido	hayamos corrido
corras	corráis	hayas corrido	hayáis corrido
corra	corran	haya corrido	hayan corrido
7 imperfecto de subjuntivo		14 pluscuamperfecto de subjuntivo	
corriera	corriéramos	hubiera corrido	hubiéramos corrido
corrieras	corrierais	hubieras corrido	hubierais corrido
corriera	corrieran	hubiera corrido	hubieran corrido
OR		OR	
corriese	corriésemos	hubiese corrido	hubiésemos corrido
corrieses	corrieseis	hubieses corrido	hubieseis corrido
corriese	corriesen	hubiese corrido	hubiesen corrido

imperativo	
—	corramos
corre; no corras	corred; no corráis
corra	corran

Words and expressions related to this verb

el correo mail, post
correo aéreo air mail
echar una carta al correo to mail (post)
  a letter
por correo aparte under separate cover (mail)

la corrida race
de corrida at full speed
recorrer to travel on, to go over
descorrer to flow (liquids); to draw
  a curtain or drape

costar	Gerundio **costando**	Part. pas. **costado**

to cost

The Seven Simple Tenses		The Seven Compound Tenses	
Singular	Plural	Singular	Plural
1 presente de indicativo		8 perfecto de indicativo	
cuesta	**cuestan**	**ha costado**	**han costado**
2 imperfecto de indicativo		9 pluscuamperfecto de indicativo	
costaba	**costaban**	**había costado**	**habían costado**
3 pretérito		10 pretérito anterior	
costó	**costaron**	**hubo costado**	**hubieron costado**
4 futuro		11 futuro perfecto	
costará	**costarán**	**habrá costado**	**habrán costado**
5 potencial simple		12 potencial compuesto	
costaría	**costarían**	**habría costado**	**habrían costado**
6 presente de subjuntivo		13 perfecto de subjuntivo	
que cueste	**que cuesten**	**que haya costado**	**que hayan costado**
7 imperfecto de subjuntivo		14 pluscuamperfecto de subjuntivo	
que costara	**que costaran**	**que hubiera costado**	**que hubieran costado**
OR		OR	
que costase	**que costasen**	**que hubiese costado**	**que hubiesen costado**

imperativo
¡Que cueste!   **¡Que cuesten!**

Sentences using this verb and words and expressions related to it

—¿**Cuánto cuesta este libro?**
—**Cuesta diez dólares.**

costoso, costosa costly, expensive	**costar un ojo de la cara** to be very expensive (to cost an arm and a leg)
el costo price, cost	**cueste lo que cueste** at any cost

100

Gerundio **creciendo**   Part. pas. **crecido**   **crecer**

The Seven Simple Tenses		The Seven Compound Tenses	
Singular	Plural	Singular	Plural
1 presente de indicativo		8 perfecto de indicativo	
crezco	crecemos	he crecido	hemos crecido
creces	crecéis	has crecido	habéis crecido
crece	crecen	ha crecido	han crecido
2 imperfecto de indicativo		9 pluscuamperfecto de indicativo	
crecía	crecíamos	había crecido	habíamos crecido
crecías	crecíais	habías crecido	habíais crecido
crecía	crecían	había crecido	habían crecido
3 pretérito		10 pretérito anterior	
crecí	crecimos	hube crecido	hubimos crecido
creciste	crecisteis	hubiste crecido	hubisteis crecido
creció	crecieron	hubo crecido	hubieron crecido
4 futuro		11 futuro perfecto	
creceré	creceremos	habré crecido	habremos crecido
crecerás	creceréis	habrás crecido	habréis crecido
crecerá	crecerán	habrá crecido	habrán crecido
5 potencial simple		12 potencial compuesto	
crecería	creceríamos	habría crecido	habríamos crecido
crecerías	creceríais	habrías crecido	habríais crecido
crecería	crecerían	habría crecido	habrían crecido
6 presente de subjuntivo		13 perfecto de subjuntivo	
crezca	crezcamos	haya crecido	hayamos crecido
crezcas	crezcáis	hayas crecido	hayáis crecido
crezca	crezcan	haya crecido	hayan crecido
7 imperfecto de subjuntivo		14 pluscuamperfecto de subjuntivo	
creciera	creciéramos	hubiera crecido	hubiéramos crecido
crecieras	crecierais	hubieras crecido	hubierais crecido
creciera	crecieran	hubiera crecido	hubieran crecido
OR		OR	
creciese	creciésemos	hubiese crecido	hubiésemos crecido
crecieses	crecieseis	hubieses crecido	hubieseis crecido
creciese	creciesen	hubiese crecido	hubiesen crecido

imperativo	
—	crezcamos
crece; no crezcas	creced; no crezcáis
crezca	crezcan

Words and expressions related to this verb
crecer como la mala hierba   to grow like a weed
crecidamente   abundantly
el crescendo   crescendo (music)

creer   Gerundio **creyendo**   Part. pas. **creído**

to believe

The Seven Simple Tenses		The Seven Compound Tenses	
Singular	Plural	Singular	Plural
1 presente de indicativo		8 perfecto de indicativo	
creo	creemos	he creído	hemos creído
crees	creéis	has creído	habéis creído
cree	creen	ha creído	han creído
2 imperfecto de indicativo		9 pluscuamperfecto de indicativo	
creía	creíamos	había creído	habíamos creído
creías	creíais	habías creído	habíais creído
creía	creían	había creído	habían creído
3 pretérito		10 pretérito anterior	
creí	creímos	hube creído	hubimos creído
creíste	creísteis	hubiste creído	hubisteis creído
creyó	creyeron	hubo creído	hubieron creído
4 futuro		11 futuro perfecto	
creeré	creeremos	habré creído	habremos creído
creerás	creeréis	habrás creído	habréis creído
creerá	creerán	habrá creído	habrán creído
5 potencial simple		12 potencial compuesto	
creería	creeríamos	habría creído	habríamos creído
creerías	creeríais	habrías creído	habríais creído
creería	creerían	habría creído	habrían creído
6 presente de subjuntivo		13 perfecto de subjuntivo	
crea	creamos	haya creído	hayamos creído
creas	creáis	hayas creído	hayáis creído
crea	crean	haya creído	hayan creído
7 imperfecto de subjuntivo		14 pluscuamperfecto de subjuntivo	
creyera	creyéramos	hubiera creído	hubiéramos creído
creyeras	creyerais	hubieras creído	hubierais creído
creyera	creyeran	hubiera creído	hubieran creído
OR		OR	
creyese	creyésemos	hubiese creído	hubiésemos creído
creyeses	creyeseis	hubieses creído	hubieseis creído
creyese	creyesen	hubiese creído	hubiesen creído

	imperativo
—	creamos
cree; no creas	creed; no creáis
crea	crean

Words and expressions related to this verb

Ver y creer Seeing is believing.   la credulidad credulity
¡Ya lo creo! Of course!   el credo creed
crédulo, crédula credulous   dar crédito to believe
descreer to disbelieve

to breed, to raise, to bring up (rear)

The Seven Simple Tenses		The Seven Compound Tenses	
Singular	Plural	Singular	Plural
1 presente de indicativo		8 perfecto de indicativo	
crío	criamos	he criado	hemos criado
crías	criáis	has criado	habéis criado
cría	crían	ha criado	han criado
2 imperfecto de indicativo		9 pluscuamperfecto de indicativo	
criaba	criábamos	había criado	habíamos criado
criabas	criabais	habías criado	habíais criado
criaba	criaban	había criado	habían criado
3 pretérito		10 pretérito anterior	
crié	criamos	hube criado	hubimos criado
criaste	criasteis	hubiste criado	hubisteis criado
crió	criaron	hubo criado	hubieron criado
4 futuro		11 futuro perfecto	
criaré	criaremos	habré criado	habremos criado
criarás	criaréis	habrás criado	habréis criado
criará	criarán	habrá criado	habrán criado
5 potencial simple		12 potencial compuesto	
criaría	criaríamos	habría criado	habríamos criado
criarías	criaríais	habrías criado	habríais criado
criaría	criarían	habría criado	habrían criado
6 presente de subjuntivo		13 perfecto de subjuntivo	
críe	criemos	haya criado	hayamos criado
críes	criéis	hayas criado	hayáis criado
críe	críen	haya criado	hayan criado
7 imperfecto de subjuntivo		14 pluscuamperfecto de subjuntivo	
criara	criáramos	hubiera criado	hubiéramos criado
criaras	criarais	hubieras criado	hubierais criado
criara	criaran	hubiera criado	hubieran criado
OR		OR	
criase	criásemos	hubiese criado	hubiésemos criado
criases	criaseis	hubieses criado	hubieseis criado
criase	criasen	hubiese criado	hubiesen criado

imperativo	
—	criemos
cría; no críes	criad; no criéis
críe	críen

Words and expressions related to this verb

la **criandera**, la **criadora**   wet nurse
el **criado**, la **criada**   servant
la **crianza**   nursing, education
dar **crianza**   to educate, to bring up

mala **crianza**   bad manners, impoliteness
Dios los cría y ellos se juntan   Birds of a
   feather flock together.

to cross

The Seven Simple Tenses		The Seven Compound Tenses	
Singular	Plural	Singular	Plural
1 presente de indicativo		8 perfecto de indicativo	
cruzo	cruzamos	he cruzado	hemos cruzado
cruzas	cruzáis	has cruzado	habéis cruzado
cruza	cruzan	ha cruzado	han cruzado
2 imperfecto de indicativo		9 pluscuamperfecto de indicativo	
cruzaba	cruzábamos	había cruzado	habíamos cruzado
cruzabas	cruzabais	habías cruzado	habíais cruzado
cruzaba	cruzaban	había cruzado	habían cruzado
3 pretérito		10 pretérito anterior	
crucé	cruzamos	hube cruzado	hubimos cruzado
cruzaste	cruzasteis	hubiste cruzado	hubisteis cruzado
cruzó	cruzaron	hubo cruzado	hubieron cruzado
4 futuro		11 futuro perfecto	
cruzaré	cruzaremos	habré cruzado	habremos cruzado
cruzarás	cruzaréis	habrás cruzado	habréis cruzado
cruzará	cruzarán	habrá cruzado	habrán cruzado
5 potencial simple		12 potencial compuesto	
cruzaría	cruzaríamos	habría cruzado	habríamos cruzado
cruzarías	cruzaríais	habrías cruzado	habríais cruzado
cruzaría	cruzarían	habría cruzado	habrían cruzado
6 presente de subjuntivo		13 perfecto de subjuntivo	
cruce	crucemos	haya cruzado	hayamos cruzado
cruces	crucéis	hayas cruzado	hayáis cruzado
cruce	crucen	haya cruzado	hayan cruzado
7 imperfecto de subjuntivo		14 pluscuamperfecto de subjuntivo	
cruzara	cruzáramos	hubiera cruzado	hubiéramos cruzado
cruzaras	cruzarais	hubieras cruzado	hubierais cruzado
cruzara	cruzaran	hubiera cruzado	hubieran cruzado
OR		OR	
cruzase	cruzásemos	hubiese cruzado	hubiésemos cruzado
cruzases	cruzaseis	hubieses cruzado	hubieseis cruzado
cruzase	cruzasen	hubiese cruzado	hubiesen cruzado

imperativo	
—	crucemos
cruza; no cruces	cruzad; no crucéis
cruce	crucen

Sentence using this verb and words related to it
El que no se aventura no cruza el mar.   Nothing ventured, nothing gained.

el cruzamiento crossing	**la cruz** cross
la cruzada crusade, crossroads	**la cruz de Malta** Maltese cross

Gerundio **cubriendo**   Part. pas. **cubierto**   **cubrir**

The Seven Simple Tenses		The Seven Compound Tenses	
Singular	Plural	Singular	Plural
1 presente de indicativo		8 perfecto de indicativo	
cubro	**cubrimos**	**he cubierto**	**hemos cubierto**
cubres	**cubrís**	**has cubierto**	**habéis cubierto**
cubre	**cubren**	**ha cubierto**	**han cubierto**
2 imperfecto de indicativo		9 pluscuamperfecto de indicativo	
cubría	**cubríamos**	**había cubierto**	**habíamos cubierto**
cubrías	**cubríais**	**habías cubierto**	**habíais cubierto**
cubría	**cubrían**	**había cubierto**	**habían cubierto**
3 pretérito		10 pretérito anterior	
cubrí	**cubrimos**	**hube cubierto**	**hubimos cubierto**
cubriste	**cubristeis**	**hubiste cubierto**	**hubisteis cubierto**
cubrió	**cubrieron**	**hubo cubierto**	**hubieron cubierto**
4 futuro		11 futuro perfecto	
cubriré	**cubriremos**	**habré cubierto**	**habremos cubierto**
cubrirás	**cubriréis**	**habrás cubierto**	**habréis cubierto**
cubrirá	**cubrirán**	**habrá cubierto**	**habrán cubierto**
5 potencial simple		12 potencial compuesto	
cubriría	**cubriríamos**	**habría cubierto**	**habríamos cubierto**
cubrirías	**cubriríais**	**habrías cubierto**	**habríais cubierto**
cubriría	**cubrirían**	**habría cubierto**	**habrían cubierto**
6 presente de subjuntivo		13 perfecto de subjuntivo	
cubra	**cubramos**	**haya cubierto**	**hayamos cubierto**
cubras	**cubráis**	**hayas cubierto**	**hayáis cubierto**
cubra	**cubran**	**haya cubierto**	**hayan cubierto**
7 imperfecto de subjuntivo		14 pluscuamperfecto de subjuntivo	
cubriera	**cubriéramos**	**hubiera cubierto**	**hubiéramos cubierto**
cubrieras	**cubrierais**	**hubieras cubierto**	**hubierais cubierto**
cubriera	**cubrieran**	**hubiera cubierto**	**hubieran cubierto**
OR		OR	
cubriese	**cubriésemos**	**hubiese cubierto**	**hubiésemos cubierto**
cubrieses	**cubrieseis**	**hubieses cubierto**	**hubieseis cubierto**
cubriese	**cubriesen**	**hubiese cubierto**	**hubiesen cubierto**

imperativo	
—	**cubramos**
cubre; no cubras	**cubrid; no cubráis**
cubra	**cubran**

Words and expressions related to this verb

la cubierta cover, wrapping
la cubierta del motor hood of an
    automobile
el cubrimiento covering
encubrir to hide, to conceal, to mask
el encubrimiento hiding, concealment

descubrir to discover
cubrir la mesa to lay the table
cubrir los gastos to pay expenses
cubiertamente under cover

105

cumplir   Gerundio **cumpliendo**   Part. pas. **cumplido**

to fulfill, to keep (a promise), to reach one's birthday (use with **años**)

The Seven Simple Tenses		The Seven Compound Tenses	
Singular	Plural	Singular	Plural
1 presente de indicativo		8 perfecto de indicativo	
cumplo	**cumplimos**	**he cumplido**	**hemos cumplido**
cumples	**cumplís**	**has cumplido**	**habéis cumplido**
cumple	**cumplen**	**ha cumplido**	**han cumplido**
2 imperfecto de indicativo		9 pluscuamperfecto de indicativo	
cumplía	**cumplíamos**	**había cumplido**	**habíamos cumplido**
cumplías	**cumplíais**	**habías cumplido**	**habíais cumplido**
cumplía	**cumplían**	**había cumplido**	**habían cumplido**
3 pretérito		10 pretérito anterior	
cumplí	**cumplimos**	**hube cumplido**	**hubimos cumplido**
cumpliste	**cumplisteis**	**hubiste cumplido**	**hubisteis cumplido**
cumplió	**cumplieron**	**hubo cumplido**	**hubieron cumplido**
4 futuro		11 futuro perfecto	
cumpliré	**cumpliremos**	**habré cumplido**	**habremos cumplido**
cumplirás	**cumpliréis**	**habrás cumplido**	**habréis cumplido**
cumplirá	**cumplirán**	**habrá cumplido**	**habrán cumplido**
5 potencial simple		12 potencial compuesto	
cumpliría	**cumpliríamos**	**habría cumplido**	**habríamos cumplido**
cumplirías	**cumpliríais**	**habrías cumplido**	**habríais cumplido**
cumpliría	**cumplirían**	**habría cumplido**	**habrían cumplido**
6 presente de subjuntivo		13 perfecto de subjuntivo	
cumpla	**cumplamos**	**haya cumplido**	**hayamos cumplido**
cumplas	**cumpláis**	**hayas cumplido**	**hayáis cumplido**
cumpla	**cumplan**	**haya cumplido**	**hayan cumplido**
7 imperfecto de subjuntivo		14 pluscuamperfecto de subjuntivo	
cumpliera	**cumpliéramos**	**hubiera cumplido**	**hubiéramos cumplido**
cumplieras	**cumplierais**	**hubieras cumplido**	**hubierais cumplido**
cumpliera	**cumplieran**	**hubiera cumplido**	**hubieran cumplido**
OR		OR	
cumpliese	**cumpliésemos**	**hubiese cumplido**	**hubiésemos cumplido**
cumplieses	**cumplieseis**	**hubieses cumplido**	**hubieseis cumplido**
cumpliese	**cumpliesen**	**hubiese cumplido**	**hubiesen cumplido**

	imperativo	
—		**cumplamos**
cumple; no cumplas		**cumplid; no cumpláis**
cumpla		**cumplan**

Words and expressions related to this verb

el cumpleaños birthday
cumplidamente completely
el cumplimiento completion
cumplir con to fulfill

cumplir . . . años to reach the age of . . .
Hoy cumplo diez y siete años Today I am seventeen years old.

106

Gerundio **dando** Part. pas. **dado** **dar**

to give

The Seven Simple Tenses		The Seven Compound Tenses	
Singular	Plural	Singular	Plural
1 presente de indicativo		8 perfecto de indicativo	
doy	damos	he dado	hemos dado
das	dais	has dado	habéis dado
da	dan	ha dado	han dado
2 imperfecto de indicativo		9 pluscuamperfecto de indicativo	
daba	dábamos	había dado	habíamos dado
dabas	dabais	habías dado	habíais dado
daba	daban	había dado	habían dado
3 pretérito		10 pretérito anterior	
di	dimos	hube dado	hubimos dado
diste	disteis	hubiste dado	hubisteis dado
dio	dieron	hubo dado	hubieron dado
4 futuro		11 futuro perfecto	
daré	daremos	habré dado	habremos dado
darás	daréis	habrás dado	habréis dado
dará	darán	habrá dado	habrán dado
5 potencial simple		12 potencial compuesto	
daría	daríamos	habría dado	habríamos dado
darías	daríais	habrías dado	habríais dado
daría	darían	habría dado	habrían dado
6 presente de subjuntivo		13 perfecto de subjuntivo	
dé	demos	haya dado	hayamos dado
des	deis	hayas dado	hayáis dado
dé	den	haya dado	hayan dado
7 imperfecto de subjuntivo		14 pluscuamperfecto de subjuntivo	
diera	diéramos	hubiera dado	hubiéramos dado
dieras	dierais	hubieras dado	hubierais dado
diera	dieran	hubiera dado	hubieran dado
OR		OR	
diese	diésemos	hubiese dado	hubiésemos dado
dieses	dieseis	hubieses dado	hubieseis dado
diese	diesen	hubiese dado	hubiesen dado

imperativo	
—	demos
da; no des	dad; no deis
dé	den

Common idiomatic expressions using this verb

A Dios rogando y con el mazo dando. Put your
faith in God and keep your powder dry.
El tiempo da buen consejo. Time will tell.
dar la mano (las manos) a alguien to shake hands with someone
dar de comer to feed
darse to give oneself up, to give in

107

deber Gerundio **debiendo** Part. pas. **debido**

to owe, must, ought

The Seven Simple Tenses		The Seven Compound Tenses	
Singular	Plural	Singular	Plural

1 presente de indicativo		8 perfecto de indicativo	
debo	debemos	he debido	hemos debido
debes	debéis	has debido	habéis debido
debe	deben	ha debido	han debido

2 imperfecto de indicativo		9 pluscuamperfecto de indicativo	
debía	debíamos	había debido	habíamos debido
debías	debíais	habías debido	habíais debido
debía	debían	había debido	habían debido

3 pretérito		10 pretérito anterior	
debí	debimos	hube debido	hubimos debido
debiste	debisteis	hubiste debido	hubisteis debido
debió	debieron	hubo debido	hubieron debido

4 futuro		11 futuro perfecto	
deberé	deberemos	habré debido	habremos debido
deberás	deberéis	habrás debido	habréis debido
deberá	deberán	habrá debido	habrán debido

5 potencial simple		12 potencial compuesto	
debería	deberíamos	habría debido	habríamos debido
deberías	deberíais	habrías debido	habríais debido
debería	deberían	habría debido	habrían debido

6 presente de subjuntivo		13 perfecto de subjuntivo	
deba	debamos	haya debido	hayamos debido
debas	debáis	hayas debido	hayáis debido
deba	deban	haya debido	hayan debido

7 imperfecto de subjuntivo		14 pluscuamperfecto de subjuntivo	
debiera	debiéramos	hubiera debido	hubiéramos debido
debieras	debierais	hubieras debido	hubierais debido
debiera	debieran	hubiera debido	hubieran debido
OR		OR	
debiese	debiésemos	hubiese debido	hubiésemos debido
debieses	debieseis	hubieses debido	hubieseis debido
debiese	debiesen	hubiese debido	hubiesen debido

imperativo	
—	debamos
debe; no debas	debed; no debáis
deba	deban

Sentence using this verb and words related to it

el deber	duty, obligation	estar en deuda con	to be indebted to
debiente	debtor	**José debe de haber llegado.** Joseph must
la deuda	debt; debido a due to	have arrived.

108

The Seven Simple Tenses		The Seven Compound Tenses	
Singular	Plural	Singular	Plural
1 presente de indicativo		**8 perfecto de indicativo**	
decido	decidimos	he decidido	hemos decidido
decides	decidís	has decidido	habéis decidido
decide	deciden	ha decidido	han decidido
2 imperfecto de indicativo		**9 pluscuamperfecto de indicativo**	
decidía	decidíamos	había decidido	habíamos decidido
decidías	decidíais	habías decidido	habíais decidido
decidía	decidían	había decidido	habían decidido
3 pretérito		**10 pretérito anterior**	
decidí	decidimos	hube decidido	hubimos decidido
decidiste	decidisteis	hubiste decidido	hubisteis decidido
decidió	decidieron	hubo decidido	hubieron decidido
4 futuro		**11 futuro perfecto**	
decidiré	decidiremos	habré decidido	habremos decidido
decidirás	decidiréis	habrás decidido	habréis decidido
decidirá	decidirán	habrá decidido	habrán decidido
5 potencial simple		**12 potencial compuesto**	
decidiría	decidiríamos	habría decidido	habríamos decidido
decidirías	decidiríais	habrías decidido	habríais decidido
decidiría	decidirían	habría decidido	habrían decidido
6 presente de subjuntivo		**13 perfecto de subjuntivo**	
decida	decidamos	haya decidido	hayamos decidido
decidas	decidáis	hayas decidido	hayáis decidido
decida	decidan	haya decidido	hayan decidido
7 imperfecto de subjuntivo		**14 pluscuamperfecto de subjuntivo**	
decidiera	decidiéramos	hubiera decidido	hubiéramos decidido
decidieras	decidierais	hubieras decidido	hubierais decidido
decidiera	decidieran	hubiera decidido	hubieran decidido
OR		OR	
decidiese	decidiésemos	hubiese decidido	hubiésemos decidido
decidieses	decidieseis	hubieses decidido	hubieseis decidido
decidiese	decidiesen	hubiese decidido	hubiesen decidido

imperativo	
—	decidamos
decide; no decidas	decidid; no decidáis
decida	decidan

Words and expressions related to this verb

la decisión decision
decidamente decidedly
decisivamente decisively
decisivo, decisiva decisive
decidir a + inf. to persuade + inf.; to decide + inf.

decidirse to make up one's mind,
to be determined
estar decidido (decidida) to make up
one's mind

109

decir	Gerundio **diciendo**	Part. pas. **dicho**

to say, to tell

The Seven Simple Tenses		The Seven Compound Tenses	
Singular	Plural	Singular	Plural
1 presente de indicativo		8 perfecto de indicativo	
digo	**decimos**	**he dicho**	**hemos dicho**
dices	**decís**	**has dicho**	**habéis dicho**
dice	**dicen**	**ha dicho**	**han dicho**
2 imperfecto de indicativo		9 pluscuamperfecto de indicativo	
decía	**decíamos**	**había dicho**	**habíamos dicho**
decías	**decíais**	**habías dicho**	**habíais dicho**
decía	**decían**	**había dicho**	**habían dicho**
3 pretérito		10 pretérito anterior	
dije	**dijimos**	**hube dicho**	**hubimos dicho**
dijiste	**dijisteis**	**hubiste dicho**	**hubisteis dicho**
dijo	**dijeron**	**hubo dicho**	**hubieron dicho**
4 futuro		11 futuro perfecto	
diré	**diremos**	**habré dicho**	**habremos dicho**
dirás	**diréis**	**habrás dicho**	**habréis dicho**
dirá	**dirán**	**habrá dicho**	**habrán dicho**
5 potencial simple		12 potencial compuesto	
diría	**diríamos**	**habría dicho**	**habríamos dicho**
dirías	**diríais**	**habrías dicho**	**habríais dicho**
diría	**dirían**	**habría dicho**	**habrían dicho**
6 presente de subjuntivo		13 perfecto de subjuntivo	
diga	**digamos**	**haya dicho**	**hayamos dicho**
digas	**digáis**	**hayas dicho**	**hayáis dicho**
diga	**digan**	**haya dicho**	**hayan dicho**
7 imperfecto de subjuntivo		14 pluscuamperfecto de subjuntivo	
dijera	**dijéramos**	**hubiera dicho**	**hubiéramos dicho**
dijeras	**dijerais**	**hubieras dicho**	**hubierais dicho**
dijera	**dijeran**	**hubiera dicho**	**hubieran dicho**
OR		OR	
dijese	**dijésemos**	**hubiese dicho**	**hubiésemos dicho**
dijeses	**dijeseis**	**hubieses dicho**	**hubieseis dicho**
dijese	**dijesen**	**hubiese dicho**	**hubiesen dicho**

imperativo	
—	**digamos**
di; no digas	**decid; no digáis**
diga	**digan**

Sentences using this verb and words related to it
Dicho y hecho. No sooner said than done.
Dime con quien andas y te diré quien eres. Tell me who your friends are and I
will tell you who you are.
querer decir to mean   **un decir** a familiar saying

Gerundio **defendiendo**   Part. pas. **defendido**   **defender**

to forbid, to defend, to prohibit

The Seven Simple Tenses		The Seven Compound Tenses	
Singular	Plural	Singular	Plural
1 presente de indicativo		8 perfecto de indicativo	
defiendo	**defendemos**	**he defendido**	**hemos defendido**
defiendes	**defendéis**	**has defendido**	**habéis defendido**
defiende	**defienden**	**ha defendido**	**han defendido**
2 imperfecto de indicativo		9 pluscuamperfecto de indicativo	
defendía	**defendíamos**	**había defendido**	**habíamos defendido**
defendías	**defendíais**	**habías defendido**	**habíais defendido**
defendía	**defendían**	**había defendido**	**habían defendido**
3 pretérito		10 pretérito anterior	
defendí	**defendimos**	**hube defendido**	**hubimos defendido**
defendiste	**defendisteis**	**hubiste defendido**	**hubisteis defendido**
defendió	**defendieron**	**hubo defendido**	**hubieron defendido**
4 futuro		11 futuro perfecto	
defenderé	**defenderemos**	**habré defendido**	**habremos defendido**
defenderás	**defenderéis**	**habrás defendido**	**habréis defendido**
defenderá	**defenderán**	**habrá defendido**	**habrán defendido**
5 potencial simple		12 potencial compuesto	
defendería	**defenderíamos**	**habría defendido**	**habríamos defendido**
defenderías	**defenderíais**	**habrías defendido**	**habríais defendido**
defendería	**defenderían**	**habría defendido**	**habrían defendido**
6 presente de subjuntivo		13 perfecto de subjuntivo	
defienda	**defendamos**	**haya defendido**	**hayamos defendido**
defiendas	**defendáis**	**hayas defendido**	**hayáis defendido**
defienda	**defiendan**	**haya defendido**	**hayan defendido**
7 imperfecto de subjuntivo		14 pluscuamperfecto de subjuntivo	
defendiera	**defendiéramos**	**hubiera defendido**	**hubiéramos defendido**
defendieras	**defendierais**	**hubieras defendido**	**hubierais defendido**
defendiera	**defendieran**	**hubiera defendido**	**hubieran defendido**
OR		OR	
defendiese	**defendiésemos**	**hubiese defendido**	**hubiésemos defendido**
defendieses	**defendieseis**	**hubieses defendido**	**hubieseis defendido**
defendiese	**defendiesen**	**hubiese defendido**	**hubiesen defendido**

imperativo

—	**defendamos**
defiende; no defiendas	**defended; no defendáis**
defienda	**defiendan**

Words related to this verb
defendible defensible   **el defensorio** defense, plea
la defensa defense
defensivo, defensiva defensive
defensor, defensora defender, supporter

dejar	Gerundio **dejando**	Part. pas. **dejado**

to let, to permit, to allow, to leave

The Seven Simple Tenses		The Seven Compound Tenses	
Singular	Plural	Singular	Plural
1 presente de indicativo		8 perfecto de indicativo	
dejo	dejamos	he dejado	hemos dejado
dejas	dejáis	has dejado	habéis dejado
deja	dejan	ha dejado	han dejado
2 imperfecto de indicativo		9 pluscuamperfecto de indicativo	
dejaba	dejábamos	había dejado	habíamos dejado
dejabas	dejabais	habías dejado	habíais dejado
dejaba	dejaban	había dejado	habían dejado
3 pretérito		10 pretérito anterior	
dejé	dejamos	hube dejado	hubimos dejado
dejaste	dejasteis	hubiste dejado	hubisteis dejado
dejó	dejaron	hubo dejado	hubieron dejado
4 futuro		11 futuro perfecto	
dejaré	dejaremos	habré dejado	habremos dejado
dejarás	dejaréis	habrás dejado	habréis dejado
dejará	dejarán	habrá dejado	habrán dejado
5 potencial simple		12 potencial compuesto	
dejaría	dejaríamos	habría dejado	habríamos dejado
dejarías	dejaríais	habrías dejado	habríais dejado
dejaría	dejarían	habría dejado	habrían dejado
6 presente de subjuntivo		13 perfecto de subjuntivo	
deje	dejemos	haya dejado	hayamos dejado
dejes	dejéis	hayas dejado	hayáis dejado
deje	dejen	haya dejado	hayan dejado
7 imperfecto de subjuntivo		14 pluscuamperfecto de subjuntivo	
dejara	dejáramos	hubiera dejado	hubiéramos dejado
dejaras	dejarais	hubieras dejado	hubierais dejado
dejara	dejaran	hubiera dejado	hubieran dejado
OR		OR	
dejase	dejásemos	hubiese dejado	hubiésemos dejado
dejases	dejaseis	hubieses dejado	hubieseis dejado
dejase	dejasen	hubiese dejado	hubiesen dejado

imperativo	
—	dejemos
deja; no dejes	dejad; no dejéis
deje	dejen

Words and expressions related to this verb

dejar caer to drop (to let fall)	**dejarse** to abandon (neglect) oneself
el dejo abandonment	**dejar atrás** to leave behind
dejado, dejada dejected	**dejar de + inf.** to stop + pres. part.

to break the law, to be guilty, to offend

The Seven Simple Tenses		The Seven Compound Tenses	
Singular	Plural	Singular	Plural
1 presente de indicativo		**8 perfecto de indicativo**	
delinco	delinquimos	he delinquido	hemos delinquido
delinques	delinquís	has delinquido	habéis delinquido
delinque	delinquen	ha delinquido	han delinquido
2 imperfecto de indicativo		**9 pluscuamperfecto de indicativo**	
delinquía	delinquíamos	había delinquido	habíamos delinquido
delinquías	delinquíais	habías delinquido	habíais delinquido
delinquía	delinquían	había delinquido	habían delinquido
3 pretérito		**10 pretérito anterior**	
delinquí	delinquimos	hube delinquido	hubimos delinquido
delinquiste	delinquisteis	hubiste delinquido	hubisteis delinquido
delinquió	delinquieron	hubo delinquido	hubieron delinquido
4 futuro		**11 futuro perfecto**	
delinquiré	delinquiremos	habré delinquido	habremos delinquido
delinquirás	delinquiréis	habrás delinquido	habréis delinquido
delinquirá	delinquirán	habrá delinquido	habrán delinquido
5 potencial simple		**12 potencial compuesto**	
delinquiría	delinquiríamos	habría delinquido	habríamos delinquido
delinquirías	delinquiríais	habrías delinquido	habríais delinquido
delinquiría	delinquirían	habría delinquido	habrían delinquido
6 presente de subjuntivo		**13 perfecto de subjuntivo**	
delinca	delincamos	haya delinquido	hayamos delinquido
delincas	delincáis	hayas delinquido	hayáis delinquido
delinca	delincan	haya delinquido	hayan delinquido
7 imperfecto de subjuntivo		**14 pluscuamperfecto de subjuntivo**	
delinquiera	delinquiéramos	hubiera delinquido	hubiéramos delinquido
delinquieras	delinquierais	hubieras delinquido	hubierais delinquido
delinquiera	delinquieran	hubiera delinquido	hubieran delinquido
OR		OR	
delinquiese	delinquiésemos	hubiese delinquido	hubiésemos delinquido
delinquieses	delinquieseis	hubieses delinquido	hubieseis delinquido
delinquiese	delinquiesen	hubiese delinquido	hubiesen delinquido

	imperativo	
—		delincamos
delinque; no delincas		delinquid; no delincáis
delinca		delincan

Words related to this verb

el delinquimiento, la delincuencia   delinquency
delincuente   delinquent

113

demostrar   Gerundio **demostrando**   Part. pas. **demostrado**

to demonstrate, to prove

The Seven Simple Tenses		The Seven Compound Tenses	
Singular	Plural	Singular	Plural
1 presente de indicativo		8 perfecto de indicativo	
demuestro	demostramos	he demostrado	hemos demostrado
demuestras	demostráis	has demostrado	habéis demostrado
demuestra	demuestran	ha demostrado	han demostrado
2 imperfecto de indicativo		9 pluscuamperfecto de indicativo	
demostraba	demostrábamos	había demostrado	habíamos demostrado
demostrabas	demostrabais	habías demostrado	habíais demostrado
demostraba	demostraban	había demostrado	habían demostrado
3 pretérito		10 pretérito anterior	
demostré	demostramos	hube demostrado	hubimos demostrado
demostraste	demostrasteis	hubiste demostrado	hubisteis demostrado
demostró	demostraron	hubo demostrado	hubieron de:nostrado
4 futuro		11 futuro perfecto	
demostraré	demostraremos	habré demostrado	habremos demostrado
demostrarás	demostraréis	habrás demostrado	habréis demostrado
demostrará	demostrarán	habrá demostrado	habrán demostrado
5 potencial simple		12 potencial compuesto	
demostraría	demostraríamos	habría demostrado	habríamos demostrado
demostrarías	demostraríais	habrías demostrado	habríais demostrado
demostraría	demostrarían	habría demostrado	habrían demostrado
6 presente de subjuntivo		13 perfecto de subjuntivo	
demuestre	demostremos	haya demostrado	hayamos demostrado
demuestres	demostréis	hayas demostrado	hayáis demostrado
demuestre	demuestren	haya demostrado	hayan demostrado
7 imperfecto de subjuntivo		14 pluscuamperfecto de subjuntivo	
demostrara	demostráramos	hubiera demostrado	hubiéramos demostrado
demostraras	demostrarais	hubieras demostrado	hubierais demostrado
demostrara	demostraran	hubiera demostrado	hubieran demostrado
OR		OR	
demostrase	demostrásemos	hubiese demostrado	hubiésemos demostrado
demostrases	demostraseis	hubieses demostrado	hubieseis demostrado
demostrase	demostrasen	hubiese demostrado	hubiesen demostrado

imperativo	
—	demostremos
demuestra; no demuestres	demostrad; no demostréis
demuestre	demuestren

Words related to this verb
demostrativo, demostrativa   demonstrative   demostrable   demonstrable
la demostración   demonstration, proof   mostrar   to show, to exhibit
demostrador, demostradora   demonstrator

Gerundio **desayunándose**   Part. pas. **desayunado**   **desayunarse**

to breakfast, to have breakfast

The Seven Simple Tenses		The Seven Compound Tenses	
Singular	Plural	Singular	Plural
1 presente de indicativo		8 perfecto de indicativo	
me desayuno	nos desayunamos	me he	nos hemos
te desayunas	os desayunáis	te has	os habéis + desayunado
se desayuna	se desayunan	se ha	se han
2 imperfecto de indicativo		9 pluscuamperfecto de indicativo	
me desayunaba	nos desayunábamos	me había	nos habíamos
te desayunabas	os desayunabais	te habías	os habíais + desayunado
se desayunaba	se desayunaban	se había	se habían
3 pretérito		10 pretérito anterior	
me desayuné	nos desayunamos	me hube	nos hubimos
te desayunaste	os desayunasteis	te hubiste	os hubisteis + desayunado
se desayunó	se desayunaron	se hubo	se hubieron
4 futuro		11 futuro perfecto	
me desayunaré	nos desayunaremos	me habré	nos habremos
te desayunarás	os desayunaréis	te habrás	os habréis + desayunado
se desayunará	se desayunarán	se habrá	se habrán
5 potencial simple		12 potencial compuesto	
me desayunaría	nos desayunaríamos	me habría	nos habríamos
te desayunarías	os desayunaríais	te habrías	os habríais + desayunado
se desayunaría	se desayunarían	se habría	se habrían
6 presente de subjuntivo		13 perfecto de subjuntivo	
me desayune	nos desayunemos	me haya	nos hayamos
te desayunes	os desayunéis	te hayas	os hayáis + desayunado
se desayune	se desayunen	se haya	se hayan
7 imperfecto de subjuntivo		14 pluscuamperfecto de subjuntivo	
me desayunara	nos desayunáramos	me hubiera	nos hubiéramos
te desayunaras	os desayunarais	te hubieras	os hubierais + desayunado
se desayunara	se desayunaran	se hubiera	se hubieran
OR		OR	
me desayunase	nos desayunásemos	me hubiese	nos hubiésemos
te desayunases	os desayunaseis	te hubieses	os hubieseis + desayunado
se desayunase	se desayunasen	se hubiese	se hubiesen

imperativo	
—	desayunémonos
desayúnate; no te desayunes	desayunaos; no os desayunéis
desayúnese	desayúnense

Sentences using this verb and words related to it
—¿Qué toma Ud. en el desayuno todas las mañanas?
—Tomo leche, café con crema, pan tostado y un huevo.

desayunar	to breakfast	ayunar	to fast (not to eat)
el desayuno	breakfast	el ayuno	fast, fasting

115

descansar — Gerundio **descansando** — Part. pas. **descansado**

to rest

The Seven Simple Tenses		The Seven Compound Tenses	
Singular	Plural	Singular	Plural
1 presente de indicativo		**8 perfecto de indicativo**	
descanso	descansamos	he descansado	hemos descansado
descansas	descansáis	has descansado	habéis descansado
descansa	descansan	ha descansado	han descansado
2 imperfecto de indicativo		**9 pluscuamperfecto de indicativo**	
descansaba	descansábamos	había descansado	habíamos descansado
descansabas	descansabais	habías descansado	habíais descansado
descansaba	descansaban	había descansado	habían descansado
3 pretérito		**10 pretérito anterior**	
descansé	descansamos	hube descansado	hubimos descansado
descansaste	descansasteis	hubiste descansado	hubisteis descansado
descansó	descansaron	hubo descansado	hubieron descansado
4 futuro		**11 futuro perfecto**	
descansaré	descansaremos	habré descansado	habremos descansado
descansarás	descansaréis	habrás descansado	habréis descansado
descansará	descansarán	habrá descansado	habrán descansado
5 potencial simple		**12 potencial compuesto**	
descansaría	descansaríamos	habría descansado	habríamos descansado
descansarías	descansaríais	habrías descansado	habríais descansado
descansaría	descansarían	habría descansado	habrían descansado
6 presente de subjuntivo		**13 perfecto de subjuntivo**	
descanse	descansemos	haya descansado	hayamos descansado
descanses	descanséis	hayas descansado	hayáis descansado
descanse	descansen	haya descansado	hayan descansado
7 imperfecto de subjuntivo		**14 pluscuamperfecto de subjuntivo**	
descansara	descansáramos	hubiera descansado	hubiéramos descansado
descansaras	descansarais	hubieras descansado	hubierais descansado
descansara	descansaran	hubiera descansado	hubieran descansado
OR		OR	
descansase	descansásemos	hubiese descansado	hubiésemos descansado
descansases	descansaseis	hubieses descansado	hubieseis descansado
descansase	descansasen	hubiese descansado	hubiesen descansado

imperativo	
—	descansemos
descansa; no descanses	descansad; no descanséis
descanse	descansen

Words and expressions related to this verb

el descanso rest, relief
el descansadero resting place
la cansera fatigue
cansar to fatigue, to tire, to weary

el descansillo landing on a staircase
el descanso a discreción at ease (military)
cansar de esperar to be tired of waiting

Gerundio **describiendo**   Part. pas. **descrito**   **describir**

to describe, to sketch, to delineate

The Seven Simple Tenses		The Seven Compound Tenses	
Singular	Plural	Singular	Plural
1 presente de indicativo		**8 perfecto de indicativo**	
describo	describimos	he descrito	hemos descrito
describes	describís	has descrito	habéis descrito
describe	describen	ha descrito	han descrito
2 imperfecto de indicativo		**9 pluscuamperfecto de indicativo**	
describía	describíamos	había descrito	habíamos descrito
describías	describíais	habías descrito	habíais descrito
describía	describían	había descrito	habían descrito
3 pretérito		**10 pretérito anterior**	
describí	describimos	hube descrito	hubimos descrito
describiste	describisteis	hubiste descrito	hubisteis descrito
describió	describieron	hubo descrito	hubieron descrito
4 futuro		**11 futuro perfecto**	
describiré	describiremos	habré descrito	habremos descrito
describirás	describiréis	habrás descrito	habréis descrito
describirá	describirán	habrá descrito	habrán descrito
5 potencial simple		**12 potencial compuesto**	
describiría	describiríamos	habría descrito	habríamos descrito
describirías	describiríais	habrías descrito	habríais descrito
describiría	describirían	habría descrito	habrían descrito
6 presente de subjuntivo		**13 perfecto de subjuntivo**	
describa	describamos	haya descrito	hayamos descrito
describas	describáis	hayas descrito	hayáis descrito
describa	describan	haya descrito	hayan descrito
7 imperfecto de subjuntivo		**14 pluscuamperfecto de subjuntivo**	
describiera	describiéramos	hubiera descrito	hubiéramos descrito
describieras	describierais	hubieras descrito	hubierais descrito
describiera	describieran	hubiera descrito	hubieran descrito
OR		OR	
describiese	describiésemos	hubiese descrito	hubiésemos descrito
describieses	describieseis	hubieses descrito	hubieseis descrito
describiese	describiesen	hubiese descrito	hubiesen descrito

imperativo	
—	describamos
describe; no describas	describid; no describáis
describa	describan

Words and expressions related to this verb
la descripción description
descriptor, descriptora describer
descriptivo, descriptiva descriptive
descripto, descripta described *(adj.)*

escribir to write
escribir a mano to write by hand
escribir a máquina to typewrite

117

descubrir   Gerundio **descubriendo**   Part. pas. **descubierto**

to discover

The Seven Simple Tenses		The Seven Compound Tenses	
Singular	Plural	Singular	Plural
1 presente de indicativo		8 perfecto de indicativo	
descubro	**descubrimos**	**he descubierto**	**hemos descubierto**
descubres	**descubrís**	**has descubierto**	**habéis descubierto**
descubre	**descubren**	**ha descubierto**	**han descubierto**
2 imperfecto de indicativo		9 pluscuamperfecto de indicativo	
descubría	**descubríamos**	**había descubierto**	**habíamos descubierto**
descubrías	**descubríais**	**habías descubierto**	**habíais descubierto**
descubría	**descubrían**	**había descubierto**	**habían descubierto**
3 pretérito		10 pretérito anterior	
descubrí	**descubrimos**	**hube descubierto**	**hubimos descubierto**
descubriste	**descubristeis**	**hubiste descubierto**	**hubisteis descubierto**
descubrió	**descubrieron**	**hubo descubierto**	**hubieron descubierto**
4 futuro		11 futuro perfecto	
descubriré	**descubriremos**	**habré descubierto**	**habremos descubierto**
descubrirás	**descubriréis**	**habrás descubierto**	**habréis descubierto**
descubrirá	**descubrirán**	**habrá descubierto**	**habrán descubierto**
5 potencial simple		12 potencial compuesto	
descubriría	**descubriríamos**	**habría descubierto**	**habríamos descubierto**
descubrirías	**descubriríais**	**habrías descubierto**	**habríais descubierto**
descubriría	**descubrirían**	**habría descubierto**	**habrían descubierto**
6 presente de subjuntivo		13 perfecto de subjuntivo	
descubra	**descubramos**	**haya descubierto**	**hayamos descubierto**
descubras	**descubráis**	**hayas descubierto**	**hayáis descubierto**
descubra	**descubran**	**haya descubierto**	**hayan descubierto**
7 imperfecto de subjuntivo		14 pluscuamperfecto de subjuntivo	
descubriera	**descubriéramos**	**hubiera descubierto**	**hubiéramos descubierto**
descubrieras	**descubrierais**	**hubieras descubierto**	**hubierais descubierto**
descubriera	**descubrieran**	**hubiera descubierto**	**hubieran descubierto**
OR		OR	
descubriese	**descubriésemos**	**hubiese descubierto**	**hubiésemos descubierto**
descubrieses	**descubrieseis**	**hubieses descubierto**	**hubieseis descubierto**
descubriese	**descubriesen**	**hubiese descubierto**	**hubiesen descubierto**

	imperativo	
—	**descubramos**
descubre; no descubras	**descubrid; no descubráis**
descubra	**descubran**

Words and expressions related to this verb

descubrirse to take off one's hat
el descubrimiento discovery
descubridor, descubridora discoverer
a la descubierta clearly, openly

cubrir to cover
cubrir el costo to cover the cost
cubrir la mesa to cover the table

Gerundio **deseando**   Part. pas. **deseado**   **desear**

to desire, to wish, to want

The Seven Simple Tenses		The Seven Compound Tenses	
Singular	Plural	Singular	Plural
1 presente de indicativo		8 perfecto de indicativo	
deseo	**deseamos**	**he deseado**	**hemos deseado**
deseas	**deseáis**	**has deseado**	**habéis deseado**
desea	**desean**	**ha deseado**	**han deseado**
2 imperfecto de indicativo		9 pluscuamperfecto de indicativo	
deseaba	**deseábamos**	**había deseado**	**habíamos deseado**
deseabas	**deseabais**	**habías deseado**	**habíais deseado**
deseaba	**deseaban**	**había deseado**	**habían deseado**
3 pretérito		10 pretérito anterior	
deseé	**deseamos**	**hube deseado**	**hubimos deseado**
deseaste	**deseasteis**	**hubiste deseado**	**hubisteis deseado**
deseó	**desearon**	**hubo deseado**	**hubieron deseado**
4 futuro		11 futuro perfecto	
desearé	**desearemos**	**habré deseado**	**habremos deseado**
desearás	**desaréis**	**habrás deseado**	**habréis deseado**
deseará	**desearán**	**habrá deseado**	**habrán deseado**
5 potencial simple		12 potencial compuesto	
desearía	**desearíamos**	**habría deseado**	**habríamos deseado**
desearías	**desearíais**	**habrías deseado**	**habríais deseado**
desearía	**desearían**	**habría deseado**	**habrían deseado**
6 presente de subjuntivo		13 perfecto de subjuntivo	
desee	**deseemos**	**haya deseado**	**hayamos deseado**
desees	**deseéis**	**hayas deseado**	**hayáis deseado**
desee	**deseen**	**haya deseado**	**hayan deseado**
7 imperfecto de subjuntivo		14 pluscuamperfecto de subjuntivo	
deseara	**deseáramos**	**hubiera deseado**	**hubiéramos deseado**
desearas	**desearais**	**hubieras deseado**	**hubierais deseado**
deseara	**desearan**	**hubiera deseado**	**hubieran deseado**
OR		OR	
desease	**deseásemos**	**hubiese deseado**	**hubiésemos deseado**
deseases	**deseaseis**	**hubieses deseado**	**hubieseis deseado**
desease	**deseasen**	**hubiese deseado**	**hubiesen deseado**

imperativo	
—	**deseemos**
desea; no desees	**desead; no deseéis**
desee	**deseen**

Words and expressions related to this verb

el deseo   desire
deseoso, deseosa   desirous
tener deseo de + inf.   to be eager + inf.
deseable   desirable

el deseador, la deseadora   desirer, wisher
deseablemente   desirably

119

despedir	Gerundio **despidiendo**	Part. pas. **despedido**

to dismiss

The Seven Simple Tenses		The Seven Compound Tenses	
Singular	Plural	Singular	Plural

1 presente de indicativo		8 perfecto de indicativo	
despido	despedimos	he despedido	hemos despedido
despides	despedís	has despedido	habéis despedido
despide	despiden	ha despedido	han despedido

2 imperfecto de indicativo		9 pluscuamperfecto de indicativo	
despedía	despedíamos	había despedido	habíamos despedido
despedías	despedíais	habías despedido	habíais despedido
despedía	despedían	había despedido	habían despedido

3 pretérito		10 pretérito anterior	
despedí	despedimos	hube despedido	hubimos despedido
despediste	despedisteis	hubiste despedido	hubisteis despedido
despidió	despidieron	hubo despedido	hubieron despedido

4 futuro		11 futuro perfecto	
despediré	despediremos	habré despedido	habremos despedido
despedirás	despediréis	habrás despedido	habréis despedido
despedirá	despedirán	habrá despedido	habrán despedido

5 potencial simple		12 potencial compuesto	
despediría	despediríamos	habría despedido	habríamos despedido
despedirías	despediríais	habrías despedido	habríais despedido
despediría	despedirían	habría despedido	habrían despedido

6 presente de subjuntivo		13 perfecto de subjuntivo	
despida	despidamos	haya despedido	hayamos despedido
despidas	despidáis	hayas despedido	hayáis despedido
despida	despidan	haya despedido	hayan despedido

7 imperfecto de subjuntivo		14 pluscuamperfecto de subjuntivo	
despidiera	despidiéramos	hubiera despedido	hubiéramos despedido
despidieras	despidierais	hubieras despedido	hubierais despedido
despidiera	despidieran	hubiera despedido	hubieran despedido
OR		OR	
despidiese	despidiésemos	hubiese despedido	hubiésemos despedido
despidieses	despidieseis	hubieses despedido	hubieseis despedido
despidiese	despidiesen	hubiese despedido	hubiesen despedido

	imperativo	
—	despidamos	
despide; no despidas	despedid; no despidáis	
despida	despidan	

Words and expressions related to this verb
un despedimiento, una despedida dismissal, discharge, farewell
despedirse to take leave of, to say good-bye to
despedirse a la francesa to take French leave

Gerundio **despidiéndose**   Part. pas. **despedido**   **despedirse**

to take leave of, to say good-bye to

The Seven Simple Tenses		The Seven Compound Tenses	
Singular	Plural	Singular	Plural

1   presente de indicativo

me despido	nos despedimos		
te despides	os despedís		
se despide	se despiden		

8   perfecto de indicativo

me he	nos hemos	
te has	os habéis	+ despedido
se ha	se han	

2   imperfecto de indicativo

me despedía	nos despedíamos
te despedías	os despedíais
se despedía	se despedían

9   pluscuamperfecto de indicativo

me había	nos habíamos	
te habías	os habíais	+ despedido
se había	se habían	

3   pretérito

me despedí	nos despedimos
te despediste	os despedisteis
se despidió	se despidieron

10   pretérito anterior

me hube	nos hubimos	
te hubiste	os hubisteis	+ despedido
se hubo	se hubieron	

4   futuro

me despediré	nos despediremos
te despedirás	os despediréis
se despedirá	se despedirán

11   futuro perfecto

me habré	nos habremos	
te habrás	os habréis	+ despedido
se habrá	se habrán	

5   potencial simple

me despediría	nos despediríamos
te despedirías	os despediríais
se despediría	se despedirían

12   potencial compuesto

me habría	nos habríamos	
te habrías	os habríais	+ despedido
se habría	se habrían	

6   presente de subjuntivo

me despida	nos despidamos
te despidas	os despidáis
se despida	se despidan

13   perfecto de subjuntivo

me haya	nos hayamos	
te hayas	os hayáis	+ despedido
se haya	se hayan	

7   imperfecto de subjuntivo

me despidiera	nos despidiéramos
te despidieras	os despidierais
se despidiera	se despidieran
OR	
me despidiese	nos despidiésemos
te despidieses	os despidieseis
se despidiese	se despidiesen

14   pluscuamperfecto de subjuntivo

me hubiera	nos hubiéramos	
te hubieras	os hubierais	+ despedido
se hubiera	se hubieran	
OR		
me hubiese	nos hubiésemos	
te hubieses	os hubieseis	+ despedido
se hubiese	se hubiesen	

imperativo

—	despidámonos
despídete; no te despidas	despedíos; no os despidáis
despídase	despídanse

Words and expressions related to this verb
despedirse a la francesa   to take French leave
despedir   to dismiss
un despedimiento, una despedida   dismissal, discharge, farewell
despedirse de   to take leave of, to say good-bye to

121

despertar   Gerundio **despertando**   Part. pas. **despertado**

to enliven, to awaken (someone)

The Seven Simple Tenses		The Seven Compound Tenses	
Singular	Plural	Singular	Plural
1 presente de indicativo		8 perfecto de indicativo	
despierto	despertamos	he despertado	hemos despertado
despiertas	despertáis	has despertado	habéis despertado
despierta	despiertan	ha despertado	han despertado
2 imperfecto de indicativo		9 pluscuamperfecto de indicativo	
despertaba	despertábamos	había despertado	habíamos despertado
despertabas	despertabais	habías despertado	habíais despertado
despertaba	despertaban	había despertado	habían despertado
3 pretérito		10 pretérito anterior	
desperté	despertamos	hube despertado	hubimos despertado
despertaste	despertasteis	hubiste despertado	hubisteis despertado
despertó	despertaron	hubo despertado	hubieron despertado
4 futuro		11 futuro perfecto	
despertaré	despertaremos	habré despertado	habremos despertado
despertarás	despertaréis	habrás despertado	habréis despertado
despertará	despertarán	habrá despertado	habrán despertado
5 potencial simple		12 potencial compuesto	
despertaría	despertaríamos	habría despertado	habríamos despertado
despertarías	despertaríais	habrías despertado	habríais despertado
despertaría	despertarían	habría despertado	habrían despertado
6 presente de subjuntivo		13 perfecto de subjuntivo	
despierte	despertemos	haya despertado	hayamos despertado
despiertes	despertéis	hayas despertado	hayáis despertado
despierte	despierten	haya despertado	hayan despertado
7 imperfecto de subjuntivo		14 pluscuamperfecto de subjuntivo	
despertara	despertáramos	hubiera despertado	hubiéramos despertado
despertaras	despertarais	hubieras despertado	hubierais despertado
despertara	despertaran	hubiera despertado	hubieran despertado
OR		OR	
despertase	despertásemos	hubiese despertado	hubiésemos despertado
despertases	despertaseis	hubieses despertado	hubieseis despertado
despertase	despertasen	hubiese despertado	hubiesen despertado

imperativo	
—	despertemos
despierta; no despiertes	despertad; no despertéis
despierte	despierten

Words related to this verb
despertarse to wake up oneself
un despertador alarm clock
el despertamiento awakening

Gerundio **despertándose**   Part. pas. **despertado**   **despertarse**

to wake up oneself

The Seven Simple Tenses		The Seven Compound Tenses	
Singular	Plural	Singular	Plural
1 presente de indicativo		**8 perfecto de indicativo**	
me despierto	**nos despertamos**	**me he**	**nos hemos**
te despiertas	**os despertáis**	**te has**	**os habéis** + **despertado**
se despierta	**se despiertan**	**se ha**	**se han**
2 imperfecto de indicativo		**9 pluscuamperfecto de indicativo**	
me despertaba	**nos despertábamos**	**me había**	**nos habíamos**
te despertabas	**os despertabais**	**te habías**	**os habíais** + **despertado**
se despertaba	**se despertaban**	**se había**	**se habían**
3 pretérito		**10 pretérito anterior**	
me desperté	**nos despertamos**	**me hube**	**nos hubimos**
te despertaste	**os despertasteis**	**te hubiste**	**os hubisteis** + **despertado**
se despertó	**se despertaron**	**se hubo**	**se hubieron**
4 futuro		**11 futuro perfecto**	
me despertaré	**nos despertaremos**	**me habré**	**nos habremos**
te despertarás	**os despertaréis**	**te habrás**	**os habréis** + **despertado**
se despertará	**se despertarán**	**se habrá**	**se habrán**
5 potencial simple		**12 potencial compuesto**	
me despertaría	**nos despertaríamos**	**me habría**	**nos habríamos**
te despertarías	**os despertaríais**	**te habrías**	**os habríais** + **despertado**
se despertaría	**se despertarían**	**se habría**	**se habrían**
6 presente de subjuntivo		**13 perfecto de subjuntivo**	
me despierte	**nos despertemos**	**me haya**	**nos hayamos**
te despiertes	**os despertéis**	**te hayas**	**os hayáis** + **despertado**
se despierte	**se despierten**	**se haya**	**se hayan**
7 imperfecto de subjuntivo		**14 pluscuamperfecto de subjuntivo**	
me despertara	**nos despertáramos**	**me hubiera**	**nos hubiéramos**
te despertaras	**os despertarais**	**te hubieras**	**os hubierais** + **despertado**
se despertara	**se despertaran**	**se hubiera**	**se hubieran**
OR		OR	
me despertase	**nos despertásemos**	**me hubiese**	**nos hubiésemos**
te despertases	**os despertaseis**	**te hubieses**	**os hubieseis** + **despertado**
se despertase	**se despertasen**	**se hubiese**	**se hubiesen**

imperativo

—	**despertémonos**
despiértate; no te despiertes	**despertaos; no os despertéis**
despiértese	**despiértense**

Words related to this verb
despertar   to awaken (someone), to enliven
un despertador   alarm clock
el despertamiento   awakening

123

destruir

Gerundio **destruyendo**   Part. pas. **destruido**

to destroy

The Seven Simple Tenses		The Seven Compound Tenses	
Singular	Plural	Singular	Plural
1 presente de indicativo		**8 perfecto de indicativo**	
destruyo	destruimos	he destruido	hemos destruido
destruyes	destruís	has destruido	habéis destruido
destruye	destruyen	ha destruido	han destruido
2 imperfecto de indicativo		**9 pluscuamperfecto de indicativo**	
destruía	destruíamos	había destruido	habíamos destruido
destruías	destruíais	habías destruido	habíais destruido
destruía	destruían	había destruido	habían destruido
3 pretérito		**10 pretérito anterior**	
destruí	destruimos	hube destruido	hubimos destruido
destruiste	destruisteis	hubiste destruido	hubisteis destruido
destruyó	destruyeron	hubo destruido	hubieron destruido
4 futuro		**11 futuro perfecto**	
destruiré	destruiremos	habré destruido	habremos destruido
destruirás	destruiréis	habrás destruido	habréis destruido
destruirá	destruirán	habrá destruido	habrán destruido
5 potencial simple		**12 potencial compuesto**	
destruiría	destruiríamos	habría destruido	habríamos destruido
destruirías	destruiríais	habrías destruido	habríais destruido
destruiría	destruirían	habría destruido	habrían destruido
6 presente de subjuntivo		**13 perfecto de subjuntivo**	
destruya	destruyamos	haya destruido	hayamos destruido
destruyas	destruyáis	hayas destruido	hayáis destruido
destruya	destruyan	haya destruido	hayan destruido
7 imperfecto de subjuntivo		**14 pluscuamperfecto de subjuntivo**	
destruyera	destruyéramos	hubiera destruido	hubiéramos destruido
destruyeras	destruyerais	hubieras destruido	hubierais destruido
destruyera	destruyeran	hubiera destruido	hubieran destruido
OR		OR	
destruyese	destruyésemos	hubiese destruido	hubiésemos destruido
destruyeses	destruyeseis	hubieses destruido	hubieseis destruido
destruyese	destruyesen	hubiese destruido	hubiesen destruido

imperativo	
—	destruyamos
destruye; no destruyas	destruid; no destruyáis
destruya	destruyan

Words related to this verb
destructor, destructora destructor, destroyer   **destructivo, destructiva**
                                                 destructive
la destrucción destruction   **destruidor, destruidora** destroyer
destruible destructible

Gerundio **desvistiéndose** Part. pas. **desvestido** **desvestirse**

to undress oneself, to get undressed

The Seven Simple Tenses		The Seven Compound Tenses	
Singular	Plural	Singular	Plural
1 presente de indicativo		8 perfecto de indicativo	
me desvisto	**nos desvestimos**	**me he**	**nos hemos**
te desvistes	**os desvestís**	**te has**	**os habéis** + desvestido
se desviste	**se desvisten**	**se ha**	**se han**
2 imperfecto de indicativo		9 pluscuamperfecto de indicativo	
me desvestía	**nos desvestíamos**	**me había**	**nos habíamos**
te desvestías	**os desvestíais**	**te habías**	**os habíais** + desvestido
se desvestía	**se desvestían**	**se había**	**se habían**
3 pretérito		10 pretérito anterior	
me desvestí	**nos desvestimos**	**me hube**	**nos hubimos**
te desvestiste	**os desvestisteis**	**te hubiste**	**os hubisteis** + desvestido
se desvistió	**se desvistieron**	**se hubo**	**se hubieron**
4 futuro		11 futuro perfecto	
me desvestiré	**nos desvestiremos**	**me habré**	**nos habremos**
te desvestirás	**os desvestiréis**	**te habrás**	**os habréis** + desvestido
se desvestirá	**se desvestirán**	**se habrá**	**se habrán**
5 potencial simple		12 potencial compuesto	
me desvestiría	**nos desvestiríamos**	**me habría**	**nos habríamos**
te desvestirías	**os desvestiríais**	**te habrías**	**os habríais** + desvestido
se desvestiría	**se desvestirían**	**se habría**	**se habrían**
6 presente de subjuntivo		13 perfecto de subjuntivo	
me desvista	**nos desvistamos**	**me haya**	**nos hayamos**
te desvistas	**os desvistáis**	**te hayas**	**os hayáis** + desvestido
se desvista	**se desvistan**	**se haya**	**se hayan**
7 imperfecto de subjuntivo		14 pluscuamperfecto de subjuntivo	
me desvistiera	**nos desvistiéramos**	**me hubiera**	**nos hubiéramos**
te desvistieras	**os desvistierais**	**te hubieras**	**os hubierais** + desvestido
se desvistiera	**se desvistieran**	**se hubiera**	**se hubieran**
OR		OR	
me desvistiese	**nos desvistiésemos**	**me hubiese**	**nos hubiésemos**
te desvistieses	**os desvistieseis**	**te hubieses**	**os hubieseis** + desvestido
se desvistiese	**se desvistiesen**	**se hubiese**	**se hubiesen**

	imperativo	
—		**desvistámonos**
desvístete; no te desvistas		**desvestíos; no os desvistáis**
desvístase		**desvístanse**

Words related to this verb
vestir   to clothe, to dress
vestirse   to clothe oneself, to dress oneself
el vestido   clothing, clothes, dress
vestidos usados   secondhand clothing

125

detenerse   Gerundio **deteniéndose**   Part. pas. **detenido**

to stop (oneself)

The Seven Simple Tenses		The Seven Compound Tenses	
Singular	Plural	Singular	Plural
1 presente de indicativo		8 perfecto de indicativo	
me detengo	nos detenemos	me he detenido	nos hemos detenido
te detienes	os detenéis	te has detenido	os habéis detenido
se detiene	se detienen	se ha detenido	se han detenido
2 imperfecto de indicativo		9 pluscuamperfecto de indicativo	
me detenía	nos deteníamos	me había detenido	nos habíamos detenido
te detenías	os deteníais	te habías detenido	os habíais detenido
se detenía	se detenían	se había detenido	se habían detenido
3 pretérito		10 pretérito anterior	
me detuve	nos detuvimos	me hube detenido	nos hubimos detenido
te detuviste	os detuvisteis	te hubiste detenido	os hubisteis detenido
se detuvo	se detuvieron	se hubo detenido	se hubieron detenido
4 futuro		11 futuro perfecto	
me detendré	nos detendremos	me habré detenido	nos habremos detenido
te detendrás	os detendréis	te habrás detenido	os habréis detenido
se detendrá	se detendrán	se habrá detenido	se habrán detenido
5 potencial simple		12 potencial compuesto	
me detendría	nos detendríamos	me habría detenido	nos habríamos detenido
te detendrías	os detendríais	te habrías detenido	os habríais detenido
se detendría	se detendrían	se habría detenido	se habrían detenido
6 presente de subjuntivo		13 perfecto de subjuntivo	
me detenga	nos detengamos	me haya detenido	nos hayamos detenido
te detengas	os detengáis	te hayas detenido	os hayáis detenido
se detenga	se detengan	se haya detenido	se hayan detenido
7 imperfecto de subjuntivo		14 pluscuamperfecto de subjuntivo	
me detuviera	nos detuviéramos	me hubiera detenido	nos hubiéramos detenido
te detuvieras	os detuvierais	te hubieras detenido	os hubierais detenido
se detuviera	se detuvieran	se hubiera detenido	se hubieran detenido
OR		OR	
me detuviese	nos detuviésemos	me hubiese detenido	nos hubiésemos detenido
te detuvieses	os detuvieseis	te hubieses detenido	os hubieseis detenido
se detuviese	se detuviesen	se hubiese detenido	se hubiesen detenido

	imperativo	
—		detengámonos
detente; no te detengas		deteneos; no os detengáis
deténgase		deténganse

Words related to this verb
detener   to stop (someone or something), to detain
detenedor, detenedora   detainer

126

to return (an object), to refund, to give back

The Seven Simple Tenses		The Seven Compound Tenses	
Singular	Plural	Singular	Plural
1 presente de indicativo		**8 perfecto de indicativo**	
devuelvo	**devolvemos**	**he devuelto**	**hemos devuelto**
devuelves	**devolvéis**	**has devuelto**	**habéis devuelto**
devuelve	**devuelven**	**ha devuelto**	**han devuelto**
2 imperfecto de indicativo		**9 pluscuamperfecto de indicativo**	
devolvía	**devolvíamos**	**había devuelto**	**habíamos devuelto**
devolvías	**devolvíais**	**habías devuelto**	**habíais devuelto**
devolvía	**devolvían**	**había devuelto**	**habían devuelto**
3 pretérito		**10 pretérito anterior**	
devolví	**devolvimos**	**hube devuelto**	**hubimos devuelto**
devolviste	**devolvisteis**	**hubiste devuelto**	**hubisteis devuelto**
devolvió	**devolvieron**	**hubo devuelto**	**hubieron devuelto**
4 futuro		**11 futuro perfecto**	
devolveré	**devolveremos**	**habré devuelto**	**habremos devuelto**
devolverás	**devolveréis**	**habrás devuelto**	**habréis devuelto**
devolverá	**devolverán**	**habrá devuelto**	**habrán devuelto**
5 potencial simple		**12 potencial compuesto**	
devolvería	**devolveríamos**	**habría devuelto**	**habríamos devuelto**
devolverías	**devolveríais**	**habrías devuelto**	**habríais devuelto**
devolvería	**devolverían**	**habría devuelto**	**habrían devuelto**
6 presente de subjuntivo		**13 perfecto de subjuntivo**	
devuelva	**devolvamos**	**haya devuelto**	**hayamos devuelto**
devuelvas	**devolváis**	**hayas devuelto**	**hayáis devuelto**
devuelva	**devuelvan**	**haya devuelto**	**hayan devuelto**
7 imperfecto de subjuntivo		**14 pluscuamperfecto de subjuntivo**	
devolviera	**devolviéramos**	**hubiera devuelto**	**hubiéramos devuelto**
devolvieras	**devolvierais**	**hubieras devuelto**	**hubierais devuelto**
devolviera	**devolvieran**	**hubiera devuelto**	**hubieran devuelto**
OR		OR	
devolviese	**devolviésemos**	**hubiese devuelto**	**hubiésemos devuelto**
devolvieses	**devolvieseis**	**hubieses devuelto**	**hubieseis devuelto**
devolviese	**devolviesen**	**hubiese devuelto**	**hubiesen devuelto**

	imperativo	
—		**devolvamos**
devuelve; no devuelvas		**devolved; no devolváis**
devuelva		**devuelvan**

Sentences using this verb and words related to it
—¿**Ha devuelto Ud. los libros a la biblioteca?**
—**Sí, señora, los devolví ayer.**

devolutivo, devolutiva   returnable   **devolver**   to vomit
volver   to return, to go back   **la devolución**   restitution

dirigir	Gerundio **dirigiendo**	Part. pas. **dirigido**

to direct

The Seven Simple Tenses		The Seven Compound Tenses	
Singular	Plural	Singular	Plural
1 presente de indicativo		8 perfecto de indicativo	
dirijo	dirigimos	he dirigido	hemos dirigido
diriges	dirigís	has dirigido	habéis dirigido
dirige	dirigen	ha dirigido	han dirigido
2 imperfecto de indicativo		9 pluscuamperfecto de indicativo	
dirigía	dirigíamos	había dirigido	habíamos dirigido
dirigías	dirigíais	habías dirigido	habíais dirigido
dirigía	dirigían	había dirigido	habían dirigido
3 pretérito		10 pretérito anterior	
dirigí	dirigimos	hube dirigido	hubimos dirigido
dirigiste	dirigisteis	hubiste dirigido	hubisteis dirigido
dirigió	dirigieron	hubo dirigido	hubieron dirigido
4 futuro		11 futuro perfecto	
dirigiré	dirigiremos	habré dirigido	habremos dirigido
dirigirás	dirigiréis	habrás dirigido	habréis dirigido
dirigirá	dirigirán	habrá dirigido	habrán dirigido
5 potencial simple		12 potencial compuesto	
dirigiría	dirigiríamos	habría dirigido	habríamos dirigido
dirigirías	dirigiríais	habrías dirigido	habríais dirigido
dirigiría	dirigirían	habría dirigido	habrían dirigido
6 presente de subjuntivo		13 perfecto de subjuntivo	
dirija	dirijamos	haya dirigido	hayamos dirigido
dirijas	dirijáis	hayas dirigido	hayáis dirigido
dirija	dirijan	haya dirigido	hayan dirigido
7 imperfecto de subjuntivo		14 pluscuamperfecto de subjuntivo	
dirigiera	dirigiéramos	hubiera dirigido	hubiéramos dirigido
dirigieras	dirigierais	hubieras dirigido	hubierais dirigido
dirigiera	dirigieran	hubiera dirigido	hubieran dirigido
OR		OR	
dirigiese	dirigiésemos	hubiese dirigido	hubiésemos dirigido
dirigieses	dirigieseis	hubieses dirigido	hubieseis dirigido
dirigiese	dirigiesen	hubiese dirigido	hubiesen dirigido

imperativo	
—	dirijamos
dirige; no dirijas	dirigid; no dirijáis
dirija	dirijan

Words and expressions related to this verb
el director, la directora   director
director de orquesta   orchestra conductor
el dirigente, la dirigente   leader
dirigir la palabra   to address, to speak to

128

to excuse, to dispense, to distribute, to exempt

The Seven Simple Tenses		The Seven Compound Tenses	
Singular	Plural	Singular	Plural
1 presente de indicativo		8 perfecto de indicativo	
dispenso	dispensamos	he dispensado	hemos dispensado
dispensas	dispensáis	has dispensado	habéis dispensado
dispensa	dispensan	ha dispensado	han dispensado
2 imperfecto de indicativo		9 pluscuamperfecto de indicativo	
dispensaba	dispensábamos	había dispensado	habíamos dispensado
dispensabas	dispensabais	habías dispensado	habíais dispensado
dispensaba	dispensaban	había dispensado	habían dispensado
3 pretérito		10 pretérito anterior	
dispensé	dispensamos	hube dispensado	hubimos dispensado
dispensaste	dispensasteis	hubiste dispensado	hubisteis dispensado
dispensó	dispensaron	hubo dispensado	hubieron dispensado
4 futuro		11 futuro perfecto	
dispensaré	dispensaremos	habré dispensado	habremos dispensado
dispensarás	dispensaréis	habrás dispensado	habréis dispensado
dispensará	dispensarán	habrá dispensado	habrán dispensado
5 potencial simple		12 potencial compuesto	
dispensaría	dispensaríamos	habría dispensado	habríamos dispensado
dispensarías	dispensaríais	habrías dispensado	habríais dispensado
dispensaría	dispensarían	habría dispensado	habrían dispensado
6 presente de subjuntivo		13 perfecto de subjuntivo	
dispense	dispensemos	haya dispensado	hayamos dispensado
dispenses	dispenséis	hayas dispensado	hayáis dispensado
dispense	dispensen	haya dispensado	hayan dispensado
7 imperfecto de subjuntivo		14 pluscuamperfecto de subjuntivo	
dispensara	dispensáramos	hubiera dispensado	hubiéramos dispensado
dispensaras	dispensarais	hubieras dispensado	hubierais dispensado
dispensara	dispensaran	hubiera dispensado	hubieran dispensado
OR		OR	
dispensase	dispensásemos	hubiese dispensado	hubiésemos dispensado
dispensases	dispensaseis	hubieses dispensado	hubieseis dispensado
dispensase	dispensasen	hubiese dispensado	hubiesen dispensado

	imperativo	
—	dispensemos
dispensa; no dispenses	dispensad; no dispenséis
dispense	dispensen

Words and expressions related to this verb
¡Dispénseme!   Excuse me!
la dispensación   dispensation
el dispensario   dispensary, clinic
dispensar de + inf.   to excuse from + pres. part.
la dispensa   privilege

129

distinguir

Gerundio **distinguiendo**   Part. pas. **distinguido**

to distinguish

The Seven Simple Tenses		The Seven Compound Tenses	
Singular	Plural	Singular	Plural
1 presente de indicativo		8 perfecto de indicativo	
distingo	distinguimos	he distinguido	hemos distinguido
distingues	distinguís	has distinguido	habéis distinguido
distingue	distinguen	ha distinguido	han distinguido
2 imperfecto de indicativo		9 pluscuamperfecto de indicativo	
distinguía	distinguíamos	había distinguido	habíamos distinguido
distinguías	distinguíais	habías distinguido	habíais distinguido
distinguía	distinguían	había distinguido	habían distinguido
3 pretérito		10 pretérito anterior	
distinguí	distinguimos	hube distinguido	hubimos distinguido
distinguiste	distinguisteis	hubiste distinguido	hubisteis distinguido
distinguió	distinguieron	hubo distinguido	hubieron distinguido
4 futuro		11 futuro perfecto	
distinguiré	distinguiremos	habré distinguido	habremos distinguido
distinguirás	distinguiréis	habrás distinguido	habréis distinguido
distinguirá	distinguirán	habrá distinguido	habrán distinguido
5 potencial simple		12 potencial compuesto	
distinguiría	distinguiríamos	habría distinguido	habríamos distinguido
distinguirías	distinguiríais	habrías distinguido	habríais distinguido
distinguiría	distinguirían	habría distinguido	habrían distinguido
6 presente de subjuntivo		13 perfecto de subjuntivo	
distinga	distingamos	haya distinguido	hayamos distinguido
distingas	distingáis	hayas distinguido	hayáis distinguido
distinga	distingan	haya distinguido	hayan distinguido
7 imperfecto de subjuntivo		14 pluscuamperfecto de subjuntivo	
distinguiera	distinguiéramos	hubiera distinguido	hubiéramos distinguido
distinguieras	distinguierais	hubieras distinguido	hubierais distinguido
distinguiera	distinguieran	hubiera distinguido	hubieran distinguido
OR		OR	
distinguiese	distinguiésemos	hubiese distinguido	hubiésemos distinguido
distinguieses	distinguieseis	hubieses distinguido	hubieseis distinguido
distinguiese	distinguiesen	hubiese distinguido	hubiesen distinguido

	imperativo	
—	distingamos	
distingue; no distingas	distinguid; no distingáis	
distinga	distingan	

Words related to this verb
distinguirse   to distinguish oneself
distintivo, distintiva   distinctive
el distingo   restriction
la distinción   distinction

to have a good time, to enjoy oneself

The Seven Simple Tenses		The Seven Compound Tenses	
Singular	Plural	Singular	Plural
1 presente de indicativo		8 perfecto de indicativo	
me divierto	**nos divertimos**	**me he divertido**	**nos hemos divertido**
te diviertes	**os divertís**	**te has divertido**	**os habéis divertido**
se divierte	**se divierten**	**se ha divertido**	**se han divertido**
2 imperfecto de indicativo		9 pluscuamperfecto de indicativo	
me divertía	**nos divertíamos**	**me había divertido**	**nos habíamos divertido**
te divertías	**os divertíais**	**te habías divertido**	**os habíais divertido**
se divertía	**se divertían**	**se había divertido**	**se habían divertido**
3 pretérito		10 pretérito anterior	
me divertí	**nos divertimos**	**me hube divertido**	**nos hubimos divertido**
te divertiste	**os divertisteis**	**te hubiste divertido**	**os hubisteis divertido**
se divirtió	**se divirtieron**	**se hubo divertido**	**se hubieron divertido**
4 futuro		11 futuro perfecto	
me divertiré	**nos divertiremos**	**me habré divertido**	**nos habremos divertido**
te divertirás	**os divertiréis**	**te habrás divertido**	**os habréis divertido**
se divertirá	**se divertirán**	**se habrá divertido**	**se habrán divertido**
5 potencial simple		12 potencial compuesto	
me divertiría	**nos divertiríamos**	**me habría divertido**	**nos habríamos divertido**
te divertirías	**os divertiríais**	**te habrías divertido**	**os habríais divertido**
se divertiría	**se divertirían**	**se habría divertido**	**se habrían divertido**
6 presente de subjuntivo		13 perfecto de subjuntivo	
me divierta	**nos divirtamos**	**me haya divertido**	**nos hayamos divertido**
te diviertas	**os divirtáis**	**te hayas divertido**	**os hayáis divertido**
se divierta	**se diviertan**	**se haya divertido**	**se hayan divertido**
7 imperfecto de subjuntivo		14 pluscuamperfecto de subjuntivo	
me divirtiera	**nos divirtiéramos**	**me hubiera divertido**	**nos hubiéramos divertido**
te divirtieras	**os divirtierais**	**te hubieras divertido**	**os hubierais divertido**
se divirtiera	**se divirtieran**	**se hubiera divertido**	**se hubieran divertido**
OR		OR	
me divirtiese	**nos divirtiésemos**	**me hubiese divertido**	**nos hubiésemos divertido**
te divirtieses	**os divirtieseis**	**te hubieses divertido**	**os hubieseis divertido**
se divirtiese	**se divirtiesen**	**se hubiese divertido**	**se hubiesen divertido**

	imperativo
—	**divirtámonos; no nos divirtamos**
diviértete; no te diviertas	**divertíos; no os divirtáis**
diviértase; no se divierta	**diviértanse; no se diviertan**

Words related to this verb
el divertimiento   amusement, diversion
diverso, diversa   diverse, different
la diversión   entertainment
divertir   to entertain

dormir

Gerundio **durmiendo**   Part. pas. **dormido**

to sleep

The Seven Simple Tenses		The Seven Compound Tenses	
Singular	Plural	Singular	Plural
1 presente de indicativo		**8 perfecto de indicativo**	
duermo	dormimos	he dormido	hemos dormido
duermes	dormís	has dormido	habéis dormido
duerme	duermen	ha dormido	han dormido
2 imperfecto de indicativo		**9 pluscuamperfecto de indicativo**	
dormía	dormíamos	había dormido	habíamos dormido
dormías	dormíais	habías dormido	habíais dormido
dormía	dormían	había dormido	habían dormido
3 pretérito		**10 pretérito anterior**	
dormí	dormimos	hube dormido	hubimos dormido
dormiste	dormisteis	hubiste dormido	hubisteis dormido
durmío	durmieron	hubo dormido	hubieron dormido
4 futuro		**11 futuro perfecto**	
dormiré	dormiremos	habré dormido	habremos dormido
dormirás	dormiréis	habrás dormido	habréis dormido
dormirá	dormirán	habrá dormido	habrán dormido
5 potencial simple		**12 potencial compuesto**	
dormiría	dormiríamos	habría dormido	habríamos dormido
dormirías	dormiríais	habrías dormido	habríais dormido
dormiría	dormirían	habría dormido	habrían dormido
6 presente de subjuntivo		**13 perfecto de subjuntivo**	
duerma	durmamos	haya dormido	hayamos dormido
duermas	durmáis	hayas dormido	hayáis dormido
duerma	duerman	haya dormido	hayan dormido
7 imperfecto de subjuntivo		**14 pluscuamperfecto de subjuntivo**	
durmiera	durmiéramos	hubiera dormido	hubiéramos dormido
durmieras	durmierais	hubieras dormido	hubierais dormido
durmiera	durmieran	hubiera dormido	hubieran dormido
OR		OR	
durmiese	durmiésemos	hubiese dormido	hubiésemos dormido
durmieses	durmieseis	hubieses dormido	hubieseis dormido
durmiese	durmiesen	hubiese dormido	hubiesen dormido

imperativo	
—	durmamos
duerme; no duermas	dormid; no durmáis
duerma	duerman

Words and expressions related to this verb
dormirse   to fall asleep; (pres. part.: **durmiéndose**)
dormir a pierna suelta   to sleep soundly
dormitar   to doze
el dormitorio   bedroom, dormitory

132

Gerundio **durmiéndose**   Part. pas. **dormido**   **dormirse**

to fall asleep

The Seven Simple Tenses		The Seven Compound Tenses	
Singular	Plural	Singular	Plural
1 presente de indicativo		8 perfecto de indicativo	
me duermo	nos dormimos	me he dormido	nos hemos dormido
te duermes	os dormís	te has dormido	os habéis dormido
se duerme	se duermen	se ha dormido	se han dormido
2 imperfecto de indicativo		9 pluscuamperfecto de indicativo	
me dormía	nos dormíamos	me había dormido	nos habíamos dormido
te dormías	os dormíais	te habías dormido	os habíais dormido
se dormía	se dormían	se había dormido	se habían dormido
3 pretérito		10 pretérito anterior	
me dormí	nos dormimos	me hube dormido	nos hubimos dormido
te dormiste	os dormisteis	te hubiste dormido	os hubisteis dormido
se durmió	se durmieron	se hubo dormido	se hubieron dormido
4 futuro		11 futuro perfecto	
me dormiré	nos dormiremos	me habré dormido	nos habremos dormido
te dormirás	os dormiréis	te habrás dormido	os habréis dormido
se dormirá	se dormirán	se habrá dormido	se habrán dormido
5 potencial simple		12 potencial compuesto	
me dormiría	nos dormiríamos	me habría dormido	nos habríamos dormido
te dormirías	os dormiríais	te habrías dormido	os habríais dormido
se dormiría	se dormirían	se habría dormido	se habrían dormido
6 presente de subjuntivo		13 perfecto de subjuntivo	
me duerma	nos durmamos	me haya dormido	nos hayamos dormido
te duermas	os durmáis	te hayas dormido	os hayáis dormido
se duerma	se duerman	se haya dormido	se hayan dormido
7 imperfecto de subjuntivo		14 pluscuamperfecto de subjuntivo	
me durmiera	nos durmiéramos	me hubiera dormido	nos hubiéramos dormido
te durmieras	os durmierais	te hubieras dormido	os hubierais dormido
se durmiera	se durmieran	se hubiera dormido	se hubieran dormido
OR		OR	
me durmiese	nos durmiésemos	me hubiese dormido	nos hubiésemos dormido
te durmieses	os durmieseis	te hubieses dormido	os hubieseis dormido
se durmiese	se durmiesen	se hubiese dormido	se hubiesen dormido

	imperativo	
—		durmámonos
duérmete; no te duermas		dormíos; no os durmáis
duérmase		duérmanse

Words and expressions related to this verb
dormir   to sleep
dormir a pierna suelta   to sleep soundly
dormitar   to doze
el dormitorio   bedroom, dormitory

133

dudar Gerundio **dudando** Part. pas. **dudado**

to doubt

The Seven Simple Tenses		The Seven Compound Tenses	
Singular	Plural	Singular	Plural
1 presente de indicativo		8 perfecto de indicativo	
dudo	dudamos	he dudado	hemos dudado
dudas	dudáis	has dudado	habéis dudado
duda	dudan	ha dudado	han dudado
2 imperfecto de indicativo		9 pluscuamperfecto de indicativo	
dudaba	dudábamos	había dudado	habíamos dudado
dudabas	dudabais	habías dudado	habíais dudado
dudaba	dudaban	había dudado	habían dudado
3 pretérito		10 pretérito anterior	
dudé	dudamos	hube dudado	hubimos dudado
dudaste	dudasteis	hubiste dudado	hubisteis dudado
dudó	dudaron	hubo dudado	hubieron dudado
4 futuro		11 futuro perfecto	
dudaré	dudaremos	habré dudado	habremos dudado
dudarás	dudaréis	habrás dudado	habréis dudado
dudará	dudarán	habrá dudado	habrán dudado
5 potencial simple		12 potencial compuesto	
dudaría	dudaríamos	habría dudado	habríamos dudado
dudarías	dudaríais	habrías dudado	habríais dudado
dudaría	dudarían	habría dudado	habrían dudado
6 presente de subjuntivo		13 perfecto de subjuntivo	
dude	dudemos	haya dudado	hayamos dudado
dudes	dudéis	hayas dudado	hayáis dudado
dude	duden	haya dudado	hayan dudado
7 imperfecto de subjuntivo		14 pluscuamperfecto de subjuntivo	
dudara	dudáramos	hubiera dudado	hubiéramos dudado
dudaras	dudarais	hubieras dudado	hubierais dudado
dudara	dudaran	hubiera dudado	hubieran dudado
OR		OR	
dudase	dudásemos	hubiese dudado	hubiésemos dudado
dudases	dudaseis	hubieses dudado	hubieseis dudado
dudase	dudasen	hubiese dudado	hubiesen dudado

imperativo	
—	dudemos
duda; no dudes	dudad; no dudéis
dude	duden

Words and expressions related to this verb
la duda doubt
sin duda undoubtedly, without a doubt
dudoso, dudosa doubtful
dudosamente doubtfully

poner en duda to doubt, to question
No cabe duda There is no doubt.

to cast, to fling, to hurl, to pitch, to throw

The Seven Simple Tenses		The Seven Compound Tenses	
Singular	Plural	Singular	Plural
1 presente de indicativo		8 perfecto de indicativo	
echo	echamos	he echado	hemos echado
echas	echáis	has echado	habéis echado
echa	echan	ha echado	han echado
2 imperfecto de indicativo		9 pluscuamperfecto de indicativo	
echaba	echábamos	había echado	habíamos echado
echabas	echabais	habías echado	habíais echado
echaba	echaban	había echado	habían echado
3 pretérito		10 pretérito anterior	
eché	echamos	hube echado	hubimos echado
echaste	echasteis	hubiste echado	hubisteis echado
echó	echaron	hubo echado	hubieron echado
4 futuro		11 futuro perfecto	
echaré	echaremos	habré echado	habremos echado
echarás	echaréis	habrás echado	habréis echado
echará	echarán	habrá echado	habrán echado
5 potencial simple		12 potencial compuesto	
echaría	echaríamos	habría echado	habríamos echado
echarías	echaríais	habrías echado	habríais echado
echaría	echarían	habría echado	habrían echado
6 presente de subjuntivo		13 perfecto de subjuntivo	
eche	echemos	haya echado	hayamos echado
eches	echéis	hayas echado	hayáis echado
eche	echen	haya echado	hayan echado
7 imperfecto de subjuntivo		14 pluscuamperfecto de subjuntivo	
echara	echáramos	hubiera echado	hubiéramos echado
echaras	echarais	hubieras echado	hubierais echado
echara	echaran	hubiera echado	hubieran echado
OR		OR	
echase	echásemos	hubiese echado	hubiésemos echado
echases	echaseis	hubieses echado	hubieseis echado
echase	echasen	hubiese echado	hubiesen echado

imperativo	
—	echemos
echa; no eches	echad; no echéis
eche	echen

Words and expressions related to this verb
echar mano a to grab; **echar de menos a una persona** to miss a person
echar una carta al correo to mail (post) a letter; **echar raíces** to take root
una echada, un echamiento cast, throw, casting, throwing
echarse to lie down, rest, stretch out (oneself)
desechar to reject

to exert, to exercise

The Seven Simple Tenses		The Seven Compound Tenses	
Singular	Plural	Singular	Plural
1 presente de indicativo		8 perfecto de indicativo	
ejerzo	ejercemos	he ejercido	hemos ejercido
ejerces	ejercéis	has ejercido	habéis ejercido
ejerce	ejercen	ha ejercido	han ejercido
2 imperfecto de indicativo		9 pluscuamperfecto de indicativo	
ejercía	ejercíamos	había ejercido	habíamos ejercido
ejercías	ejercíais	habías ejercido	habíais ejercido
ejercía	ejercían	había ejercido	habían ejercido
3 pretérito		10 pretérito anterior	
ejercí	ejercimos	hube ejercido	hubimos ejercido
ejerciste	ejercisteis	hubiste ejercido	hubisteis ejercido
ejerció	ejercieron	hubo ejercido	hubieron ejercido
4 futuro		11 futuro perfecto	
ejerceré	ejerceremos	habré ejercido	habremos ejercido
ejercerás	ejerceréis	habrás ejercido	habréis ejercido
ejercerá	ejercerán	habrá ejercido	habrán ejercido
5 potencial simple		12 potencial compuesto	
ejercería	ejerceríamos	habría ejercido	habríamos ejercido
ejercerías	ejerceríais	habrías ejercido	habríais ejercido
ejercería	ejercerían	habría ejercido	habrían ejercido
6 presente de subjuntivo		13 perfecto de subjuntivo	
ejerza	ejerzamos	haya ejercido	hayamos ejercido
ejerzas	ejerzáis	hayas ejercido	hayáis ejercido
ejerza	ejerzan	haya ejercido	hayan ejercido
7 imperfecto de subjuntivo		14 pluscuamperfecto de subjuntivo	
ejerciera	ejerciéramos	hubiera ejercido	hubiéramos ejercido
ejercieras	ejercierais	hubieras ejercido	hubierais ejercido
ejerciera	ejercieran	hubiera ejercido	hubieran ejercido
OR		OR	
ejerciese	ejerciésemos	hubiese ejercido	hubiésemos ejercido
ejercieses	ejercieseis	hubieses ejercido	hubieseis ejercido
ejerciese	ejerciesen	hubiese ejercido	hubiesen ejercido

	imperativo	
—	ejerzamos
ejerce; no ejerzas	ejerced; no ejerzáis
ejerza	ejerzan

Words and expressions related to this verb
el ejercicio exercise
hacer ejercicio to drill, to exercise
el ejército army
ejercitar to drill, to exercise, to train

136

Gerundio **eligiendo**   Part. pas. **elegido**   **elegir**

to elect, to select, to choose

The Seven Simple Tenses		The Seven Compound Tenses	
Singular	Plural	Singular	Plural
1 presente de indicativo		8 perfecto de indicativo	
elijo	elegimos	he elegido	hemos elegido
eliges	elegís	has elegido	habéis elegido
elige	eligen	ha elegido	han elegido
2 imperfecto de indicativo		9 pluscuamperfecto de indicativo	
elegía	elegíamos	había elegido	habíamos elegido
elegías	elegíais	habías elegido	habíais elegido
elegía	elegían	había elegido	habían elegido
3 pretérito		10 pretérito anterior	
elegí	elegimos	hube elegido	hubimos elegido
elegiste	elegisteis	hubiste elegido	hubisteis elegido
eligió	eligieron	hubo elegido	hubieron elegido
4 futuro		11 futuro perfecto	
elegiré	elegiremos	habré elegido	habremos elegido
elegirás	elegiréis	habrás elegido	habréis elegido
elegirá	elegirán	habrá elegido	habrán elegido
5 potencial simple		12 potencial compuesto	
elegiría	elegiríamos	habría elegido	habríamos elegido
elegirías	elegiríais	habrías elegido	habríais elegido
elegiría	elegirían	habría elegido	habrían elegido
6 presente de subjuntivo		13 perfecto de subjuntivo	
elija	elijamos	haya elegido	hayamos elegido
elijas	elijáis	hayas elegido	hayáis elegido
elija	elijan	haya elegido	hayan elegido
7 imperfecto de subjuntivo		14 pluscuamperfecto de subjuntivo	
eligiera	eligiéramos	hubiera elegido	hubiéramos elegido
eligieras	eligierais	hubieras elegido	hubierais elegido
eligiera	eligieran	hubiera elegido	hubieran elegido
OR		OR	
eligiese	eligiésemos	hubiese elegido	hubiésemos elegido
eligieses	eligieseis	hubieses elegido	hubieseis elegido
eligiese	eligiesen	hubiese elegido	hubiesen elegido

imperativo	
—	elijamos
elige; no elijas	elegid; no elijáis
elija	elijan

Words related to this verb
elegible eligible
la elegibilidad eligibility
la elección election

elegir + inf.   to choose + inf.
reelegir to reelect
el elector, la electora elector

137

empezar   Gerundio **empezando**   Part. pas. **empezado**

to begin, to start

The Seven Simple Tenses		The Seven Compound Tenses	
Singular	Plural	Singular	Plural
1 presente de indicativo		8 perfecto de indicativo	
empiezo	empezamos	he empezado	hemos empezado
empiezas	empezáis	has empezado	habéis empezado
empieza	empiezan	ha empezado	han empezado
2 imperfecto de indicativo		9 pluscuamperfecto de indicativo	
empezaba	empezábamos	había empezado	habíamos empezado
empezabas	empezabais	habías empezado	habíais empezado
empezaba	empezaban	había empezado	habían empezado
3 pretérito		10 pretérito anterior	
empecé	empezamos	hube empezado	hubimos empezado
empezaste	empezasteis	hubiste empezado	hubisteis empezado
empezó	empezaron	hubo empezado	hubieron empezado
4 futuro		11 futuro perfecto	
empezaré	empezaremos	habré empezado	habremos empezado
empezarás	empezaréis	habrás empezado	habréis empezado
empezará	empezarán	habrá empezado	habrán empezado
5 potencial simple		12 potencial compuesto	
empezaría	empezaríamos	habría empezado	habríamos empezado
empezarías	empezaríais	habrías empezado	habríais empezado
empezaría	empezarían	habría empezado	habrían empezado
6 presente de subjuntivo		13 perfecto de subjuntivo	
empiece	empecemos	haya empezado	hayamos empezado
empieces	empecéis	hayas empezado	hayáis empezado
empiece	empiecen	haya empezado	hayan empezado
7 imperfecto de subjuntivo		14 pluscuamperfecto de subjuntivo	
empezara	empezáramos	hubiera empezado	hubiéramos empezado
empezaras	empezarais	hubieras empezado	hubierais empezado
empezara	empezaran	hubiera empezado	hubieran empezado
OR		OR	
empezase	empezásemos	hubiese empezado	hubiésemos empezado
empezases	empezaseis	hubieses empezado	hubieseis empezado
empezase	empezasen	hubiese empezado	hubiesen empezado

imperativo	
—	empecemos
empieza; no empieces	empezad; no empecéis
empiece	empiecen

Common idiomatic expressions using this verb

empezar por + inf.   to begin by + pres. part.
empezar a + inf.   to begin + inf.; **Ricardo empieza a escribir en inglés.**
para empezar   to begin with

The Seven Simple Tenses		The Seven Compound Tenses	
Singular	Plural	Singular	Plural

1 presente de indicativo		8 perfecto de indicativo	
empleo	**empleamos**	**he empleado**	**hemos empleado**
empleas	**empleáis**	**has empleado**	**habéis empleado**
emplea	**emplean**	**ha empleado**	**han empleado**

2 imperfecto de indicativo		9 pluscuamperfecto de indicativo	
empleaba	**empleábamos**	**había empleado**	**habíamos empleado**
empleabas	**empleabais**	**habías empleado**	**habíais empleado**
empleaba	**empleaban**	**había empleado**	**habían empleado**

3 pretérito		10 pretérito anterior	
empleé	**empleamos**	**hube empleado**	**hubimos empleado**
empleaste	**empleasteis**	**hubiste empleado**	**hubisteis empleado**
empleó	**emplearon**	**hubo empleado**	**hubieron empleado**

4 futuro		11 futuro perfecto	
emplearé	**emplearemos**	**habré empleado**	**habremos empleado**
emplearás	**emplearéis**	**habrás empleado**	**habréis empleado**
empleará	**emplearán**	**habrá empleado**	**habrán empleado**

5 potencial simple		12 potencial compuesto	
emplearía	**emplearíamos**	**habría empleado**	**habríamos empleado**
emplearías	**emplearíais**	**habrías empleado**	**habríais empleado**
emplearía	**emplearían**	**habría empleado**	**habrían empleado**

6 presente de subjuntivo		13 perfecto de subjuntivo	
emplee	**empleemos**	**haya empleado**	**hayamos empleado**
emplees	**empleéis**	**hayas empleado**	**hayáis empleado**
emplee	**empleen**	**haya empleado**	**hayan empleado**

7 imperfecto de subjuntivo		14 pluscuamperfecto de subjuntivo	
empleara	**empleáramos**	**hubiera empleado**	**hubiéramos empleado**
emplearas	**emplearais**	**hubieras empleado**	**hubierais empleado**
empleara	**emplearan**	**hubiera empleado**	**hubieran empleado**
OR		OR	
emplease	**empleásemos**	**hubiese empleado**	**hubiésemos empleado**
empleases	**empleaseis**	**hubieses empleado**	**hubieseis empleado**
emplease	**empleasen**	**hubiese empleado**	**hubiesen empleado**

imperativo	
—	**empleemos**
emplea; no emplees	**emplead; no empleéis**
emplee	**empleen**

Words and expressions related to this verb
un empleado, una empleada   employee
el empleo   job, employment, occupation, use
un empleador, una empleadora   employer
EMPLEO SOLICITADO   POSITION WANTED

encontrar   Gerundio **encontrando**   Part. pas. **encontrado**

to meet, to encounter, to find

The Seven Simple Tenses		The Seven Compound Tenses	
Singular	Plural	Singular	Plural
1 presente de indicativo		**8 perfecto de indicativo**	
encuentro	encontramos	he encontrado	hemos encontrado
encuentras	encontráis	has encontrado	habéis encontrado
encuentra	encuentran	ha encontrado	han encontrado
2 imperfecto de indicativo		**9 pluscuamperfecto de indicativo**	
encontraba	encontrábamos	había encontrado	habíamos encontrado
encontrabas	encontrabais	habías encontrado	habíais encontrado
encontraba	encontraban	había encontrado	habían encontrado
3 pretérito		**10 pretérito anterior**	
encontré	encontramos	hube encontrado	hubimos encontrado
encontraste	encontrasteis	hubiste encontrado	hubisteis encontrado
encontró	encontraron	hubo encontrado	hubieron encontrado
4 futuro		**11 futuro perfecto**	
encontraré	encontraremos	habré encontrado	habremos encontrado
encontrarás	encontraréis	habrás encontrado	habréis encontrado
encontrará	encontrarán	habrá encontrado	habrán encontrado
5 potencial simple		**12 potencial compuesto**	
encontraría	encontraríamos	habría encontrado	habríamos encontrado
encontrarías	encontraríais	habrías encontrado	habríais encontrado
encontraría	encontrarían	habría encontrado	habrían encontrado
6 presente de subjuntivo		**13 perfecto de subjuntivo**	
encuentre	encontremos	haya encontrado	hayamos encontrado
encuentres	encontréis	hayas encontrado	hayáis encontrado
encuentre	encuentren	haya encontrado	hayan encontrado
7 imperfecto de subjuntivo		**14 pluscuamperfecto de subjuntivo**	
encontrara	encontráramos	hubiera encontrado	hubiéramos encontrado
encontraras	encontrarais	hubieras encontrado	hubierais encontrado
encontrara	encontraran	hubiera encontrado	hubieran encontrado
OR		OR	
encontrase	encontrásemos	hubiese encontrado	hubiésemos encontrado
encontrases	encontraseis	hubieses encontrado	hubieseis encontrado
encontrase	encontrasen	hubiese encontrado	hubiesen encontrado

imperativo	
—	encontremos
encuentra; no encuentres	encontrad; no encontréis
encuentre	encuentren

Words and expressions related to this verb
un encuentro encounter, meeting
salir al encuentro de to go to meet
encontrarse con alguien to meet someone, to run across someone

to find, to meet, to come across or upon

The Seven Simple Tenses		The Seven Compound Tenses	
Singular	Plural	Singular	Plural
1 presente de indicativo		8 perfecto de indicativo	
me encuentro	nos encontramos	me he	nos hemos
te encuentras	os encontráis	te has	os habéis + encontrado
se encuentra	se encuentran	se ha	se han
2 imperfecto de indicativo		9 pluscuamperfecto de indicativo	
me encontraba	nos encontrábamos	me había	nos habíamos
te encontrabas	os encontrabais	te habías	os habíais + encontrado
se encontraba	se encontraban	se había	se habían
3 pretérito		10 pretérito anterior	
me encontré	nos encontramos	me hube	nos hubimos
te encontraste	os encontrasteis	te hubiste	os hubisteis + encontrado
se encontró	se encontraron	se hubo	se hubieron
4 futuro		11 futuro perfecto	
me encontraré	nos encontraremos	me habré	nos habremos
te encontrarás	os encontraréis	te habrás	os habréis + encontrado
se encontrará	se encontrarán	se habrá	se habrán
5 potencial simple		12 potencial compuesto	
me encontraría	nos encontraríamos	me habría	nos habríamos
te encontrarías	os encontraríais	te habrías	os habríais + encontrado
se encontraría	se encontrarían	se habría	se habrían
6 presente de subjuntivo		13 perfecto de subjuntivo	
me encuentre	nos encontremos	me haya	nos hayamos
te encuentres	os encontréis	te hayas	os hayáis + encontrado
se encuentre	se encuentren	se haya	se hayan
7 imperfecto de subjuntivo		14 pluscuamperfecto de subjuntivo	
me encontrara	nos encontráramos	me hubiera	nos hubiéramos
te encontraras	os encontrarais	te hubieras	os hubierais + encontrado
se encontrara	se encontraran	se hubiera	se hubieran
OR		OR	
me encontrase	nos encontrásemos	me hubiese	nos hubiésemos
te encontrases	os encontraseis	te hubieses	os hubieseis + encontrado
se encontrase	se encontrasen	se hubiese	se hubiesen

imperativo	
—	encontrémonos
encuéntrate; no te encuentres	encontraos; no os encontréis
encuéntrese	encuéntrense

Words and expressions related to this verb
encontrar to meet, to encounter, to find
un encuentro encounter, meeting
salir al encuentro de to go to meet
encontrarse con alguien to meet someone, to run across someone

enfadarse   Gerundio enfadándose   Part. pas. enfadado

to become angry

The Seven Simple Tenses		The Seven Compound Tenses	
Singular	Plural	Singular	Plural
1 presente de indicativo		8 perfecto de indicativo	
me enfado	nos enfadamos	me he enfadado	nos hemos enfadado
te enfadas	os enfadáis	te has enfadado	os habéis enfadado
se enfada	se enfadan	se ha enfadado	se han enfadado
2 imperfecto de indicativo		9 pluscuamperfecto de indicativo	
me enfadaba	nos enfadábamos	me había enfadado	nos habíamos enfadado
te enfadabas	os enfadabais	te habías enfadado	os habíais enfadado
se enfadaba	se enfadaban	se había enfadado	se habían enfadado
3 pretérito		10 pretérito anterior	
me enfadé	nos enfadamos	me hube enfadado	nos hubimos enfadado
te enfadaste	os enfadasteis	te hubiste enfadado	os hubisteis enfadado
se enfadó	se enfadaron	se hubo enfadado	se hubieron enfadado
4 futuro		11 futuro perfecto	
me enfadaré	nos enfadaremos	me habré enfadado	nos habremos enfadado
te enfadarás	os enfadaréis	te habrás enfadado	os habréis enfadado
se enfadará	se enfadarán	se habrá enfadado	se habrán enfadado
5 potencial simple		12 potencial compuesto	
me enfadaría	nos enfadaríamos	me habría enfadado	nos habríamos enfadado
te enfadarías	os enfadaríais	te habrías enfadado	os habríais enfadado
se enfadaría	se enfadarían	se habría enfadado	se habrían enfadado
6 presente de subjuntivo		13 perfecto de subjuntivo	
me enfade	nos enfademos	me haya enfadado	nos hayamos enfadado
te enfades	os enfadéis	te hayas enfadado	os hayáis enfadado
se enfade	se enfaden	se haya enfadado	se hayan enfadado
7 imperfecto de subjuntivo		14 pluscuamperfecto de subjuntivo	
me enfadara	nos enfadáramos	me hubiera enfadado	nos hubiéramos enfadado
te enfadaras	os enfadarais	te hubieras enfadado	os hubierais enfadado
se enfadara	se enfadaran	se hubiera enfadado	se hubieran enfadado
OR		OR	
me enfadase	nos enfadásemos	me hubiese enfadado	nos hubiésemos enfadado
te enfadases	os enfadaseis	te hubieses enfadado	os hubieseis enfadado
se enfadase	se enfadasen	se hubiese enfadado	se hubiesen enfadado

imperativo	
—	enfadémonos
enfádate; no te enfades	enfadaos; no os enfadéis
enfádese	enfádense

Words related to this verb
enfadoso, enfadosa annoying   enfadosamente annoyingly
el enfado anger, vexation   enfadar to anger
enfadadizo, enfadadiza irritable

142

to become angry, to get angry, to get cross

The Seven Simple Tenses		The Seven Compound Tenses	
Singular	Plural	Singular	Plural
1 presente de indicativo		**8 perfecto de indicativo**	
me enojo	nos enojamos	me he enojado	nos hemos enojado
te enojas	os enojáis	te has enojado	os habéis enojado
se enoja	se enojan	se ha enojado	se han enojado
2 imperfecto de indicativo		**9 pluscuamperfecto de indicativo**	
me enojaba	nos enojábamos	me había enojado	nos habíamos enojado
te enojabas	os enojabais	te habías enojado	os habíais enojado
se enojaba	se enojaban	se había enojado	se habían enojado
3 pretérito		**10 pretérito anterior**	
me enojé	nos enojamos	me hube enojado	nos hubimos enojado
te enojaste	os enojasteis	te hubiste enojado	os hubisteis enojado
se enojó	se enojaron	se hubo enojado	se hubieron enojado
4 futuro		**11 futuro perfecto**	
me enojaré	nos enojaremos	me habré enojado	nos habremos enojado
te enojarás	os enojaréis	te habrás enojado	os habréis enojado
se enojará	se enojarán	se habrá enojado	se habrán enojado
5 potencial simple		**12 potencial compuesto**	
me enojaría	nos enojaríamos	me habría enojado	nos habríamos enojado
te enojarías	os enojaríais	te habrías enojado	os habríais enojado
se enojaría	se enojarían	se habría enojado	se habrían enojado
6 presente de subjuntivo		**13 perfecto de subjuntivo**	
me enoje	nos enojemos	me haya enojado	nos hayamos enojado
te enojes	os enojéis	te hayas enojado	os hayáis enojado
se enoje	se enojen	se haya enojado	se hayan enojado
7 imperfecto de subjuntivo		**14 pluscuamperfecto de subjuntivo**	
me enojara	nos enojáramos	me hubiera enojado	nos hubiéramos enojado
te enojaras	os enojarais	te hubieras enojado	os hubierais enojado
se enojara	se enojaran	se hubiera enojado	se hubieran enojado
OR		OR	
me enojase	nos enojásemos	me hubiese enojado	nos hubiésemos enojado
te enojases	os enojaseis	te hubieses enojado	os hubieseis enojado
se enojase	se enojasen	se hubiese enojado	se hubiesen enojado

	imperativo	
—	enojémonos	
enójate; no te enojes	enojaos; no os enojéis	
enójese	enójense	

Words and expressions related to this verb
enojar   to annoy, to irritate, to make angry, to vex; **enojarse de**   to become
   angry at someone
el enojo   anger, annoyance; **enojadizo, enojadiza**   ill-tempered, irritable
enojoso, enojosa   irritating, troublesome   **enojosamente**   angrily
enojado, enojada   angry; **una enojada**   fit of anger

143

enseñar

Gerundio **enseñando**   Part. pas. **enseñado**

to teach, to show, to point out

The Seven Simple Tenses		The Seven Compound Tenses	
Singular	Plural	Singular	Plural
1 presente de indicativo		**8 perfecto de indicativo**	
enseño	enseñamos	he enseñado	hemos enseñado
enseñas	enseñáis	has enseñado	habéis enseñado
enseña	enseñan	ha enseñado	han enseñado
2 imperfecto de indicativo		**9 pluscuamperfecto de indicativo**	
enseñaba	enseñábamos	había enseñado	habíamos enseñado
enseñabas	enseñabais	habías enseñado	habíais enseñado
enseñaba	enseñaban	había enseñado	habían enseñado
3 pretérito		**10 pretérito anterior**	
enseñé	enseñamos	hube enseñado	hubimos enseñado
enseñaste	enseñasteis	hubiste enseñado	hubisteis enseñado
enseñó	enseñaron	hubo enseñado	hubieron enseñado
4 futuro		**11 futuro perfecto**	
enseñaré	enseñaremos	habré enseñado	habremos enseñado
enseñarás	enseñaréis	habrás enseñado	habréis enseñado
enseñará	enseñarán	habrá enseñado	habrán enseñado
5 potencial simple		**12 potencial compuesto**	
enseñaría	enseñaríamos	habría enseñado	habríamos enseñado
enseñarías	enseñaríais	habrías enseñado	habríais enseñado
enseñaría	enseñarían	habría enseñado	habrían enseñado
6 presente de subjuntivo		**13 perfecto de subjuntivo**	
enseñe	enseñemos	haya enseñado	hayamos enseñado
enseñes	enseñéis	hayas enseñado	hayáis enseñado
enseñe	enseñen	haya enseñado	hayan enseñado
7 imperfecto de subjuntivo		**14 pluscuamperfecto de subjuntivo**	
enseñara	enseñáramos	hubiera enseñado	hubiéramos enseñado
enseñaras	enseñarais	hubieras enseñado	hubierais enseñado
enseñara	enseñaran	hubiera enseñado	hubieran enseñado
OR		OR	
enseñase	enseñásemos	hubiese enseñado	hubiésemos enseñado
enseñases	enseñaseis	hubieses enseñado	hubieseis enseñado
enseñase	enseñasen	hubiese enseñado	hubiesen enseñado

imperativo	
—	enseñemos
enseña; no enseñes	enseñad; no enseñéis
enseñe	enseñen

Words and expressions related to this verb

enseñarse   to teach oneself
el enseño   teaching
diseñar   to design
el diseño   design

el enseñamiento, la enseñanza   teaching, education
la enseñanza primaria   primary education
la enseñanza superior   higher education
el enseñador, la enseñadora   instructor

144

The Seven Simple Tenses		The Seven Compound Tenses	
Singular	Plural	Singular	Plural
1 presente de indicativo		**8 perfecto de indicativo**	
entiendo	entendemos	he entendido	hemos entendido
entiendes	entendéis	has entendido	habéis entendido
entiende	entienden	ha entendido	han entendido
2 imperfecto de indicativo		**9 pluscuamperfecto de indicativo**	
entendía	entendíamos	había entendido	habíamos entendido
entendías	entendíais	habías entendido	habíais entendido
entendía	entendían	había entendido	habían entendido
3 pretérito		**10 pretérito anterior**	
entendí	entendimos	hube entendido	hubimos entendido
entendiste	entendisteis	hubiste entendido	hubisteis entendido
entendió	entendieron	hubo entendido	hubieron entendido
4 futuro		**11 futuro perfecto**	
entenderé	entenderemos	habré entendido	habremos entendido
entenderás	entenderéis	habrás entendido	habréis entendido
entenderá	entenderán	habrá entendido	habrán entendido
5 potencial simple		**12 potencial compuesto**	
entendería	entenderíamos	habría entendido	habríamos entendido
entenderías	entenderíais	habrías entendido	habríais entendido
entendería	entenderían	habría entendido	habrían entendido
6 presente de subjuntivo		**13 perfecto de subjuntivo**	
entienda	entendamos	haya entendido	hayamos entendido
entiendas	entendáis	hayas entendido	hayáis entendido
entienda	entiendan	haya entendido	hayan entendido
7 imperfecto de subjuntivo		**14 pluscuamperfecto de subjuntivo**	
entendiera	entendiéramos	hubiera entendido	hubiéramos entendido
entendieras	entendierais	hubieras entendido	hubierais entendido
entendiera	entendieran	hubiera entendido	hubieran entendido
OR		OR	
entendiese	entendiésemos	hubiese entendido	hubiésemos entendido
entendieses	entendieseis	hubieses entendido	hubieseis entendido
entendiese	entendiesen	hubiese entendido	hubiesen entendido

imperativo	
—	entendamos
entiende; no entiendas	entended; no entendáis
entienda	entiendan

Words and expressions related to this verb

dar a entender to insinuate, to hint
el entender understanding
según mi entender according to my understanding
el entendimiento comprehension, understanding

entenderse to understand each other
desentenderse de to pay no attention to

entrar

Gerundio **entrando**   Part. pas. **entrado**

to enter, to go (in), to come (in)

The Seven Simple Tenses		The Seven Compound Tenses	
Singular	Plural	Singular	Plural
1 presente de indicativo		**8 perfecto de indicativo**	
entro	entramos	he entrado	hemos entrado
entras	entráis	has entrado	habéis entrado
entra	entran	ha entrado	han entrado
2 imperfecto de indicativo		**9 pluscuamperfecto de indicativo**	
entraba	entrábamos	había entrado	habíamos entrado
entrabas	entrabais	habías entrado	habíais entrado
entraba	entraban	había entrado	habían entrado
3 pretérito		**10 pretérito anterior**	
entré	entramos	hube entrado	hubimos entrado
entraste	entrasteis	hubiste entrado	hubisteis entrado
entró	entraron	hubo entrado	hubieron entrado
4 futuro		**11 futuro perfecto**	
entraré	entraremos	habré entrado	habremos entrado
entrarás	entraréis	habrás entrado	habréis entrado
entrará	entrarán	habrá entrado	habrán entrado
5 potencial simple		**12 potencial compuesto**	
entraría	entraríamos	habría entrado	habríamos entrado
entrarías	entraríais	habrías entrado	habríais entrado
entraría	entrarían	habría entrado	habrían entrado
6 presente de subjuntivo		**13 perfecto de subjuntivo**	
entre	entremos	haya entrado	hayamos entrado
entres	entréis	hayas entrado	hayáis entrado
entre	entren	haya entrado	hayan entrado
7 imperfecto de subjuntivo		**14 pluscuamperfecto de subjuntivo**	
entrara	entráramos	hubiera entrado	hubiéramos entrado
entraras	entrarais	hubieras entrado	hubierais entrado
entrara	entraran	hubiera entrado	hubieran entrado
OR		OR	
entrase	entrásemos	hubiese entrado	hubiésemos entrado
entrases	entraseis	hubieses entrado	hubieseis entrado
entrase	entrasen	hubiese entrado	hubiesen entrado

imperativo	
—	entremos
entra; no entres	entrad; no entréis
entre	entren

Words and expressions related to this verb
la entrada   entrance
entrada general   standing room (theater, movies)
entrado (entrada) en años   advanced in years

146

to enunciate, to state

The Seven Simple Tenses		The Seven Compound Tenses	
Singular	Plural	Singular	Plural
1 presente de indicativo		8 perfecto de indicativo	
enuncio	**enunciamos**	**he enunciado**	**hemos enunciado**
enuncias	**enunciáis**	**has enunciado**	**habéis enunciado**
enuncia	**enuncian**	**ha enunciado**	**han enunciado**
2 imperfecto de indicativo		9 pluscuamperfecto de indicativo	
enunciaba	**enunciábamos**	**había enunciado**	**habíamos enunciado**
enunciabas	**enunciabais**	**habías enunciado**	**habíais enunciado**
enunciaba	**enunciaban**	**había enunciado**	**habían enunciado**
3 pretérito		10 pretérito anterior	
enuncié	**enunciamos**	**hube enunciado**	**hubimos enunciado**
enunciaste	**enunciasteis**	**hubiste enunciado**	**hubisteis enunciado**
enunció	**enunciaron**	**hubo enunciado**	**hubieron enunciado**
4 futuro		11 futuro perfecto	
enunciaré	**enunciaremos**	**habré enunciado**	**habremos enunciado**
enunciarás	**enunciaréis**	**habrás enunciado**	**habréis enunciado**
enunciará	**enunciarán**	**habrá enunciado**	**habrán enunciado**
5 potencial simple		12 potencial compuesto	
enunciaría	**enunciaríamos**	**habría enunciado**	**habríamos enunciado**
enunciarías	**enunciaríais**	**habrías enunciado**	**habríais enunciado**
enunciaría	**enunciarían**	**habría enunciado**	**habrían enunciado**
6 presente de subjuntivo		13 perfecto de subjuntivo	
enuncie	**enunciemos**	**haya enunciado**	**hayamos enunciado**
enuncies	**enunciéis**	**hayas enunciado**	**hayáis enunciado**
enuncie	**enuncien**	**haya enunciado**	**hayan enunciado**
7 imperfecto de subjuntivo		14 pluscuamperfecto de subjuntivo	
enunciara	**enunciáramos**	**hubiera enunciado**	**hubiéramos enunciado**
enunciaras	**enunciarais**	**hubieras enunciado**	**hubierais enunciado**
enunciara	**enunciaran**	**hubiera enunciado**	**hubieran enunciado**
OR		OR	
enunciase	**enunciásemos**	**hubiese enunciado**	**hubiésemos enunciado**
enunciases	**enunciaseis**	**hubieses enunciado**	**hubieseis enunciado**
enunciase	**enunciasen**	**hubiese enunciado**	**hubiesen enunciado**

imperativo

—	**enunciemos**
enuncia; no enuncies	**enunciad; no enunciéis**
enuncie	**enuncien**

Words related to this verb
la enunciación   enunciation, statement, declaration
enunciativo, enunciativa   enunciative

enviar

Gerundio **enviando**　　　Part. pas. **enviado**

to send

The Seven Simple Tenses	
Singular	Plural

The Seven Compound Tenses	
Singular	Plural

1 presente de indicativo

envío	enviamos
envías	enviáis
envía	envían

8 perfecto de indicativo

he enviado	hemos enviado
has enviado	habéis enviado
ha enviado	han enviado

2 imperfecto de indicativo

enviaba	enviábamos
enviabas	enviabais
enviaba	enviaban

9 pluscuamperfecto de indicativo

había enviado	habíamos enviado
habías enviado	habíais enviado
había enviado	habían enviado

3 pretérito

envié	enviamos
enviaste	enviasteis
envió	enviaron

10 pretérito anterior

hube enviado	hubimos enviado
hubiste enviado	hubisteis enviado
hubo enviado	hubieron enviado

4 futuro

enviaré	enviaremos
enviarás	enviaréis
enviará	enviarán

11 futuro perfecto

habré enviado	habremos enviado
habrás enviado	habréis enviado
habrá enviado	habrán enviado

5 potencial simple

enviaría	enviaríamos
enviarías	enviaríais
enviaría	enviarían

12 potencial compuesto

habría enviado	habríamos enviado
habrías enviado	habríais enviado
habría enviado	habrían enviado

6 presente de subjuntivo

envíe	enviemos
envíes	enviéis
envíe	envíen

13 perfecto de subjuntivo

haya enviado	hayamos enviado
hayas enviado	hayáis enviado
haya enviado	hayan enviado

7 imperfecto de subjuntivo

enviara	enviáramos
enviaras	enviarais
enviara	enviaran
OR	
enviase	enviásemos
enviases	enviaseis
enviase	enviasen

14 pluscuamperfecto de subjuntivo

hubiera enviado	hubiéramos enviado
hubieras enviado	hubierais enviado
hubiera enviado	hubieran enviado
OR	
hubiese enviado	hubiésemos enviado
hubieses enviado	hubieseis enviado
hubiese enviado	hubiesen enviado

imperativo

—	enviemos
envía; no envíes	enviad; no enviéis
envíe	envíen

Words and expressions related to this verb

enviar a alguien a pasear to send someone to take a walk
enviador, enviadora sender; **un enviado** envoy
la enviada shipment
reenviar to send back; to forward

148

The Seven Simple Tenses		The Seven Compound Tenses	
Singular	Plural	Singular	Plural
1 presente de indicativo		8 perfecto de indicativo	
me equivoco	**nos equivocamos**	**me he**	**nos hemos**
te equivocas	**os equivocáis**	**te has**	**os habéis** + equivocado
se equivoca	**se equivocan**	**se ha**	**se han**
2 imperfecto de indicativo		9 pluscuamperfecto de indicativo	
me equivocaba	**nos equivocábamos**	**me había**	**nos habíamos**
te equivocabas	**os equivocabais**	**te habías**	**os habíais** + equivocado
se equivocaba	**se equivocaban**	**se había**	**se habían**
3 pretérito		10 pretérito anterior	
me equivoqué	**nos equivocamos**	**me hube**	**nos hubimos**
te equivocaste	**os equivocasteis**	**te hubiste**	**os hubisteis** + equivocado
se equivocó	**se equivocaron**	**se hubo**	**se hubieron**
4 futuro		11 futuro perfecto	
me equivocaré	**nos equivocaremos**	**me habré**	**nos habremos**
te equivocarás	**os equivocaréis**	**te habrás**	**os habréis** + equivocado
se equivocará	**se equivocarán**	**se habrá**	**se habrán**
5 potencial simple		12 potencial compuesto	
me equivocaría	**nos equivocaríamos**	**me habría**	**nos habríamos**
te equivocarías	**os equivocaríais**	**te habrías**	**os habríais** + equivocado
se equivocaría	**se equivocarían**	**se habría**	**se habrían**
6 presente de subjuntivo		13 perfecto de subjuntivo	
me equivoque	**nos equivoquemos**	**me haya**	**nos hayamos**
te equivoques	**os equivoquéis**	**te hayas**	**os hayáis** + equivocado
se equivoque	**se equivoquen**	**se haya**	**se hayan**
7 imperfecto de subjuntivo		14 pluscuamperfecto de subjuntivo	
me equivocara	**nos equivocáramos**	**me hubiera**	**nos hubiéramos**
te equivocaras	**os equivocarais**	**te hubieras**	**os hubierais** + equivocado
se equivocara	**se equivocaran**	**se hubiera**	**se hubieran**
OR		OR	
me equivocase	**nos equivocásemos**	**me hubiese**	**nos hubiésemos**
te equivocases	**os equivocaseis**	**te hubieses**	**os hubieseis** + equivocado
se equivocase	**se equivocasen**	**se hubiese**	**se hubiesen**

imperativo	
—	**equivoquémonos**
equivócate; no te equivoques	**equivocaos; no os equivoquéis**
equivóquese	**equivóquense**

Words related to this verb
equivoquista quibbler
equivocado, equivocada mistaken
una equivocación error, mistake, equivocation

errar	Gerundio errando	Part. pas. errado

to err, to wander, to roam, to miss

The Seven Simple Tenses		The Seven Compound Tenses	
Singular	Plural	Singular	Plural
1 presente de indicativo		8 perfecto de indicativo	
yerro	erramos	he errado	hemos errado
yerras	erráis	has errado	habéis errado
yerra	yerran	ha errado	han errado
2 imperfecto de indicativo		9 pluscuamperfecto de indicativo	
erraba	errábamos	había errado	habíamos errado
errabas	errabais	habías errado	habíais errado
erraba	erraban	había errado	habían errado
3 pretérito		10 pretérito anterior	
erré	erramos	hube errado	hubimos errado
erraste	errasteis	hubiste errado	hubisteis errado
erró	erraron	hubo errado	hubieron errado
4 futuro		11 futuro perfecto	
erraré	erraremos	habré errado	habremos errado
errarás	erraréis	habrás errado	habréis errado
errará	errarán	habrá errado	habrán errado
5 potencial simple		12 potencial compuesto	
erraría	erraríamos	habría errado	habríamos errado
errarías	erraríais	habrías errado	habríais errado
erraría	errarían	habría errado	habrían errado
6 presente de subjuntivo		13 perfecto de subjuntivo	
yerre	erremos	haya errado	hayamos errado
yerres	erréis	hayas errado	hayáis errado
yerre	yerren	haya errado	hayan errado
7 imperfecto de subjuntivo		14 pluscuamperfecto de subjuntivo	
errara	erráramos	hubiera errado	hubiéramos errado
erraras	errarais	hubieras errado	hubierais errado
errara	erraran	hubiera errado	hubieran errado
OR		OR	
errase	errásemos	hubiese errado	hubiésemos errado
errases	erraseis	hubieses errado	hubieseis errado
errase	errasen	hubiese errado	hubiesen errado

imperativo	
—	erremos
yerra; no yerres	errad; no erréis
yerre	yerren

Words and expressions related to this verb
una errata   erratum, typographical error
errante   errant, wandering
un error   error, mistake

un yerro   error, fault, mistake
deshacer un yerro   to amend an error

to choose, to select

The Seven Simple Tenses		The Seven Compound Tenses	
Singular	Plural	Singular	Plural
1 presente de indicativo		8 perfecto de indicativo	
escojo	escogemos	he escogido	hemos escogido
escoges	escogéis	has escogido	habéis escogido
escoge	escogen	ha escogido	han escogido
2 imperfecto de indicativo		9 pluscuamperfecto de indicativo	
escogía	escogíamos	había escogido	habíamos escogido
escogías	escogíais	habías escogido	habíais escogido
escogía	escogían	había escogido	habían escogido
3 pretérito		10 pretérito anterior	
escogí	escogimos	hube escogido	hubimos escogido
escogiste	escogisteis	hubiste escogido	hubisteis escogido
escogió	escogieron	hubo escogido	hubieron escogido
4 futuro		11 futuro perfecto	
escogeré	escogeremos	habré escogido	habremos escogido
escogerás	escogeréis	habrás escogido	habréis escogido
escogerá	escogerán	habrá escogido	habrán escogido
5 potencial simple		12 potencial compuesto	
escogería	escogeríamos	habría escogido	habríamos escogido
escogerías	escogeríais	habrías escogido	habríais escogido
escogería	escogerían	habría escogido	habrían escogido
6 presente de subjuntivo		13 perfecto de subjuntivo	
escoja	escojamos	haya escogido	hayamos escogido
escojas	escojáis	hayas escogido	hayáis escogido
escoja	escojan	haya escogido	hayan escogido
7 imperfecto de subjuntivo		14 pluscuamperfecto de subjuntivo	
escogiera	escogiéramos	hubiera escogido	hubiéramos escogido
escogieras	escogierais	hubieras escogido	hubierais escogido
escogiera	escogieran	hubiera escogido	hubieran escogido
OR		OR	
escogiese	escogiésemos	hubiese escogido	hubiésemos escogido
escogieses	escogieseis	hubieses escogido	hubieseis escogido
escogiese	escogiesen	hubiese escogido	hubiesen escogido

imperativo	
—	escojamos
escoge; no escojas	escoged; no escojáis
escoja	escojan

Words related to this verb
un escogimiento   choice, selection
escogido, escogida   chosen
See also coger.

escribir	Gerundio **escribiendo**	Part. pas. **escrito**

to write

The Seven Simple Tenses	The Seven Compound Tenses

Singular	Plural	Singular	Plural
1 presente de indicativo		8 perfecto de indicativo	
escribo	escribimos	he escrito	hemos escrito
escribes	escribís	has escrito	habéis escrito
escribe	escriben	ha escrito	han escrito
2 imperfecto de indicativo		9 pluscuamperfecto de indicativo	
escribía	escribíamos	había escrito	habíamos escrito
escribías	escribíais	habías escrito	habíais escrito
escribía	escribían	había escrito	habían escrito
3 pretérito		10 pretérito anterior	
escribí	escribimos	hube escrito	hubimos escrito
escribiste	escribisteis	hubiste escrito	hubisteis escrito
escribió	escribieron	hubo escrito	hubieron escrito
4 futuro		11 futuro perfecto	
escribiré	escribiremos	habré escrito	habremos escrito
escribirás	escribiréis	habrás escrito	habréis escrito
escribirá	escribirán	habrá escrito	habrán escrito
5 potencial simple		12 potencial compuesto	
escribiría	escribiríamos	habría escrito	habríamos escrito
escribirías	escribiríais	habrías escrito	habríais escrito
escribiría	escribirían	habría escrito	habrían escrito
6 presente de subjuntivo		13 perfecto de subjuntivo	
escriba	escribamos	haya escrito	hayamos escrito
escribas	escribáis	hayas escrito	hayáis escrito
escriba	escriban	haya escrito	hayan escrito
7 imperfecto de subjuntivo		14 pluscuamperfecto de subjuntivo	
escribiera	escribiéramos	hubiera escrito	hubiéramos escrito
escribieras	escribierais	hubieras escrito	hubierais escrito
escribiera	escribieran	hubiera escrito	hubieran escrito
OR		OR	
escribiese	escribiésemos	hubiese escrito	hubiésemos escrito
escribieses	escribieseis	hubieses escrito	hubieseis escrito
escribiese	escribiesen	hubiese escrito	hubiesen escrito

imperativo	
—	escribamos
escribe; no escribas	escribid; no escribáis
escriba	escriban

Words and expressions related to this verb

una máquina de escribir typewriter	por escrito in writing
escribir a máquina to typewrite	escribir a mano to write by hand
un escritorio writing desk	describir to describe
escritor, escritora writer, author	la descripción description

152

Gerundio **escuchando**   Part. pas. **escuchado**   **escuchar**

to listen (to)

The Seven Simple Tenses		The Seven Compound Tenses	
Singular	Plural	Singular	Plural
1 presente de indicativo		8 perfecto de indicativo	
escucho	**escuchamos**	**he escuchado**	**hemos escuchado**
escuchas	**escucháis**	**has escuchado**	**habéis escuchado**
escucha	**escuchan**	**ha escuchado**	**han escuchado**
2 imperfecto de indicativo		9 pluscuamperfecto de indicativo	
escuchaba	**escuchábamos**	**había escuchado**	**habíamos escuchado**
escuchabas	**escuchabais**	**habías escuchado**	**habíais escuchado**
escuchaba	**escuchaban**	**había escuchado**	**habían escuchado**
3 pretérito		10 pretérito anterior	
escuché	**escuchamos**	**hube escuchado**	**hubimos escuchado**
escuchaste	**escuchasteis**	**hubiste escuchado**	**hubisteis escuchado**
escuchó	**escucharon**	**hubo escuchado**	**hubieron escuchado**
4 futuro		11 futuro perfecto	
escucharé	**escucharemos**	**habré escuchado**	**habremos escuchado**
escucharás	**escucharéis**	**habrás escuchado**	**habréis escuchado**
escuchará	**escucharán**	**habrá escuchado**	**habrán escuchado**
5 potencial simple		12 potencial compuesto	
escucharía	**escucharíamos**	**habría escuchado**	**habríamos escuchado**
escucharías	**escucharíais**	**habrías escuchado**	**habríais escuchado**
escucharía	**escucharían**	**habría escuchado**	**habrían escuchado**
6 presente de subjuntivo		13 perfecto de subjuntivo	
escuche	**escuchemos**	**haya escuchado**	**hayamos escuchado**
escuches	**escuchéis**	**hayas escuchado**	**hayáis escuchado**
escuche	**escuchen**	**haya escuchado**	**hayan escuchado**
7 imperfecto de subjuntivo		14 pluscuamperfecto de subjuntivo	
escuchara	**escucháramos**	**hubiera escuchado**	**hubiéramos escuchado**
escucharas	**escucharais**	**hubieras escuchado**	**hubierais escuchado**
escuchara	**escucharan**	**hubiera escuchado**	**hubieran escuchado**
OR		OR	
escuchase	**escuchásemos**	**hubiese escuchado**	**hubiésemos escuchado**
escuchases	**escuchaseis**	**hubieses escuchado**	**hubieseis escuchado**
escuchase	**escuchasen**	**hubiese escuchado**	**hubiesen escuchado**

	imperativo	
—	**escuchemos**	
escucha; no escuches	**escuchad; no escuchéis**	
escuche	**escuchen**	

Words related to this verb

escuchar + noun   to listen to + noun
Escucho la música.   I'm listening to the music.
escuchador, escuchadora, escuchante   listener

153

to scatter, to spread

The Seven Simple Tenses		The Seven Compound Tenses	
Singular	Plural	Singular	Plural
1 presente de indicativo		8 perfecto de indicativo	
esparzo	esparcimos	he esparcido	hemos esparcido
esparces	esparcís	has esparcido	habéis esparcido
esparce	esparcen	ha esparcido	han esparcido
2 imperfecto de indicativo		9 pluscuamperfecto de indicativo	
esparcía	esparcíamos	había esparcido	habíamos esparcido
esparcías	esparcíais	habías esparcido	habíais esparcido
esparcía	esparcían	había esparcido	habian esparcido
3 pretérito		10 pretérito anterior	
esparcí	esparcimos	hube esparcido	hubimos esparcido
esparciste	esparcisteis	hubiste esparcido	hubisteis esparcido
esparció	esparcieron	hubo esparcido	hubieron esparcido
4 futuro		11 futuro perfecto	
esparciré	esparciremos	habré esparcido	habremos esparcido
esparcirás	esparciréis	habrás esparcido	habréis esparcido
esparcirá	esparcirán	habrá esparcido	habrán esparcido
5 potencial simple		12 potencial compuesto	
esparciría	esparciríamos	habría esparcido	habríamos esparcido
esparcirías	esparciríais	habrías esparcido	habríais esparcido
esparciría	esparcirían	habría esparcido	habrían esparcido
6 presente de subjuntivo		13 perfecto de subjuntivo	
esparza	esparzamos	haya esparcido	hayamos esparcido
esparzas	esparzáis	hayas esparcido	hayáis esparcido
esparza	esparzan	haya esparcido	hayan esparcido
7 imperfecto de subjuntivo		14 pluscuamperfecto de subjuntivo	
esparciera	esparciéramos	hubiera esparcido	hubiéramos esparcido
esparcieras	esparcierais	hubieras esparcido	hubierais esparcido
esparciera	esparcieran	hubiera esparcido	hubieran esparcido
OR		OR	
esparciese	esparciésemos	hubiese esparcido	hubiésemos esparcido
esparcieses	esparcieseis	hubieses esparcido	hubieseis esparcido
esparciese	esparciesen	hubiese esparcido	hubiesen esparcido

	imperativo	
—		esparzamos
esparce; no esparzas		esparcid; no esparzáis
esparza		esparzan

Words related to this verb

el esparcimiento scattering, spreading
esparcidamente separately, here and there
el esparcidor, la esparcidora spreader, scatterer

Gerundio **esperando**   Part. pas. **esperado**   **esperar**

to expect, to hope, to wait (for)

The Seven Simple Tenses		The Seven Compound Tenses	
Singular	Plural	Singular	Plural
1 presente de indicativo		**8 perfecto de indicativo**	
espero	esperamos	he esperado	hemos esperado
esperas	esperáis	has esperado	habéis esperado
espera	esperan	ha esperado	han esperado
2 imperfecto de indicativo		**9 pluscuamperfecto de indicativo**	
esperaba	esperábamos	había esperado	habíamos esperado
esperabas	esperabais	habías esperado	habíais esperado
esperaba	esperaban	había esperado	habían esperado
3 pretérito		**10 pretérito anterior**	
esperé	esperamos	hube esperado	hubimos esperado
esperaste	esperasteis	hubiste esperado	hubisteis esperado
esperó	esperaron	hubo esperado	hubieron esperado
4 futuro		**11 futuro perfecto**	
esperaré	esperaremos	habré esperado	habremos esperado
esperarás	esperaréis	habrás esperado	habréis esperado
esperará	esperarán	habrá esperado	habrán esperado
5 potencial simple		**12 potencial compuesto**	
esperaría	esperaríamos	habría esperado	habríamos esperado
esperarías	esperaríais	habrías esperado	habríais esperado
esperaría	esperarían	habría esperado	habrían esperado
6 presente de subjuntivo		**13 perfecto de subjuntivo**	
espere	esperemos	haya esperado	hayamos esperado
esperes	esperéis	hayas esperado	hayáis esperado
espere	esperen	haya esperado	hayan esperado
7 imperfecto de subjuntivo		**14 pluscuamperfecto de subjuntivo**	
esperara	esperáramos	hubiera esperado	hubiéramos esperado
esperaras	esperarais	hubieras esperado	hubierais esperado
esperara	esperaran	hubiera esperado	hubieran esperado
OR		OR	
esperase	esperásemos	hubiese esperado	hubiésemos esperado
esperases	esperaseis	hubieses esperado	hubieseis esperado
esperase	esperasen	hubiese esperado	hubiesen esperado

imperativo	
—	esperemos
espera; no esperes	esperad; no esperéis
espere	esperen

Sentences using this verb and words related to it
Mientras hay vida hay esperanza.   Where there is life there is hope.
la esperanza hope
No hay esperanza.   There is no hope.
dar esperanzas to give encouragement
desesperar to despair

estar	Gerundio **estando**	Part. pas. **estado**

to be

The Seven Simple Tenses		The Seven Compound Tenses	
Singular	Plural	Singular	Plural
1 presente de indicativo		8 perfecto de indicativo	
estoy	estamos	he estado	hemos estado
estás	estáis	has estado	habéis estado
está	están	ha estado	han estado
2 imperfecto de indicativo		9 pluscuamperfecto de indicativo	
estaba	estábamos	había estado	habíamos estado
estabas	estabais	habías estado	habíais estado
estaba	estaban	había estado	habían estado
3 pretérito		10 pretérito anterior	
estuve	estuvimos	hube estado	hubimos estado
estuviste	estuvisteis	hubiste estado	hubisteis estado
estuvo	estuvieron	hubo estado	hubieron estado
4 futuro		11 futuro perfecto	
estaré	estaremos	habré estado	habremos estado
estarás	estaréis	habrás estado	habréis estado
estará	estarán	habrá estado	habrán estado
5 potencial simple		12 potencial compuesto	
estaría	estaríamos	habría estado	habríamos estado
estarías	estaríais	habrías estado	habríais estado
estaría	estarían	habría estado	habrían estado
6 presente de subjuntivo		13 perfecto de subjuntivo	
esté	estemos	haya estado	hayamos estado
estés	estéis	hayas estado	hayáis estado
esté	estén	haya estado	hayan estado
7 imperfecto de subjuntivo		14 pluscuamperfecto de subjuntivo	
estuviera	estuviéramos	hubiera estado	hubiéramos estado
estuvieras	estuvierais	hubieras estado	hubierais estado
estuviera	estuvieran	hubiera estado	hubieran estado
OR		OR	
estuviese	estuviésemos	hubiese estado	hubiésemos estado
estuvieses	estuvieseis	hubieses estado	hubieseis estado
estuviese	estuviesen	hubiese estado	hubiesen estado

	imperativo	
—	estemos	
está; no estés	estad; no estéis	
esté	estén	

Common idiomatic expressions using this verb
—¿Cómo está Ud.?
—Estoy muy bien, gracias. ¿Y usted?
—Estoy enfermo hoy.

estar para + inf.   to be about + inf.
Estoy para salir.   I am about to go out.
estar por   to be in favor of

156

Gerundio **estudiando**   Part. pas. **estudiado**   **estudiar**

to study

The Seven Simple Tenses		The Seven Compound Tenses	
Singular	Plural	Singular	Plural
1 presente de indicativo		8 perfecto de indicativo	
estudio	**estudiamos**	**he estudiado**	**hemos estudiado**
estudias	**estudiáis**	**has estudiado**	**habéis estudiado**
estudia	**estudian**	**ha estudiado**	**han estudiado**
2 imperfecto de indicativo		9 pluscuamperfecto de indicativo	
estudiaba	**estudiábamos**	**había estudiado**	**habíamos estudiado**
estudiabas	**estudiabais**	**habías estudiado**	**habíais estudiado**
estudiaba	**estudiaban**	**había estudiado**	**habían estudiado**
3 pretérito		10 pretérito anterior	
estudié	**estudiamos**	**hube estudiado**	**hubimos estudiado**
estudiaste	**estudiasteis**	**hubiste estudiado**	**hubisteis estudiado**
estudió	**estudiaron**	**hubo estudiado**	**hubieron estudiado**
4 futuro		11 futuro perfecto	
estudiaré	**estudiaremos**	**habré estudiado**	**habremos estudiado**
estudiarás	**estudiaréis**	**habrás estudiado**	**habréis estudiado**
estudiará	**estudiarán**	**habrá estudiado**	**habrán estudiado**
5 potencial simple		12 potencial compuesto	
estudiaría	**estudiaríamos**	**habría estudiado**	**habríamos estudiado**
estudiarías	**estudiaríais**	**habrías estudiado**	**habríais estudiado**
estudiaría	**estudiarían**	**habría estudiado**	**habrían estudiado**
6 presente de subjuntivo		13 perfecto de subjuntivo	
estudie	**estudiemos**	**haya estudiado**	**hayamos estudiado**
estudies	**estudiéis**	**hayas estudiado**	**hayáis estudiado**
estudie	**estudien**	**haya estudiado**	**hayan estudiado**
7 imperfecto de subjuntivo		14 pluscuamperfecto de subjuntivo	
estudiara	**estudiáramos**	**hubiera estudiado**	**hubiéramos estudiado**
estudiaras	**estudiarais**	**hubieras estudiado**	**hubierais estudiado**
estudiara	**estudiaran**	**hubiera estudiado**	**hubieran estudiado**
OR		OR	
estudiase	**estudiásemos**	**hubiese estudiado**	**hubiésemos estudiado**
estudiases	**estudiaseis**	**hubieses estudiado**	**hubieseis estudiado**
estudiase	**estudiasen**	**hubiese estudiado**	**hubiesen estudiado**

	imperativo	
—		**estudiemos**
estudia; no estudies		**estudiad; no estudiéis**
estudie		**estudien**

Words related to this verb

un, una estudiante   student
el estudio   study, studio, study room
estudioso, estudiosa   studious

altos estudios   advanced studies
estudiosamente   studiously

exigir Gerundio **exigiendo** Part. pas. **exigido**

to demand, to urge, to require

The Seven Simple Tenses		The Seven Compound Tenses	
Singular	Plural	Singular	Plural
1 presente de indicativo		**8 perfecto de indicativo**	
exijo	exigimos	he exigido	hemos exigido
exiges	exigís	has exigido	habéis exigido
exige	exigen	ha exigido	han exigido
2 imperfecto de indicativo		**9 pluscuamperfecto de indicativo**	
exigía	exigíamos	había exigido	habíamos exigido
exigías	exigíais	habías exigido	habíais exigido
exigía	exigían	había exigido	habían exigido
3 pretérito		**10 pretérito anterior**	
exigí	exigimos	hube exigido	hubimos exigido
exigiste	exigisteis	hubiste exigido	hubisteis exigido
exigió	exigieron	hubo exigido	hubieron exigido
4 futuro		**11 futuro perfecto**	
exigiré	exigiremos	habré exigido	habremos exigido
exigirás	exigiréis	habrás exigido	habréis exigido
exigirá	exigirán	habrá exigido	habrán exigido
5 potencial simple		**12 potencial compuesto**	
exigiría	exigiríamos	habría exigido	habríamos exigido
exigirías	exigiríais	habrías exigido	habríais exigido
exigiría	exigirían	habría exigido	habrían exigido
6 presente de subjuntivo		**13 perfecto de subjuntivo**	
exija	exijamos	haya exigido	hayamos exigido
exijas	exijáis	hayas exigido	hayáis exigido
exija	exijan	haya exigido	hayan exigido
7 imperfecto de subjuntivo		**14 pluscuamperfecto de subjuntivo**	
exigiera	exigiéramos	hubiera exigido	hubiéramos exigido
exigieras	exigierais	hubieras exigido	hubierais exigido
exigiera	exigieran	hubiera exigido	hubieran exigido
OR		OR	
exigiese	exigiésemos	hubiese exigido	hubiésemos exigido
exigieses	exigieseis	hubieses exigido	hubieseis exigido
exigiese	exigiesen	hubiese exigido	hubiesen exigido

imperativo	
—	exijamos
exige; no exijas	exigid; no exijáis
exija	exijan

Words and expressions related to this verb
exigente exacting, demanding
la exigencia exigency, requirement
exigir el pago to demand payment

Gerundio **explicando**   Part. pas. **explicado**   **explicar**

to explain

The Seven Simple Tenses		The Seven Compound Tenses	
Singular	Plural	Singular	Plural
1 presente de indicativo		8 perfecto de indicativo	
explico	explicamos	he explicado	hemos explicado
explicas	explicáis	has explicado	habéis explicado
explica	explican	ha explicado	han explicado
2 imperfecto de indicativo		9 pluscuamperfecto de indicativo	
explicaba	explicábamos	había explicado	habíamos explicado
explicabas	explicabais	habías explicado	habíais explicado
explicaba	explicaban	había explicado	habían explicado
3 pretérito		10 pretérito anterior	
expliqué	explicamos	hube explicado	hubimos explicado
explicaste	explicasteis	hubiste explicado	hubisteis explicado
explicó	explicaron	hubo explicado	hubieron explicado
4 futuro		11 futuro perfecto	
explicaré	explicaremos	habré explicado	habremos explicado
explicarás	explicaréis	habrás explicado	habréis explicado
explicará	explicarán	habrá explicado	habrán explicado
5 potencial simple		12 potencial compuesto	
explicaría	explicaríamos	habría explicado	habríamos explicado
explicarías	explicaríais	habrías explicado	habríais explicado
explicaría	explicarían	habría explicado	habrían explicado
6 presente de subjuntivo		13 perfecto de subjuntivo	
explique	expliquemos	haya explicado	hayamos explicado
expliques	expliquéis	hayas explicado	hayáis explicado
explique	expliquen	haya explicado	hayan explicado
7 imperfecto de subjuntivo		14 pluscuamperfecto de subjuntivo	
explicara	explicáramos	hubiera explicado	hubiéramos explicado
explicaras	explicarais	hubieras explicado	hubierais explicado
explicara	explicaran	hubiera explicado	hubieran explicado
OR		OR	
explicase	explicásemos	hubiese explicado	hubiésemos explicado
explicases	explicaseis	hubieses explicado	hubieseis explicado
explicase	explicasen	hubiese explicado	hubiesen explicado

imperativo	
—	expliquemos
explica; no expliques	explicad; no expliquéis
explique	expliquen

Words and expressions related to this verb
una explicación   explanation
explícito, explícita   explicit   **explicativo, explicativa**   explanatory
explícitamente   explicitly   **pedir explicaciones**   to demand an explanation

expresar　　　　　　　Gerundio **expresando**　　　Part. pas. **expresado**

to express

The Seven Simple Tenses		The Seven Compound Tenses	
Singular	Plural	Singular	Plural
1　presente de indicativo		8　perfecto de indicativo	
expreso	expresamos	he expresado	hemos expresado
expresas	expresáis	has expresado	habéis expresado
expresa	expresan	ha expresado	han expresado
2　imperfecto de indicativo		9　pluscuamperfecto de indicativo	
expresaba	expresábamos	había expresado	habíamos expresado
expresabas	expresabais	habías expresado	habíais expresado
expresaba	expresaban	había expresado	habían expresado
3　pretérito		10　pretérito anterior	
expresé	expresamos	hube expresado	hubimos expresado
expresaste	expresasteis	hubiste expresado	hubisteis expresado
expresó	expresaron	hubo expresado	hubieron expresado
4　futuro		11　futuro perfecto	
expresaré	expresaremos	habré expresado	habremos expresado
expresarás	expresaréis	habrás expresado	habréis expresado
expresará	expresarán	habrá expresado	habrán expresado
5　potencial simple		12　potencial compuesto	
expresaría	expresaríamos	habría expresado	habríamos expresado
expresarías	expresaríais	habrías expresado	habríais expresado
expresaría	expresarían	habría expresado	habrían expresado
6　presente de subjuntivo		13　perfecto de subjuntivo	
exprese	expresemos	haya expresado	hayamos expresado
expreses	expreséis	hayas expresado	hayáis expresado
exprese	expresen	haya expresado	hayan expresado
7　imperfecto de subjuntivo		14　pluscuamperfecto de subjuntivo	
expresara	expresáramos	hubiera expresado	hubiéramos expresado
expresaras	expresarais	hubieras expresado	hubierais expresado
expresara	expresaran	hubiera expresado	hubieran expresado
OR		OR	
expresase	expresásemos	hubiese expresado	hubiésemos expresado
expresases	expresaseis	hubieses expresado	hubieseis expresado
expresase	expresasen	hubiese expresado	hubiesen expresado

	imperativo	
—	expresemos	
expresa; no expreses	expresad; no expreséis	
exprese	expresen	

Words and expressions related to this verb

expresarse　to express oneself
una expresión　expression, phrase
expresamente　expressly, on purpose
expresivamente　expressively

expresiones de mi parte　kindest regards
el expresionismo　expressionism
expreso　express (train, etc.)

to be lacking, to be wanting, to lack, to miss, to need

The Seven Simple Tenses		The Seven Compound Tenses	
Singular	Plural	Singular	Plural
1 presente de indicativo		8 perfecto de indicativo	
falto	faltamos	he faltado	hemos faltado
faltas	faltáis	has faltado	habéis faltado
falta	faltan	ha faltado	han faltado
2 imperfecto de indicativo		9 pluscuamperfecto de indicativo	
faltaba	faltábamos	había faltado	habíamos faltado
faltabas	faltabais	habías faltado	habíais faltado
faltaba	faltaban	había faltado	habían faltado
3 pretérito		10 pretérito anterior	
falté	faltamos	hube faltado	hubimos faltado
faltaste	faltasteis	hubiste faltado	hubisteis faltado
faltó	faltaron	hubo faltado	hubieron faltado
4 futuro		11 futuro perfecto	
faltaré	faltaremos	habré faltado	habremos faltado
faltarás	faltaréis	habrás faltado	habréis faltado
faltará	faltarán	habrá faltado	habrán faltado
5 potencial simple		12 potencial compuesto	
faltaría	faltaríamos	habría faltado	habríamos faltado
faltarías	faltaríais	habrías faltado	habríais faltado
faltaría	faltarían	habría faltado	habrían faltado
6 presente de subjuntivo		13 perfecto de subjuntivo	
falte	faltemos	haya faltado	hayamos faltado
faltes	faltéis	hayas faltado	hayáis faltado
falte	falten	haya faltado	hayan faltado
7 imperfecto de subjuntivo		14 pluscuamperfecto de subjuntivo	
faltara	faltáramos	hubiera faltado	hubiéramos faltado
faltaras	faltarais	hubieras faltado	hubierais faltado
faltara	faltaran	hubiera faltado	hubieran faltado
OR		OR	
faltase	faltásemos	hubiese faltado	hubiésemos faltado
faltases	faltaseis	hubieses faltado	hubieseis faltado
faltase	faltasen	hubiese faltado	hubiesen faltado

imperativo	
—	faltemos
falta; no faltes	faltad; no faltéis
falte	falten

Common idiomatic expressions using this verb

a falta de   for lack of
sin falta   without fail, without fault
la falta   lack, want
faltante   lacking, wanting

poner faltas a   to find fault with
¡No faltaba más!   That's the limit!
hacer falta   to be necessary

felicitar Gerundio **felicitando** Part. pas. **felicitado**

to congratulate, to felicitate

The Seven Simple Tenses		The Seven Compound Tenses	
Singular	Plural	Singular	Plural
1 presente de indicativo		**8 perfecto de indicativo**	
felicito	felicitamos	he felicitado	hemos felicitado
felicitas	felicitáis	has felicitado	habéis felicitado
felicita	felicitan	ha felicitado	han felicitado
2 imperfecto de indicativo		**9 pluscuamperfecto de indicativo**	
felicitaba	felicitábamos	había felicitado	habíamos felicitado
felicitabas	felicitabais	habías felicitado	habíais felicitado
felicitaba	felicitaban	había felicitado	habían felicitado
3 pretérito		**10 pretérito anterior**	
felicité	felicitamos	hube felicitado	hubimos felicitado
felicitaste	felicitasteis	hubiste felicitado	hubisteis felicitado
felicitó	felicitaron	hubo felicitado	hubieron felicitado
4 futuro		**11 futuro perfecto**	
felicitaré	felicitaremos	habré felicitado	habremos felicitado
felicitarás	felicitaréis	habrás felicitado	habréis felicitado
felicitará	felicitarán	habrá felicitado	habrán felicitado
5 potencial simple		**12 potencial compuesto**	
felicitaría	felicitaríamos	habría felicitado	habríamos felicitado
felicitarías	felicitaríais	habrías felicitado	habríais felicitado
felicitaría	felicitarían	habría felicitado	habrían felicitado
6 presente de subjuntivo		**13 perfecto de subjuntivo**	
felicite	felicitemos	haya felicitado	hayamos felicitado
felicites	felicitéis	hayas felicitado	hayáis felicitado
felicite	feliciten	haya felicitado	hayan felicitado
7 imperfecto de subjuntivo		**14 pluscuamperfecto de subjuntivo**	
felicitara	felicitáramos	hubiera felicitado	hubiéramos felicitado
felicitaras	felicitarais	hubieras felicitado	hubierais felicitado
felicitara	felicitaran	hubiera felicitado	hubieran felicitado
OR		OR	
felicitase	felicitásemos	hubiese felicitado	hubiésemos felicitado
felicitases	felicitaseis	hubieses felicitado	hubieseis felicitado
felicitase	felicitasen	hubiese felicitado	hubiesen felicitado

imperativo	
—	felicitemos
felicita; no felicites	felicitad; no felicitéis
felicite	feliciten

Words related to this verb
la felicitación, las felicitaciones congratulations **feliz** happy, fortunate, lucky
la felicidad happiness, good fortune *(pl.* felices)
felizmente happily, fortunately **Felices Fiestas** Happy Holidays

Gerundio **fiando** Part. pas. **fiado** **fiar**

to confide, to trust

The Seven Simple Tenses		The Seven Compound Tenses	
Singular	Plural	Singular	Plural
1 presente de indicativo		8 perfecto de indicativo	
fío	fiamos	he fiado	hemos fiado
fías	fiáis	has fiado	habéis fiado
fía	fían	ha fiado	han fiado
2 imperfecto de indicativo		9 pluscuamperfecto de indicativo	
fiaba	fiábamos	había fiado	habíamos fiado
fiabas	fiabais	habías fiado	habíais fiado
fiaba	fiaban	había fiado	habían fiado
3 pretérito		10 pretérito anterior	
fié	fiamos	hube fiado	hubimos fiado
fiaste	fiasteis	hubiste fiado	hubisteis fiado
fió	fiaron	hubo fiado	hubieron fiado
4 futuro		11 futuro perfecto	
fiaré	fiaremos	habré fiado	habremos fiado
fiarás	fiaréis	habrás fiado	habréis fiado
fiará	fiarán	habrá fiado	habrán fiado
5 potencial simple		12 potencial compuesto	
fiaría	fiaríamos	habría fiado	habríamos fiado
fiarías	fiaríais	habrías fiado	habríais fiado
fiaría	fiarían	habría fiado	habrían fiado
6 presente de subjuntivo		13 perfecto de subjuntivo	
fíe	fiemos	haya fiado	hayamos fiado
fíes	fiéis	hayas fiado	hayáis fiado
fíe	fíen	haya fiado	hayan fiado
7 imperfecto de subjuntivo		14 pluscuamperfecto de subjuntivo	
fiara	fiáramos	hubiera fiado	hubiéramos fiado
fiaras	fiarais	hubieras fiado	hubierais fiado
fiara	fiaran	hubiera fiado	hubieran fiado
OR		OR	
fiase	fiásemos	hubiese fiado	hubiésemos fiado
fiases	fiaseis	hubieses fiado	hubieseis fiado
fiase	fiasen	hubiese fiado	hubiesen fiado

	imperativo	
—	fiemos	
fía; no fíes	fiad; no fiéis	
fíe	fíen	

Words and expressions related to this verb

fiarse de   to have confidence in
la fianza   security, surety, guarantee
al fiado   on credit, on trust

fiable   trustworthy
fiar en   to trust in
el fiat   consent, fiat

163

fijar   Gerundio **fijando**   Part. pas. **fijado** (**fijo,** when used as an *adj.*)

to clinch, to fasten, to fix

The Seven Simple Tenses		The Seven Compound Tenses	
Singular	Plural	Singular	Plural
1 presente de indicativo		8 perfecto de indicativo	
fijo	fijamos	he fijado	hemos fijado
fijas	fijáis	has fijado	habéis fijado
fija	fijan	ha fijado	han fijado
2 imperfecto de indicativo		9 pluscuamperfecto de indicativo	
fijaba	fijábamos	había fijado	habíamos fijado
fijabas	fijabais	habías fijado	habíais fijado
fijaba	fijaban	había fijado	habían fijado
3 pretérito		10 pretérito anterior	
fijé	fijamos	hube fijado	hubimos fijado
fijaste	fijasteis	hubiste fijado	hubisteis fijado
fijó	fijaron	hubo fijado	hubieron fijado
4 futuro		11 futuro perfecto	
fijaré	fijaremos	habré fijado	habremos fijado
fijarás	fijaréis	habrás fijado	habréis fijado
fijará	fijarán	habrá fijado	habrán fijado
5 potencial simple		12 potencial compuesto	
fijaría	fijaríamos	habría fijado	habríamos fijado
fijarías	fijaríais	habrías fijado	habríais fijado
fijaría	fijarían	habría fijado	habrían fijado
6 presente de subjuntivo		13 perfecto de subjuntivo	
fije	fijemos	haya fijado	hayamos fijado
fijes	fijéis	hayas fijado	hayáis fijado
fije	fijen	haya fijado	hayan fijado
7 imperfecto de subjuntivo		14 pluscuamperfecto de subjuntivo	
fijara	fijáramos	hubiera fijado	hubiéramos fijado
fijaras	fijarais	hubieras fijado	hubierais fijado
fijara	fijaran	hubiera fijado	hubieran fijado
OR		OR	
fijase	fijásemos	hubiese fijado	hubiésemos fijado
fijases	fijaseis	hubieses fijado	hubieseis fijado
fijase	fijasen	hubiese fijado	hubiesen fijado

imperativo	
—	fijemos
fija; no fijes	fijad; no fijéis
fije	fijen

Words related to this verb

hora fija   set time, set hour, time agreed on
fijamente   fixedly, assuredly
una fija   door hinge
fijarse en   to take notice of, to pay attention to, to settle in

164

Gerundio **fijándose**   Part. pas. **fijado**   **fijarse**

to take notice, to pay attention, to settle

The Seven Simple Tenses		The Seven Compound Tenses	
Singular	Plural	Singular	Plural
1 presente de indicativo		8 perfecto de indicativo	
me fijo	nos fijamos	me he fijado	nos hemos fijado
te fijas	os fijáis	te has fijado	os habéis fijado
se fija	se fijan	se ha fijado	se han fijado
2 imperfecto de indicativo		9 pluscuamperfecto de indicativo	
me fijaba	nos fijábamos	me había fijado	nos habíamos fijado
te fijabas	os fijabais	te habías fijado	os habíais fijado
se fijaba	se fijaban	se había fijado	se habían fijado
3 pretérito		10 pretérito anterior	
me fijé	nos fijamos	me hube fijado	nos hubimos fijado
te fijaste	os fijasteis	te hubiste fijado	os hubisteis fijado
se fijó	se fijaron	se hubo fijado	se hubieron fijado
4 futuro		11 futuro perfecto	
me fijaré	nos fijaremos	me habré fijado	nos habremos fijado
te fijarás	os fijaréis	te habrás fijado	os habréis fijado
se fijará	se fijarán	se habrá fijado	se habrán fijado
5 potencial simple		12 potencial compuesto	
me fijaría	nos fijaríamos	me habría fijado	nos habríamos fijado
te fijarías	os fijaríais	te habrías fijado	os habríais fijado
se fijaría	se fijarían	se habría fijado	se habrían fijado
6 presente de subjuntivo		13 perfecto de subjuntivo	
me fije	nos fijemos	me haya fijado	nos hayamos fijado
te fijes	os fijéis	te hayas fijado	os hayáis fijado
se fije	se fijen	se haya fijado	se hayan fijado
7 imperfecto de subjuntivo		14 pluscuamperfecto de subjuntivo	
me fijara	nos fijáramos	me hubiera fijado	nos hubiéramos fijado
te fijaras	os fijarais	te hubieras fijado	os hubierais fijado
se fijara	se fijaran	se hubiera fijado	se hubieran fijado
OR		OR	
me fijase	nos fijásemos	me hubiese fijado	nos hubiésemos fijado
te fijases	os fijaseis	te hubieses fijado	os hubieseis fijado
se fijase	se fijasen	se hubiese fijado	se hubiesen fijado

imperativo	
—	fijémonos
fíjate; no te fijes	fijaos; no os fijéis
fíjese	fíjense

Words and expressions related to this verb

fijar   to clinch, to fasten, to fix; **fijo** (when used as an adj.)
fijarse en   to take notice of, to pay attention to, to settle in
hora fija   set time, set hour, time agreed on; **de fijo** surely
fijamente   fixedly, assuredly; **fijar el precio**   to fix the price

freír   Gerundio **friendo**   Part. pas. **frito** *or* **freído**

to fry

The Seven Simple Tenses		The Seven Compound Tenses	
Singular	Plural	Singular	Plural
1 presente de indicativo		8 perfecto de indicativo	
frío	freímos	he frito	hemos frito
fríes	freís	has frito	habéis frito
fríe	fríen	ha frito	han frito
2 imperfecto de indicativo		9 pluscuamperfecto de indicativo	
freía	freíamos	había frito	habíamos frito
freías	freíais	habías frito	habíais frito
freía	freían	había frito	habían frito
3 pretérito		10 pretérito anterior	
freí	freímos	hube frito	hubimos frito
freíste	freísteis	hubiste frito	hubisteis frito
frió	frieron	hubo frito	hubieron frito
4 futuro		11 futuro perfecto	
freiré	freiremos	habré frito	habremos frito
freirás	freiréis	habrás frito	habréis frito
freirá	freirán	habrá frito	habrán frito
5 potencial simple		12 potencial compuesto	
freiría	freiríamos	habría frito	habríamos frito
freirías	freiríais	habrías frito	habríais frito
freiría	freirían	habría frito	habrían frito
6 presente de subjuntivo		13 perfecto de subjuntivo	
fría	friamos	haya frito	hayamos frito
frías	friáis	hayas frito	hayáis frito
fría	frían	haya frito	hayan frito
7 imperfecto de subjuntivo		14 pluscuamperfecto de subjuntivo	
friera	friéramos	hubiera frito	hubiéramos frito
frieras	frierais	hubieras frito	hubierais frito
friera	frieran	hubiera frito	hubieran frito
OR		OR	
friese	friésemos	hubiese frito	hubiésemos frito
frieses	frieseis	hubieses frito	hubieseis frito
friese	friesen	hubiese frito	hubiesen frito

	imperativo	
—	friamos	
fríe; no frías	freíd; no friáis	
fría	frían	

Words and expressions related to this verb
patatas fritas fried potatoes, French fries   **la fritada** fried food
patatas fritas a la inglesa potato chips   **la fritura** fry

Gerundio **ganando**   Part. pas. **ganado**   **ganar**

to earn, to gain, to win

The Seven Simple Tenses		The Seven Compound Tenses	
Singular	Plural	Singular	Plural
1 presente de indicativo		8 perfecto de indicativo	
gano	ganamos	he ganado	hemos ganado
ganas	ganáis	has ganado	habéis ganado
gana	ganan	ha ganado	han ganado
2 imperfecto de indicativo		9 pluscuamperfecto de indicativo	
ganaba	ganábamos	había ganado	habíamos ganado
ganabas	ganabais	habías ganado	habíais ganado
ganaba	ganaban	había ganado	habían ganado
3 pretérito		10 pretérito anterior	
gané	ganamos	hube ganado	hubimos ganado
ganaste	ganasteis	hubiste ganado	hubisteis ganado
ganó	ganaron	hubo ganado	hubieron ganado
4 futuro		11 futuro perfecto	
ganaré	ganaremos	habré ganado	habremos ganado
ganarás	ganaréis	habrás ganado	habréis ganado
ganará	ganarán	habrá ganado	habrán ganado
5 potencial simple		12 potencial compuesto	
ganaría	ganaríamos	habría ganado	habríamos ganado
ganarías	ganaríais	habrías ganado	habríais ganado
ganaría	ganarían	habría ganado	habrían ganado
6 presente de subjuntivo		13 perfecto de subjuntivo	
gane	ganemos	haya ganado	hayamos ganado
ganes	ganéis	hayas ganado	hayáis ganado
gane	ganen	haya ganado	hayan ganado
7 imperfecto de subjuntivo		14 pluscuamperfecto de subjuntivo	
ganara	ganáramos	hubiera ganado	hubiéramos ganado
ganaras	ganarais	hubieras ganado	hubierais ganado
ganara	ganaran	hubiera ganado	hubieran ganado
OR		OR	
ganase	ganásemos	hubiese ganado	hubiésemos ganado
ganases	ganaseis	hubieses ganado	hubieseis ganado
ganase	ganasen	hubiese ganado	hubiesen ganado

	imperativo
—	ganemos
gana; no ganes	ganad; no ganéis
gane	ganen

Words and expressions related to this verb
ganar el pan, ganar la vida   to earn a living
la ganancia   profit, gain
ganador, ganadora   winner
ganar dinero   to earn (make) money

desganar   to dissuade
desganarse   to lose one's appetite; to be bored

gemir Gerundio **gimiendo** Part. pas. **gemido**

to grieve, to groan, to moan

The Seven Simple Tenses		The Seven Compound Tenses	
Singular	Plural	Singular	Plural
1 presente de indicativo		8 perfecto de indicativo	
gimo	gemimos	he gemido	hemos gemido
gimes	gemís	has gemido	habéis gemido
gime	gimen	ha gemido	han gemido
2 imperfecto de indicativo		9 pluscuamperfecto de indicativo	
gemía	gemíamos	había gemido	habíamos gemido
gemías	gemíais	habías gemido	habíais gemido
gemía	gemían	había gemido	habían gemido
3 pretérito		10 pretérito anterior	
gemí	gemimos	hube gemido	hubimos gemido
gemiste	gemisteis	hubiste gemido	hubisteis gemido
gimió	gimieron	hubo gemido	hubieron gemido
4 futuro		11 futuro perfecto	
gemiré	gemiremos	habré gemido	habremos gemido
gemirás	gemiréis	habrás gemido	habréis gemido
gemirá	gemirán	habrá gemido	habrán gemido
5 potencial simple		12 potencial compuesto	
gemiría	gemiríamos	habría gemido	habríamos gemido
gemirías	gemiríais	habrías gemido	habríais gemido
gemiría	gemirían	habría gemido	habrían gemido
6 presente de subjuntivo		13 perfecto de subjuntivo	
gima	gimamos	haya gemido	hayamos gemido
gimas	gimáis	hayas gemido	hayáis gemido
gima	giman	haya gemido	hayan gemido
7 imperfecto de subjuntivo		14 pluscuamperfecto de subjuntivo	
gimiera	gimiéramos	hubiera gemido	hubiéramos gemido
gimieras	gimierais	hubieras gemido	hubierais gemido
gimiera	gimieran	hubiera gemido	hubieran gemido
OR		OR	
gimiese	gimiésemos	hubiese gemido	hubiésemos gemido
gimieses	gimieseis	hubieses gemido	hubieseis gemido
gimiese	gimiesen	hubiese gemido	hubiesen gemido

imperativo	
—	gimamos
gime; no gimas	gemid; no gimáis
gima	giman

Words related to this verb
gemidor, gemidora lamenter, griever **gemiquear** to whine
el gemido lamentation, howl, groan, moan **el gemiqueo** whining

Gerundio **gozando**   Part. pas. **gozado**   **gozar**

The Seven Simple Tenses		The Seven Compound Tenses	
Singular	Plural	Singular	Plural
1 presente de indicativo		8 perfecto de indicativo	
gozo	gozamos	he gozado	hemos gozado
gozas	gozáis	has gozado	habéis gozado
goza	gozan	ha gozado	han gozado
2 imperfecto de indicativo		9 pluscuamperfecto de indicativo	
gozaba	gozábamos	había gozado	habíamos gozado
gozabas	gozabais	habías gozado	habíais gozado
gozaba	gozaban	había gozado	habían gozado
3 pretérito		10 pretérito anterior	
gocé	gozamos	hube gozado	hubimos gozado
gozaste	gozasteis	hubiste gozado	hubisteis gozado
gozó	gozaron	hubo gozado	hubieron gozado
4 futuro		11 futuro perfecto	
gozaré	gozaremos	habré gozado	habremos gozado
gozarás	gozaréis	habrás gozado	habréis gozado
gozará	gozarán	habrá gozado	habrán gozado
5 potencial simple		12 potencial compuesto	
gozaría	gozaríamos	habría gozado	habríamos gozado
gozarías	gozaríais	habrías gozado	habríais gozado
gozaría	gozarían	habría gozado	habrían gozado
6 presente de subjuntivo		13 perfecto de subjuntivo	
goce	gocemos	haya gozado	hayamos gozado
goces	gocéis	hayas gozado	hayáis gozado
goce	gocen	haya gozado	hayan gozado
7 imperfecto de subjuntivo		14 pluscuamperfecto de subjuntivo	
gozara	gozáramos	hubiera gozado	hubiéramos gozado
gozaras	gozarais	hubieras gozado	hubierais gozado
gozara	gozaran	hubiera gozado	hubieran gozado
OR		OR	
gozase	gozásemos	hubiese gozado	hubiésemos gozado
gozases	gozaseis	hubieses gozado	hubieseis gozado
gozase	gozasen	hubiese gozado	hubiesen gozado

	imperativo	
—	gocemos
goza; no goces	gozad; no gocéis
goce	gocen

Words and expressions related to this verb

el goce enjoyment	**saltar de gozo** to jump with joy
gozador, gozadora, gozante enjoyer	**gozosamente** joyfully
el gozo joy, pleasure	

169

gritar   Gerundio **gritando**   Part. pas. **gritado**

to shout, to scream, to shriek, to cry out

The Seven Simple Tenses		The Seven Compound Tenses	
Singular	Plural	Singular	Plural
1 presente de indicativo		8 perfecto de indicativo	
grito	gritamos	he gritado	hemos gritado
gritas	gritáis	has gritado	habéis gritado
grita	gritan	ha gritado	han gritado
2 imperfecto de indicativo		9 pluscuamperfecto de indicativo	
gritaba	gritábamos	había gritado	habíamos gritado
gritabas	gritabais	habías gritado	habíais gritado
gritaba	gritaban	había gritado	habían gritado
3 pretérito		10 pretérito anterior	
grité	gritamos	hube gritado	hubimos gritado
gritaste	gritasteis	hubiste gritado	hubisteis gritado
gritó	gritaron	hubo gritado	hubieron gritado
4 futuro		11 futuro perfecto	
gritaré	gritaremos	habré gritado	habremos gritado
gritarás	gritaréis	habrás gritado	habréis gritado
gritará	gritarán	habrá gritado	habrán gritado
5 potencial simple		12 potencial compuesto	
gritaría	gritaríamos	habría gritado	habríamos gritado
gritarías	gritaríais	habrías gritado	habríais gritado
gritaría	gritarían	habría gritado	habrían gritado
6 presente de subjuntivo		13 perfecto de subjuntivo	
grite	gritemos	haya gritado	hayamos gritado
grites	gritéis	hayas gritado	hayáis gritado
grite	griten	haya gritado	hayan gritado
7 imperfecto de subjuntivo		14 pluscuamperfecto de subjuntivo	
gritara	gritáramos	hubiera gritado	hubiéramos gritado
gritaras	gritarais	hubieras gritado	hubierais gritado
gritara	gritaran	hubiera gritado	hubieran gritado
OR		OR	
gritase	gritásemos	hubiese gritado	hubiésemos gritado
gritases	gritaseis	hubieses gritado	hubieseis gritado
gritase	gritasen	hubiese gritado	hubiesen gritado

	imperativo
—	gritemos
grita; no grites	gritad; no gritéis
grite	griten

Words and expressions related to this verb
el grito cry, scream, shout
a gritos at the top of one's voice, loudly
la grita, la gritería outcry, shouting

un gritón, una gritona screamer
dar grita a to hoot at

Gerundio **gruñendo**   Part. pas. **gruñido**   **gruñir**

to grumble, to grunt, to growl, to creak

The Seven Simple Tenses		The Seven Compound Tenses	
Singular	Plural	Singular	Plural
1 presente de indicativo		8 perfecto de indicativo	
gruño	**gruñimos**	**he gruñido**	**hemos gruñido**
gruñes	**gruñís**	**has gruñido**	**habéis gruñido**
gruñe	**gruñen**	**ha gruñido**	**han gruñido**
2 imperfecto de indicativo		9 pluscuamperfecto de indicativo	
gruñía	**gruñíamos**	**había gruñido**	**habíamos gruñido**
gruñías	**gruñíais**	**habías gruñido**	**habíais gruñido**
gruñía	**gruñían**	**había gruñido**	**habían gruñido**
3 pretérito		10 pretérito anterior	
gruñí	**gruñimos**	**hube gruñido**	**hubimos gruñido**
gruñiste	**gruñisteis**	**hubiste gruñido**	**hubisteis gruñido**
gruñó	**gruñeron**	**hubo gruñido**	**hubieron gruñido**
4 futuro		11 futuro perfecto	
gruñiré	**gruñiremos**	**habré gruñido**	**habremos gruñido**
gruñirás	**gruñiréis**	**habrás gruñido**	**habréis gruñido**
gruñirá	**gruñirán**	**habrá gruñido**	**habrán gruñido**
5 potencial simple		12 potencial compuesto	
gruñiría	**gruñiríamos**	**habría gruñido**	**habríamos gruñido**
gruñirías	**gruñiríais**	**habrías gruñido**	**habríais gruñido**
gruñiría	**gruñirían**	**habría gruñido**	**habrían gruñido**
6 presente de subjuntivo		13 perfecto de subjuntivo	
gruña	**gruñamos**	**haya gruñido**	**hayamos gruñido**
gruñas	**gruñáis**	**hayas gruñido**	**hayáis gruñido**
gruña	**gruñan**	**haya gruñido**	**hayan gruñido**
7 imperfecto de subjuntivo		14 pluscuamperfecto de subjuntivo	
gruñera	**gruñéramos**	**hubiera gruñido**	**hubiéramos gruñido**
gruñeras	**gruñerais**	**hubieras gruñido**	**hubierais gruñido**
gruñera	**gruñeran**	**hubiera gruñido**	**hubieran gruñido**
OR		OR	
gruñese	**gruñésemos**	**hubiese gruñido**	**hubiésemos gruñido**
gruñeses	**gruñeseis**	**hubieses gruñido**	**hubieseis gruñido**
gruñese	**gruñesen**	**hubiese gruñido**	**hubiesen gruñido**

imperativo	
—	**gruñamos**
gruñe; no gruñas	**gruñid; no gruñáis**
gruña	**gruñan**

Words related to this verb
gruñón, gruñona cranky
el gruñido, el gruñimiento grunting, grunt, growling, growl
gruñidor, gruñidora growler, grumbler

171

guiar Gerundio **guiando** Part. pas. **guiado**

to lead, to guide

The Seven Simple Tenses		The Seven Compound Tenses	
Singular	Plural	Singular	Plural
1 presente de indicativo		8 perfecto de indicativo	
guío	guiamos	he guiado	hemos guiado
guías	guiáis	has guiado	habéis guiado
guía	guían	ha guiado	han guiado
2 imperfecto de indicativo		9 pluscuamperfecto de indicativo	
guiaba	guiábamos	había guiado	habíamos guiado
guiabas	guiabais	habías guiado	habíais guiado
guiaba	guiaban	había guiado	habían guiado
3 pretérito		10 pretérito anterior	
guié	guiamos	hube guiado	hubimos guiado
guiaste	guiasteis	hubiste guiado	hubisteis guiado
guió	guiaron	hubo guiado	hubieron guiado
4 futuro		11 futuro perfecto	
guiaré	guiaremos	habré guiado	habremos guiado
guiarás	guiaréis	habrás guiado	habréis guiado
guiará	guiarán	habrá guiado	habrán guiado
5 potencial simple		12 potencial compuesto	
guiaría	guiaríamos	habría guiado	habríamos guiado
guiarías	guiaríais	habrías guiado	habríais guiado
guiaría	guiarían	habría guiado	habrían guiado
6 presente de subjuntivo		13 perfecto de subjuntivo	
guíe	guiemos	haya guiado	hayamos guiado
guíes	guiéis	hayas guiado	hayáis guiado
guíe	guíen	haya guiado	hayan guiado
7 imperfecto de subjuntivo		14 pluscuamperfecto de subjuntivo	
guiara	guiáramos	hubiera guiado	hubiéramos guiado
guiaras	guiarais	hubieras guiado	hubierais guiado
guiara	guiaran	hubiera guiado	hubieran guiado
OR		OR	
guiase	guiásemos	hubiese guiado	hubiésemos guiado
guiases	guiaseis	hubieses guiado	hubieseis guiado
guiase	guiasen	hubiese guiado	hubiesen guiado

imperativo	
—	guiemos
guía; no guíes	guiad; no guiéis
guíe	guíen

Words and expressions related to this verb
el guía guide, leader
la guía guidebook
guiarse por to be guided by, to be governed by

Gerundio **gustando**   Part. pas. **gustado**   **gustar**

to be pleasing (to), to like

The Seven Simple Tenses	The Seven Compound Tenses

Singular	Plural	Singular	Plural
1 presente de indicativo		8 perfecto de indicativo	
gusta	**gustan**	**ha gustado**	**han gustado**
2 imperfecto de indicativo		9 pluscuamperfecto de indicativo	
gustaba	**gustaban**	**había gustado**	**habían gustado**
3 pretérito		10 pretérito anterior	
gustó	**gustaron**	**hubo gustado**	**hubieron gustado**
4 futuro		11 futuro perfecto	
gustará	**gustarán**	**habrá gustado**	**habrán gustado**
5 potencial simple		12 potencial compuesto	
gustaría	**gustarían**	**habría gustado**	**habrían gustado**
6 presente de subjuntivo		13 perfecto de subjuntivo	
que guste	**que gusten**	**que haya gustado**	**que hayan gustado**
7 imperfecto de subjuntivo		14 pluscuamperfecto de subjuntivo	
que gustara	**que gustaran**	**que hubiera gustado**	**que hubieran gustado**
OR		OR	
que gustase	**que gustasen**	**que hubiese gustado**	**que hubiesen gustado**

imperativo
¡Que guste!   ¡Que gusten!

Sentences using this verb and words and expressions related to it
Me gusta el café.   I like coffee.
  Me gustan la leche y el café.   I like milk and coffee.
  A María le gustan los dulces.   Mary likes candy.
  A José y a Elena les gustan los deportes.   Joseph and Helen like sports.
el gusto taste, pleasure, liking   **dar gusto** to please
gustoso, gustosa tasty, pleasing   **tener gusto en** to be glad to
This verb is commonly used in the third person singular or plural, as in the above
examples.   **173**

haber   Gerundio **habiendo**   Part. pas. **habido**

to have (as an auxiliary, helping verb to form the compound tenses)

The Seven Simple Tenses		The Seven Compound Tenses	
Singular	Plural	Singular	Plural
1 presente de indicativo		8 perfecto de indicativo	
he	hemos	he habido	hemos habido
has	habéis	has habido	habéis habido
ha	han	ha habido	han habido
2 imperfecto de indicativo		9 pluscuamperfecto de indicativo	
había	habíamos	había habido	habíamos habido
habías	habíais	habías habido	habíais habido
había	habían	había habido	habían habido
3 pretérito		10 pretérito anterior	
hube	hubimos	hube habido	hubimos habido
hubiste	hubisteis	hubiste habido	hubisteis habido
hubo	hubieron	hubo habido	hubieron habido
4 futuro		11 futuro perfecto	
habré	habremos	habré habido	habremos habido
habrás	habréis	habrás habido	habréis habido
habrá	habrán	habrá habido	habrán habido
5 potencial simple		12 potencial compuesto	
habría	habríamos	habría habido	habríamos habido
habrías	habríais	habrías habido	habríais habido
habría	habrían	habría habido	habrían habido
6 presente de subjuntivo		13 perfecto de subjuntivo	
haya	hayamos	haya habido	hayamos habido
hayas	hayáis	hayas habido	hayáis habido
haya	hayan	haya habido	hayan habido
7 imperfecto de subjuntivo		14 pluscuamperfecto de subjuntivo	
hubiera	hubiéramos	hubiera habido	hubiéramos habido
hubieras	hubierais	hubieras habido	hubierais habido
hubiera	hubieran	hubiera habido	hubieran habido
OR		OR	
hubiese	hubiésemos	hubiese habido	hubiésemos habido
hubieses	hubieseis	hubieses habido	hubieseis habido
hubiese	hubiesen	hubiese habido	hubiesen habido

	imperativo	
—	hayamos	
hé; no hayas	habed; no hayáis	
haya	hayan	

Words and expressions related to this verb
el haber   credit (in bookkeeping); **hay . . .**   there is . . . , there are . . .
los haberes   assets, possessions, property   **No hay de qué.**   You're welcome.
habérselas con alguien   to have a showdown with someone

to inhabit, to dwell, to live, to reside

The Seven Simple Tenses		The Seven Compound Tenses	
Singular	Plural	Singular	Plural
1 presente de indicativo		8 perfecto de indicativo	
habito	**habitamos**	**he habitado**	**hemos habitado**
habitas	**habitáis**	**has habitado**	**habéis habitado**
habita	**habitan**	**ha habitado**	**han habitado**
2 imperfecto de indicativo		9 pluscuamperfecto de indicativo	
habitaba	**habitábamos**	**había habitado**	**habíamos habitado**
habitabas	**habitabais**	**habías habitado**	**habíais habitado**
habitaba	**habitaban**	**había habitado**	**habían habitado**
3 pretérito		10 pretérito anterior	
habité	**habitamos**	**hube habitado**	**hubimos habitado**
habitaste	**habitasteis**	**hubiste habitado**	**hubisteis habitado**
habitó	**habitaron**	**hubo habitado**	**hubieron habitado**
4 futuro		11 futuro perfecto	
habitaré	**habitaremos**	**habré habitado**	**habremos habitado**
habitarás	**habitaréis**	**habrás habitado**	**habréis habitado**
habitará	**habitarán**	**habrá habitado**	**habrán habitado**
5 potencial simple		12 potencial compuesto	
habitaría	**habitaríamos**	**habría habitado**	**habríamos habitado**
habitarías	**habitaríais**	**habrías habitado**	**habríais habitado**
habitaría	**habitarían**	**habría habitado**	**habrían habitado**
6 presente de subjuntivo		13 perfecto de subjuntivo	
habite	**habitemos**	**haya habitado**	**hayamos habitado**
habites	**habitéis**	**hayas habitado**	**hayáis habitado**
habite	**habiten**	**haya habitado**	**hayan habitado**
7 imperfecto de subjuntivo		14 pluscuamperfecto de subjuntivo	
habitara	**habitáramos**	**hubiera habitado**	**hubiéramos habitado**
habitaras	**habitarais**	**hubieras habitado**	**hubierais habitado**
habitara	**habitaran**	**hubiera habitado**	**hubieran habitado**
OR		OR	
habitase	**habitásemos**	**hubiese habitado**	**hubiésemos habitado**
habitases	**habitaseis**	**hubieses habitado**	**hubieseis habitado**
habitase	**habitasen**	**hubiese habitado**	**hubiesen habitado**

imperativo	
—	**habitemos**
habita; no habites	**habitad; no habitéis**
habite	**habiten**

Words related to this verb
la habitación   habitation, residence, dwelling, abode
habitador, habitadora   inhabitant
la habitabilidad   habitability
el, la habitante   inhabitant

hablar

Gerundio **hablando**   Part. pas. **hablado**

to talk, to speak

The Seven Simple Tenses		The Seven Compound Tenses	
Singular	Plural	Singular	Plural
1 presente de indicativo		**8 perfecto de indicativo**	
hablo	hablamos	he hablado	hemos hablado
hablas	habláis	has hablado	habéis hablado
habla	hablan	ha hablado	han hablado
2 imperfecto de indicativo		**9 pluscuamperfecto de indicativo**	
hablaba	hablábamos	había hablado	habíamos hablado
hablabas	hablabais	habías hablado	habíais hablado
hablaba	hablaban	había hablado	habían hablado
3 pretérito		**10 pretérito anterior**	
hablé	hablamos	hube hablado	hubimos hablado
hablaste	hablasteis	hubiste hablado	hubisteis hablado
habló	hablaron	hubo hablado	hubieron hablado
4 futuro		**11 futuro perfecto**	
hablaré	hablaremos	habré hablado	habremos hablado
hablarás	hablaréis	habrás hablado	habréis hablado
hablará	hablarán	habrá hablado	habrán hablado
5 potencial simple		**12 potencial compuesto**	
hablaría	hablaríamos	habría hablado	habríamos hablado
hablarías	hablaríais	habrías hablado	habríais hablado
hablaría	hablarían	habría hablado	habrían hablado
6 presente de subjuntivo		**13 perfecto de subjuntivo**	
hable	hablemos	haya hablado	hayamos hablado
hables	habléis	hayas hablado	hayáis hablado
hable	hablen	haya hablado	hayan hablado
7 imperfecto de subjuntivo		**14 pluscuamperfecto de subjuntivo**	
hablara	habláramos	hubiera hablado	hubiéramos hablado
hablaras	hablarais	hubieras hablado	hubierais hablado
hablara	hablaran	hubiera hablado	hubieran hablado
OR		OR	
hablase	hablásemos	hubiese hablado	hubiésemos hablado
hablases	hablaseis	hubieses hablado	hubieseis hablado
hablase	hablasen	hubiese hablado	hubiesen hablado

imperativo	
—	hablemos
habla; no hables	hablad; no habléis
hable	hablen

Words and expressions related to this verb

hablador, habladora talkative, chatterbox   **hablar al oído** to whisper in one's ear
hablar a gritos to shout   **la habladuría** gossip, idle rumor
hablar entre dientes to mumble   **de habla española** Spanish-speaking
de habla inglesa English-speaking

176

to do, to make

The Seven Simple Tenses		The Seven Compound Tenses	
Singular	Plural	Singular	Plural
1 presente de indicativo		8 perfecto de indicativo	
hago	**hacemos**	**he hecho**	**hemos hecho**
haces	**hacéis**	**has hecho**	**habéis hecho**
hace	**hacen**	**ha hecho**	**han hecho**
2 imperfecto de indicativo		9 pluscuamperfecto de indicativo	
hacía	**hacíamos**	**había hecho**	**habíamos hecho**
hacías	**hacíais**	**habías hecho**	**habíais hecho**
hacía	**hacían**	**había hecho**	**habían hecho**
3 pretérito		10 pretérito anterior	
hice	**hicimos**	**hube hecho**	**hubimos hecho**
hiciste	**hicisteis**	**hubiste hecho**	**hubisteis hecho**
hizo	**hicieron**	**hubo hecho**	**hubieron hecho**
4 futuro		11 futuro perfecto	
haré	**haremos**	**habré hecho**	**habremos hecho**
harás	**haréis**	**habrás hecho**	**habréis hecho**
hará	**harán**	**habrá hecho**	**habrán hecho**
5 potencial simple		12 potencial compuesto	
haría	**haríamos**	**habría hecho**	**habríamos hecho**
harías	**haríais**	**habrías hecho**	**habríais hecho**
haría	**harían**	**habría hecho**	**habrían hecho**
6 presente de subjuntivo		13 perfecto de subjuntivo	
haga	**hagamos**	**haya hecho**	**hayamos hecho**
hagas	**hagáis**	**hayas hecho**	**hayáis hecho**
haga	**hagan**	**haya hecho**	**hayan hecho**
7 imperfecto de subjuntivo		14 pluscuamperfecto de subjuntivo	
hiciera	**hiciéramos**	**hubiera hecho**	**hubiéramos hecho**
hicieras	**hicierais**	**hubieras hecho**	**hubierais hecho**
hiciera	**hicieran**	**hubiera hecho**	**hubieran hecho**
OR		OR	
hiciese	**hiciésemos**	**hubiese hecho**	**hubiésemos hecho**
hicieses	**hicieseis**	**hubieses hecho**	**hubieseis hecho**
hiciese	**hiciesen**	**hubiese hecho**	**hubiesen hecho**

	imperativo	
	—	**hagamos**
	haz; no hagas	**haced; no hagáis**
	haga	**hagan**

Common idiomatic expressions using this verb
Dicho y hecho.   No sooner said than done.
La práctica hace maestro al novicio.   Practice makes perfect
Si a Roma fueres, haz como vieres.   When in Rome do as the Romans do.
[See **irse,** page 189, bottom]

hallar   Gerundio **hallando**   Part. pas. **hallado**

to find, to come across

The Seven Simple Tenses		The Seven Compound Tenses	
Singular	Plural	Singular	Plural
1 presente de indicativo		8 perfecto de indicativo	
hallo	hallamos	he hallado	hemos hallado
hallas	halláis	has hallado	habéis hallado
halla	hallan	ha hallado	han hallado
2 imperfecto de indicativo		9 pluscuamperfecto de indicativo	
hallaba	hallábamos	había hallado	habíamos hallado
hallabas	hallabais	habías hallado	habíais hallado
hallaba	hallaban	había hallado	habían hallado
3 pretérito		10 pretérito anterior	
hallé	hallamos	hube hallado	hubimos hallado
hallaste	hallasteis	hubiste hallado	hubisteis hallado
halló	hallaron	hubo hallado	hubieron hallado
4 futuro		11 futuro perfecto	
hallaré	hallaremos	habré hallado	habremos hallado
hallarás	hallaréis	habrás hallado	habréis hallado
hallará	hallarán	habrá hallado	habrán hallado
5 potencial simple		12 potencial compuesto	
hallaría	hallaríamos	habría hallado	habríamos hallado
hallarías	hallaríais	habrías hallado	habríais hallado
hallaría	hallarían	habría hallado	habrían hallado
6 presente de subjuntivo		13 perfecto de subjuntivo	
halle	hallemos	haya hallado	hayamos hallado
halles	halléis	hayas hallado	hayáis hallado
halle	hallen	haya hallado	hayan hallado
7 imperfecto de subjuntivo		14 pluscuamperfecto de subjuntivo	
hallara	halláramos	hubiera hallado	hubiéramos hallado
hallaras	hallarais	hubieras hallado	hubierais hallado
hallara	hallaran	hubiera hallado	hubieran hallado
OR		OR	
hallase	hallásemos	hubiese hallado	hubiésemos hallado
hallases	hallaseis	hubieses hallado	hubieseis hallado
hallase	hallasen	hubiese hallado	hubiesen hallado

imperativo	
—	hallemos
halla; no halles	hallad; no halléis
halle	hallen

Words and expressions related to this verb
hallar bien con   to be well pleased with
un hallazgo   a find, something found
hallador, halladora   discoverer, finder

Gerundio **hiriendo**   Part. pas. **herido**   **herir**

to harm, to hurt, to wound

The Seven Simple Tenses		The Seven Compound Tenses	
Singular	Plural	Singular	Plural
1 presente de indicativo		8 perfecto de indicativo	
hiero	herimos	he herido	hemos herido
hieres	herís	has herido	habéis herido
hiere	hieren	ha herido	han herido
2 imperfecto de indicativo		9 pluscuamperfecto de indicativo	
hería	heríamos	había herido	habíamos herido
herías	heríais	habías herido	habíais herido
hería	herían	había herido	habían herido
3 pretérito		10 pretérito anterior	
herí	herimos	hube herido	hubimos herido
heriste	heristeis	hubiste herido	hubisteis herido
hirió	hirieron	hubo herido	hubieron herido
4 futuro		11 futuro perfecto	
heriré	heriremos	habré herido	habremos herido
herirás	heriréis	habrás herido	habréis herido
herirá	herirán	habrá herido	habrán herido
5 potencial simple		12 potencial compuesto	
heriría	heriríamos	habría herido	habríamos herido
herirías	heriríais	habrías herido	habríais herido
heriría	herirían	habría herido	habrían herido
6 presente de subjuntivo		13 perfecto de subjuntivo	
hiera	hiramos	haya herido	hayamos herido
hieras	hiráis	hayas herido	hayáis herido
hiera	hieran	haya herido	hayan herido
7 imperfecto de subjuntivo		14 pluscuamperfecto de subjuntivo	
hiriera	hiriéramos	hubiera herido	hubiéramos herido
hirieras	hirierais	hubieras herido	hubierais herido
hiriera	hirieran	hubiera herido	hubieran herido
OR		OR	
hiriese	hiriésemos	hubiese herido	hubiésemos herido
hirieses	hirieseis	hubieses herido	hubieseis herido
hiriese	hiriesen	hubiese herido	hubiesen herido

imperativo	
—	hiramos
hiere; no hieras	herid; no hiráis
hiera	hieran

Words and expressions related to this verb
la herida   wound
mal herido, mal herida   seriously wounded

una herida abierta   open wound
a grito herido   in loud cries

179

to escape, to flee, to run away, to slip away

The Seven Simple Tenses		The Seven Compound Tenses	
Singular	Plural	Singular	Plural

1 presente de indicativo		8 perfecto de indicativo	
huyo	huimos	he huido	hemos huido
huyes	huís	has huido	habéis huido
huye	huyen	ha huido	han huido

2 imperfecto de indicativo		9 pluscuamperfecto de indicativo	
huía	huíamos	había huido	habíamos huido
huías	huíais	habías huido	habíais huido
huía	huían	había huido	habían huido

3 pretérito		10 pretérito anterior	
huí	huimos	hube huido	hubimos huido
huiste	huisteis	hubiste huido	hubisteis huido
huyó	huyeron	hubo huido	hubieron huido

4 futuro		11 futuro perfecto	
huiré	huiremos	habré huido	habremos huido
huirás	huiréis	habrás huido	habréis huido
huirá	huirán	habrá huido	habrán huido

5 potencial simple		12 potencial compuesto	
huiría	huiríamos	habría huido	habríamos huido
huirías	huiríais	habrías huido	habríais huido
huiría	huirían	habría huido	habrían huido

6 presente de subjuntivo		13 perfecto de subjuntivo	
huya	huyamos	haya huido	hayamos huido
huyas	huyáis	hayas huido	hayáis huido
huya	huyan	haya huido	hayan huido

7 imperfecto de subjuntivo		14 pluscuamperfecto de subjuntivo	
huyera	huyéramos	hubiera huido	hubiéramos huido
huyeras	huyerais	hubieras huido	hubierais huido
huyera	huyeran	hubiera huido	hubieran huido
OR		OR	
huyese	huyésemos	hubiese huido	hubiésemos huido
huyeses	huyeseis	hubieses huido	hubieseis huido
huyese	huyesen	hubiese huido	hubiesen huido

imperativo	
—	huyamos
huye; no huyas	huid; no huyáis
huya	huyan

Words and expressions related to this verb
huir de to keep away from
la huida escape, flight
huidizo, huidiza fugitive

huidor, huidora fleeing, fugitive
rehuir to avoid, refuse, shun

Gerundio **importando**   Part. pas. **importado**   **importar**

to matter, to be important

The Seven Simple Tenses	The Seven Compound Tenses

Singular	Plural	Singular	Plural
1 presente de indicativo		8 perfecto de indicativo	
importa	**importan**	**ha importado**	**han importado**
2 imperfecto de indicativo		9 pluscuamperfecto de indicativo	
importaba	**importaban**	**había importado**	**habían importado**
3 pretérito		10 pretérito anterior	
importó	**importaron**	**hubo importado**	**hubieron importado**
4 futuro		11 futuro perfecto	
importará	**importarán**	**habrá importado**	**habrán importado**
5 potencial simple		12 potencial compuesto	
importaría	**importarían**	**habría importado**	**habrían importado**
6 presente de subjuntivo		13 perfecto de subjuntivo	
que importe	**que importen**	**que haya importado**	**que hayan importado**
7 imperfecto de subjuntivo		14 pluscuamperfecto de subjuntivo	
que importara **que importaran**		**que hubiera importado** **que hubieran importado**	
OR		OR	
que importase **que importasen**		**que hubiese importado** **que hubiesen importado**	

imperativo
¡Que importe!   **¡Que importen!**

Words and expressions related to this verb
No importa. It does not matter.   **Eso no importa.** That does not
                                                        matter.

No me importaría. It wouldn't matter to me.   **la importancia** importance
importante important   **dar importancia a** to value
de gran importancia of great importance   **darse importancia** to be
                                                        pretentious

¿Qué importa? What difference does it make?
This verb can be conjugated regularly in all the persons but it is used most commonly
as an impersonal verb in the third person.

incluir

Gerundio **incluyendo**   Part. pas. **incluido**

to include, to enclose

The Seven Simple Tenses		The Seven Compound Tenses	
Singular	Plural	Singular	Plural
1 presente de indicativo		8 perfecto de indicativo	
incluyo	incluimos	he incluido	hemos incluido
incluyes	incluís	has incluido	habéis incluido
incluye	incluyen	ha incluido	han incluido
2 imperfecto de indicativo		9 pluscuamperfecto de indicativo	
incluía	incluíamos	había incluido	habíamos incluido
incluías	incluíais	habías incluido	habíais incluido
incluía	incluían	había incluido	habían incluido
3 pretérito		10 pretérito anterior	
incluí	incluimos	hube incluido	hubimos incluido
incluiste	incluisteis	hubiste incluido	hubisteis incluido
incluyó	incluyeron	hubo incluido	hubieron incluido
4 futuro		11 futuro perfecto	
incluiré	incluiremos	habré incluido	habremos incluido
incluirás	incluiréis	habrás incluido	habréis incluido
incluirá	incluirán	habrá incluido	habrán incluido
5 potencial simple		12 potencial compuesto	
incluiría	incluiríamos	habría incluido	habríamos incluido
incluirías	incluiríais	habrías incluido	habríais incluido
incluiría	incluirían	habría incluido	habrían incluido
6 presente de subjuntivo		13 perfecto de subjuntivo	
incluya	incluyamos	haya incluido	hayamos incluido
incluyas	incluyáis	hayas incluido	hayáis incluido
incluya	incluyan	haya incluido	hayan incluido
7 imperfecto de subjuntivo		14 pluscuamperfecto de subjuntivo	
incluyera	incluyéramos	hubiera incluido	hubiéramos incluido
incluyeras	incluyerais	hubieras incluido	hubierais incluido
incluyera	incluyeran	hubiera incluido	hubieran incluido
OR		OR	
incluyese	incluyésemos	hubiese incluido	hubiésemos incluido
incluyeses	incluyeseis	hubieses incluido	hubieseis incluido
incluyese	incluyesen	hubiese incluido	hubiesen incluido

	imperativo	
—	incluyamos	
incluye; no incluyas	incluid; no incluyáis	
incluya	incluyan	

Words related to this verb
inclusivo, inclusiva inclusive, including
la inclusión inclusion
una inclusa foundling home

to indicate, to point out

The Seven Simple Tenses		The Seven Compound Tenses	
Singular	Plural	Singular	Plural
1 presente de indicativo		8 perfecto de indicativo	
indico	indicamos	he indicado	hemos indicado
indicas	indicáis	has indicado	habéis indicado
indica	indican	ha indicado	han indicado
2 imperfecto de indicativo		9 pluscuamperfecto de indicativo	
indicaba	indicábamos	había indicado	habíamos indicado
indicabas	indicabais	habías indicado	habíais indicado
indicaba	indicaban	había indicado	habían indicado
3 pretérito		10 pretérito anterior	
indiqué	indicamos	hube indicado	hubimos indicado
indicaste	indicasteis	hubiste indicado	hubisteis indicado
indicó	indicaron	hubo indicado	hubieron indicado
4 futuro		11 futuro perfecto	
indicaré	indicaremos	habré indicado	habremos indicado
indicarás	indicaréis	habrás indicado	habréis indicado
indicará	indicarán	habrá indicado	habrán indicado
5 potencial simple		12 potencial compuesto	
indicaría	indicaríamos	habría indicado	habríamos indicado
indicarías	indicaríais	habrías indicado	habríais indicado
indicaría	indicarían	habría indicado	habrían indicado
6 presente de subjuntivo		13 perfecto de subjuntivo	
indique	indiquemos	haya indicado	hayamos indicado
indiques	indiquéis	hayas indicado	hayáis indicado
indique	indiquen	haya indicado	hayan indicado
7 imperfecto de subjuntivo		14 pluscuamperfecto de subjuntivo	
indicara	indicáramos	hubiera indicado	hubiéramos indicado
indicaras	indicarais	hubieras indicado	hubierais indicado
indicara	indicaran	hubiera indicado	hubieran indicado
OR		OR	
indicase	indicásemos	hubiese indicado	hubiésemos indicado
indicases	indicaseis	hubieses indicado	hubieseis indicado
indicase	indicasen	hubiese indicado	hubiesen indicado

	imperativo	
—	indiquemos	
indica; no indiques	indicad; no indiquéis	
indique	indiquen	

Words and expressions related to this verb
indicativo, indicativa   indicative
la indicación   indication
el indicador   indicator; **el indicador de incendios**   fire alarm

inducir Gerundio **induciendo** Part. pas. **inducido**

to induce, to influence, to persuade

The Seven Simple Tenses		The Seven Compound Tenses	
Singular	Plural	Singular	Plural
1 presente de indicativo		**8 perfecto de indicativo**	
induzco	inducimos	he inducido	hemos inducido
induces	inducís	has inducido	habéis inducido
induce	inducen	ha inducido	han inducido
2 imperfecto de indicativo		**9 pluscuamperfecto de indicativo**	
inducía	inducíamos	había inducido	habíamos inducido
inducías	inducíais	habías inducido	habíais inducido
inducía	inducían	había inducido	habían inducido
3 pretérito		**10 pretérito anterior**	
induje	indujimos	hube inducido	hubimos inducido
indujiste	indujisteis	hubiste inducido	hubisteis inducido
indujo	indujeron	hubo inducido	hubieron inducido
4 futuro		**11 futuro perfecto**	
induciré	induciremos	habré inducido	habremos inducido
inducirás	induciréis	habrás inducido	habréis inducido
inducirá	inducirán	habrá inducido	habrán inducido
5 potencial simple		**12 potencial compuesto**	
induciría	induciríamos	habría inducido	habríamos inducido
inducirías	induciríais	habrías inducido	habríais inducido
induciría	inducirían	habría inducido	habrían inducido
6 presente de subjuntivo		**13 perfecto de subjuntivo**	
induzca	induzcamos	haya inducido	hayamos inducido
induzcas	induzcáis	hayas inducido	hayáis inducido
induzca	induzcan	haya inducido	hayan inducido
7 imperfecto de subjuntivo		**14 pluscuamperfecto de subjuntivo**	
indujera	indujéramos	hubiera inducido	hubiéramos inducido
indujeras	indujerais	hubieras inducido	hubierais inducido
indujera	indujeran	hubiera inducido	hubieran inducido
OR		OR	
indujese	indujésemos	hubiese inducido	hubiésemos inducido
indujeses	indujeseis	hubieses inducido	hubieseis inducido
indujese	indujesen	hubiese inducido	hubiesen inducido

imperativo	
—	induzcamos
induce; no induzcas	inducid; no induzcáis
induzca	induzcan

Words related to this verb
inducidor, inducidora inducer
el inducimiento inducement
la inducción inducement, induction

to influence

The Seven Simple Tenses		The Seven Compound Tenses	
Singular	Plural	Singular	Plural
1 presente de indicativo		8 perfecto de indicativo	
influyo	influimos	he influido	hemos influido
influyes	influís	has influido	habéis influido
influye	influyen	ha influido	han influido
2 imperfecto de indicativo		9 pluscuamperfecto de indicativo	
influía	influíamos	había influido	habíamos influido
influías	influíais	habías influido	habíais influido
influía	influían	había influido	habían influido
3 pretérito		10 pretérito anterior	
influí	influimos	hube influido	hubimos influido
influiste	influisteis	hubiste influido	hubisteis influido
influyó	influyeron	hubo influido	hubieron influido
4 futuro		11 futuro perfecto	
influiré	influiremos	habré influido	habremos influido
influirás	influiréis	habrás influido	habréis influido
influirá	influirán	habrá influido	habrán influido
5 potencial simple		12 potencial compuesto	
influiría	influiríamos	habría influido	habríamos influido
influirías	influiríais	habrías influido	habríais influido
influiría	influirían	habría influido	habrían influido
6 presente de subjuntivo		13 perfecto de subjuntivo	
influya	influyamos	haya influido	hayamos influido
influyas	influyáis	hayas influido	hayáis influido
influya	influyan	haya influido	hayan influido
7 imperfecto de subjuntivo		14 pluscuamperfecto de subjuntivo	
influyera	influyéramos	hubiera influido	hubiéramos influido
influyeras	influyerais	hubieras influido	hubierais influido
influyera	influyeran	hubiera influido	hubieran influido
OR		OR	
influyese	influyésemos	hubiese influido	hubiésemos influido
influyeses	influyeseis	hubieses influido	hubieseis influido
influyese	influyesen	hubiese influido	hubiesen influido

	imperativo	
—	influyamos	
influye; no influyas	influid; no influyáis	
influya	influyan	

Words related to this verb
la influencia   influence
influente   influential, influencing
influir en   to affect, to have an influence on, upon

insistir

Gerundio **insistiendo**   Part. pas. **insistido**

to insist, to persist

The Seven Simple Tenses		The Seven Compound Tenses	
Singular	Plural	Singular	Plural
1 presente de indicativo		**8 perfecto de indicativo**	
insisto	insistimos	he insistido	hemos insistido
insistes	insistís	has insistido	habéis insistido
insiste	insisten	ha insistido	han insistido
2 imperfecto de indicativo		**9 pluscuamperfecto de indicativo**	
insistía	insistíamos	había insistido	habíamos insistido
insistías	insistíais	habías insistido	habíais insistido
insistía	insistían	había insistido	habían insistido
3 pretérito		**10 pretérito anterior**	
insistí	insistimos	hube insistido	hubimos insistido
insististe	insististeis	hubiste insistido	hubisteis insistido
insistió	insistieron	hubo insistido	hubieron insistido
4 futuro		**11 futuro perfecto**	
insistiré	insistiremos	habré insistido	habremos insistido
insistirás	insistiréis	habrás insistido	habréis insistido
insistirá	insistirán	habrá insistido	habrán insistido
5 potencial simple		**12 potencial compuesto**	
insistiría	insistiríamos	habría insistido	habríamos insistido
insistirías	insistiríais	habrías insistido	habríais insistido
insistiría	insistirían	habría insistido	habrían insistido
6 presente de subjuntivo		**13 perfecto de subjuntivo**	
insista	insistamos	haya insistido	hayamos insistido
insistas	insistáis	hayas insistido	hayáis insistido
insista	insistan	haya insistido	hayan insistido
7 imperfecto de subjuntivo		**14 pluscuamperfecto de subjuntivo**	
insistiera	insistiéramos	hubiera insistido	hubiéramos insistido
insistieras	insistierais	hubieras insistido	hubierais insistido
insistiera	insistieran	hubiera insistido	hubieran insistido
OR		OR	
insistiese	insistiésemos	hubiese insistido	hubiésemos insistido
insistieses	insistieseis	hubieses insistido	hubieseis insistido
insistiese	insistiesen	hubiese insistido	hubiesen insistido

imperativo	
—	insistamos
insiste; no insistas	insistid; no insistáis
insista	insistan

Words related to this verb

insistir en to insist on, to persist in
la insistencia insistence, persistence

insistente insistent

to introduce

The Seven Simple Tenses		The Seven Compound Tenses	
Singular	Plural	Singular	Plural
1 presente de indicativo		8 perfecto de indicativo	
introduzco	**introducimos**	**he introducido**	**hemos introducido**
introduces	**introducís**	**has introducido**	**habéis introducido**
introduce	**introducen**	**ha introducido**	**han introducido**
2 imperfecto de indicativo		9 pluscuamperfecto de indicativo	
introducía	**introducíamos**	**había introducido**	**habíamos introducido**
introducías	**introducíais**	**habías introducido**	**habíais introducido**
introducía	**introducían**	**había introducido**	**habían introducido**
3 pretérito		10 pretérito anterior	
introduje	**introdujimos**	**hube introducido**	**hubimos introducido**
introdujiste	**introdujisteis**	**hubiste introducido**	**hubisteis introducido**
introdujo	**introdujeron**	**hubo introducido**	**hubieron introducido**
4 futuro		11 futuro perfecto	
introduciré	**introduciremos**	**habré introducido**	**habremos introducido**
introducirás	**introduciréis**	**habrás introducido**	**habréis introducido**
introducirá	**introducirán**	**habrá introducido**	**habrán introducido**
5 potencial simple		12 potencial compuesto	
introduciría	**introduciríamos**	**habría introducido**	**habríamos introducido**
introducirías	**introduciríais**	**habrías introducido**	**habríais introducido**
introduciría	**introducirían**	**habría introducido**	**habrían introducido**
6 presente de subjuntivo		13 perfecto de subjuntivo	
introduzca	**introduzcamos**	**haya introducido**	**hayamos introducido**
introduzcas	**introduzcáis**	**hayas introducido**	**hayáis introducido**
introduzca	**introduzcan**	**haya introducido**	**hayan introducido**
7 imperfecto de subjuntivo		14 pluscuamperfecto de subjuntivo	
introdujera	**introdujéramos**	**hubiera introducido**	**hubiéramos introducido**
introdujeras	**introdujerais**	**hubieras introducido**	**hubierais introducido**
introdujera	**introdujeran**	**hubiera introducido**	**hubieran introducido**
OR		OR	
introdujese	**introdujésemos**	**hubiese introducido**	**hubiésemos introducido**
introdujeses	**introdujeseis**	**hubieses introducido**	**hubieseis introducido**
introdujese	**introdujesen**	**hubiese introducido**	**hubiesen introducido**

imperativo	
—	**introduzcamos**
introduce; no introduzcas	**introducid; no introduzcáis**
introduzca	**introduzcan**

Words related to this verb
la introducción introduction
introductor, introductora introducer
introductivo, introductiva introductive, introductory

ir	Gerundio **yendo**	Part. pas. **ido**

to go

The Seven Simple Tenses		The Seven Compound Tenses	
Singular	Plural	Singular	Plural
1 presente de indicativo		8 perfecto de indicativo	
voy	**vamos**	**he ido**	**hemos ido**
vas	**vais**	**has ido**	**habéis ido**
va	**van**	**ha ido**	**han ido**
2 imperfecto de indicativo		9 pluscuamperfecto de indicativo	
iba	**íbamos**	**había ido**	**habíamos ido**
ibas	**ibais**	**habías ido**	**habíais ido**
iba	**iban**	**había ido**	**habían ido**
3 pretérito		10 pretérito anterior	
fui	**fuimos**	**hube ido**	**hubimos ido**
fuiste	**fuisteis**	**hubiste ido**	**hubisteis ido**
fue	**fueron**	**hubo ido**	**hubieron ido**
4 futuro		11 futuro perfecto	
iré	**iremos**	**habré ido**	**habremos ido**
irás	**iréis**	**habrás ido**	**habréis ido**
irá	**irán**	**habrá ido**	**habrán ido**
5 potencial simple		12 potencial compuesto	
iría	**iríamos**	**habría ido**	**habríamos ido**
irías	**iríais**	**habrías ido**	**habríais ido**
iría	**irían**	**habría ido**	**habrían ido**
6 presente de subjuntivo		13 perfecto de subjuntivo	
vaya	**vayamos**	**haya ido**	**hayamos ido**
vayas	**vayáis**	**hayas ido**	**hayáis ido**
vaya	**vayan**	**haya ido**	**hayan ido**
7 imperfecto de subjuntivo		14 pluscuamperfecto de subjuntivo	
fuera	**fuéramos**	**hubiera ido**	**hubiéramos ido**
fueras	**fuerais**	**hubieras ido**	**hubierais ido**
fuera	**fueran**	**hubiera ido**	**hubieran ido**
OR		OR	
fuese	**fuésemos**	**hubiese ido**	**hubiésemos ido**
fueses	**fueseis**	**hubieses ido**	**hubieseis ido**
fuese	**fuesen**	**hubiese ido**	**hubiesen ido**

imperativo	
—	**vamos (no vayamos)**
ve; no vayas	**id; no vayáis**
vaya	**vayan**

Common idiomatic expressions using this verb

ir de compras to go shopping
ir de brazo to walk arm in arm
¿Cómo le va? How goes it? How are you?

ir a caballo to ride horseback
un billete de ida y vuelta return ticket
¡Qué va! Nonsense!

to go away

The Seven Simple Tenses		The Seven Compound Tenses	
Singular	Plural	Singular	Plural
1 presente de indicativo		**8 perfecto de indicativo**	
me voy	nos vamos	me he ido	nos hemos ido
te vas	os vais	te has ido	os habéis ido
se va	se van	se ha ido	se han ido
2 imperfecto de indicativo		**9 pluscuamperfecto de indicativo**	
me iba	nos íbamos	me había ido	nos habíamos ido
te ibas	os ibais	te habías ido	os habíais ido
se iba	se iban	se había ido	se habían ido
3 pretérito		**10 pretérito anterior**	
me fui	nos fuimos	me hube ido	nos hubimos ido
te fuiste	os fuisteis	te hubiste ido	os hubisteis ido
se fue	se fueron	se hubo ido	se hubieron ido
4 futuro		**11 futuro perfecto**	
me iré	nos iremos	me habré ido	nos habremos ido
te irás	os iréis	te habrás ido	os habréis ido
se irá	se irán	se habrá ido	se habrán ido
5 potencial simple		**12 potencial compuesto**	
me iría	nos iríamos	me habría ido	nos habríamos ido
te irías	os iríais	te habrías ido	os habríais ido
se iría	se irían	se habría ido	se habrían ido
6 presente de subjuntivo		**13 perfecto de subjuntivo**	
me vaya	nos vayamos	me haya ido	nos hayamos ido
te vayas	os vayáis	te hayas ido	os hayáis ido
se vaya	se vayan	se haya ido	se hayan ido
7 imperfecto de subjuntivo		**14 pluscuamperfecto de subjuntivo**	
me fuera	nos fuéramos	me hubiera ido	nos hubiéramos ido
te fueras	os fuerais	te hubieras ido	os hubierais ido
se fuera	se fueran	se hubiera ido	se hubieran ido
OR		OR	
me fuese	nos fuésemos	me hubiese ido	nos hubiésemos ido
te fueses	os fueseis	te hubieses ido	os hubieseis ido
se fuese	se fuesen	se hubiese ido	se hubiesen ido

	imperativo	
—	vámonos; no nos vayamos	
vete; no te vayas	idos; no os vayáis	
váyase; no se vaya	váyanse; no se vayan	

Common idiomatic expressions using this verb
¡Vámonos!   Let's go! Let's leave! ¡Vete!   Go away! ¡Váyase!   Go away!
Si a Roma fueres, haz como vieres.   When in Rome do as the Romans do. [Note that it is not uncommon to use the future subjunctive in proverbs, as in *fueres* (**ir** or **ser**) and *vieres* (**ver**); see p. xxxii.]

189

jugar	Gerundio **jugando**	Part. pas. **jugado**

to play (a game, sport)

The Seven Simple Tenses		The Seven Compound Tenses	
Singular	Plural	Singular	Plural
1 presente de indicativo		8 perfecto de indicativo	
juego	jugamos	he jugado	hemos jugado
juegas	jugáis	has jugado	habéis jugado
juega	juegan	ha jugado	han jugado
2 imperfecto de indicativo		9 pluscuamperfecto de indicativo	
jugaba	jubábamos	había jugado	habíamos jugado
jugabas	jugabais	habías jugado	habíais jugado
jugaba	jugaban	había jugado	habían jugado
3 pretérito		10 pretérito anterior	
jugué	jugamos	hube jugado	hubimos jugado
jugaste	jugasteis	hubiste jugado	hubisteis jugado
jugó	jugaron	hubo jugado	hubieron jugado
4 futuro		11 futuro perfecto	
jugaré	jugaremos	habré jugado	habremos jugado
jugarás	jugaréis	habrás jugado	habréis jugado
jugará	jugarán	habrá jugado	habrán jugado
5 potencial simple		12 potencial compuesto	
jugaría	jugaríamos	habría jugado	habríamos jugado
jugarías	jugaríais	habrías jugado	habríais jugado
jugaría	jugarían	habría jugado	habrían jugado
6 presente de subjuntivo		13 perfecto de subjuntivo	
juegue	juguemos	haya jugado	hayamos jugado
juegues	juguéis	hayas jugado	hayáis jugado
juegue	jueguen	haya jugado	hayan jugado
7 imperfecto de subjuntivo		14 pluscuamperfecto de subjuntivo	
jugara	jugáramos	hubiera jugado	hubiéramos jugado
jugaras	jugarais	hubieras jugado	hubierais jugado
jugara	jugaran	hubiera jugado	hubieran jugado
OR		OR	
jugase	jugásemos	hubiese jugado	hubiésemos jugado
jugases	jugaseis	hubieses jugado	hubieseis jugado
jugase	jugasen	hubiese jugado	hubiesen jugado

imperativo	
—	juguemos
juega; no juegues	jugad; no juguéis
juegue	jueguen

Words and expressions related to this verb

un juguete toy, plaything	jugar a los naipes to play cards
jugador, jugadora player	jugar al tenis to play tennis
un juego game	jugar al béisbol to play baseball

Gerundio **lanzando**   Part. pas. **lanzado**   **lanzar**

to throw, to hurl, to fling, to launch

The Seven Simple Tenses		The Seven Compound Tenses	
Singular	Plural	Singular	Plural
1 presente de indicativo		8 perfecto de indicativo	
lanzo	lanzamos	he lanzado	hemos lanzado
lanzas	lanzáis	has lanzado	habéis lanzado
lanza	lanzan	ha lanzado	han lanzado
2 imperfecto de indicativo		9 pluscuamperfecto de indicativo	
lanzaba	lanzábamos	había lanzado	habíamos lanzado
lanzabas	lanzabais	habías lanzado	habíais lanzado
lanzaba	lanzaban	había lanzado	habían lanzado
3 pretérito		10 pretérito anterior	
lancé	lanzamos	hube lanzado	hubimos lanzado
lanzaste	lanzasteis	hubiste lanzado	hubisteis lanzado
lanzó	lanzaron	hubo lanzado	hubieron lanzado
4 futuro		11 futuro perfecto	
lanzaré	lanzaremos	habré lanzado	habremos lanzado
lanzarás	lanzaréis	habrás lanzado	habréis lanzado
lanzará	lanzarán	habrá lanzado	habrán lanzado
5 potencial simple		12 potencial compuesto	
lanzaría	lanzaríamos	habría lanzado	habríamos lanzado
lanzarías	lanzaríais	habrías lanzado	habríais lanzado
lanzaría	lanzarían	habría lanzado	habrían lanzado
6 presente de subjuntivo		13 perfecto de subjuntivo	
lance	lancemos	haya lanzado	hayamos lanzado
lances	lancéis	hayas lanzado	hayáis lanzado
lance	lancen	haya lanzado	hayan lanzado
7 imperfecto de subjuntivo		14 pluscuamperfecto de subjuntivo	
lanzara	lanzáramos	hubiera lanzado	hubiéramos lanzado
lanzaras	lanzarais	hubieras lanzado	hubierais lanzado
lanzara	lanzaran	hubiera lanzado	hubieran lanzado
OR		OR	
lanzase	lanzásemos	hubiese lanzado	hubiésemos lanzado
lanzases	lanzaseis	hubieses lanzado	hubieseis lanzado
lanzase	lanzasen	hubiese lanzado	hubiesen lanzado

	imperativo	
—	lancemos	
lanza; no lances	lanzad; no lancéis	
lance	lancen	

Words related to this verb
la lanza   lance, spear
el lanzamiento   casting, throwing, launching

lavar   Gerundio **lavando**   Part. pas. **lavado**

to wash

The Seven Simple Tenses		The Seven Compound Tenses	
Singular	Plural	Singular	Plural
1 presente de indicativo		**8 perfecto de indicativo**	
lavo	lavamos	he lavado	hemos lavado
lavas	laváis	has lavado	habéis lavado
lava	lavan	ha lavado	han lavado
2 imperfecto de indicativo		**9 pluscuamperfecto de indicativo**	
lavaba	lavábamos	había lavado	habíamos lavado
lavabas	lavabais	habías lavado	habíais lavado
lavaba	lavaban	había lavado	habían lavado
3 pretérito		**10 pretérito anterior**	
lavé	lavamos	hube lavado	hubimos lavado
lavaste	lavasteis	hubiste lavado	hubisteis lavado
lavó	lavaron	hubo lavado	hubieron lavado
4 futuro		**11 futuro perfecto**	
lavaré	lavaremos	habré lavado	habremos lavado
lavarás	lavaréis	habrás lavado	habréis lavado
lavará	lavarán	habrá lavado	habrán lavado
5 potencial simple		**12 potencial compuesto**	
lavaría	lavaríamos	habría lavado	habríamos lavado
lavarías	lavaríais	habrías lavado	habríais lavado
lavaría	lavarían	habría lavado	habrían lavado
6 presente de subjuntivo		**13 perfecto de subjuntivo**	
lave	lavemos	haya lavado	hayamos lavado
laves	lavéis	hayas lavado	hayáis lavado
lave	laven	haya lavado	hayan lavado
7 imperfecto de subjuntivo		**14 pluscuamperfecto de subjuntivo**	
lavara	laváramos	hubiera lavado	hubiéramos lavado
lavaras	lavarais	hubieras lavado	hubierais lavado
lavara	lavaran	hubiera lavado	hubieran lavado
OR		OR	
lavase	lavásemos	hubiese lavado	hubiésemos lavado
lavases	lavaseis	hubieses lavado	hubieseis lavado
lavase	lavasen	hubiese lavado	hubiesen lavado

imperativo	
—	lavemos
lava; no laves	lavad; no lavéis
lave	laven

Words and expressions related to this verb

el lavatorio, el lavabo lavatory, washroom, washstand
lavandero, lavandera launderer
See also **lavarse.**

la lavandería laundry
el lavamanos washstand, washbowl
lavar en seco to dry clean
el lavarropa, la lavadora clothes washing machine

Gerundio **lavándose**   Part. pas. **lavado**   **lavarse**

to wash oneself

The Seven Simple Tenses		The Seven Compound Tenses	
Singular	Plural	Singular	Plural
1 presente de indicativo		8 perfecto de indicativo	
me lavo	nos lavamos	me he lavado	nos hemos lavado
te lavas	os laváis	te has lavado	os habéis lavado
se lava	se lavan	se ha lavado	se han lavado
2 imperfecto de indicativo		9 pluscuamperfecto de indicativo	
me lavaba	nos lavábamos	me había lavado	nos habíamos lavado
te lavabas	os lavabais	te habías lavado	os habíais lavado
se lavaba	se lavaban	se había lavado	se habían lavado
3 pretérito		10 pretérito anterior	
me lavé	nos lavamos	me hube lavado	nos hubimos lavado
te lavaste	os lavasteis	te hubiste lavado	os hubisteis lavado
se lavó	se lavaron	se hubo lavado	se hubieron lavado
4 futuro		11 futuro perfecto	
me lavaré	nos lavaremos	me habré lavado	nos habremos lavado
te lavarás	os lavaréis	te habrás lavado	os habréis lavado
se lavará	se lavarán	se habrá lavado	se habrán lavado
5 potencial simple		12 potencial compuesto	
me lavaría	nos lavaríamos	me habría lavado	nos habríamos lavado
te lavarías	os lavaríais	te habrías lavado	os habríais lavado
se lavaría	se lavarían	se habría lavado	se habrían lavado
6 presente de subjuntivo		13 perfecto de subjuntivo	
me lave	nos lavemos	me haya lavado	nos hayamos lavado
te laves	os lavéis	te hayas lavado	os hayáis lavado
se lave	se laven	se haya lavado	se hayan lavado
7 imperfecto de subjuntivo		14 pluscuamperfecto de subjuntivo	
me lavara	nos laváramos	me hubiera lavado	nos hubiéramos lavado
te lavaras	os lavarais	te hubieras lavado	os hubierais lavado
se lavara	se lavaran	se hubiera lavado	se hubieran lavado
OR		OR	
me lavase	nos lavásemos	me hubiese lavado	nos hubiésemos lavado
te lavases	os lavaseis	te hubieses lavado	os hubieseis lavado
se lavase	se lavasen	se hubiese lavado	se hubiesen lavado

	imperativo
—	lavémonos; no nos lavemos
lávate; no te laves	lavaos; no os lavéis
lávese; no se lave	lávense; no se laven

Words related to this verb
el lavatorio, el lavabo   lavatory, washroom, washstand
lavandero, lavandera   launderer
la lavandería   laundry
For other words and expressions related to this verb, see **lavar.**

leer Gerundio **leyendo** Part. pas. **leído**

to read

The Seven Simple Tenses		The Seven Compound Tenses	
Singular	Plural	Singular	Plural

1 presente de indicativo

leo	leemos
lees	leéis
lee	leen

2 imperfecto de indicativo

leía	leíamos
leías	leíais
leía	leían

3 pretérito

leí	leímos
leíste	leísteis
leyó	leyeron

4 futuro

leeré	leeremos
leerás	leeréis
leerá	leerán

5 potencial simple

leería	leeríamos
leerías	leeríais
leería	leerían

6 presente de subjuntivo

lea	leamos
leas	leáis
lea	lean

7 imperfecto de subjuntivo

leyera	leyéramos
leyeras	leyerais
leyera	leyeran
OR	
leyese	leyésemos
leyeses	leyeseis
leyese	leyesen

8 perfecto de indicativo

he leído	hemos leído
has leído	habéis leído
ha leído	han leído

9 pluscuamperfecto de indicativo

había leído	habíamos leído
habías leído	habíais leído
había leído	habían leído

10 pretérito anterior

hube leído	hubimos leído
hubiste leído	hubisteis leído
hubo leído	hubieron leído

11 futuro perfecto

habré leído	habremos leído
habrás leído	habréis leído
habrá leído	habrán leído

12 potencial compuesto

habría leído	habríamos leído
habrías leído	habríais leído
habría leído	habrían leído

13 perfecto de subjuntivo

haya leído	hayamos leído
hayas leído	hayáis leído
haya leído	hayan leído

14 pluscuamperfecto de subjuntivo

hubiera leído	hubiéramos leído
hubieras leído	hubierais leído
hubiera leído	hubieran leído
OR	
hubiese leído	hubiésemos leído
hubieses leído	hubieseis leído
hubiese leído	hubiesen leído

imperativo

—	leamos
lee; no leas	leed; no leáis
lea	lean

Words and expressions related to this verb

la lectura   reading
Me gusta la lectura.   I like reading.
la lección   lesson
lector, lectora   reader

releer   to read again, to reread
leer entre líneas   to read between the lines
un, una leccionista   private tutor
leer para sí   to read to oneself
leer mal   to misread

to lift, to raise

The Seven Simple Tenses		The Seven Compound Tenses	
Singular	Plural	Singular	Plural
1 presente de indicativo		8 perfecto de indicativo	
levanto	**levantamos**	**he levantado**	**hemos levantado**
levantas	**levantáis**	**has levantado**	**habéis levantado**
levanta	**levantan**	**ha levantado**	**han levantado**
2 imperfecto de indicativo		9 pluscuamperfecto de indicativo	
levantaba	**levantábamos**	**había levantado**	**habíamos levantado**
levantabas	**levantabais**	**habías levantado**	**habíais levantado**
levantaba	**levantaban**	**había levantado**	**habían levantado**
3 pretérito		10 pretérito anterior	
levanté	**levantamos**	**hube levantado**	**hubimos levantado**
levantaste	**levantasteis**	**hubiste levantado**	**hubisteis levantado**
levantó	**levantaron**	**hubo levantado**	**hubieron levantado**
4 futuro		11 futuro perfecto	
levantaré	**levantaremos**	**habré levantado**	**habremos levantado**
levantarás	**levantaréis**	**habrás levantado**	**habréis levantado**
levantará	**levantarán**	**habrá levantado**	**habrán levantado**
5 potencial simple		12 potencial compuesto	
levantaría	**levantaríamos**	**habría levantado**	**habríamos levantado**
levantarías	**levantaríais**	**habrías levantado**	**habríais levantado**
levantaría	**levantarían**	**habría levantado**	**habrían levantado**
6 presente de subjuntivo		13 perfecto de subjuntivo	
levante	**levantemos**	**haya levantado**	**hayamos levantado**
levantes	**levantéis**	**hayas levantado**	**hayáis levantado**
levante	**levanten**	**haya levantado**	**hayan levantado**
7 imperfecto de subjuntivo		14 pluscuamperfecto de subjuntivo	
levantara	**levantáramos**	**hubiera levantado**	**hubiéramos levantado**
levantaras	**levantarais**	**hubieras levantado**	**hubierais levantado**
levantara	**levantaran**	**hubiera levantado**	**hubieran levantado**
OR		OR	
levantase	**levantásemos**	**hubiese levantado**	**hubiésemos levantado**
levantases	**levantaseis**	**hubieses levantado**	**hubieseis levantado**
levantase	**levantasen**	**hubiese levantado**	**hubiesen levantado**

imperativo	
—	**levantemos**
levanta; no levantes	**levantad; no levantéis**
levante	**levanten**

Words and expressions related to this verb

levantar los manteles   to clear the table
levantar con algo   to get away with
    something
el levante   Levant, East
See also **levantarse.**

levantar fuego   to make a disturbance
levantar la cabeza   to take heart
    (courage)
el levantamiento   elevation, raising

levantarse Gerundio **levantándose** Part. pas. **levantado**

to get up, to rise

The Seven Simple Tenses		The Seven Compound Tenses	
Singular	Plural	Singular	Plural

1 presente de indicativo		8 perfecto de indicativo	
me levanto	nos levantamos	me he levantado	nos hemos levantado
te levantas	os levantáis	te has levantado	os habéis levantado
se levanta	se levantan	se ha levantado	se han levantado

2 imperfecto de indicativo		9 pluscuamperfecto de indicativo	
me levantaba	nos levantábamos	me había levantado	nos habíamos levantado
te levantabas	os levantabais	te habías levantado	os habíais levantado
se levantaba	se levantaban	se había levantado	se habían levantado

3 pretérito		10 pretérito anterior	
me levanté	nos levantamos	me hube levantado	nos hubimos levantado
te levantaste	os levantasteis	te hubiste levantado	os hubisteis levantado
se levantó	se levantaron	se hubo levantado	se hubieron levantado

4 futuro		11 futuro perfecto	
me levantaré	nos levantaremos	me habré levantado	nos habremos levantado
te levantarás	os levantaréis	te habrás levantado	os habréis levantado
se levantará	se levantarán	se habrá levantado	se habrán levantado

5 potencial simple		12 potencial compuesto	
me levantaría	nos levantaríamos	me habría levantado	nos habríamos levantado
te levantarías	os levantaríais	te habrías levantado	os habríais levantado
se levantaría	se levantarían	se habría levantado	se habrían levantado

6 presente de subjuntivo		13 perfecto de subjuntivo	
me levante	nos levantemos	me haya levantado	nos hayamos levantado
te levantes	os levantéis	te hayas levantado	os hayáis levantado
se levante	se levanten	se haya levantado	se hayan levantado

7 imperfecto de subjuntivo		14 pluscuamperfecto de subjuntivo	
me levantara	nos levantáramos	me hubiera levantado	nos hubiéramos levantado
te levantaras	os levantarais	te hubieras levantado	os hubierais levantado
se levantara	se levantaran	se hubiera levantado	se hubieran levantado
OR		OR	
me levantase	nos levantásemos	me hubiese levantado	nos hubiésemos levantado
te levantases	os levantaseis	te hubieses levantado	os hubieseis levantado
se levantase	se levantasen	se hubiese levantado	se hubiesen levantado

imperativo	
—	levantémonos; no nos levantemos
levántate; no te levantes	levantaos; no os levantéis
levántese; no se levante	levántense; no se levanten

Words and expressions related to this verb

levantar los manteles to clear the table
levantar con algo to get away with something
levantar la voz to raise one's voice
el levantamiento elevation, raising

levantar la sesión to adjourn
el levante Levant, East
See also **levantar**.

Gerundio **llamando**   Part. pas. **llamado**   **llamar**

to call, to name

The Seven Simple Tenses		The Seven Compound Tenses	
Singular	Plural	Singular	Plural
1 presente de indicativo		8 perfecto de indicativo	
llamo	llamamos	he llamado	hemos llamado
llamas	llamáis	has llamado	habéis llamado
llama	llaman	ha llamado	han llamado
2 imperfecto de indicativo		9 pluscuamperfecto de indicativo	
llamaba	llamábamos	había llamado	habíamos llamado
llamabas	llamabais	habías llamado	habíais llamado
llamaba	llamaban	había llamado	habían llamado
3 pretérito		10 pretérito anterior	
llamé	llamamos	hube llamado	hubimos llamado
llamaste	llamasteis	hubiste llamado	hubisteis llamado
llamó	llamaron	hubo llamado	hubieron llamado
4 futuro		11 futuro perfecto	
llamaré	llamaremos	habré llamado	habremos llamado
llamarás	llamaréis	habrás llamado	habréis llamado
llamará	llamarán	habrá llamado	habrán llamado
5 potencial simple		12 potencial compuesto	
llamaría	llamaríamos	habría llamado	habríamos llamado
llamarías	llamaríais	habrías llamado	habríais llamado
llamaría	llamarían	habría llamado	habrían llamado
6 presente de subjuntivo		13 perfecto de subjuntivo	
llame	llamemos	haya llamado	hayamos llamado
llames	llaméis	hayas llamado	hayáis llamado
llame	llamen	haya llamado	hayan llamado
7 imperfecto de subjuntivo		14 pluscuamperfecto de subjuntivo	
llamara	llamáramos	hubiera llamado	hubiéramos llamado
llamaras	llamarais	hubieras llamado	hubierais llamado
llamara	llamaran	hubiera llamado	hubieran llamado
OR		OR	
llamase	llamásemos	hubiese llamado	hubiésemos llamado
llamases	llamaseis	hubieses llamado	hubieseis llamado
llamase	llamasen	hubiese llamado	hubiesen llamado

imperativo		
—	llamemos	
llama; no llames	llamad; no llaméis	
llame	llamen	

Words and expressions related to this verb
llamar al doctor   to call the doctor
llamar por teléfono   to telephone
llamar la atención sobre   to call attention to
See also **llamarse.**

llamar por los nombres   to call
   the roll
una llamada   call, knock, ring
una llamada de emergencia
   emergency call

llamarse   Gerundio **llamándose**   Part. pas. **llamado**

to be called, to be named

The Seven Simple Tenses		The Seven Compound Tenses	
Singular	Plural	Singular	Plural
1 presente de indicativo		**8 perfecto de indicativo**	
me llamo	nos llamamos	me he llamado	nos hemos llamado
te llamas	os llamáis	te has llamado	os habéis llamado
se llama	se llaman	se ha llamado	se han llamado
2 imperfecto de indicativo		**9 pluscuamperfecto de indicativo**	
me llamaba	nos llamábamos	me había llamado	nos habíamos llamado
te llamabas	os llamabais	te habías llamado	os habíais llamado
se llamaba	se llamaban	se había llamado	se habían llamado
3 pretérito		**10 pretérito anterior**	
me llamé	nos llamamos	me hube llamado	nos hubimos llamado
te llamaste	os llamasteis	te hubiste llamado	os hubisteis llamado
se llamó	se llamaron	se hubo llamado	se hubieron llamado
4 futuro		**11 futuro perfecto**	
me llamaré	nos llamaremos	me habré llamado	nos habremos llamado
te llamarás	os llamaréis	te habrás llamado	os habréis llamado
se llamará	se llamarán	se habrá llamado	se habrán llamado
5 potencial simple		**12 potencial compuesto**	
me llamaría	nos llamaríamos	me habría llamado	nos habríamos llamado
te llamarías	os llamaríais	te habrías llamado	os habríais llamado
se llamaría	se llamarían	se habría llamado	se habrían llamado
6 presente de subjuntivo		**13 perfecto de subjuntivo**	
me llame	nos llamemos	me haya llamado	nos hayamos llamado
te llames	os llaméis	te hayas llamado	os hayáis llamado
se llame	se llamen	se haya llamado	se hayan llamado
7 imperfecto de subjuntivo		**14 pluscuamperfecto de subjuntivo**	
me llamara	nos llamáramos	me hubiera llamado	nos hubiéramos llamado
te llamaras	os llamarais	te hubieras llamado	os hubierais llamado
se llamara	se llamaran	se hubiera llamado	se hubieran llamado
OR		OR	
me llamase	nos llamásemos	me hubiese llamado	nos hubiésemos llamado
te llamases	os llamaseis	te hubieses llamado	os hubieseis llamado
se llamase	se llamasen	se hubiese llamado	se hubiesen llamado

imperativo	
—	llamémonos; no nos llamemos
llámate; no te llames	llamaos; no os llaméis
llámese; no se llame	llámense; no se llamen

Common idiomatic expressions using this verb

—**¿Cómo se llama usted?** What is your name? (How do you call yourself?)
—**Me llamo Juan Morales.** My name is Juan Morales.
—**¿Y cómo se llaman sus hermanos?** And what are your brothers' names?
—**Se llaman Luis y Pedro.** Their names are Louis and Peter.

to arrive

The Seven Simple Tenses		The Seven Compound Tenses	
Singular	Plural	Singular	Plural
1 presente de indicativo		8 perfecto de indicativo	
llego	llegamos	he llegado	hemos llegado
llegas	llegáis	has llegado	habéis llegado
llega	llegan	ha llegado	han llegado
2 imperfecto de indicativo		9 pluscuamperfecto de indicativo	
llegaba	llegábamos	había llegado	habíamos llegado
llegabas	llegabais	habías llegado	habíais llegado
llegaba	llegaban	había llegado	habían llegado
3 pretérito		10 pretérito anterior	
llegué	llegamos	hube llegado	hubimos llegado
llegaste	llegasteis	hubiste llegado	hubisteis llegado
llegó	llegaron	hubo llegado	hubieron llegado
4 futuro		11 futuro perfecto	
llegaré	llegaremos	habré llegado	habremos llegado
llegarás	llegaréis	habrás llegado	habréis llegado
llegará	llegarán	habrá llegado	habrán llegado
5 potencial simple		12 potencial compuesto	
llegaría	llegaríamos	habría llegado	habríamos llegado
llegarías	llegaríais	habrías llegado	habríais llegado
llegaría	llegarían	habría llegado	habrían llegado
6 presente de subjuntivo		13 perfecto de subjuntivo	
llegue	lleguemos	haya llegado	hayamos llegado
llegues	lleguéis	hayas llegado	hayáis llegado
llegue	lleguen	haya llegado	hayan llegado
7 imperfecto de subjuntivo		14 pluscuamperfecto de subjuntivo	
llegara	llegáramos	hubiera llegado	hubiéramos llegado
llegaras	llegarais	hubieras llegado	hubierais llegado
llegara	llegaran	hubiera llegado	hubieran llegado
OR		OR	
llegase	llegásemos	hubiese llegado	hubiésemos llegado
llegases	llegaseis	hubieses llegado	hubieseis llegado
llegase	llegasen	hubiese llegado	hubiesen llegado

	imperativo
—	lleguemos
llega; no llegues	llegad; no lleguéis
llegue	lleguen

Words and expressions related to this verb

llegar a ser to become
  Luis y Luisa quieren llegar a ser médicos.
  Louis and Louise want to become doctors.
llegar a saber to find out

llegar a to reach
al llegar on arrival, upon arriving
la llegada arrival
llegar tarde to arrive late

llenar	Gerundio **llenando**	Part. pas. **llenado**

to fill

The Seven Simple Tenses	The Seven Compound Tenses

Singular	Plural	Singular	Plural
1 presente de indicativo		8 perfecto de indicativo	
lleno	llenamos	he llenado	hemos llenado
llenas	llenáis	has llenado	habéis llenado
llena	llenan	ha llenado	han llenado
2 imperfecto de indicativo		9 pluscuamperfecto de indicativo	
llenaba	llenábamos	había llenado	habíamos llenado
llenabas	llenabais	habías llenado	habíais llenado
llenaba	llenaban	había llenado	habían llenado
3 pretérito		10 pretérito anterior	
llené	llenamos	hube llenado	hubimos llenado
llenaste	llenasteis	hubiste llenado	hubisteis llenado
llenó	llenaron	hubo llenado	hubieron llenado
4 futuro		11 futuro perfecto	
llenaré	llenaremos	habré llenado	habremos llenado
llenarás	llenaréis	habrás llenado	habréis llenado
llenará	llenarán	habrá llenado	habrán llenado
5 potencial simple		12 potencial compuesto	
llenaría	llenaríamos	habría llenado	habríamos llenado
llenarías	llenaríais	habrías llenado	habríais llenado
llenaría	llenarían	habría llenado	habrían llenado
6 presente de subjuntivo		13 perfecto de subjuntivo	
llene	llenemos	haya llenado	hayamos llenado
llenes	llenéis	hayas llenado	hayáis llenado
llene	llenen	haya llenado	hayan llenado
7 imperfecto de subjuntivo		14 pluscuamperfecto de subjuntivo	
llenara	llenáramos	hubiera llenado	hubiéramos llenado
llenaras	llenarais	hubieras llenado	hubierais llenado
llenara	llenaran	hubiera llenado	hubieran llenado
OR		OR	
llenase	llenásemos	hubiese llenado	hubiésemos llenado
llenases	llenaseis	hubieses llenado	hubieseis llenado
llenase	llenasen	hubiese llenado	hubiesen llenado

imperativo	
—	llenemos
llena; no llenes	llenad; no llenéis
llene	llenen

Words and expressions related to this verb
lleno, llena full, filled
la llenura abundance, fullness
llenamente fully

lleno de bote en bote full to the brim
llenar un pedido to fill an order
llenar un formulario to fill out a form

to carry (away), to take (away), to wear

The Seven Simple Tenses		The Seven Compound Tenses	
Singular	Plural	Singular	Plural
1 presente de indicativo		**8 perfecto de indicativo**	
llevo	llevamos	he llevado	hemos llevado
llevas	lleváis	has llevado	habéis llevado
lleva	llevan	ha llevado	han llevado
2 imperfecto de indicativo		**9 pluscuamperfecto de indicativo**	
llevaba	llevábamos	había llevado	habíamos llevado
llevabas	llevabais	habías llevado	habíais llevado
llevaba	llevaban	había llevado	habían llevado
3 pretérito		**10 pretérito anterior**	
llevé	llevamos	hube llevado	hubimos llevado
llevaste	llevasteis	hubiste llevado	hubisteis llevado
llevó	llevaron	hubo llevado	hubieron llevado
4 futuro		**11 futuro perfecto**	
llevaré	llevaremos	habré llevado	habremos llevado
llevarás	llevaréis	habrás llevado	habréis llevado
llevará	llevarán	habrá llevado	habrán llevado
5 potencial simple		**12 potencial compuesto**	
llevaría	llevaríamos	habría llevado	habríamos llevado
llevarías	llevaríais	habrías llevado	habríais llevado
llevaría	llevarían	habría llevado	habrían llevado
6 presente de subjuntivo		**13 perfecto de subjuntivo**	
lleve	llevemos	haya llevado	hayamos llevado
lleves	llevéis	hayas llevado	hayáis llevado
lleve	lleven	haya llevado	hayan llevado
7 imperfecto de subjuntivo		**14 pluscuamperfecto de subjuntivo**	
llevara	lleváramos	hubiera llevado	hubiéramos llevado
llevaras	llevarais	hubieras llevado	hubierais llevado
llevara	llevaran	hubiera llevado	hubieran llevado
OR		OR	
llevase	llevásemos	hubiese llevado	hubiésemos llevado
llevases	llevaseis	hubieses llevado	hubieseis llevado
llevase	llevasen	hubiese llevado	hubiesen llevado

imperativo	
—	llevemos
lleva; no lleves	llevad; no llevéis
lleve	lleven

Words and expressions related to this verb

llevar a cabo   to carry through, to accomplish   **llevador, llevadora**   carrier
llevar una caída   to have a fall   **llevar puesto**   to wear
llevarse algo de alguien   to take something from someone

llorar	Gerundio **llorando**	Part. pas. **llorado**

to weep, to cry, to whine

The Seven Simple Tenses		The Seven Compound Tenses	
Singular	Plural	Singular	Plural
1 presente de indicativo		8 perfecto de indicativo	
lloro	lloramos	he llorado	hemos llorado
lloras	lloráis	has llorado	habéis llorado
llora	lloran	ha llorado	han llorado
2 imperfecto de indicativo		9 pluscuamperfecto de indicativo	
lloraba	llorábamos	había llorado	habíamos llorado
llorabas	llorabais	habías llorado	habíais llorado
lloraba	lloraban	había llorado	habían llorado
3 pretérito		10 pretérito anterior	
lloré	lloramos	hube llorado	hubimos llorado
lloraste	llorasteis	hubiste llorado	hubisteis llorado
lloró	lloraron	hubo llorado	hubieron llorado
4 futuro		11 futuro perfecto	
lloraré	lloraremos	habré llorado	habremos llorado
llorarás	lloraréis	habrás llorado	habréis llorado
llorará	llorarán	habrá llorado	habrán llorado
5 potencial simple		12 potencial compuesto	
lloraría	lloraríamos	habría llorado	habríamos llorado
llorarías	lloraríais	habrías llorado	habríais llorado
lloraría	llorarían	habría llorado	habrían llorado
6 presente de subjuntivo		13 perfecto de subjuntivo	
llore	lloremos	haya llorado	hayamos llorado
llores	lloréis	hayas llorado	hayáis llorado
llore	lloren	haya llorado	hayan llorado
7 imperfecto de subjuntivo		14 pluscuamperfecto de subjuntivo	
llorara	lloráramos	hubiera llorado	hubiéramos llorado
lloraras	llorarais	hubieras llorado	hubierais llorado
llorara	lloraran	hubiera llorado	hubieran llorado
OR		OR	
llorase	llorásemos	hubiese llorado	hubiésemos llorado
llorases	lloraseis	hubieses llorado	hubieseis llorado
llorase	llorasen	hubiese llorado	hubiesen llorado

	imperativo	
—	lloremos
llora; no llores	llorad; no lloréis
llore	lloren

Words and expressions related to this verb

lloroso, llorosa tearful, sorrowful
el lloro weeping, crying
llorador, lloradora weeper
lloriquear to cry constantly

llorar con un ojo to shed crocodile tears
llorar por to weep (cry) for
llorar por cualquier cosa to cry about anything

Gerundio **lloviendo**	Part. pas. **llovido**	**llover**
		to rain

The Seven Simple Tenses	The Seven Compound Tenses
Singular Plural	Singular Plural
1 presente de indicativo **llueve** OR **está lloviendo**	8 perfecto de indicativo **ha llovido**
2 imperfecto de indicativo **llovía** OR **estaba lloviendo**	9 pluscuamperfecto de indicativo **había llovido**
3 pretérito **llovió**	10 pretérito anterior **hubo llovido**
4 futuro **lloverá**	11 futuro perfecto **habrá llovido**
5 potencial simple **llovería**	12 potencial compuesto **habría llovido**
6 presente de subjuntivo **llueva**	13 perfecto de subjuntivo **haya llovido**
7 imperfecto de subjuntivo **lloviera** OR **lloviese**	14 pluscuamperfecto de subjuntivo **hubiera llovido** OR **hubiese llovido**

imperativo
¡Que llueva! Let it rain!

Words and expressions related to this verb
la lluvia rain
lluvioso, lluviosa rainy
llover a cántaros to rain in torrents
llueva o no rain or shine
la llovizna drizzle

llover chuzos to rain pitchforks (cats and dogs)
tiempo lluvioso rainy weather
lloviznar to drizzle

marchar   Gerundio **marchando**   Part. pas. **marchado**

to walk, to march, to function (machine), to run (machine)

The Seven Simple Tenses		The Seven Compound Tenses	
Singular	Plural	Singular	Plural
1 presente de indicativo		8 perfecto de indicativo	
marcho	marchamos	he marchado	hemos marchado
marchas	marcháis	has marchado	habéis marchado
marcha	marchan	ha marchado	han marchado
2 imperfecto de indicativo		9 pluscuamperfecto de indicativo	
marchaba	marchábamos	había marchado	habíamos marchado
marchabas	marchabais	habías marchado	habíais marchado
marchaba	marchaban	había marchado	habían marchado
3 pretérito		10 pretérito anterior	
marché	marchamos	hube marchado	hubimos marchado
marchaste	marchasteis	hubiste marchado	hubisteis marchado
marchó	marcharon	hubo marchado	hubieron marchado
4 futuro		11 futuro perfecto	
marcharé	marcharemos	habré marchado	habremos marchado
marcharás	marcharéis	habrás marchado	habréis marchado
marchará	marcharán	habrá marchado	habrán marchado
5 potencial simple		12 potencial compuesto	
marcharía	marcharíamos	habría marchado	habríamos marchado
marcharías	marcharíais	habrías marchado	habríais marchado
marcharía	marcharían	habría marchado	habrían marchado
6 presente de subjuntivo		13 perfecto de subjuntivo	
marche	marchemos	haya marchado	hayamos marchado
marches	marchéis	hayas marchado	hayáis marchado
marche	marchen	haya marchado	hayan marchado
7 imperfecto de subjuntivo		14 pluscuamperfecto de subjuntivo	
marchara	marcháramos	hubiera marchado	hubiéramos marchado
marcharas	marcharais	hubieras marchado	hubierais marchado
marchara	marcharan	hubiera marchado	hubieran marchado
OR		OR	
marchase	marchásemos	hubiese marchado	hubiésemos marchado
marchases	marchaseis	hubieses marchado	hubieseis marchado
marchase	marchasen	hubiese marchado	hubiesen marchado

imperativo	
—	marchemos
marcha; no marches	marchad; no marchéis
marche	marchen

Words and expressions related to this verb
la marcha march
a largas marchas speedily, with speed
¡En marcha! Forward march!

poner en marcha to put in motion,
    to start
Esto no marcha That won't work;
    That will not do.

Gerundio **marchándose**   Part. pas. **marchado**   **marcharse**

to go away, to leave

The Seven Simple Tenses		The Seven Compound Tenses	
Singular	Plural	Singular	Plural
1 presente de indicativo		8 perfecto de indicativo	
me marcho	nos marchamos	me he	nos hemos
te marchas	os marcháis	te has	os habéis + marchado
se marcha	se marchan	se ha	se han
2 imperfecto de indicativo		9 pluscuamperfecto de indicativo	
me marchaba	nos marchábamos	me había	nos habíamos
te marchabas	os marchabais	te habías	os habíais + marchado
se marchaba	se marchaban	se había	se habían
3 pretérito		10 pretérito anterior	
me marché	nos marchamos	me hube	nos hubimos
te marchaste	os marchasteis	te hubiste	os hubisteis + marchado
se marchó	se marcharon	se hubo	se hubieron
4 futuro		11 futuro perfecto	
me marcharé	nos marcharemos	me habré	nos habremos
te marcharás	os marcharéis	te habrás	os habréis + marchado
se marchará	se marcharán	se habrá	se habrán
5 potencial simple		12 potencial compuesto	
me marcharía	nos marcharíamos	me habría	nos habríamos
te marcharías	os marcharíais	te habrías	os habríais + marchado
se marcharía	se marcharían	se habría	se habrían
6 presente de subjuntivo		13 perfecto de subjuntivo	
me marche	nos marchemos	me haya	nos hayamos
te marches	os marchéis	te hayas	os hayáis + marchado
se marche	se marchen	se haya	se hayan
7 imperfecto de subjuntivo		14 pluscuamperfecto de subjuntivo	
me marchara	nos marcháramos	me hubiera	nos hubiéramos
te marcharas	os marcharais	te hubieras	os hubierais + marchado
se marchara	se marcharan	se hubiera	se hubieran
OR		OR	
me marchase	nos marchásemos	me hubiese	nos hubiésemos
te marchases	os marchaseis	te hubieses	os hubieseis + marchado
se marchase	se marchasen	se hubiese	se hubiesen

imperativo	
—	marchémonos
márchate; no te marches	marchaos; no os marchéis
márchese	márchense

For words and expressions related to this verb, see **marchar,** which is related to it.

matar	Gerundio **matando**	Part. pas. **matado**

to kill

The Seven Simple Tenses		The Seven Compound Tenses	
Singular	Plural	Singular	Plural
1 presente de indicativo		**8 perfecto de indicativo**	
mato	matamos	he matado	hemos matado
matas	matáis	has matado	habéis matado
mata	matan	ha matado	han matado
2 imperfecto de indicativo		**9 pluscuamperfecto de indicativo**	
mataba	matábamos	había matado	habíamos matado
matabas	matabais	habías matado	habíais matado
mataba	mataban	había matado	habían matado
3 pretérito		**10 pretérito anterior**	
maté	matamos	hube matado	hubimos matado
mataste	matasteis	hubiste matado	hubisteis matado
mató	mataron	hubo matado	hubieron matado
4 futuro		**11 futuro perfecto**	
mataré	mataremos	habré matado	habremos matado
matarás	mataréis	habrás matado	habréis matado
matará	matarán	habrá matado	habrán matado
5 potencial simple		**12 potencial compuesto**	
mataría	mataríamos	habría matado	habríamos matado
matarías	mataríais	habrías matado	habríais matado
mataría	matarían	habría matado	habrían matado
6 presente de subjuntivo		**13 perfecto de subjuntivo**	
mate	matemos	haya matado	hayamos matado
mates	matéis	hayas matado	hayáis matado
mate	maten	haya matado	hayan matado
7 imperfecto de subjuntivo		**14 pluscuamperfecto de subjuntivo**	
matara	matáramos	hubiera matado	hubiéramos matado
mataras	matarais	hubieras matado	hubierais matado
matara	mataran	hubiera matado	hubieran matado
OR		OR	
matase	matásemos	hubiese matado	hubiésemos matado
matases	mataseis	hubieses matado	hubieseis matado
matase	matasen	hubiese matado	hubiesen matado

imperativo	
—	matemos
mata; no mates	matad; no matéis
mate	maten

Words and expressions related to this verb
el mate   checkmate (chess)
dar mate a   to checkmate (chess)
matador, matadora   killer; el matador
   bullfighter (kills the bull)

matar el tiempo   to kill time
estar a matar con alguien   to be
   angry at someone

206

Gerundio **mintiendo**   Part. pas. **mentido**   **mentir**

to lie, to tell a lie

The Seven Simple Tenses		The Seven Compound Tenses	
Singular	Plural	Singular	Plural
1 presente de indicativo		8 perfecto de indicativo	
miento	mentimos	he mentido	hemos mentido
mientes	mentís	has mentido	habéis mentido
miente	mienten	ha mentido	han mentido
2 imperfecto de indicativo		9 pluscuamperfecto de indicativo	
mentía	mentíamos	había mentido	habíamos mentido
mentías	mentíais	habías mentido	habíais mentido
mentía	mentían	había mentido	habían mentido
3 pretérito		10 pretérito anterior	
mentí	mentimos	hube mentido	hubimos mentido
mentiste	mentisteis	hubiste mentido	hubisteis mentido
mintió	mintieron	hubo mentido	hubieron mentido
4 futuro		11 futuro perfecto	
mentiré	mentiremos	habré mentido	habremos mentido
mentirás	mentiréis	habrás mentido	habréis mentido
mentirá	mentirán	habrá mentido	habrán mentido
5 potencial simple		12 potencial compuesto	
mentiría	mentiríamos	habría mentido	habríamos mentido
mentirías	mentiríais	habrías mentido	habríais mentido
mentiría	mentirían	habría mentido	habrían mentido
6 presente de subjuntivo		13 perfecto de subjuntivo	
mienta	mintamos	haya mentido	hayamos mentido
mientas	mintáis	hayas mentido	hayáis mentido
mienta	mientan	haya mentido	hayan mentido
7 imperfecto de subjuntivo		14 pluscuamperfecto de subjuntivo	
mintiera	mintiéramos	hubiera mentido	hubiéramos mentido
mintieras	mintierais	hubieras mentido	hubierais mentido
mintiera	mintieran	hubiera mentido	hubieran mentido
OR		OR	
mintiese	mintiésemos	hubiese mentido	hubiésemos mentido
mintieses	mintieseis	hubieses mentido	hubieseis mentido
mintiese	mintiesen	hubiese mentido	hubiesen mentido

imperativo

—	mintamos
miente; no mientas	mentid; no mintáis
mienta	mientan

Words and expressions related to this verb

una mentira	to lie	**mentido, mentida**	deceptive, false
un mentirón	a great lie	**mentirosamente**	falsely
una mentirilla	a fib	**¡Parece mentira¡**	I just don't believe it!

mirar	Gerundio **mirando**	Part. pas. **mirado**

to look, to look at, to watch

The Seven Simple Tenses		The Seven Compound Tenses	
Singular	Plural	Singular	Plural
1 presente de indicativo		8 perfecto de indicativo	
miro	miramos	he mirado	hemos mirado
miras	miráis	has mirado	habéis mirado
mira	miran	ha mirado	han mirado
2 imperfecto de indicativo		9 pluscuamperfecto de indicativo	
miraba	mirábamos	había mirado	habíamos mirado
mirabas	mirabais	habías mirado	habíais mirado
miraba	miraban	había mirado	habían mirado
3 pretérito		10 pretérito anterior	
miré	miramos	hube mirado	hubimos mirado
miraste	mirasteis	hubiste mirado	hubisteis mirado
miró	miraron	hubo mirado	hubieron mirado
4 futuro		11 futuro perfecto	
miraré	miraremos	habré mirado	habremos mirado
mirarás	miraréis	habrás mirado	habréis mirado
mirará	mirarán	habrá mirado	habrán mirado
5 potencial simple		12 potencial compuesto	
miraría	miraríamos	habría mirado	habríamos mirado
mirarías	miraríais	habrías mirado	habríais mirado
miraría	mirarían	habría mirado	habrían mirado
6 presente de subjuntivo		13 perfecto de subjuntivo	
mire	miremos	haya mirado	hayamos mirado
mires	miréis	hayas mirado	hayáis mirado
mire	miren	haya mirado	hayan mirado
7 imperfecto de subjuntivo		14 pluscuamperfecto de subjuntivo	
mirara	miráramos	hubiera mirado	hubiéramos mirado
miraras	mirarais	hubieras mirado	hubierais mirado
mirara	miraran	hubiera mirado	hubieran mirado
OR		OR	
mirase	mirásemos	hubiese mirado	hubiésemos mirado
mirases	miraseis	hubieses mirado	hubieseis mirado
mirase	mirasen	hubiese mirado	hubiesen mirado

	imperativo	
—	miremos	
mira; no mires	mirad; no miréis	
mire	miren	

Words and expressions related to this verb
mirar la televisión to watch television
¡Mira! Look! Look out! See here! Listen!

mira por to look after
mirador, miradora spectator
mirar de través to squint

to bite

The Seven Simple Tenses		The Seven Compound Tenses	
Singular	Plural	Singular	Plural
1 presente de indicativo		8 perfecto de indicativo	
muerdo	mordemos	he mordido	hemos mordido
muerdes	mordéis	has mordido	habéis mordido
muerde	muerden	ha mordido	han mordido
2 imperfecto de indicativo		9 pluscuamperfecto de indicativo	
mordía	mordíamos	había mordido	habíamos mordido
mordías	mordíais	habías mordido	habíais mordido
mordía	mordían	había mordido	habían mordido
3 pretérito		10 pretérito anterior	
mordí	mordimos	hube mordido	hubimos mordido
mordiste	mordisteis	hubiste mordido	hubisteis mordido
mordió	mordieron	hubo mordido	hubieron mordido
4 futuro		11 futuro perfecto	
morderé	morderemos	habré mordido	habremos mordido
morderás	morderéis	habrás mordido	habréis mordido
morderá	morderán	habrá mordido	habrán mordido
5 potencial simple		12 potencial compuesto	
mordería	morderíamos	habría mordido	habríamos mordido
morderías	morderíais	habrías mordido	habríais mordido
mordería	morderían	habría mordido	habrían mordido
6 presente de subjuntivo		13 perfecto de subjuntivo	
muerda	mordamos	haya mordido	hayamos mordido
muerdas	mordáis	hayas mordido	hayáis mordido
muerda	muerdan	haya mordido	hayan mordido
7 imperfecto de subjuntivo		14 pluscuamperfecto de subjuntivo	
mordiera	mordiéramos	hubiera mordido	hubiéramos mordido
mordieras	mordierais	hubieras mordido	hubierais mordido
mordiera	mordieran	hubiera mordido	hubieran mordido
OR		OR	
mordiese	mordiésemos	hubiese mordido	hubiésemos mordido
mordieses	mordieseis	hubieses mordido	hubieseis mordido
mordiese	mordiesen	hubiese mordido	hubiesen mordido

imperativo	
—	mordamos
muerde; no muerdas	morded; no mordáis
muerda	muerdan

Sentence using this verb and words related to it

Perro que ladra no muerde.   A barking dog does not bite.

una mordaza   muzzle   **mordazmente**   bitingly
la mordacidad   mordancy   **una mordedura**   a bite

morir	Gerundio **muriendo**	Part. pas. **muerto**

to die

The Seven Simple Tenses		The Seven Compound Tenses	
Singular	Plural	Singular	Plural

1 presente de indicativo		8 perfecto de indicativo	
muero	**morimos**	**he muerto**	**hemos muerto**
mueres	**morís**	**has muerto**	**habéis muerto**
muere	**mueren**	**ha muerto**	**han muerto**

2 imperfecto de indicativo		9 pluscuamperfecto de indicativo	
moría	**moríamos**	**había muerto**	**habíamos muerto**
morías	**moríais**	**habías muerto**	**habíais muerto**
moría	**morían**	**había muerto**	**habían muerto**

3 pretérito		10 pretérito anterior	
morí	**morimos**	**hube muerto**	**hubimos muerto**
moriste	**moristeis**	**hubiste muerto**	**hubisteis muerto**
murió	**murieron**	**hubo muerto**	**hubieron muerto**

4 futuro		11 futuro perfecto	
moriré	**moriremos**	**habré muerto**	**habremos muerto**
morirás	**moriréis**	**habrás muerto**	**habréis muerto**
morirá	**morirán**	**habrá muerto**	**habrán muerto**

5 potencial simple		12 potencial compuesto	
moriría	**moriríamos**	**habría muerto**	**habríamos muerto**
morirías	**moriríais**	**habrías muerto**	**habríais muerto**
moriría	**morirían**	**habría muerto**	**habrían muerto**

6 presente de subjuntivo		13 perfecto de subjuntivo	
muera	**muramos**	**haya muerto**	**hayamos muerto**
mueras	**muráis**	**hayas muerto**	**hayáis muerto**
muera	**mueran**	**haya muerto**	**hayan muerto**

7 imperfecto de subjuntivo		14 pluscuamperfecto de subjuntivo	
muriera	**muriéramos**	**hubiera muerto**	**hubiéramos muerto**
murieras	**murierais**	**hubieras muerto**	**hubierais muerto**
muriera	**murieran**	**hubiera muerto**	**hubieran muerto**
OR		OR	
muriese	**muriésemos**	**hubiese muerto**	**hubiésemos muerto**
murieses	**murieseis**	**hubieses muerto**	**hubieseis muerto**
muriese	**muriesen**	**hubiese muerto**	**hubiesen muerto**

imperativo	
—	**muramos**
muere; no mueras	**morid; no muráis**
muera	**mueran**

Words and expressions related to this verb

la muerte death	**entremorir** to burn out, to flicker
mortal fatal, mortal	**morir de repente** to drop dead
la mortalidad mortality	**hasta morir** until death
morir de risa to die laughing	**morirse de miedo** to be scared to death

to show, to point out

The Seven Simple Tenses		The Seven Compound Tenses	
Singular	Plural	Singular	Plural
1 presente de indicativo		8 perfecto de indicativo	
muestro	**mostramos**	**he mostrado**	**hemos mostrado**
muestras	**mostráis**	**has mostrado**	**habéis mostrado**
muestra	**muestran**	**ha mostrado**	**han mostrado**
2 imperfecto de indicativo		9 pluscuamperfecto de indicativo	
mostraba	**mostrábamos**	**había mostrado**	**habíamos mostrado**
mostrabas	**mostrabais**	**habías mostrado**	**habíais mostrado**
mostraba	**mostraban**	**había mostrado**	**habían mostrado**
3 pretérito		10 pretérito anterior	
mostré	**mostramos**	**hube mostrado**	**hubimos mostrado**
mostraste	**mostrasteis**	**hubiste mostrado**	**hubisteis mostrado**
mostró	**mostraron**	**hubo mostrado**	**hubieron mostrado**
4 futuro		11 futuro perfecto	
mostraré	**mostraremos**	**habré mostrado**	**habremos mostrado**
mostrarás	**mostraréis**	**habrás mostrado**	**habréis mostrado**
mostrará	**mostrarán**	**habrá mostrado**	**habrán mostrado**
5 potencial simple		12 potencial compuesto	
mostraría	**mostraríamos**	**habría mostrado**	**habríamos mostrado**
mostrarías	**mostraríais**	**habrías mostrado**	**habríais mostrado**
mostraría	**mostrarían**	**habría mostrado**	**habrían mostrado**
6 presente de subjuntivo		13 perfecto de subjuntivo	
muestre	**mostremos**	**haya mostrado**	**hayamos mostrado**
muestres	**mostréis**	**hayas mostrado**	**hayáis mostrado**
muestre	**muestren**	**haya mostrado**	**hayan mostrado**
7 imperfecto de subjuntivo		14 pluscuamperfecto de subjuntivo	
mostrara	**mostráramos**	**hubiera mostrado**	**hubiéramos mostrado**
mostraras	**mostrarais**	**hubieras mostrado**	**hubierais mostrado**
mostrara	**mostraran**	**hubiera mostrado**	**hubieran mostrado**
OR		OR	
mostrase	**mostrásemos**	**hubiese mostrado**	**hubiésemos mostrado**
mostrases	**mostraseis**	**hubieses mostrado**	**hubieseis mostrado**
mostrase	**mostrasen**	**hubiese mostrado**	**hubiesen mostrado**

imperative	
—	**mostremos**
muestra; no muestres	**mostrad; no mostréis**
muestre	**muestren**

Words related to this verb
mostrador, mostradora   demonstrator, counter (in a store where merchandise is
displayed under a glass case)
mostrarse   to show oneself, to appear
See also **demostrar**.

to be born

The Seven Simple Tenses		The Seven Compound Tenses	
Singular	Plural	Singular	Plural
1 presente de indicativo		8 perfecto de indicativo	
nazco	nacemos	he nacido	hemos nacido
naces	nacéis	has nacido	habéis nacido
nace	nacen	ha nacido	han nacido
2 imperfecto de indicativo		9 pluscuamperfecto de indicativo	
nacía	nacíamos	había nacido	habíamos nacido
nacías	nacíais	habías nacido	habíais nacido
nacía	nacían	había nacido	habían nacido
3 pretérito		10 pretérito anterior	
nací	nacimos	hube nacido	hubimos nacido
naciste	nacisteis	hubiste nacido	hubisteis nacido
nació	nacieron	hubo nacido	hubieron nacido
4 futuro		11 futuro perfecto	
naceré	naceremos	habré nacido	habremos nacido
nacerás	naceréis	habrás nacido	habréis nacido
nacerá	nacerán	habrá nacido	habrán nacido
5 potencial simple		12 potencial compuesto	
nacería	naceríamos	habría nacido	habríamos nacido
nacerías	naceríais	habrías nacido	habríais nacido
nacería	nacerían	habría nacido	habrían nacido
6 presente de subjuntivo		13 perfecto de subjuntivo	
nazca	nazcamos	haya nacido	hayamos nacido
nazcas	nazcáis	hayas nacido	hayáis nacido
nazca	nazcan	haya nacido	hayan nacido
7 imperfecto de subjuntivo		14 pluscuamperfecto de subjuntivo	
naciera	naciéramos	hubiera nacido	hubiéramos nacido
nacieras	nacierais	hubieras nacido	hubierais nacido
naciera	nacieran	hubiera nacido	hubieran nacido
OR		OR	
naciese	naciésemos	hubiese nacido	hubiésemos nacido
nacieses	nacieseis	hubieses nacido	hubieseis nacido
naciese	naciesen	hubiese nacido	hubiesen nacido

imperativo	
—	nazcamos
nace; no nazcas	naced; no nazcáis
nazca	nazcan

Words and expressions related to this verb
bien nacido (nacida) well bred;
  mal nacido (nacida) ill bred
el nacimiento birth
renacer to be born again, to be reborn

nacer tarde to be born yesterday
  (not much intelligence)
nacer de pies to be born with a
  silver spoon in one's mouth

The Seven Simple Tenses		The Seven Compound Tenses	
Singular	Plural	Singular	Plural
1 presente de indicativo		8 perfecto de indicativo	
nado	nadamos	he nadado	hemos nadado
nadas	nadáis	has nadado	habéis nadado
nada	nadan	ha nadado	han nadado
2 imperfecto de indicativo		9 pluscuamperfecto de indicativo	
nadaba	nadábamos	había nadado	habíamos nadado
nadabas	nadabais	habías nadado	habíais nadado
nadaba	nadaban	había nadado	habían nadado
3 pretérito		10 pretérito anterior	
nadé	nadamos	hube nadado	hubimos nadado
nadaste	nadasteis	hubiste nadado	hubisteis nadado
nadó	nadaron	hubo nadado	hubieron nadado
4 futuro		11 futuro perfecto	
nadaré	nadaremos	habré nadado	habremos nadado
nadarás	nadaréis	habrás nadado	habréis nadado
nadará	nadarán	habrá nadado	habrán nadado
5 potencial simple		12 potencial compuesto	
nadaría	nadaríamos	habría nadado	habríamos nadado
nadarías	nadaríais	habrías nadado	habríais nadado
nadaría	nadarían	habría nadado	habrían nadado
6 presente de subjuntivo		13 perfecto de subjuntivo	
nade	nademos	haya nadado	hayamos nadado
nades	nadéis	hayas nadado	hayáis nadado
nade	naden	haya nadado	hayan nadado
7 imperfecto de subjuntivo		14 pluscuamperfecto de subjuntivo	
nadara	nadáramos	hubiera nadado	hubiéramos nadado
nadaras	nadarais	hubieras nadado	hubierais nadado
nadara	nadaran	hubiera nadado	hubieran nadado
OR		OR	
nadase	nadásemos	hubiese nadado	hubiésemos nadado
nadases	nadaseis	hubieses nadado	hubieseis nadado
nadase	nadasen	hubiese nadado	hubiesen nadado

imperativo	
—	nademos
nada; no nades	nadad; no nadéis
nade	naden

Words and expressions related to this verb
nadador, nadadora swimmer
la natación swimming

nadar entre dos aguas to be undecided
nader en to revel in, to delight in, to take great
pleasure in

necesitar	Gerundio **necesitando**	Part. pas. **necesitado**

to need

The Seven Simple Tenses	The Seven Compound Tenses

Singular	Plural	Singular	Plural
1 presente de indicativo		8 perfecto de indicativo	
necesito	**necesitamos**	**he necesitado**	**hemos necesitado**
necesitas	**necesitáis**	**has necesitado**	**habéis necesitado**
necesita	**necesitan**	**ha necesitado**	**han necesitado**
2 imperfecto de indicativo		9 pluscuamperfecto de indicativo	
necesitaba	**necesitábamos**	**había necesitado**	**habíamos necesitado**
necesitabas	**necesitabais**	**habías necesitado**	**habíais necesitado**
necesitaba	**necesitaban**	**había necesitado**	**habían necesitado**
3 pretérito		10 pretérito anterior	
necesité	**necesitamos**	**hube necesitado**	**hubimos necesitado**
necesitaste	**necesitasteis**	**hubiste necesitado**	**hubisteis necesitado**
necesitó	**necesitaron**	**hubo necesitado**	**hubieron necesitado**
4 futuro		11 futuro perfecto	
necesitaré	**necesitaremos**	**habré necesitado**	**habremos necesitado**
necesitarás	**necesitaréis**	**habrás necesitado**	**habréis necesitado**
necesitará	**necesitarán**	**habrá necesitado**	**habrán necesitado**
5 potencial simple		12 potencial compuesto	
necesitaría	**necesitaríamos**	**habría necesitado**	**habríamos necesitado**
necesitarías	**necesitaríais**	**habrías necesitado**	**habríais necesitado**
necesitaría	**necesitarían**	**habría necesitado**	**habrían necesitado**
6 presente de subjuntivo		13 perfecto de subjuntivo	
necesite	**necesitemos**	**haya necesitado**	**hayamos necesitado**
necesites	**necesitéis**	**hayas necesitado**	**hayáis necesitado**
necesite	**necesiten**	**haya necesitado**	**hayan necesitado**
7 imperfecto de subjuntivo		14 pluscuamperfecto de subjuntivo	
necesitara	**necesitáramos**	**hubiera necesitado**	**hubiéramos necesitado**
necesitaras	**necesitarais**	**hubieras necesitado**	**hubierais necesitado**
necesitara	**necesitaran**	**hubiera necesitado**	**hubieran necesitado**
OR		OR	
necesitase	**necesitásemos**	**hubiese necesitado**	**hubiésemos necesitado**
necesitases	**necesitaseis**	**hubieses necesitado**	**hubieseis necesitado**
necesitase	**necesitasen**	**hubiese necesitado**	**hubiesen necesitado**

imperativo	
—	**necesitemos**
necesita; no necesites	**necesitad; no necesitéis**
necesite	**necesiten**

Words and expressions related to this verb

la necesidad necessity
por necesidad from necessity
necesario, necesaria necessary

necesitar + inf. to have + inf., to need + inf.
un necesitado, una necesitada needy person
necesariamente necessarily

to deny

The Seven Simple Tenses		The Seven Compound Tenses	
Singular	Plural	Singular	Plural
1 presente de indicativo		**8 perfecto de indicativo**	
niego	negamos	he negado	hemos negado
niegas	negáis	has negado	habéis negado
niega	niegan	ha negado	han negado
2 imperfecto de indicativo		**9 pluscuamperfecto de indicativo**	
negaba	negábamos	había negado	habíamos negado
negabas	negabais	habías negado	habíais negado
negaba	negaban	había negado	habían negado
3 pretérito		**10 pretérito anterior**	
negué	negamos	hube negado	hubimos negado
negaste	negasteis	hubiste negado	hubisteis negado
negó	negaron	hubo negado	hubieron negado
4 futuro		**11 futuro perfecto**	
negaré	negaremos	habré negado	habremos negado
negarás	negaréis	habrás negado	habréis negado
negará	negarán	habrá negado	habrán negado
5 potencial simple		**12 potencial compuesto**	
negaría	negaríamos	habría negado	habríamos negado
negarías	negaríais	habrías negado	habríais negado
negaría	negarían	habría negado	habrían negado
6 presente de subjuntivo		**13 perfecto de subjuntivo**	
niegue	neguemos	haya negado	hayamos negado
niegues	neguéis	hayas negado	hayáis negado
niegue	nieguen	haya negado	hayan negado
7 imperfecto de subjuntivo		**14 pluscuamperfecto de subjuntivo**	
negara	negáramos	hubiera negado	hubiéramos negado
negaras	negarais	hubieras negado	hubierais negado
negara	negaran	hubiera negado	hubieran negado
OR		OR	
negase	negásemos	hubiese negado	hubiésemos negado
negases	negaseis	hubieses negado	hubieseis negado
negase	negasen	hubiese negado	hubiesen negado

imperativo	
—	neguemos
niega; no niegues	negad; no neguéis
niegue	nieguen

Words and expressions related to this verb

negador, negadora denier
negativo, negativa negative
la negación denial, negation
negable deniable

negar haber + past part. to deny having + past part.
negarse a to refuse
renegar to abhor, to deny vehemently

215

nevar   Gerundio **nevando**   Part. pas. **nevado**

to snow

The Seven Simple Tenses	The Seven Compound Tenses
Singular Plural	Singular Plural
1 presente de indicativo **nieva** OR **está nevando**	8 perfecto de indicativo **ha nevado**
2 imperfecto de indicativo **nevaba** OR **estaba nevando**	9 pluscuamperfecto de indicativo **había nevado**
3 pretérito **nevó**	10 pretérito anterior **hubo nevado**
4 futuro **nevará**	11 futuro perfecto **habrá nevado**
5 potencial simple **nevaría**	12 potencial compuesto **habría nevado**
6 presente de subjuntivo **nieve**	13 perfecto de subjuntivo **haya nevado**
7 imperfecto de subjuntivo **nevara** OR **nevase**	14 pluscuamperfecto de subjuntivo **hubiera nevado** OR **hubiese nevado**

imperativo
¡Que nieve! Let it snow!

Words and expressions related to this verb
la nieve snow
   Me gusta la nieve. I like snow.
nevado, nevada snowy, snow covered
la nevada snowfall; the state of Nevada, U.S.A.

la nevera refrigerator
un copo de nieve snowflake
una bola de nieve snowball

to obey

The Seven Simple Tenses		The Seven Compound Tenses	
Singular	Plural	Singular	Plural
1 presente de indicativo		8 perfecto de indicativo	
obedezco	obedecemos	he obedecido	hemos obedecido
obedeces	obedecéis	has obedecido	habéis obedecido
obedece	obedecen	ha obedecido	han obedecido
2 imperfecto de indicativo		9 pluscuamperfecto de indicativo	
obedecía	obedecíamos	había obedecido	habíamos obedecido
obedecías	obedecíais	habías obedecido	habíais obedecido
obedecía	obedecían	había obedecido	habían obedecido
3 pretérito		10 pretérito anterior	
obedecí	obedecimos	hube obedecido	hubimos obedecido
obedeciste	obedecisteis	hubiste obedecido	hubisteis obedecido
obedeció	obedecieron	hubo obedecido	hubieron obedecido
4 futuro		11 futuro perfecto	
obedeceré	obedeceremos	habré obedecido	habremos obedecido
obedecerás	obedeceréis	habrás obedecido	habréis obedecido
obedecerá	obedecerán	habrá obedecido	habrán obedecido
5 potencial simple		12 potencial compuesto	
obedecería	obedeceríamos	habría obedecido	habríamos obedecido
obedecerías	obedeceríais	habrías obedecido	habríais obedecido
obedecería	obedecerían	habría obedecido	habrían obedecido
6 presente de subjuntivo		13 perfecto de subjuntivo	
obedezca	obedezcamos	haya obedecido	hayamos obedecido
obedezcas	obedezcáis	hayas obedecido	hayáis obedecido
obedezca	obedezcan	haya obedecido	hayan obedecido
7 imperfecto de subjuntivo		14 pluscuamperfecto de subjuntivo	
obedeciera	obedeciéramos	hubiera obedecido	hubiéramos obedecido
obedecieras	obedecierais	hubieras obedecido	hubierais obedecido
obedeciera	obedecieran	hubiera obedecido	hubieran obedecido
OR		OR	
obedeciese	obedeciésemos	hubiese obedecido	hubiésemos obedecido
obedecieses	obedecieseis	hubieses obedecido	hubieseis obedecido
obedeciese	obedeciesen	hubiese obedecido	hubiesen obedecido

	imperativo	
—		obedezcamos
obedece; no obedezcas		obedeced; no obedezcáis
obedezca		obedezcan

Words related to this verb
el obedecimiento, la obediencia   obedience   **obedientemente** obediently
obediente   obedient   **desobedecer** to disobey

obtener Gerundio **obteniendo** Part. pas. **obtenido**

to obtain, to get

The Seven Simple Tenses		The Seven Compound Tenses	
Singular	Plural	Singular	Plural
1 presente de indicativo		8 perfecto de indicativo	
obtengo	obtenemos	he obtenido	hemos obtenido
obtienes	obtenéis	has obtenido	habéis obtenido
obtiene	obtienen	ha obtenido	han obtenido
2 imperfecto de indicativo		9 pluscuamperfecto de indicativo	
obtenía	obteníamos	había obtenido	habíamos obtenido
obtenías	obteníais	habías obtenido	habíais obtenido
obtenía	obtenían	había obtenido	habían obtenido
3 pretérito		10 pretérito anterior	
obtuve	obtuvimos	hube obtenido	hubimos obtenido
obtuviste	obtuvisteis	hubiste obtenido	hubisteis obtenido
obtuvo	obtuvieron	hubo obtenido	hubieron obtenido
4 futuro		11 futuro perfecto	
obtendré	obtendremos	habré obtenido	habremos obtenido
obtendrás	obtendréis	habrás obtenido	habréis obtenido
obtendrá	obtendrán	habrá obtenido	habrán obtenido
5 potencial simple		12 potencial compuesto	
obtendría	obtendríamos	habría obtenido	habríamos obtenido
obtendrías	obtendríais	habrías obtenido	habríais obtenido
obtendría	obtendrían	habría obtenido	habrían obtenido
6 presente de subjuntivo		13 perfecto de subjuntivo	
obtenga	obtengamos	haya obtenido	hayamos obtenido
obtengas	obtengáis	hayas obtenido	hayáis obtenido
obtenga	obtengan	haya obtenido	hayan obtenido
7 imperfecto de subjuntivo		14 pluscuamperfecto de subjuntivo	
obtuviera	obtuviéramos	hubiera obtenido	hubiéramos obtenido
obtuvieras	obtuvierais	hubieras obtenido	hubierais obtenido
obtuviera	obtuvieran	hubiera obtenido	hubieran obtenido
OR		OR	
obtuviese	obtuviésemos	hubiese obtenido	hubiésemos obtenido
obtuvieses	obtuvieseis	hubieses obtenido	hubieseis obtenido
obtuviese	obtuviesen	hubiese obtenido	hubiesen obtenido

imperativo	
—	obtengamos
obtén; no obtengas	obtened; obtengáis
obtenga	obtengan

Words related to this verb
obtenible obtainable, available
obtener una colocación to get a job
la obtención obtainment

Gerundio **ocupando**   Part. pas. **ocupado**   **ocupar**

to occupy

The Seven Simple Tenses		The Seven Compound Tenses	
Singular	Plural	Singular	Plural
1 presente de indicativo		8 perfecto de indicativo	
ocupo	ocupamos	he ocupado	hemos ocupado
ocupas	ocupáis	has ocupado	habéis ocupado
ocupa	ocupan	ha ocupado	han ocupado
2 imperfecto de indicativo		9 pluscuamperfecto de indicativo	
ocupaba	ocupábamos	había ocupado	habíamos ocupado
ocupabas	ocupabais	habías ocupado	habíais ocupado
ocupaba	ocupaban	había ocupado	habían ocupado
3 pretérito		10 pretérito anterior	
ocupé	ocupamos	hube ocupado	hubimos ocupado
ocupaste	ocupasteis	hubiste ocupado	hubisteis ocupado
ocupó	ocuparon	hubo ocupado	hubieron ocupado
4 futuro		11 futuro perfecto	
ocuparé	ocuparemos	habré ocupado	habremos ocupado
ocuparás	ocuparéis	habrás ocupado	habréis ocupado
ocupará	ocuparán	habrá ocupado	habrán ocupado
5 potencial simple		12 potencial compuesto	
ocuparía	ocuparíamos	habría ocupado	habríamos ocupado
ocuparías	ocuparíais	habrías ocupado	habríais ocupado
ocuparía	ocuparían	habría ocupado	habrían ocupado
6 presente de subjuntivo		13 perfecto de subjuntivo	
ocupe	ocupemos	haya ocupado	hayamos ocupado
ocupes	ocupéis	hayas ocupado	hayáis ocupado
ocupe	ocupen	haya ocupado	hayan ocupado
7 imperfecto de subjuntivo		14 pluscuamperfecto de subjuntivo	
ocupara	ocupáramos	hubiera ocupado	hubiéramos ocupado
ocuparas	ocuparais	hubieras ocupado	hubierais ocupado
ocupara	ocuparan	hubiera ocupado	hubieran ocupado
OR		OR	
ocupase	ocupásemos	hubiese ocupado	hubiésemos ocupado
ocupases	ocupaseis	hubieses ocupado	hubieseis ocupado
ocupase	ocupasen	hubiese ocupado	hubiesen ocupado

imperativo	
—	ocupemos
ocupa; no ocupes	ocupad; no ocupéis
ocupe	ocupen

Words and expressions related to this verb
ocupado, ocupada busy, occupied
la ocupación occupation
ocuparse de (en) to be busy with, in, to be engaged in
un, una ocupante occupant

desocupar to vacate
ocuparse con algo to
be busy with
something

ocurrir	Gerundio **ocurriendo**	Part. pas. **ocurrido**

to occur, to happen

The Seven Simple Tenses		The Seven Compound Tenses	
Singular	Plural	Singular	Plural
1 presente de indicativo		8 perfecto de indicativo	
ocurre	**ocurren**	**ha ocurrido**	**han ocurrido**
2 imperfecto de indicativo		9 pluscuamperfecto de indicativo	
ocurría	**ocurrían**	**había ocurrido**	**habían ocurrido**
3 pretérito		10 pretérito anterior	
ocurrió	**ocurrieron**	**hubo ocurrido**	**hubieron ocurrido**
4 futuro		11 futuro perfecto	
ocurrirá	**ocurrirán**	**habrá ocurrido**	**habrán ocurrido**
5 potencial simple		12 potencial compuesto	
ocurriría	**ocurrirían**	**habría ocurrido**	**habrían ocurrido**
6 presente de subjuntivo		13 perfecto de subjuntivo	
ocurra	**ocurran**	**haya ocurrido**	**hayan ocurrido**
7 imperfecto de subjuntivo		14 pluscuamperfecto de subjuntivo	
ocurriera	**ocurrieran**	**hubiera ocurrido**	**hubieran ocurrido**
OR		OR	
ocurriese	**ocurriesen**	**hubiese ocurrido**	**hubiesen ocurrido**

imperativo
¡Que ocurra! **¡Que ocurran!**
Let it occur!   Let them occur!

Words related to this verb
ocurrente occurring; funny, witty, humorous
la ocurrencia occurrence, happening, event; witticism
This verb is generally used in the third person singular and plural.

to offer

The Seven Simple Tenses		The Seven Compound Tenses	
Singular	Plural	Singular	Plural
1 presente de indicativo		8 perfecto de indicativo	
ofrezco	**ofrecemos**	**he ofrecido**	**hemos ofrecido**
ofreces	**ofrecéis**	**has ofrecido**	**habéis ofrecido**
ofrece	**ofrecen**	**ha ofrecido**	**han ofrecido**
2 imperfecto de indicativo		9 pluscuamperfecto de indicativo	
ofrecía	**ofrecíamos**	**había ofrecido**	**habíamos ofrecido**
ofrecías	**ofrecíais**	**habías ofrecido**	**habíais ofrecido**
ofrecía	**ofrecían**	**había ofrecido**	**habían ofrecido**
3 pretérito		10 pretérito anterior	
ofrecí	**ofrecimos**	**hube ofrecido**	**hubimos ofrecido**
ofreciste	**ofrecisteis**	**hubiste ofrecido**	**hubisteis ofrecido**
ofreció	**ofrecieron**	**hubo ofrecido**	**hubieron ofrecido**
4 futuro		11 futuro perfecto	
ofreceré	**ofreceremos**	**habré ofrecido**	**habremos ofrecido**
ofrecerás	**ofreceréis**	**habrás ofrecido**	**habréis ofrecido**
ofrecerá	**ofrecerán**	**habrá ofrecido**	**habrán ofrecido**
5 potencial simple		12 potencial compuesto	
ofrecería	**ofreceríamos**	**habría ofrecido**	**habríamos ofrecido**
ofrecerías	**ofreceríais**	**habrías ofrecido**	**habríais ofrecido**
ofrecería	**ofrecerían**	**habría ofrecido**	**habrían ofrecido**
6 presente de subjuntivo		13 perfecto de subjuntivo	
ofrezca	**ofrezcamos**	**haya ofrecido**	**hayamos ofrecido**
ofrezcas	**ofrezcáis**	**hayas ofrecido**	**hayáis ofrecido**
ofrezca	**ofrezcan**	**haya ofrecido**	**hayan ofrecido**
7 imperfecto de subjuntivo		14 pluscuamperfecto de subjuntivo	
ofreciera	**ofreciéramos**	**hubiera ofrecido**	**hubiéramos ofrecido**
ofrecieras	**ofrecierais**	**hubieras ofrecido**	**hubierais ofrecido**
ofreciera	**ofrecieran**	**hubiera ofrecido**	**hubieran ofrecido**
OR		OR	
ofreciese	**ofreciésemos**	**hubiese ofrecido**	**hubiésemos ofrecido**
ofrecieses	**ofrecieseis**	**hubieses ofrecido**	**hubieseis ofrecido**
ofreciese	**ofreciesen**	**hubiese ofrecido**	**hubiesen ofrecido**

	imperativo	
—	**ofrezcamos**	
ofrece; no ofrezcas	**ofreced; no ofrezcáis**	
ofrezca	**ofrezcan**	

Words related to this verb
ofreciente offering
el ofrecimiento offer, offering
la ofrenda gift, oblation

ofrecer + inf. to offer + inf.
el ofrecedor, la ofrecedora offerer

oír	Gerundio **oyendo**	Part. pas. **oído**

to hear

The Seven Simple Tenses		The Seven Compound Tenses	
Singular	Plural	Singular	Plural
1 presente de indicativo		8 perfecto de indicativo	
oigo	oímos	he oído	hemos oído
oyes	oís	has oído	habéis oído
oye	oyen	ha oído	han oído
2 imperfecto de indicativo		9 pluscuamperfecto de indicativo	
oía	oíamos	había oído	habíamos oído
oías	oíais	habías oído	habíais oído
oía	oían	había oído	habían oído
3 pretérito		10 pretérito anterior	
oí	oímos	hube oído	hubimos oído
oíste	oísteis	hubiste oído	hubisteis oído
oyó	oyeron	hubo oído	hubieron oído
4 futuro		11 futuro perfecto	
oiré	oiremos	habré oído	habremos oído
oirás	oiréis	habrás oído	habréis oído
oirá	oirán	habrá oído	habrán oído
5 potencial simple		12 potencial compuesto	
oiría	oiríamos	habría oído	habríamos oído
oirías	oiríais	habrías oído	habríais oído
oiría	oirían	habría oído	habrían oído
6 presente de subjuntivo		13 perfecto de subjuntivo	
oiga	oigamos	haya oído	hayamos oído
oigas	oigáis	hayas oído	hayáis oído
oiga	oigan	haya oído	hayan oído
7 imperfecto de subjuntivo		14 pluscuamperfecto de subjuntivo	
oyera	oyéramos	hubiera oído	hubiéramos oído
oyeras	oyerais	hubieras oído	hubierais oído
oyera	oyeran	hubiera oído	hubieran oído
OR		OR	
oyese	oyésemos	hubiese oído	hubiésemos oído
oyeses	oyeseis	hubieses oído	hubieseis oído
oyese	oyesen	hubiese oído	hubiesen oído

	imperativo	
—	oigamos	
oye; no oigas	oíd; no oigáis	
oiga	oigan	

Words and expressions related to this verb

la oída hearing; **de oídas** by hearsay
dar oídos to lend an ear
oír decir to hear tell, to hear say
oír hablar de to hear of, to hear talk of

por oídos, de oídos by hearing
al oído confidentially
el oído hearing (sense)
desoír to ignore, to be deaf to

to smell, to scent

The Seven Simple Tenses		The Seven Compound Tenses	
Singular	Plural	Singular	Plural
1 presente de indicativo		8 perfecto de indicativo	
huelo	**olemos**	**he olido**	**hemos olido**
hueles	**oléis**	**has olido**	**habéis olido**
huele	**huelen**	**ha olido**	**han olido**
2 imperfecto de indicativo		9 pluscuamperfecto de indicativo	
olía	**olíamos**	**había olido**	**habíamos olido**
olías	**olíais**	**habías olido**	**habíais olido**
olía	**olían**	**había olido**	**habían olido**
3 pretérito		10 pretérito anterior	
olí	**olimos**	**hube olido**	**hubimos olido**
oliste	**olisteis**	**hubiste olido**	**hubisteis olido**
olió	**olieron**	**hubo olido**	**hubieron olido**
4 futuro		11 futuro perfecto	
oleré	**oleremos**	**habré olido**	**habremos olido**
olerás	**oleréis**	**habrás olido**	**habréis olido**
olerá	**olerán**	**habrá olido**	**habrán olido**
5 potencial simple		12 potencial compuesto	
olería	**oleríamos**	**habría olido**	**habríamos olido**
olerías	**oleríais**	**habrías olido**	**habríais olido**
olería	**olerían**	**habría olido**	**habrían olido**
6 presente de subjuntivo		13 perfecto de subjuntivo	
huela	**olamos**	**haya olido**	**hayamos olido**
huelas	**oláis**	**hayas olido**	**hayáis olido**
huela	**huelan**	**haya olido**	**hayan olido**
7 imperfecto de subjuntivo		14 pluscuamperfecto de subjuntivo	
oliera	**oliéramos**	**hubiera olido**	**hubiéramos olido**
olieras	**olierais**	**hubieras olido**	**hubierais olido**
oliera	**olieran**	**hubiera olido**	**hubieran olido**
OR		OR	
oliese	**oliésemos**	**hubiese olido**	**hubiésemos olido**
olieses	**olieseis**	**hubieses olido**	**hubieseis olido**
oliese	**oliesen**	**hubiese olido**	**hubiesen olido**

	imperativo
—	**olamos**
huele; no huelas	**oled; no oláis**
huela	**huelan**

Words and expressions related to this verb
el olfato, la olfacción   olfaction (the sense of smelling, act of smelling)
olfatear   to sniff
oler a   to smell of
No huele bien   It looks fishy (It doesn't smell good.)

olvidar Gerundio **olvidando** Part. pas. **olvidado**

to forget

The Seven Simple Tenses		The Seven Compound Tenses	
Singular	Plural	Singular	Plural
1 presente de indicativo		8 perfecto de indicativo	
olvido	olvidamos	he olvidado	hemos olvidado
olvidas	olvidáis	has olvidado	habéis olvidado
olvida	olvidan	ha olvidado	han olvidado
2 imperfecto de indicativo		9 pluscuamperfecto de indicativo	
olvidaba	olvidábamos	había olvidado	habíamos olvidado
olvidabas	olvidabais	habías olvidado	habíais olvidado
olvidaba	olvidaban	había olvidado	habían olvidado
3 pretérito		10 pretérito anterior	
olvidé	olvidamos	hube olvidado	hubimos olvidado
olvidaste	olvidasteis	hubiste olvidado	hubisteis olvidado
olvidó	olvidaron	hubo olvidado	hubieron olvidado
4 futuro		11 futuro perfecto	
olvidaré	olvidaremos	habré olvidado	habremos olvidado
olvidarás	olvidaréis	habrás olvidado	habréis olvidado
olvidará	olvidarán	habrá olvidado	habrán olvidado
5 potencial simple		12 potencial compuesto	
olvidaría	olvidaríamos	habría olvidado	habríamos olvidado
olvidarías	olvidaríais	habrías olvidado	habríais olvidado
olvidaría	olvidarían	habría olvidado	habrían olvidado
6 presente de subjuntivo		13 perfecto de subjuntivo	
olvide	olvidemos	haya olvidado	hayamos olvidado
olvides	olvidéis	hayas olvidado	hayáis olvidado
olvide	olviden	haya olvidado	hayan olvidado
7 imperfecto de subjuntivo		14 pluscuamperfecto de subjuntivo	
olvidara	olvidáramos	hubiera olvidado	hubiéramos olvidado
olvidaras	olvidarais	hubieras olvidado	hubierais olvidado
olvidara	olvidaran	hubiera olvidado	hubieran olvidado
OR		OR	
olvidase	olvidásemos	hubiese olvidado	hubiésemos olvidado
olvidases	olvidaseis	hubieses olvidado	hubieseis olvidado
olvidase	olvidasen	hubiese olvidado	hubiesen olvidado

	imperativo	
—	olvidemos	
olvida; no olvides	olvidad; no olvidéis	
olvide	olviden	

Words and expressions related to this verb
olvidado, olvidada forgotten
olvidadizo, olvidadiza forgetful
el olvido forgetfulness, oblivion
Se me olvidó It slipped my mind.

olvidar + inf. to forget + inf.
olvidarse de to forget
olvidarse de + inf. to forget + inf.

Gerundio **ordenando**   Part. pas. **ordenado**   **ordenar**

to order, to command, to put in order, to arrange

The Seven Simple Tenses		The Seven Compound Tenses	
Singular	Plural	Singular	Plural
1 presente de indicativo		**8 perfecto de indicativo**	
ordeno	**ordenamos**	**he ordenado**	**hemos ordenado**
ordenas	**ordenáis**	**has ordenado**	**habéis ordenado**
ordena	**ordenan**	**ha ordenado**	**han ordenado**
2 imperfecto de indicativo		**9 pluscuamperfecto de indicativo**	
ordenaba	**ordenábamos**	**había ordenado**	**habíamos ordenado**
ordenabas	**ordenabais**	**habías ordenado**	**habíais ordenado**
ordenaba	**ordenaban**	**había ordenado**	**habían ordenado**
3 pretérito		**10 pretérito anterior**	
ordené	**ordenamos**	**hube ordenado**	**hubimos ordenado**
ordenaste	**ordenasteis**	**hubiste ordenado**	**hubisteis ordenado**
ordenó	**ordenaron**	**hubo ordenado**	**hubieron ordenado**
4 futuro		**11 futuro perfecto**	
ordenaré	**ordenaremos**	**habré ordenado**	**habremos ordenado**
ordenarás	**ordenaréis**	**habrás ordenado**	**habréis ordenado**
ordenará	**ordenarán**	**habrá ordenado**	**habrán ordenado**
5 potencial simple		**12 potencial compuesto**	
ordenaría	**ordenaríamos**	**habría ordenado**	**habríamos ordenado**
ordenarías	**ordenaríais**	**habrías ordenado**	**habríais ordenado**
ordenaría	**ordenarían**	**habría ordenado**	**habrían ordenado**
6 presente de subjuntivo		**13 perfecto de subjuntivo**	
ordene	**ordenemos**	**haya ordenado**	**hayamos ordenado**
ordenes	**ordenéis**	**hayas ordenado**	**hayáis ordenado**
ordene	**ordenen**	**haya ordenado**	**hayan ordenado**
7 imperfecto de subjuntivo		**14 pluscuamperfecto de subjuntivo**	
ordenara	**ordenáramos**	**hubiera ordenado**	**hubiéramos ordenado**
ordenaras	**ordenarais**	**hubieras ordenado**	**hubierais ordenado**
ordenara	**ordenaran**	**hubiera ordenado**	**hubieran ordenado**
OR		OR	
ordenase	**ordenásemos**	**hubiese ordenado**	**hubiésemos ordenado**
ordenases	**ordenaseis**	**hubieses ordenado**	**hubieseis ordenado**
ordenase	**ordenasen**	**hubiese ordenado**	**hubiesen ordenado**

imperativo	
—	**ordenemos**
ordena; no ordenes	**ordenad; no ordenéis**
ordene	**ordenen**

Words and expressions related to this verb

el orden, los órdenes   order, orders
el orden del día   order of the day
ordenadamente   in order, orderly,
   methodically

ordenarse   to become ordained,
   to take orders
llamar al orden   to call to order

organizar   Gerundio **organizando**   Part. pas. **organizado**

to organize, to arrange, to set up

The Seven Simple Tenses		The Seven Compound Tenses	
Singular	Plural	Singular	Plural
1 presente de indicativo		8 perfecto de indicativo	
organizo	organizamos	he organizado	hemos organizado
organizas	organizáis	has organizado	habéis organizado
organiza	organizan	ha organizado	han organizado
2 imperfecto de indicativo		9 pluscuamperfecto de indicativo	
organizaba	organizábamos	había organizado	habíamos organizado
organizabas	organizabais	habías organizado	habíais organizado
organizaba	organizaban	había organizado	habían organizado
3 pretérito		10 pretérito anterior	
organicé	organizamos	hube organizado	hubimos organizado
organizaste	organizasteis	hubiste organizado	hubisteis organizado
organizó	organizaron	hubo organizado	hubieron organizado
4 futuro		11 futuro perfecto	
organizaré	organizaremos	habré organizado	habremos organizado
organizarás	organizaréis	habrás organizado	habréis organizado
organizará	organizarán	habrá organizado	habrán organizado
5 potencial simple		12 potencial compuesto	
organizaría	organizaríamos	habría organizado	habríamos organizado
organizarías	organizaríais	habrías organizado	habríais organizado
organizaría	organizarían	habría organizado	habrían organizado
6 presente de subjuntivo		13 perfecto de subjuntivo	
organice	organicemos	haya organizado	hayamos organizado
organices	organicéis	hayas organizado	hayáis organizado
organice	organicen	haya organizado	hayan organizado
7 imperfecto de subjuntivo		14 pluscuamperfecto de subjuntivo	
organizara	organizáramos	hubiera organizado	hubiéramos organizado
organizaras	organizarais	hubieras organizado	hubierais organizado
organizara	organizaran	hubiera organizado	hubieran organizado
OR		OR	
organizase	organizásemos	hubiese organizado	hubiésemos organizado
organizases	organizaseis	hubieses organizado	hubieseis organizado
organizase	organizasen	hubiese organizado	hubiesen organizado

	imperativo
—	organicemos
organiza; no organices	organizad; no organicéis
organice	organicen

Words related to this verb
organizado, organizada organized   **el organizador, la organizadora** organizer
la organización organization   **organizable** organizable

to dare, to venture

The Seven Simple Tenses		The Seven Compound Tenses	
Singular	Plural	Singular	Plural
1 presente de indicativo		8 perfecto de indicativo	
oso	osamos	he osado	hemos osado
osas	osáis	has osado	habéis osado
osa	osan	ha osado	han osado
2 imperfecto de indicativo		9 pluscuamperfecto de indicativo	
osaba	osábamos	había osado	habíamos osado
osabas	osabais	habías osado	habíais osado
osaba	osaban	había osado	habían osado
3 pretérito		10 pretérito anterior	
osé	osamos	hube osado	hubimos osado
osaste	osasteis	hubiste osado	hubisteis osado
osó	osaron	hubo osado	hubieron osado
4 futuro		11 futuro perfecto	
osaré	osaremos	habré osado	habremos osado
osarás	osaréis	habrás osado	habréis osado
osará	osarán	habrá osado	habrán osado
5 potencial simple		12 potencial compuesto	
osaría	osaríamos	habría osado	habríamos osado
osarías	osaríais	habrías osado	habríais osado
osaría	osarían	habría osado	habrían osado
6 presente de subjuntivo		13 perfecto de subjuntivo	
ose	osemos	haya osado	hayamos osado
oses	oséis	hayas osado	hayáis osado
ose	osen	haya osado	hayan osado
7 imperfecto de subjuntivo		14 pluscuamperfecto de subjuntivo	
osara	osáramos	hubiera osado	hubiéramos osado
osaras	osarais	hubieras osado	hubierais osado
osara	osaran	hubiera osado	hubieran osado
OR		OR	
osase	osásemos	hubiese osado	hubiésemos osado
osases	osaseis	hubieses osado	hubieseis osado
osase	osasen	hubiese osado	hubiesen osado

	imperativo	
—	osemos	
osa; no oses	osad; no oséis	
ose	osen	

Words related to this verb
osado, osada   audacious, bold, daring
osadamente   boldly, daring
la osadía   audacity, boldness

pagar   Gerundio **pagando**   Part. pas. **pagado**

to pay

The Seven Simple Tenses		The Seven Compound Tenses	
Singular	Plural	Singular	Plural
1 presente de indicativo		8 perfecto de indicativo	
pago	pagamos	he pagado	hemos pagado
pagas	pagáis	has pagado	habéis pagado
paga	pagan	ha pagado	han pagado
2 imperfecto de indicativo		9 pluscuamperfecto de indicativo	
pagaba	pagábamos	había pagado	habíamos pagado
pagabas	pagabais	habías pagado	habíais pagado
pagaba	pagaban	había pagado	habían pagado
3 pretérito		10 pretérito anterior	
pagué	pagamos	hube pagado	hubimos pagado
pagaste	pagasteis	hubiste pagado	hubisteis pagado
pagó	pagaron	hubo pagado	hubieron pagado
4 futuro		11 futuro perfecto	
pagaré	pagaremos	habré pagado	habremos pagado
pagarás	pagaréis	habrás pagado	habréis pagado
pagará	pagarán	habrá pagado	habrán pagado
5 potencial simple		12 potencial compuesto	
pagaría	pagaríamos	habría pagado	habríamos pagado
pagarías	pagaríais	habrías pagado	habríais pagado
pagaría	pagarían	habría pagado	habrían pagado
6 presente de subjuntivo		13 perfecto de subjuntivo	
pague	paguemos	haya pagado	hayamos pagado
pagues	paguéis	hayas pagado	hayáis pagado
pague	paguen	haya pagado	hayan pagado
7 imperfecto de subjuntivo		14 pluscuamperfecto de subjuntivo	
pagara	pagáramos	hubiera pagado	hubiéramos pagado
pagaras	pagarais	hubieras pagado	hubierais pagado
pagara	pagaran	hubiera pagado	hubieran pagado
OR		OR	
pagase	pagásemos	hubiese pagado	hubiésemos pagado
pagases	pagaseis	hubieses pagado	hubieseis pagado
pagase	pagasen	hubiese pagado	hubiesen pagado

imperativo	
—	paguemos
paga; no pagues	pagad; no paguéis
pague	paguen

Words and expressions related to this verb

la paga   payment
pagable   payable
pagador, pagadora   payer
el pagaré   promissory note, I.O.U.

pagar al contado   to pay in cash
pagar contra entrega   C.O.D. (Collect on delivery)
pagar la cuenta   to pay the bill

Gerundio **parándose**   Part. pas. **parado**   **pararse**

to stop (oneself)

The Seven Simple Tenses		The Seven Compound Tenses	
Singular	Plural	Singular	Plural

1   presente de indicativo

me paro	nos paramos
te paras	os paráis
se para	se paran

8   perfecto de indicativo

me he parado	nos hemos parado
te has parado	os habéis parado
se ha parado	se han parado

2   imperfecto de indicativo

me paraba	nos parábamos
te parabas	os parabais
se paraba	se paraban

9   pluscuamperfecto de indicativo

me había parado	nos habíamos parado
te habías parado	os habíais parado
se había parado	se habían parado

3   pretérito

me paré	nos paramos
te paraste	os parasteis
se paró	se pararon

10   pretérito anterior

me hube parado	nos hubimos parado
te hubiste parado	os hubisteis parado
se hubo parado	se hubieron parado

4   futuro

me pararé	nos pararemos
te pararás	os pararéis
se parará	se pararán

11   futuro perfecto

me habré parado	nos habremos parado
te habrás parado	os habréis parado
se habrá parado	se habrán parado

5   potencial simple

me pararía	nos pararíamos
te pararías	os pararíais
se pararía	se pararían

12   potencial compuesto

me habría parado	nos habríamos parado
te habrías parado	os habríais parado
se habría parado	se habrían parado

6   presente de subjuntivo

me pare	nos paremos
te pares	os paréis
se pare	se paren

13   perfecto de subjuntivo

me haya parado	nos hayamos parado
te hayas parado	os hayáis parado
se haya parado	se hayan parado

7   imperfecto de subjuntivo

me parara	nos paráramos
te pararas	os pararais
se parara	se pararan
OR	
me parase	nos parásemos
te parases	os paraseis
se parase	se parasen

14   pluscuamperfecto de subjuntivo

me hubiera parado	nos hubiéramos parado
te hubieras parado	os hubierais parado
se hubiera parado	se hubieran parado
OR	
me hubiese parado	nos hubiésemos parado
te hubieses parado	os hubieseis parado
se hubiese parado	se hubiesen parado

imperativo

—	parémonos
párate; no te pares	paraos; no os paréis
párese	párense

Words and expressions related to this verb

la parada   stop
una paradeta, una paradilla   pause
una parada en seco   dead stop

parar   to stop (someone or something)
no poder parar   to be restless
parar en mal   to end badly

229

parecer Gerundio **pareciendo** Part. pas. **parecido**

to seem, to appear

The Seven Simple Tenses		The Seven Compound Tenses	
Singular	Plural	Singular	Plural
1 presente de indicativo		8 perfecto de indicativo	
parezco	parecemos	he parecido	hemos parecido
pareces	parecéis	has parecido	habéis parecido
parece	parecen	ha parecido	han parecido
2 imperfecto de indicativo		9 pluscuamperfecto de indicativo	
parecía	parecíamos	había parecido	habíamos parecido
parecías	parecíais	habías parecido	habíais parecido
parecía	parecían	había parecido	habían parecido
3 pretérito		10 pretérito anterior	
parecí	parecimos	hube parecido	hubimos parecido
pareciste	parecisteis	hubiste parecido	hubisteis parecido
pareció	parecieron	hubo parecido	hubieron parecido
4 futuro		11 futuro perfecto	
pareceré	pareceremos	habré parecido	habremos parecido
parecerás	pareceréis	habrás parecido	habréis parecido
parecerá	parecerán	habrá parecido	habrán parecido
5 potencial simple		12 potencial compuesto	
parecería	pareceríamos	habría parecido	habríamos parecido
parecerías	pareceríais	habrías parecido	habríais parecido
parecería	parecerían	habría parecido	habrían parecido
6 presente de subjuntivo		13 perfecto de subjuntivo	
parezca	parezcamos	haya parecido	hayamos parecido
parezcas	parezcáis	hayas parecido	hayáis parecido
parezca	parezcan	haya parecido	hayan parecido
7 imperfecto de subjuntivo		14 pluscuamperfecto de subjuntivo	
pareciera	pareciéramos	hubiera parecido	hubiéramos parecido
parecieras	parecierais	hubieras parecido	hubierais parecido
pareciera	parecieran	hubiera parecido	hubieran parecido
OR		OR	
pareciese	pareciésemos	hubiese parecido	hubiésemos parecido
parecieses	parecieseis	hubieses parecido	hubieseis parecido
pareciese	pareciesen	hubiese parecido	hubiesen parecido

	imperativo	
—		parezcamos
parece; no parezcas		pareced; no parezcáis
parezca		parezcan

Words and expressions related to this verb
a lo que parece according to what it seems
al parecer seemingly, apparently
pareciente similar
See also **parecerse.**

parecerse a to resemble each other, to look alike
Me parece ... It seems to me ...
por el bien parecer for the sake of appearances

Gerundio **pareciéndose**   Part. pas. **parecido**   **parecerse**

to resemble each other, to look alike

The Seven Simple Tenses		The Seven Compound Tenses	
Singular	Plural	Singular	Plural

1 presente de indicativo

me parezco	nos parecemos
te pareces	os parecéis
se parece	se parecen

8 perfecto de indicativo

me he parecido	nos hemos parecido
te has parecido	os habéis parecido
se ha parecido	se han parecido

2 imperfecto de indicativo

me parecía	nos parecíamos
te parecías	os parecíais
se parecía	se parecían

9 pluscuamperfecto de indicativo

me había parecido	nos habíamos parecido
te habías parecido	os habíais parecido
se había parecido	se habían parecido

3 pretérito

me parecí	nos parecimos
te pareciste	os parecisteis
se pareció	se parecieron

10 pretérito anterior

me hube parecido	nos hubimos parecido
te hubiste parecido	os hubisteis parecido
se hubo parecido	se hubieron parecido

4 futuro

me pareceré	nos pareceremos
te parecerás	os pareceréis
se parecerá	se parecerán

11 futuro perfecto

me habré parecido	nos habremos parecido
te habrás parecido	os habréis parecido
se habrá parecido	se habrán parecido

5 potencial simple

me parecería	nos pareceríamos
te parecerías	os pareceríais
se parecería	se parecerían

12 potencial compuesto

me habría parecido	nos habríamos parecido
te habrías parecido	os habríais parecido
se habría parecido	se habrían parecido

6 presente de subjuntivo

me parezca	nos parezcamos
te parezcas	os parezcáis
se parezca	se parezcan

13 perfecto de subjuntivo

me haya parecido	nos hayamos parecido
te hayas parecido	os hayáis parecido
se haya parecido	se hayan parecido

7 imperfecto de subjuntivo

me pareciera	nos pareciéramos
te parecieras	os parecierais
se pareciera	se parecieran
OR	
me pareciese	nos pareciésemos
te parecieses	os parecieseis
se pareciese	se pareciesen

14 pluscuamperfecto de subjuntivo

me hubiera parecido	nos hubiéramos parecido
te hubieras parecido	os hubierais parecido
se hubiera parecido	se hubieran parecido
OR	
me hubiese parecido	nos hubiésemos parecido
te hubieses parecido	os hubieseis parecido
se hubiese parecido	se hubiesen parecido

imperativo

—	parezcámonos
parécete; no te parezcas	pareceos; no os parezcáis
parézcase	parézcanse

Words and expressions related to this verb
parecer to seem, to appear
a lo que parece according to what it seems
See also **parecer.**

al parecer seemingly, apparently
pareciente similar

partir Gerundio **partiendo** Part. pas. **partido**

to leave, to depart, to divide, to split

The Seven Simple Tenses		The Seven Compound Tenses	
Singular	Plural	Singular	Plural
1 presente de indicativo		8 perfecto de indicativo	
parto	**partimos**	**he partido**	**hemos partido**
partes	**partís**	**has partido**	**habéis partido**
parte	**parten**	**ha partido**	**han partido**
2 imperfecto de indicativo		9 pluscuamperfecto de indicativo	
partía	**partíamos**	**había partido**	**habíamos partido**
partías	**partíais**	**habías partido**	**habíais partido**
partía	**partían**	**había partido**	**habían partido**
3 pretérito		10 pretérito anterior	
partí	**partimos**	**hube partido**	**hubimos partido**
partiste	**partisteis**	**hubiste partido**	**hubisteis partido**
partió	**partieron**	**hubo partido**	**hubieron partido**
4 futuro		11 futuro perfecto	
partiré	**partiremos**	**habré partido**	**habremos partido**
partirás	**partiréis**	**habrás partido**	**habréis partido**
partirá	**partirán**	**habrá partido**	**habrán partido**
5 potencial simple		12 potencial compuesto	
partiría	**partiríamos**	**habría partido**	**habríamos partido**
partirías	**partiríais**	**habrías partido**	**habríais partido**
partiría	**partirían**	**habría partido**	**habrían partido**
6 presente de subjuntivo		13 perfecto de subjuntivo	
parta	**partamos**	**haya partido**	**hayamos partido**
partas	**partáis**	**hayas partido**	**hayáis partido**
parta	**partan**	**haya partido**	**hayan partido**
7 imperfecto de subjuntivo		14 pluscuamperfecto de subjuntivo	
partiera	**partiéramos**	**hubiera partido**	**hubiéramos partido**
partieras	**partierais**	**hubieras partido**	**hubierais partido**
partiera	**partieran**	**hubiera partido**	**hubieran partido**
OR		OR	
partiese	**partiésemos**	**hubiese partido**	**hubiésemos partido**
partieses	**partieseis**	**hubieses partido**	**hubieseis partido**
partiese	**partiesen**	**hubiese partido**	**hubiesen partido**

imperativo	
—	**partamos**
parte; no partas	**partid; no partáis**
parta	**partan**

Words and expressions related to this verb

a partir de beginning with, starting from
tomar partido to take sides, to make up
   one's mind

la partida departure
partirse to become divided
repartir to distribute

Gerundio **pasando**   Part. pas. **pasado**   **pasar**

to pass (by), to happen, to spend (time)

The Seven Simple Tenses		The Seven Compound Tenses	
Singular	Plural	Singular	Plural
1 presente de indicativo		8 perfecto de indicativo	
paso	pasamos	he pasado	hemos pasado
pasas	pasáis	has pasado	habéis pasado
pasa	pasan	ha pasado	han pasado
2 imperfecto de indicativo		9 pluscuamperfecto de indicativo	
pasaba	pasábamos	había pasado	habíamos pasado
pasabas	pasabais	habías pasado	habíais pasado
pasaba	pasaban	había pasado	habían pasado
3 pretérito		10 pretérito anterior	
pasé	pasamos	hube pasado	hubimos pasado
pasaste	pasasteis	hubiste pasado	hubisteis pasado
pasó	pasaron	hubo pasado	hubieron pasado
4 futuro		11 futuro perfecto	
pasaré	pasaremos	habré pasado	habremos pasado
pasarás	pasaréis	habrás pasado	habréis pasado
pasará	pasarán	habrá pasado	habrán pasado
5 potencial simple		12 potencial compuesto	
pasaría	pasaríamos	habría pasado	habríamos pasado
pasarías	pasaríais	habrías pasado	habríais pasado
pasaría	pasarían	habría pasado	habrían pasado
6 presente de subjuntivo		13 perfecto de subjuntivo	
pase	pasemos	haya pasado	hayamos pasado
pases	paséis	hayas pasado	hayáis pasado
pase	pasen	haya pasado	hayan pasado
7 imperfecto de subjuntivo		14 pluscuamperfecto de subjuntivo	
pasara	pasáramos	hubiera pasado	hubiéramos pasado
pasaras	pasarais	hubieras pasado	hubierais pasado
pasara	pasaran	hubiera pasado	hubieran pasado
OR		OR	
pasase	pasásemos	hubiese pasado	hubiésemos pasado
pasases	pasaseis	hubieses pasado	hubieseis pasado
pasase	pasasen	hubiese pasado	hubiesen pasado

	imperativo	
—	pasemos	
pasa; no pases	pasad; no paséis	
pase	pasen	

Words and expressions related to this verb
pasajero, pasajera   passenger, traveler
¡Que lo pase Ud. bien!   Good luck, good-bye!
¿Qué pasa?   What's happening? What's going on?
el pasatiempo   amusement, pastime

pasearse   Gerundio **paseándose**   Part. pas. **paseado**

to take a walk, to parade

The Seven Simple Tenses		The Seven Compound Tenses	
Singular	Plural	Singular	Plural
1 presente de indicativo		8 perfecto de indicativo	
me paseo	nos paseamos	me he paseado	nos hemos paseado
te paseas	os paseáis	te has paseado	os habéis paseado
se pasea	se pasean	se ha paseado	se han paseado
2 imperfecto de indicativo		9 pluscuamperfecto de indicativo	
me paseaba	nos paseábamos	me había paseado	nos habíamos paseado
te paseabas	os paseabais	te habías paseado	os habíais paseado
se paseaba	se paseaban	se había paseado	se habían paseado
3 pretérito		10 pretérito anterior	
me paseé	nos paseamos	me hube paseado	nos hubimos paseado
te paseaste	os paseasteis	te hubiste paseado	os hubisteis paseado
se paseó	se pasearon	se hubo paseado	se hubieron paseado
4 futuro		11 futuro perfecto	
me pasearé	nos pasearemos	me habré paseado	nos habremos paseado
te pasearás	os pasearéis	te habrás paseado	os habréis paseado
se paseará	se pasearán	se habrá paseado	se habrán paseado
5 potencial simple		12 potencial compuesto	
me pasearía	nos pasearíamos	me habría paseado	nos habríamos paseado
te pasearías	os pasearíais	te habrías paseado	os habríais paseado
se pasearía	se pasearían	se habría paseado	se habrían paseado
6 presente de subjuntivo		13 perfecto de subjuntivo	
me pasee	nos paseemos	me haya paseado	nos hayamos paseado
te pasees	os paseéis	te hayas paseado	os hayáis paseado
se pasee	se paseen	se haya paseado	se hayan paseado
7 imperfecto de subjuntivo		14 pluscuamperfecto de subjuntivo	
me paseara	nos paseáramos	me hubiera paseado	nos hubiéramos paseado
te pasearas	os pasearais	te hubieras paseado	os hubierais paseado
se paseara	se pasearan	se hubiera paseado	se hubieran paseado
OR		OR	
me pasease	nos paseásemos	me hubiese paseado	nos hubiésemos paseado
te paseases	os paseaseis	te hubieses paseado	os hubieseis paseado
se pasease	se paseasen	se hubiese paseado	se hubiesen paseado

imperativo	
—	paseémonos
paséate; no te pasees	paseaos; no os paseéis
paséese	paséense

Words and expressions related to this verb
un pase pass, permit
un, una paseante stroller
un paseo a walk
dar un paseo to take a walk

ir de paseo to go out for a walk
un paseo campestre picnic
sacar a paseo to take out for a walk
pasear to walk (a child, etc.)

234

Gerundio **pidiendo**   Part. pas. **pedido**   **pedir**

to ask for, to request

The Seven Simple Tenses		The Seven Compound Tenses	
Singular	Plural	Singular	Plural
1 presente de indicativo		**8 perfecto de indicativo**	
pido	pedimos	he pedido	hemos pedido
pides	pedís	has pedido	habéis pedido
pide	piden	ha pedido	han pedido
2 imperfecto de indicativo		**9 pluscuamperfecto de indicativo**	
pedía	pedíamos	había pedido	habíamos pedido
pedías	pedíais	habías pedido	habíais pedido
pedía	pedían	había pedido	habían pedido
3 pretérito		**10 pretérito anterior**	
pedí	pedimos	hube pedido	hubimos pedido
pediste	pedisteis	hubiste pedido	hubisteis pedido
pidió	pidieron	hubo pedido	hubieron pedido
4 futuro		**11 futuro perfecto**	
pediré	pediremos	habré pedido	habremos pedido
pedirás	pediréis	habrás pedido	habréis pedido
pedirá	pedirán	habrá pedido	habrán pedido
5 potencial simple		**12 potencial compuesto**	
pediría	pediríamos	habría pedido	habríamos pedido
pedirías	pediríais	habrías pedido	habríais pedido
pediría	pedirían	habría pedido	habrían pedido
6 presente de subjuntivo		**13 perfecto de subjuntivo**	
pida	pidamos	haya pedido	hayamos pedido
pidas	pidáis	hayas pedido	hayáis pedido
pida	pidan	haya pedido	hayan pedido
7 imperfecto de subjuntivo		**14 pluscuamperfecto de subjuntivo**	
pidiera	pidiéramos	hubiera pedido	hubiéramos pedido
pidieras	pidierais	hubieras pedido	hubierais pedido
pidiera	pidieran	hubiera pedido	hubieran pedido
OR		OR	
pidiese	pidiésemos	hubiese pedido	hubiésemos pedido
pidieses	pidieseis	hubieses pedido	hubieseis pedido
pidiese	pidiesen	hubiese pedido	hubiesen pedido

imperativo	
—	pidamos
pide; no pidas	pedid; no pidáis
pida	pidan

Words and expressions related to this verb
un pedimento petition
hacer un pedido to place an order
See also **despedir.**

un pedido request, order
colocar un pedido to place an order
pedir prestado to borrow

235

peinarse Gerundio **peinándose** Part. pas. **peinado**

to comb one's hair

The Seven Simple Tenses		The Seven Compound Tenses	
Singular	Plural	Singular	Plural
1 presente de indicativo		8 perfecto de indicativo	
me peino	nos peinamos	me he peinado	nos hemos peinado
te peinas	os peináis	te has peinado	os habéis peinado
se peina	se peinan	se ha peinado	se han peinado
2 imperfecto de indicativo		9 pluscuamperfecto de indicativo	
me peinaba	nos peinábamos	me había peinado	nos habíamos peinado
te peinabas	os peinabais	te habías peinado	os habíais peinado
se peinaba	se peinaban	se había peinado	se habían peinado
3 pretérito		10 pretérito anterior	
me peiné	nos peinamos	me hube peinado	nos hubimos peinado
te peinaste	os peinasteis	te hubiste peinado	os hubisteis peinado
se peinó	se peinaron	se hubo peinado	se hubieron peinado
4 futuro		11 futuro perfecto	
me peinaré	nos peinaremos	me habré peinado	nos habremos peinado
te peinarás	os peinaréis	te habrás peinado	os habréis peinado
se peinará	se peinarán	se habrá peinado	se habrán peinado
5 potencial simple		12 potencial compuesto	
me peinaría	nos peinaríamos	me habría peinado	nos habríamos peinado
te peinarías	os peinaríais	te habrías peinado	os habríais peinado
se peinaría	se peinarían	se habría peinado	se habrían peinado
6 presente de subjuntivo		13 perfecto de subjuntivo	
me peine	nos peinemos	me haya peinado	nos hayamos peinado
te peines	os peinéis	te hayas peinado	os hayáis peinado
se peine	se peinen	se haya peinado	se hayan peinado
7 imperfecto de subjuntivo		14 pluscuamperfecto de subjuntivo	
me peinara	nos peináramos	me hubiera peinado	nos hubiéramos peinado
te peinaras	os peinarais	te hubieras peinado	os hubierais peinado
se peinara	se peinaran	se hubiera peinado	se hubieran peinado
OR		OR	
me peinase	nos peinásemos	me hubiese peinado	nos hubiésemos peinado
te peinases	os peinaseis	te hubieses peinado	os hubieseis peinado
se peinase	se peinasen	se hubiese peinado	se hubiesen peinado

imperativo	
—	peinémonos
péinate; no te peines	peinaos; no os peinéis
péinese	péinense

Words related to this verb
un peine a comb   **peinar** to comb; **peinarse** to comb one's hair
un peinado hairdo, hairstyle   **despeinarse** to dishevel, to take down one's hair
una peineta shell comb (used by women as an ornament in the hair)

236

Gerundio **pensando**   Part. pas. **pensado**   **pensar**

to think

The Seven Simple Tenses		The Seven Compound Tenses	
Singular	Plural	Singular	Plural
1 presente de indicativo		**8 perfecto de indicativo**	
pienso	pensamos	he pensado	hemos pensado
piensas	pensáis	has pensado	habéis pensado
piensa	piensan	ha pensado	han pensado
2 imperfecto de indicativo		**9 pluscuamperfecto de indicativo**	
pensaba	pensábamos	había pensado	habíamos pensado
pensabas	pensabais	habías pensado	habíais pensado
pensaba	pensaban	había pensado	habían pensado
3 pretérito		**10 pretérito anterior**	
pensé	pensamos	hube pensado	hubimos pensado
pensaste	pensasteis	hubiste pensado	hubisteis pensado
pensó	pensaron	hubo pensado	hubieron pensado
4 futuro		**11 futuro perfecto**	
pensaré	pensaremos	habré pensado	habremos pensado
pensarás	pensaréis	habrás pensado	habréis pensado
pensará	pensarán	habrá pensado	habrán pensado
5 potencial simple		**12 potencial compuesto**	
pensaría	pensaríamos	habría pensado	habríamos pensado
pensarías	pensaríais	habrías pensado	habríais pensado
pensaría	pensarían	habría pensado	habrían pensado
6 presente de subjuntivo		**13 perfecto de subjuntivo**	
piense	pensemos	haya pensado	hayamos pensado
pienses	penséis	hayas pensado	hayáis pensado
piense	piensen	haya pensado	hayan pensado
7 imperfecto de subjuntivo		**14 pluscuamperfecto de subjuntivo**	
pensara	pensáramos	hubiera pensado	hubiéramos pensado
pensaras	pensarais	hubieras pensado	hubierais pensado
pensara	pensaran	hubiera pensado	hubieran pensado
OR		OR	
pensase	pensásemos	hubiese pensado	hubiésemos pensado
pensases	pensaseis	hubieses pensado	hubieseis pensado
pensase	pensasen	hubiese pensado	hubiesen pensado

imperativo	
—	pensemos
piensa; no pienses	pensad; no penséis
piense	piensen

Words and expressions related to this verb

pensar + inf. to intend + inf.
¿En qué piensa Ud.? What are you thinking of?
pensativo, pensativa thoughtful, pensive
un pensador, una pensadora thinker

pensar en to think of, about
sin pensar thoughtlessly
repensar to think over (again)

237

perder	Gerundio **perdiendo**	Part. pas. **perdido**

to lose

The Seven Simple Tenses		The Seven Compound Tenses	
Singular	Plural	Singular	Plural
1 presente de indicativo		**8 perfecto de indicativo**	
pierdo	perdemos	he perdido	hemos perdido
pierdes	perdéis	has perdido	habéis perdido
pierde	pierden	ha perdido	han perdido
2 imperfecto de indicativo		**9 pluscuamperfecto de indicativo**	
perdía	perdíamos	había perdido	habíamos perdido
perdías	perdíais	habías perdido	habíais perdido
perdía	perdían	había perdido	habían perdido
3 pretérito		**10 pretérito anterior**	
perdí	perdimos	hube perdido	hubimos perdido
perdiste	perdisteis	hubiste perdido	hubisteis perdido
perdió	perdieron	hubo perdido	hubieron perdido
4 futuro		**11 futuro perfecto**	
perderé	perderemos	habré perdido	habremos perdido
perderás	perderéis	habrás perdido	habréis perdido
perderá	perderán	habrá perdido	habrán perdido
5 potencial simple		**12 potencial compuesto**	
perdería	perderíamos	habría perdido	habríamos perdido
perderías	perderíais	habrías perdido	habríais perdido
perdería	perderían	habría perdido	habrían perdido
6 presente de subjuntivo		**13 perfecto de subjuntivo**	
pierda	perdamos	haya perdido	hayamos perdido
pierdas	perdáis	hayas perdido	hayáis perdido
pierda	pierdan	haya perdido	hayan perdido
7 imperfecto de subjuntivo		**14 pluscuamperfecto de subjuntivo**	
perdiera	perdiéramos	hubiera perdido	hubiéramos perdido
perdieras	perdierais	hubieras perdido	hubierais perdido
perdiera	perdieran	hubiera perdido	hubieran perdido
OR		OR	
perdiese	perdiésemos	hubiese perdido	hubiésemos perdido
perdieses	perdieseis	hubieses perdido	hubieseis perdido
perdiese	perdiesen	hubiese perdido	hubiesen perdido

imperativo	
—	perdamos
pierde; no pierdas	perded; no perdáis
pierda	pierdan

Words and expressions related to this verb
un perdedor, una perdedora loser
la pérdida loss
¡Pierda Ud. cuidado! Don't worry!

perder el juicio to go mad (crazy)
perder los estribos to lose self control
perderse to lose one's way, to get lost

Gerundio **permitiendo**   Part. pas. **permitido**   **permitir**

to permit, to admit, to allow, to grant

The Seven Simple Tenses		The Seven Compound Tenses	
Singular	Plural	Singular	Plural
1 presente de indicativo		**8 perfecto de indicativo**	
permito	permitimos	he permitido	hemos permitido
permites	permitís	has permitido	habéis permitido
permite	permiten	ha permitido	han permitido
2 imperfecto de indicativo		**9 pluscuamperfecto de indicativo**	
permitía	permitíamos	había permitido	habíamos permitido
permitías	permitíais	habías permitido	habíais permitido
permitía	permitían	había permitido	habían permitido
3 pretérito		**10 pretérito anterior**	
permití	permitimos	hube permitido	hubimos permitido
permitiste	permitisteis	hubiste permitido	hubisteis permitido
permitió	permitieron	hubo permitido	hubieron permitido
4 futuro		**11 futuro perfecto**	
permitiré	permitiremos	habré permitido	habremos permitido
permitirás	permitiréis	habrás permitido	habréis permitido
permitirá	permitirán	habrá permitido	habrán permitido
5 potencial simple		**12 potencial compuesto**	
permitiría	permitiríamos	habría permitido	habríamos permitido
permitirías	permitiríais	habrías permitido	habríais permitido
permitiría	permitirían	habría permitido	habrían permitido
6 presente de subjuntivo		**13 perfecto de subjuntivo**	
permita	permitamos	haya permitido	hayamos permitido
permitas	permitáis	hayas permitido	hayáis permitido
permita	permitan	haya permitido	hayan permitido
7 imperfecto de subjuntivo		**14 pluscuamperfecto de subjuntivo**	
permitiera	permitiéramos	hubiera permitido	hubiéramos permitido
permitieras	permitierais	hubieras permitido	hubierais permitido
permitiera	permitieran	hubiera permitido	hubieran permitido
OR		OR	
permitiese	permitiésemos	hubiese permitido	hubiésemos permitido
permitieses	permitieseis	hubieses permitido	hubieseis permitido
permitiese	permitiesen	hubiese permitido	hubiesen permitido

	imperativo
—	permitamos
permite; no permitas	permitid; no permitáis
permita	permitan

Words and expressions related to this verb

el permiso permit, permission	**admitir** to admit
¡Con permiso! Excuse me!	**permitirse + inf.** to take the liberty + inf.
la permisión permission	**el permiso de conducir** driver's license
emitir to emit	**transmitir** to transmit

to be able, can

The Seven Simple Tenses		The Seven Compound Tenses	
Singular	Plural	Singular	Plural
1 presente de indicativo		8 perfecto de indicativo	
puedo	**podemos**	**he podido**	**hemos podido**
puedes	**podéis**	**has podido**	**habéis podido**
puede	**pueden**	**ha podido**	**han podido**
2 imperfecto de indicativo		9 pluscuamperfecto de indicativo	
podía	**podíamos**	**había podido**	**habíamos podido**
podías	**podíais**	**habías podido**	**habíais podido**
podía	**podían**	**había podido**	**habían podido**
3 pretérito		10 pretérito anterior	
pude	**pudimos**	**hube podido**	**hubimos podido**
pudiste	**pudisteis**	**hubiste podido**	**hubisteis podido**
pudo	**pudieron**	**hubo podido**	**hubieron podido**
4 futuro		11 futuro perfecto	
podré	**podremos**	**habré podido**	**habremos podido**
podrás	**podréis**	**habrás podido**	**habréis podido**
podrá	**podrán**	**habrá podido**	**habrán podido**
5 potencial simple		12 potencial compuesto	
podría	**podríamos**	**habría podido**	**habríamos podido**
podrías	**podríais**	**habrías podido**	**habríais podido**
podría	**podrían**	**habría podido**	**habrían podido**
6 presente de subjuntivo		13 perfecto de subjuntivo	
pueda	**podamos**	**haya podido**	**hayamos podido**
puedas	**podáis**	**hayas podido**	**hayáis podido**
pueda	**puedan**	**haya podido**	**hayan podido**
7 imperfecto de subjuntivo		14 pluscuamperfecto de subjuntivo	
pudiera	**pudiéramos**	**hubiera podido**	**hubiéramos podido**
pudieras	**pudierais**	**hubieras podido**	**hubierais podido**
pudiera	**pudieran**	**hubiera podido**	**hubieran podido**
OR		OR	
pudiese	**pudiésemos**	**hubiese podido**	**hubiésemos podido**
pudieses	**pudieseis**	**hubieses podido**	**hubieseis podido**
pudiese	**pudiesen**	**hubiese podido**	**hubiesen podido**

	imperativo	
—	**podamos**	
puede; no puedas	**poded; no podáis**	
pueda	**puedan**	

Words and expressions related to this verb
el poder power
apoderar to empower
apoderarse de to take possession, to take over
poderoso, poderosa powerful

No se puede. It can't be done.
estar en el poder to be in power
Querer es poder Where there's a will there's a way.

Gerundio **poniendo**   Part. pas. **puesto**   **poner**

to put, to place

The Seven Simple Tenses		The Seven Compound Tenses	
Singular	Plural	Singular	Plural
1 presente de indicativo		**8 perfecto de indicativo**	
pongo	ponemos	he puesto	hemos puesto
pones	ponéis	has puesto	habéis puesto
pone	ponen	ha puesto	han puesto
2 imperfecto de indicativo		**9 pluscuamperfecto de indicativo**	
ponía	poníamos	había puesto	habíamos puesto
ponías	poníais	habías puesto	habíais puesto
ponía	ponían	había puesto	habían puesto
3 pretérito		**10 pretérito anterior**	
puse	pusimos	hube puesto	hubimos puesto
pusiste	pusisteis	hubiste puesto	hubisteis puesto
puso	pusieron	hubo puesto	hubieron puesto
4 futuro		**11 futuro perfecto**	
pondré	pondremos	habré puesto	habremos puesto
pondrás	pondréis	habrás puesto	habréis puesto
pondrá	pondrán	habrá puesto	habrán puesto
5 potencial simple		**12 potencial compuesto**	
pondría	pondríamos	habría puesto	habríamos puesto
pondrías	pondríais	habrías puesto	habríais puesto
pondría	pondrían	habría puesto	habrían puesto
6 presente de subjuntivo		**13 perfecto de subjuntivo**	
ponga	pongamos	haya puesto	hayamos puesto
pongas	pongáis	hayas puesto	hayáis puesto
ponga	pongan	haya puesto	hayan puesto
7 imperfecto de subjuntivo		**14 pluscuamperfecto de subjuntivo**	
pusiera	pusiéramos	hubiera puesto	hubiéramos puesto
pusieras	pusierais	hubieras puesto	hubierais puesto
pusiera	pusieran	hubiera puesto	hubieran puesto
OR		OR	
pusiese	pusiésemos	hubiese puesto	hubiésemos puesto
pusieses	pusieseis	hubieses puesto	hubieseis puesto
pusiese	pusiesen	hubiese puesto	hubiesen puesto

imperativo	
—	pongamos
pon; no pongas	poned; pongáis
ponga	pongan

Common idiomatic expressions using this verb

poner fin a   to put a stop to   **la puesta de sol**   sunset
poner la mesa   to set the table   **bien puesto, bien puesta**   well placed
poner de acuerdo   to reach an agreement   **reponer**   to replace, to put back
For additional words and expressions related to this verb, see **ponerse** and **componer.**

241

ponerse Gerundio **poniéndose** Part. pas. **puesto**

to put on (clothing), to become, to set (of sun)

The Seven Simple Tenses		The Seven Compound Tenses	
Singular	Plural	Singular	Plural

1   presente de indicativo

me pongo	nos ponemos	
te pones	os ponéis	
se pone	se ponen	

8   perfecto de indicativo

me he puesto	nos hemos puesto
te has puesto	os habéis puesto
se ha puesto	se han puesto

2   imperfecto de indicativo

me ponía	nos poníamos
te ponías	os poníais
se ponía	se ponían

9   pluscuamperfecto de indicativo

me había puesto	nos habíamos puesto
te habías puesto	os habíais puesto
se había puesto	se habían puesto

3   pretérito

me puse	nos pusimos
te pusiste	os pusisteis
se puso	se pusieron

10   pretérito anterior

me hube puesto	nos hubimos puesto
te hubiste puesto	os hubisteis puesto
se hubo puesto	se hubieron puesto

4   futuro

me pondré	nos pondremos
te pondrás	os pondréis
se pondrá	se pondrán

11   futuro perfecto

me habré puesto	nos habremos puesto
te habrás puesto	os habréis puesto
se habrá puesto	se habrán puesto

5   potencial simple

me pondría	nos pondríamos
te pondrías	os pondríais
se pondría	se pondrían

12   potencial compuesto

me habría puesto	nos habríamos puesto
te habrías puesto	os habríais puesto
se habría puesto	se habrían puesto

6   presente de subjuntivo

me ponga	nos pongamos
te pongas	os pongáis
se ponga	se pongan

13   perfecto de subjuntivo

me haya puesto	nos hayamos puesto
te hayas puesto	os hayáis puesto
se haya puesto	se hayan puesto

7   imperfecto de subjuntivo

me pusiera	nos pusiéramos
te pusieras	os pusierais
se pusiera	se pusieran
OR	
me pusiese	nos pusiésemos
te pusieses	os pusieseis
se pusiese	se pusiesen

14   pluscuamperfecto de subjuntivo

me hubiera puesto	nos hubiéramos puesto
te hubieras puesto	os hubierais puesto
se hubiera puesto	se hubieran puesto
OR	
me hubiese puesto	nos hubiésemos puesto
te hubieses puesto	os hubieseis puesto
se hubiese puesto	se hubiesen puesto

imperativo

—	pongámonos
ponte; no te pongas	poneos; no os pongáis
póngase	pónganse

Common idiomatic expressions using this verb

ponerse el abrigo   to put on one's overcoat
ponerse a + inf.   to begin, to start + inf.
María se puso pálida.   Mary became pale.

reponerse   to calm down,
   to recover (one's health)
indisponerse   to become ill

For additional words and expressions related to this verb, see **poner** and **componer**.

242

to practice

The Seven Simple Tenses		The Seven Compound Tenses	
Singular	Plural	Singular	Plural
1 presente de indicativo		8 perfecto de indicativo	
practico	practicamos	he practicado	hemos practicado
practicas	practicáis	has practicado	habéis practicado
practica	practican	ha practicado	han practicado
2 imperfecto de indicativo		9 pluscuamperfecto de indicativo	
practicaba	practicábamos	había practicado	habíamos practicado
practicabas	practicabais	habías practicado	habíais practicado
practicaba	practicaban	había practicado	habían practicado
3 pretérito		10 pretérito anterior	
practiqué	practicamos	hube practicado	hubimos practicado
practicaste	practicasteis	hubiste practicado	hubisteis practicado
practicó	practicaron	hubo practicado	hubieron practicado
4 futuro		11 futuro perfecto	
practicaré	practicaremos	habré practicado	habremos practicado
practicarás	practicaréis	habrás practicado	habréis practicado
practicará	practicarán	habrá practicado	habrán practicado
5 potencial simple		12 potencial compuesto	
practicaría	practicaríamos	habría practicado	habríamos practicado
practicarías	practicaríais	habrías practicado	habríais practicado
practicaría	practicarían	habría practicado	habrían practicado
6 presente de subjuntivo		13 perfecto de subjuntivo	
practique	practiquemos	haya practicado	hayamos practicado
practiques	practiquéis	hayas practicado	hayáis practicado
practique	practiquen	haya practicado	hayan practicado
7 imperfecto de subjuntivo		14 pluscuamperfecto de subjuntivo	
practicara	practicáramos	hubiera practicado	hubiéramos practicado
practicaras	practicarais	hubieras practicado	hubierais practicado
practicara	practicaran	hubiera practicado	hubieran practicado
OR		OR	
practicase	practicásemos	hubiese practicado	hubiésemos practicado
practicases	practicaseis	hubieses practicado	hubieseis practicado
practicase	practicasen	hubiese practicado	hubiesen practicado

	imperativo	
—	practiquemos	
practica; no practiques	practicad; no practiquéis	
practique	practiquen	

Words and expressions related to this verb

práctico, práctica   practical
la práctica   practice, habit
en la práctica   in practice

practicar investigaciones   to look into,
   to investigate
practicar un informe   to make a report

243

preferir   Gerundio **prefiriendo**   Part. pas. **preferido**

to prefer

The Seven Simple Tenses		The Seven Compound Tenses	
Singular	Plural	Singular	Plural
1 presente de indicativo		8 perfecto de indicativo	
prefiero	preferimos	he preferido	hemos preferido
prefieres	preferís	has preferido	habéis preferido
prefiere	prefieren	ha preferido	han preferido
2 imperfecto de indicativo		9 pluscuamperfecto de indicativo	
prefería	preferíamos	había preferido	habíamos preferido
preferías	preferíais	habías preferido	habíais preferido
prefería	preferían	había preferido	habían preferido
3 pretérito		10 pretérito anterior	
preferí	preferimos	hube preferido	hubimos preferido
preferiste	preferisteis	hubiste preferido	hubisteis preferido
prefirió	prefirieron	hubo preferido	hubieron preferido
4 futuro		11 futuro perfecto	
preferiré	preferiremos	habré preferido	habremos preferido
preferirás	preferiréis	habrás preferido	habréis preferido
preferirá	preferirán	habrá preferido	habrán preferido
5 potencial simple		12 potencial compuesto	
preferiría	preferiríamos	habría preferido	habríamos preferido
preferirías	preferiríais	habrías preferido	habríais preferido
preferiría	preferirían	habría preferido	habrían preferido
6 presente de subjuntivo		13 perfecto de subjuntivo	
prefiera	prefiramos	haya preferido	hayamos preferido
prefieras	prefiráis	hayas preferido	hayáis preferido
prefiera	prefieran	haya preferido	hayan preferido
7 imperfecto de subjuntivo		14 pluscuamperfecto de subjuntivo	
prefiriera	prefiriéramos	hubiera preferido	hubiéramos preferido
prefirieras	prefirierais	hubieras preferido	hubierais preferido
prefiriera	prefirieran	hubiera preferido	hubieran preferido
OR		OR	
prefiriese	prefiriésemos	hubiese preferido	hubiésemos preferido
prefirieses	prefirieseis	hubieses preferido	hubieseis preferido
prefiriese	prefiriesen	hubiese preferido	hubiesen preferido

	imperativo	
—		prefiramos
prefiere; no prefieras		preferid; no prefiráis
prefiera		prefieran

Words related to this verb

preferiblemente preferably
preferible preferable
la preferencia preference
preferido, preferida preferred

de preferencia preferably
preferentemente preferably
referir to refer, to relate

244

to ask, to inquire, to question

The Seven Simple Tenses		The Seven Compound Tenses	
Singular	Plural	Singular	Plural
1 presente de indicativo		8 perfecto de indicativo	
pregunto	**preguntamos**	**he preguntado**	**hemos preguntado**
preguntas	**preguntáis**	**has preguntado**	**habéis preguntado**
pregunta	**preguntan**	**ha preguntado**	**han preguntado**
2 imperfecto de indicativo		9 pluscuamperfecto de indicativo	
preguntaba	**preguntábamos**	**había preguntado**	**habíamos preguntado**
preguntabas	**preguntabais**	**habías preguntado**	**habíais preguntado**
preguntaba	**preguntaban**	**había preguntado**	**habían preguntado**
3 pretérito		10 pretérito anterior	
pregunté	**preguntamos**	**hube preguntado**	**hubimos preguntado**
preguntaste	**preguntasteis**	**hubiste preguntado**	**hubisteis preguntado**
preguntó	**preguntaron**	**hubo preguntado**	**hubieron preguntado**
4 futuro		11 futuro perfecto	
preguntaré	**preguntaremos**	**habré preguntado**	**habremos preguntado**
preguntarás	**preguntaréis**	**habrás preguntado**	**habréis preguntado**
preguntará	**preguntarán**	**habrá preguntado**	**habrán preguntado**
5 potencial simple		12 potencial compuesto	
preguntaría	**preguntaríamos**	**habría preguntado**	**habríamos preguntado**
preguntarías	**preguntaríais**	**habrías preguntado**	**habríais preguntado**
preguntaría	**preguntarían**	**habría preguntado**	**habrían preguntado**
6 presente de subjuntivo		13 perfecto de subjuntivo	
pregunte	**preguntemos**	**haya preguntado**	**hayamos preguntado**
preguntes	**preguntéis**	**hayas preguntado**	**hayáis preguntado**
pregunte	**pregunten**	**haya preguntado**	**hayan preguntado**
7 imperfecto de subjuntivo		14 pluscuamperfecto de subjuntivo	
preguntara	**preguntáramos**	**hubiera preguntado**	**hubiéramos preguntado**
preguntaras	**preguntarais**	**hubieras preguntado**	**hubierais preguntado**
preguntara	**preguntaran**	**hubiera preguntado**	**hubieran preguntado**
OR		OR	
preguntase	**preguntásemos**	**hubiese preguntado**	**hubiésemos preguntado**
preguntases	**preguntaseis**	**hubieses preguntado**	**hubieseis preguntado**
preguntase	**preguntasen**	**hubiese preguntado**	**hubiesen preguntado**

	imperativo	
—		**preguntemos**
pregunta; no preguntes		**preguntad; no preguntéis**
pregunte		**pregunten**

Words and expressions related to this verb

una pregunta   question
hacer una pregunta   to ask a question
un preguntón, una preguntona
  inquisitive individual

preguntarse   to wonder, to ask oneself
preguntante   inquiring

preparar	Gerundio **preparando**	Part. pas. **preparado**

to prepare

The Seven Simple Tenses		The Seven Compound Tenses	
Singular	Plural	Singular	Plural
1 presente de indicativo		8 perfecto de indicativo	
preparo	preparamos	he preparado	hemos preparado
preparas	preparáis	has preparado	habéis preparado
prepara	preparan	ha preparado	han preparado
2 imperfecto de indicativo		9 pluscuamperfecto de indicativo	
preparaba	preparábamos	había preparado	habíamos preparado
preparabas	preparabais	habías preparado	habíais preparado
preparaba	preparaban	había preparado	habían preparado
3 pretérito		10 pretérito anterior	
preparé	preparamos	hube preparado	hubimos preparado
preparaste	preparasteis	hubiste preparado	hubisteis preparado
preparó	prepararon	hubo preparado	hubieron preparado
4 futuro		11 futuro perfecto	
prepararé	prepararemos	habré preparado	habremos preparado
prepararás	prepararéis	habrás preparado	habréis preparado
preparará	prepararán	habrá preparado	habrán preparado
5 potencial simple		12 potencial compuesto	
prepararía	prepararíamos	habría preparado	habríamos preparado
prepararías	prepararíais	habrías preparado	habríais preparado
prepararía	prepararían	habría preparado	habrían preparado
6 presente de subjuntivo		13 perfecto de subjuntivo	
prepare	preparemos	haya preparado	hayamos preparado
prepares	preparéis	hayas preparado	hayáis preparado
prepare	preparen	haya preparado	hayan preparado
7 imperfecto de subjuntivo		14 pluscuamperfecto de subjuntivo	
preparara	preparáramos	hubiera preparado	hubiéramos preparado
prepararas	prepararais	hubieras preparado	hubierais preparado
preparara	prepararan	hubiera preparado	hubieran preparado
OR		OR	
preparase	preparásemos	hubiese preparado	hubiésemos preparado
preparases	preparaseis	hubieses preparado	hubieseis preparado
preparase	preparasen	hubiese preparado	hubiesen preparado

	imperativo	
—	preparemos	
prepara; no prepares	preparad; no preparéis	
prepare	preparen	

Words related to this verb

preparatorio, preparatoria preparatory   **la preparación** preparation
el preparativo preparation, preparative   **prepararse** to prepare oneself

The Seven Simple Tenses		The Seven Compound Tenses	
Singular	Plural	Singular	Plural
1 presente de indicativo		8 perfecto de indicativo	
presto	**prestamos**	**he prestado**	**hemos prestado**
prestas	**prestáis**	**has prestado**	**habéis prestado**
presta	**prestan**	**ha prestado**	**han prestado**
2 imperfecto de indicativo		9 pluscuamperfecto de indicativo	
prestaba	**prestábamos**	**había prestado**	**habíamos prestado**
prestabas	**prestabais**	**habías prestado**	**habíais prestado**
prestaba	**prestaban**	**había prestado**	**habían prestado**
3 pretérito		10 pretérito anterior	
presté	**prestamos**	**hube prestado**	**hubimos prestado**
prestaste	**prestasteis**	**hubiste prestado**	**hubisteis prestado**
prestó	**prestaron**	**hubo prestado**	**hubieron prestado**
4 futuro		11 futuro perfecto	
prestaré	**prestaremos**	**habré prestado**	**habremos prestado**
prestarás	**prestaréis**	**habrás prestado**	**habréis prestado**
prestará	**prestarán**	**habrá prestado**	**habrán prestado**
5 potencial simple		12 potencial compuesto	
prestaría	**prestaríamos**	**habría prestado**	**habríamos prestado**
prestarías	**prestaríais**	**habrías prestado**	**habríais prestado**
prestaría	**prestarían**	**habría prestado**	**habrían prestado**
6 presente de subjuntivo		13 perfecto de subjuntivo	
preste	**prestemos**	**haya prestado**	**hayamos prestado**
prestes	**prestéis**	**hayas prestado**	**hayáis prestado**
preste	**presten**	**haya prestado**	**hayan prestado**
7 imperfecto de subjuntivo		14 pluscuamperfecto de subjuntivo	
prestara	**prestáramos**	**hubiera prestado**	**hubiéramos prestado**
prestaras	**prestarais**	**hubieras prestado**	**hubierais prestado**
prestara	**prestaran**	**hubiera prestado**	**hubieran prestado**
OR		OR	
prestase	**prestásemos**	**hubiese prestado**	**hubiésemos prestado**
prestases	**prestaseis**	**hubieses prestado**	**hubieseis prestado**
prestase	**prestasen**	**hubiese prestado**	**hubiesen prestado**

imperativo	
—	**prestemos**
presta; no prestes	**prestad; no prestéis**
preste	**presten**

Words and expressions related to this verb

pedir prestado   to borrow
tomar prestado   to borrow
prestador, prestadora   lender
un préstamo   loan

prestar atención   to pay attention
una casa de préstamos   pawn shop
un, una prestamista   money lender

probar	Gerundio **probando**	Part. pas. **probado**

to test, to prove, to try, to try on

The Seven Simple Tenses		The Seven Compound Tenses	
Singular	Plural	Singular	Plural
1 presente de indicativo		8 perfecto de indicativo	
pruebo	**probamos**	**he probado**	**hemos probado**
pruebas	**probáis**	**has probado**	**habéis probado**
prueba	**prueban**	**ha probado**	**han probado**
2 imperfecto de indicativo		9 pluscuamperfecto de indicativo	
probaba	**probábamos**	**había probado**	**habíamos probado**
probabas	**probabais**	**habías probado**	**habíais probado**
probaba	**probaban**	**había probado**	**habían probado**
3 pretérito		10 pretérito anterior	
probé	**probamos**	**hube probado**	**hubimos probado**
probaste	**probasteis**	**hubiste probado**	**hubisteis probado**
probó	**probaron**	**hubo probado**	**hubieron probado**
4 futuro		11 futuro perfecto	
probaré	**probaremos**	**habré probado**	**habremos probado**
probarás	**probaréis**	**habrás probado**	**habréis probado**
probará	**probarán**	**habrá probado**	**habrán probado**
5 potencial simple		12 potencial compuesto	
probaría	**probaríamos**	**habría probado**	**habríamos probado**
probarías	**probaríais**	**habrías probado**	**habríais probado**
probaría	**probarían**	**habría probado**	**habrían probado**
6 presente de subjuntivo		13 perfecto de subjuntivo	
pruebe	**probemos**	**haya probado**	**hayamos probado**
pruebes	**probéis**	**hayas probado**	**hayáis probado**
pruebe	**prueben**	**haya probado**	**hayan probado**
7 imperfecto de subjuntivo		14 pluscuamperfecto de subjuntivo	
probara	**probáramos**	**hubiera probado**	**hubiéramos probado**
probaras	**probarais**	**hubieras probado**	**hubierais probado**
probara	**probaran**	**hubiera probado**	**hubieran probado**
OR		OR	
probase	**probásemos**	**hubiese probado**	**hubiésemos probado**
probases	**probaseis**	**hubieses probado**	**hubieseis probado**
probase	**probasen**	**hubiese probado**	**hubiesen probado**

imperativo	
—	**probemos**
prueba; no pruebes	**probad; no probéis**
pruebe	**prueben**

Words and expressions related to this verb

la prueba proof, evidence, test
poner a prueba to put to the test, to try out
probable probable

probablemente probably
probar de to taste, to take a taste of
la probatura test, experiment
la probabilidad probability

to try on

The Seven Simple Tenses		The Seven Compound Tenses	
Singular	Plural	Singular	Plural

1   presente de indicativo

me pruebo	nos probamos		
te pruebas	os probáis		
se prueba	se prueban		

8   perfecto de indicativo

me he probado	nos hemos probado		
te has probado	os habéis probado		
se ha probado	se han probado		

2   imperfecto de indicativo

me probaba	nos probábamos
te probabas	os probabais
se probaba	se probaban

9   pluscuamperfecto de indicativo

me había probado	nos habíamos probado
te habías probado	os habíais probado
se había probado	se habían probado

3   pretérito

me probé	nos probamos
te probaste	os probasteis
se probó	se probaron

10   pretérito anterior

me hube probado	nos hubimos probado
te hubiste probado	os hubisteis probado
se hubo probado	se hubieron probado

4   futuro

me probaré	nos probaremos
te probarás	os probaréis
se probará	se probarán

11   futuro perfecto

me habré probado	nos habremos probado
te habrás probado	os habréis probado
se habrá probado	se habrán probado

5   potencial simple

me probaría	nos probaríamos
te probarías	os probaríais
se probaría	se probarían

12   potencial compuesto

me habría probado	nos habríamos probado
te habrías probado	os habríais probado
se habría probado	se habrían probado

6   presente de subjuntivo

me pruebe	nos probemos
te pruebes	os probéis
se pruebe	se prueben

13   perfecto de subjuntivo

me haya probado	nos hayamos probado
te hayas probado	os hayáis probado
se haya probado	se hayan probado

7   imperfecto de subjuntivo

me probara	nos probáramos
te probaras	os probarais
se probara	se probaran
OR	
me probase	nos probásemos
te probases	os probaseis
se probase	se probasen

14   pluscuamperfecto de subjuntivo

me hubiera probado	nos hubiéramos probado
te hubieras probado	os hubierais probado
se hubiera probado	se hubieran probado
OR	
me hubiese probado	nos hubiésemos probado
te hubieses probado	os hubieseis probado
se hubiese probado	se hubiesen probado

imperativo

—	probémonos
pruébate; no te pruebes	probaos; no os probéis
pruébese	pruébense

For words and expressions related to this verb, see **probar**.

pronunciar   Gerundio **pronunciando**   Part. pas. **pronunciado**

to pronounce

The Seven Simple Tenses		The Seven Compound Tenses	
Singular	Plural	Singular	Plural
1 presente de indicativo		8 perfecto de indicativo	
pronuncio	**pronunciamos**	**he pronunciado**	**hemos pronunciado**
pronuncias	**pronunciáis**	**has pronunciado**	**habéis pronunciado**
pronuncia	**pronuncian**	**ha pronunciado**	**han pronunciado**
2 imperfecto de indicativo		9 pluscuamperfecto de indicativo	
pronunciaba	**pronunciábamos**	**había pronunciado**	**habíamos pronunciado**
pronunciabas	**pronunciabais**	**habías pronunciado**	**habíais pronunciado**
pronunciaba	**pronunciaban**	**había pronunciado**	**habían pronunciado**
3 pretérito		10 pretérito anterior	
pronuncié	**pronunciamos**	**hube pronunciado**	**hubimos pronunciado**
pronunciaste	**pronunciasteis**	**hubiste pronunciado**	**hubisteis pronunciado**
pronunció	**pronunciaron**	**hubo pronunciado**	**hubieron pronunciado**
4 futuro		11 futuro perfecto	
pronunciaré	**pronunciaremos**	**habré pronunciado**	**habremos pronunciado**
pronunciarás	**pronunciaréis**	**habrás pronunciado**	**habréis pronunciado**
pronunciará	**pronunciarán**	**habrá pronunciado**	**habrán pronunciado**
5 potencial simple		12 potencial compuesto	
pronunciaría	**pronunciaríamos**	**habría pronunciado**	**habríamos pronunciado**
pronunciarías	**pronunciaríais**	**habrías pronunciado**	**habríais pronunciado**
pronunciaría	**pronunciarían**	**habría pronunciado**	**habrían pronunciado**
6 presente de subjuntivo		13 perfecto de subjuntivo	
pronuncie	**pronunciemos**	**haya pronunciado**	**hayamos pronunciado**
pronuncies	**pronunciéis**	**hayas pronunciado**	**hayáis pronunciado**
pronuncie	**pronuncien**	**haya pronunciado**	**hayan pronunciado**
7 imperfecto de subjuntivo		14 pluscuamperfecto de subjuntivo	
pronunciara	**pronunciáramos**	**hubiera pronunciado**	**hubiéramos pronunciado**
pronunciaras	**pronunciarais**	**hubieras pronunciado**	**hubierais pronunciado**
pronunciara	**pronunciaran**	**hubiera pronunciado**	**hubieran pronunciado**
OR		OR	
pronunciase	**pronunciásemos**	**hubiese pronunciado**	**hubiésemos pronunciado**
pronunciases	**pronunciaseis**	**hubieses pronunciado**	**hubieseis pronunciado**
pronunciase	**pronunciasen**	**hubiese pronunciado**	**hubiesen pronunciado**

imperativo	
—	**pronunciemos**
pronuncia; no pronuncies	**pronunciad; no pronunciéis**
pronuncie	**pronuncien**

Words and expressions related to this verb

la pronunciación pronunciation
pronunciado, pronunciada pronounced
pronunciar un discurso to make a speech
pronunciar una conferencia to deliver a lecture

enunciar to enunciate
anunciar to announce
denunciar to denounce
renunciar to renounce

to protect

The Seven Simple Tenses		The Seven Compound Tenses	
Singular	Plural	Singular	Plural

1   presente de indicativo

protejo	**protegemos**	
proteges	**protegéis**	
protege	**protegen**	

8   perfecto de indicativo

he protegido	**hemos protegido**
has protegido	**habéis protegido**
ha protegido	**han protegido**

2   imperfecto de indicativo

protegía	**protegíamos**
protegías	**protegíais**
protegía	**protegían**

9   pluscuamperfecto de indicativo

había protegido	**habíamos protegido**
habías protegido	**habíais protegido**
había protegido	**habían protegido**

3   pretérito

protegí	**protegimos**
protegiste	**protegisteis**
protegió	**protegieron**

10   pretérito anterior

hube protegido	**hubimos protegido**
hubiste protegido	**hubisteis protegido**
hubo protegido	**hubieron protegido**

4   futuro

protegeré	**protegeremos**
protegerás	**protegeréis**
protegerá	**protegerán**

11   futuro perfecto

habré protegido	**habremos protegido**
habrás protegido	**habréis protegido**
habrá protegido	**habrán protegido**

5   potencial simple

protegería	**protegeríamos**
protegerías	**protegeríais**
protegería	**protegerían**

12   potencial compuesto

habría protegido	**habríamos protegido**
habrías protegido	**habríais protegido**
habría protegido	**habrían protegido**

6   presente de subjuntivo

proteja	**protejamos**
protejas	**protejáis**
proteja	**protejan**

13   perfecto de subjuntivo

haya protegido	**hayamos protegido**
hayas protegido	**hayáis protegido**
haya protegido	**hayan protegido**

7   imperfecto de subjuntivo

protegiera	**protegiéramos**
protegieras	**protegierais**
protegiera	**protegieran**
OR	
protegiese	**protegiésemos**
protegieses	**protegieseis**
protegiese	**protegiesen**

14   pluscuamperfecto de subjuntivo

hubiera protegido	**hubiéramos protegido**
hubieras protegido	**hubierais protegido**
hubiera protegido	**hubieran protegido**
OR	
hubiese protegido	**hubiésemos protegido**
hubieses protegido	**hubieseis protegido**
hubiese protegido	**hubiesen protegido**

imperativo

—	**protejamos**
protege; no protejas	**proteged; no protejáis**
proteja	**protejan**

Words and expressions related to this verb
la protección   protection
protegido, protegida   protected, favorite, protégé
el protector, la protectriz   protector, protectress
protectorio, protectoria   protective

251

quedarse	Gerundio **quedándose**	Part. pas. **quedado**

to remain, to stay

The Seven Simple Tenses	The Seven Compound Tenses

Singular	Plural	Singular	Plural
1 presente de indicativo		**8 perfecto de indicativo**	
me quedo	nos quedamos	me he quedado	nos hemos quedado
te quedas	os quedáis	te has quedado	os habéis quedado
se queda	se quedan	se ha quedado	se han quedado
2 imperfecto de indicativo		**9 pluscuamperfecto de indicativo**	
me quedaba	nos quedábamos	me había quedado	nos habíamos quedado
te quedabas	os quedabais	te habías quedado	os habíais quedado
se quedaba	se quedaban	se había quedado	se habían quedado
3 pretérito		**10 pretérito anterior**	
me quedé	nos quedamos	me hube quedado	nos hubimos quedado
te quedaste	os quedasteis	te hubiste quedado	os hubisteis quedado
se quedó	se quedaron	se hubo quedado	se hubieron quedado
4 futuro		**11 futuro perfecto**	
me quedaré	nos quedaremos	me habré quedado	nos habremos quedado
te quedarás	os quedaréis	te habrás quedado	os habréis quedado
se quedará	se quedarán	se habrá quedado	se habrán quedado
5 potencial simple		**12 potencial compuesto**	
me quedaría	nos quedaríamos	me habría quedado	nos habríamos quedado
te quedarías	os quedaríais	te habrías quedado	os habríais quedado
se quedaría	se quedarían	se habría quedado	se habrían quedado
6 presente de subjuntivo		**13 perfecto de subjuntivo**	
me quede	nos quedemos	me haya quedado	nos hayamos quedado
te quedes	os quedéis	te hayas quedado	os hayáis quedado
se quede	se queden	se haya quedado	se hayan quedado
7 imperfecto de subjuntivo		**14 pluscuamperfecto de subjuntivo**	
me quedara	nos quedáramos	me hubiera quedado	nos hubiéramos quedado
te quedaras	os quedarais	te hubieras quedado	os hubierais quedado
se quedara	se quedaran	se hubiera quedado	se hubieran quedado
OR		OR	
me quedase	nos quedásemos	me hubiese quedado	nos hubiésemos quedado
te quedases	os quedaseis	te hubieses quedado	os hubieseis quedado
se quedase	se quedasen	se hubiese quedado	se hubiesen quedado

imperativo	
—	quedémonos
quédate; no te quedes	quedaos; no os quedéis
quédese	quédense

Words and expressions related to this verb
la quedada residence, stay
quedar to remain, to be left;
  ¿Cuánto dinero queda? How much money is left?
  Me quedan dos dólares. I have two dollars left (remaining).

Gerundio **queriendo**   Part. pas. **querido**   **querer**

to want, to wish

The Seven Simple Tenses		The Seven Compound Tenses	
Singular	Plural	Singular	Plural
1 presente de indicativo		8 perfecto de indicativo	
quiero	**queremos**	**he querido**	**hemos querido**
quieres	**queréis**	**has querido**	**habéis querido**
quiere	**quieren**	**ha querido**	**han querido**
2 imperfecto de indicativo		9 pluscuamperfecto de indicativo	
quería	**queríamos**	**había querido**	**habíamos querido**
querías	**queríais**	**habías querido**	**habíais querido**
quería	**querían**	**había querido**	**habían querido**
3 pretérito		10 pretérito anterior	
quise	**quisimos**	**hube querido**	**hubimos querido**
quisiste	**quisisteis**	**hubiste querido**	**hubisteis querido**
quiso	**quisieron**	**hubo querido**	**hubieron querido**
4 futuro		11 futuro perfecto	
querré	**querremos**	**habré querido**	**habremos querido**
querrás	**querréis**	**habrás querido**	**habréis querido**
querrá	**querrán**	**habrá querido**	**habrán querido**
5 potencial simple		12 potencial compuesto	
querría	**querríamos**	**habría querido**	**habríamos querido**
querrías	**querríais**	**habrías querido**	**habríais querido**
querría	**querrían**	**habría querido**	**habrían querido**
6 presente de subjuntivo		13 perfecto de subjuntivo	
quiera	**queramos**	**haya querido**	**hayamos querido**
quieras	**queráis**	**hayas querido**	**hayáis querido**
quiera	**quieran**	**haya querido**	**hayan querido**
7 imperfecto de subjuntivo		14 pluscuamperfecto de subjuntivo	
quisiera	**quisiéramos**	**hubiera querido**	**hubiéramos querido**
quisieras	**quisierais**	**hubieras querido**	**hubierais querido**
quisiera	**quisieran**	**hubiera querido**	**hubieran querido**
OR		OR	
quisiese	**quisiésemos**	**hubiese querido**	**hubiésemos querido**
quisieses	**quisieseis**	**hubieses querido**	**hubieseis querido**
quisiese	**quisiesen**	**hubiese querido**	**hubiesen querido**

imperativo

—	**queramos**
quiere; no quieras	**quered; no queráis**
quiera	**quieran**

Words and expressions related to this verb
querer decir   to mean;   **¿Qué quiere Ud. decir?**   What do you mean?
   ¿Qué quiere decir esto?   What does this mean?
querido, querida   dear;   **querido amigo, querida amiga**   dear friend
querido mío, querida mía   my dear
querer bien a   to love

253

| quitarse | Gerundio **quitándose** | Part. pas. **quitado** |

to take off (clothing), to remove oneself, to withdraw

The Seven Simple Tenses		The Seven Compound Tenses	
Singular	Plural	Singular	Plural
1 presente de indicativo		8 perfecto de indicativo	
me quito	**nos quitamos**	**me he quitado**	**nos hemos quitado**
te quitas	**os quitáis**	**te has quitado**	**os habéis quitado**
se quita	**se quitan**	**se ha quitado**	**se han quitado**
2 imperfecto de indicativo		9 pluscuamperfecto de indicativo	
me quitaba	**nos quitábamos**	**me había quitado**	**nos habíamos quitado**
te quitabas	**os quitabais**	**te habías quitado**	**os habíais quitado**
se quitaba	**se quitaban**	**se había quitado**	**se habían quitado**
3 pretérito		10 pretérito anterior	
me quité	**nos quitamos**	**me hube quitado**	**nos hubimos quitado**
te quitaste	**os quitasteis**	**te hubiste quitado**	**os hubisteis quitado**
se quitó	**se quitaron**	**se hubo quitado**	**se hubieron quitado**
4 futuro		11 futuro perfecto	
me quitaré	**nos quitaremos**	**me habré quitado**	**nos habremos quitado**
te quitarás	**os quitaréis**	**te habrás quitado**	**os habréis quitado**
se quitará	**se quitarán**	**se habrá quitado**	**se habrán quitado**
5 potencial simple		12 potencial compuesto	
me quitaría	**nos quitaríamos**	**me habría quitado**	**nos habríamos quitado**
te quitarías	**os quitaríais**	**te habrías quitado**	**os habríais quitado**
se quitaría	**se quitarían**	**se habría quitado**	**se habrían quitado**
6 presente de subjuntivo		13 perfecto de subjuntivo	
me quite	**nos quitemos**	**me haya quitado**	**nos hayamos quitado**
te quites	**os quitéis**	**te hayas quitado**	**os hayáis quitado**
se quite	**se quiten**	**se haya quitado**	**se hayan quitado**
7 imperfecto de subjuntivo		14 pluscuamperfecto de subjuntivo	
me quitara	**nos quitáramos**	**me hubiera quitado**	**nos hubiéramos quitado**
te quitaras	**os quitarais**	**te hubieras quitado**	**os hubierais quitado**
se quitara	**se quitaran**	**se hubiera quitado**	**se hubieran quitado**
OR		OR	
me quitase	**nos quitásemos**	**me hubiese quitado**	**nos hubiésemos quitado**
te quitases	**os quitaseis**	**te hubieses quitado**	**os hubieseis quitado**
se quitase	**se quitasen**	**se hubiese quitado**	**se hubiesen quitado**

	imperativo	
	—	**quitémonos**
	quítate; no te quites	**quitaos; no os quitéis**
	quítese	**quítense**

Words and expressions related to this verb
la quita release (from owing money), acquittance
¡Quita de ahí! Get away from here!
quitar to remove, to take away; to rob, to strip
el quite removal; **el quitasol** parasol (sunshade)

Gerundio **recibiendo**   Part. pas. **recibido**   **recibir**

The Seven Simple Tenses		The Seven Compound Tenses	
Singular	Plural	Singular	Plural
1 presente de indicativo		8 perfecto de indicativo	
recibo	**recibimos**	**he recibido**	**hemos recibido**
recibes	**recibís**	**has recibido**	**habéis recibido**
recibe	**reciben**	**ha recibido**	**han recibido**
2 imperfecto de indicativo		9 pluscuamperfecto de indicativo	
recibía	**recibíamos**	**había recibido**	**habíamos recibido**
recibías	**recibíais**	**habías recibido**	**habíais recibido**
recibía	**recibían**	**había recibido**	**habían recibido**
3 pretérito		10 pretérito anterior	
recibí	**recibimos**	**hube recibido**	**hubimos recibido**
recibiste	**recibisteis**	**hubiste recibido**	**hubisteis recibido**
recibió	**recibieron**	**hubo recibido**	**hubieron recibido**
4 futuro		11 futuro perfecto	
recibiré	**recibiremos**	**habré recibido**	**habremos recibido**
recibirás	**recibiréis**	**habrás recibido**	**habréis recibido**
recibirá	**recibirán**	**habrá recibido**	**habrán recibido**
5 potencial simple		12 potencial compuesto	
recibiría	**recibiríamos**	**habría recibido**	**habríamos recibido**
recibirías	**recibiríais**	**habrías recibido**	**habríais recibido**
recibiría	**recibirían**	**habría recibido**	**habrían recibido**
6 presente de subjuntivo		13 perfecto de subjuntivo	
reciba	**recibamos**	**haya recibido**	**hayamos recibido**
recibas	**recibáis**	**hayas recibido**	**hayáis recibido**
reciba	**reciban**	**haya recibido**	**hayan recibido**
7 imperfecto de subjuntivo		14 pluscuamperfecto de subjuntivo	
recibiera	**recibiéramos**	**hubiera recibido**	**hubiéramos recibido**
recibieras	**recibierais**	**hubieras recibido**	**hubierais recibido**
recibiera	**recibieran**	**hubiera recibido**	**hubieran recibido**
OR		OR	
recibiese	**recibiésemos**	**hubiese recibido**	**hubiésemos recibido**
recibieses	**recibieseis**	**hubieses recibido**	**hubieseis recibido**
recibiese	**recibiesen**	**hubiese recibido**	**hubiesen recibido**

imperativo	
—	**recibamos**
recibe; no recibas	**recibid; no recibáis**
reciba	**reciban**

Words and expressions related to this verb
un recibo   receipt
acusar recibo   to acknowledge receipt
la recepción   reception
recibir a cuenta   to receive on account

de recibo   acceptable; **ser de recibo**   to be acceptable
recibirse   to be admitted, to be received

recordar	Gerundio **recordando**	Part. pas. **recordado**

to remember, to recall, to remind

The Seven Simple Tenses		The Seven Compound Tenses	
Singular	Plural	Singular	Plural
1 presente de indicativo		8 perfecto de indicativo	
recuerdo	recordamos	he recordado	hemos recordado
recuerdas	recordáis	has recordado	habéis recordado
recuerda	recuerdan	ha recordado	han recordado
2 imperfecto de indicativo		9 pluscuamperfecto de indicativo	
recordaba	recordábamos	había recordado	habíamos recordado
recordabas	recordabais	habías recordado	habíais recordado
recordaba	recordaban	había recordado	habían recordado
3 pretérito		10 pretérito anterior	
recordé	recordamos	hube recordado	hubimos recordado
recordaste	recordasteis	hubiste recordado	hubisteis recordado
recordó	recordaron	hubo recordado	hubieron recordado
4 futuro		11 futuro perfecto	
recordaré	recordaremos	habré recordado	habremos recordado
recordarás	recordaréis	habrás recordado	habréis recordado
recordará	recordarán	habrá recordado	habrán recordado
5 potencial simple		12 potencial compuesto	
recordaría	recordaríamos	habría recordado	habríamos recordado
recordarías	recordaríais	habrías recordado	habríais recordado
recordaría	recordarían	habría recordado	habrían recordado
6 presente de subjuntivo		13 perfecto de subjuntivo	
recuerde	recordemos	haya recordado	hayamos recordado
recuerdes	recordéis	hayas recordado	hayáis recordado
recuerde	recuerden	haya recordado	hayan recordado
7 imperfecto de subjuntivo		14 pluscuamperfecto de subjuntivo	
recordara	recordáramos	hubiera recordado	hubiéramos recordado
recordaras	recordarais	hubieras recordado	hubierais recordado
recordara	recordaran	hubiera recordado	hubieran recordado
OR		OR	
recordase	recordásemos	hubiese recordado	hubiésemos recordado
recordases	recordaseis	hubieses recordado	hubieseis recordado
recordase	recordasen	hubiese recordado	hubiesen recordado

imperativo	
—	recordemos
recuerda; no recuerdes	recordad; no recordéis
recuerde	recuerden

Words and expressions related to this verb
el recuerdo   memory, recollection
los recuerdos   regards, compliments
recordable   memorable

recordar algo a uno   to remind someone
   of something
un recordatorio   memento, reminder

Gerundio **refiriendo**   Part. pas. **referido**   **referir**

to refer, to relate

The Seven Simple Tenses		The Seven Compound Tenses	
Singular	Plural	Singular	Plural
1 presente de indicativo		8 perfecto de indicativo	
refiero	**referimos**	**he referido**	**hemos referido**
refieres	**referís**	**has referido**	**habéis referido**
refiere	**refieren**	**ha referido**	**han referido**
2 imperfecto de indicativo		9 pluscuamperfecto de indicativo	
refería	**referíamos**	**había referido**	**habíamos referido**
referías	**referíais**	**habías referido**	**habíais referido**
refería	**referían**	**había referido**	**habían referido**
3 pretérito		10 pretérito anterior	
referí	**referimos**	**hube referido**	**hubimos referido**
referiste	**referisteis**	**hubiste referido**	**hubisteis referido**
refirió	**refirieron**	**hubo referido**	**hubieron referido**
4 futuro		11 futuro perfecto	
referiré	**referiremos**	**habré referido**	**habremos referido**
referirás	**referiréis**	**habrás referido**	**habréis referido**
referirá	**referirán**	**habrá referido**	**habrán referido**
5 potencial simple		12 potencial compuesto	
referiría	**referiríamos**	**habría referido**	**habríamos referido**
referirías	**referiríais**	**habrías referido**	**habríais referido**
referiría	**referirian**	**habría referido**	**habrían referido**
6 presente de subjuntivo		13 perfecto de subjuntivo	
refiera	**refiramos**	**haya referido**	**hayamos referido**
refieras	**refiráis**	**hayas referido**	**hayáis referido**
refiera	**refieran**	**haya referido**	**hayan referido**
7 imperfecto de subjuntivo		14 pluscuamperfecto de subjuntivo	
refiriera	**refiriéramos**	**hubiera referido**	**hubiéramos referido**
refirieras	**refirieras**	**hubieras referido**	**hubierais referido**
refiriera	**refirieran**	**hubiera referido**	**hubieran referido**
OR		OR	
refiriese	**refiriésemos**	**hubiese referido**	**hubiésemos referido**
refirieses	**refirieseis**	**hubieses referido**	**hubieseis referido**
refiriese	**refiriesen**	**hubiese referido**	**hubiesen referido**

imperativo	
—	**refiramos**
refiere; no refieras	**referid; no refiráis**
refiera	**refieran**

Words related to this verb

la referencia   reference, account (narration)
referente   concerning, referring, relating (to)
el referéndum   referendum
preferir   to prefer
el referido, la referida   the person referred to

reír	Gerundio **riendo**	Part. pas. **reído**

to laugh

The Seven Simple Tenses	The Seven Compound Tenses

Singular	Plural	Singular	Plural
1 presente de indicativo		8 perfecto de indicativo	
río	reímos	he reído	hemos reído
ríes	reís	has reído	habéis reído
ríe	ríen	ha reído	han reído
2 imperfecto de indicativo		9 pluscuamperfecto de indicativo	
reía	reíamos	había reído	habíamos reído
reías	reíais	habías reído	habíais reído
reía	reían	había reído	habían reído
3 pretérito		10 pretérito anterior	
reí	reímos	hube reído	hubimos reído
reiste	reísteis	hubiste reído	hubisteis reído
rió	rieron	hubo reído	hubieron reído
4 futuro		11 futuro perfecto	
reiré	reiremos	habré reído	habremos reído
reirás	reiréis	habrás reído	habréis reído
reirá	reirán	habrá reído	habrán reído
5 potencial simple		12 potencial compuesto	
reiría	reiríamos	habría reído	habríamos reído
reirías	reiríais	habrías reído	habríais reído
reiría	reirían	habría reído	habrían reído
6 presente de subjuntivo		13 perfecto de subjuntivo	
ría	riamos	haya reído	hayamos reído
rías	riáis	hayas reído	hayáis reído
ría	rían	haya reído	hayan reído
7 imperfecto de subjuntivo		14 pluscuamperfecto de subjuntivo	
riera	riéramos	hubiera reído	hubiéramos reído
rieras	rierais	hubieras reído	hubierais reído
riera	rieran	hubiera reído	hubieran reído
OR		OR	
riese	riésemos	hubiese reído	hubiésemos reído
rieses	rieseis	hubieses reído	hubieseis reído
riese	riesen	hubiese reído	hubiesen reído

imperativo	
—	riamos
ríe; no rías	reíd; no riáis
ría	rían

Common idiomatic expressions using this verb

reír a carcajadas to laugh loudly
reír de to laugh at, to make fun of
la risa laugh, laughter

risible laughable
risueño, risueña smiling

For additional words and expressions related to this verb, see **sonreír.**

Gerundio **riñendo**	Part. pas. **reñido**	**reñir**

to scold, to quarrel

The Seven Simple Tenses		The Seven Compound Tenses	
Singular	Plural	Singular	Plural
1 presente de indicativo		8 perfecto de indicativo	
riño	**reñimos**	**he reñido**	**hemos reñido**
riñes	**reñís**	**has reñido**	**habéis reñido**
riñe	**riñen**	**ha reñido**	**han reñido**
2 imperfecto de indicativo		9 pluscuamperfecto de indicativo	
reñía	**reñíamos**	**había reñido**	**habíamos reñido**
reñías	**reñías**	**habías reñido**	**habíais reñido**
reñía	**reñían**	**había reñido**	**habían reñido**
3 pretérito		10 pretérito anterior	
reñí	**reñimos**	**hube reñido**	**hubimos reñido**
reñiste	**reñisteis**	**hubiste reñido**	**hubisteis reñido**
riñó	**riñeron**	**hubo reñido**	**hubieron reñido**
4 futuro		11 futuro perfecto	
reñiré	**reñiremos**	**habré reñido**	**habremos reñido**
reñirás	**reñiréis**	**habrás reñido**	**habréis reñido**
reñirá	**reñirán**	**habrá reñido**	**habrán reñido**
5 potencial simple		12 potencial compuesto	
reñiría	**reñiríamos**	**habría reñido**	**habríamos reñido**
reñirías	**reñiríais**	**habrías reñido**	**habríais reñido**
reñiría	**reñirían**	**habría reñido**	**habrían reñido**
6 presente de subjuntivo		13 perfecto de subjuntivo	
riña	**riñamos**	**haya reñido**	**hayamos reñido**
riñas	**riñáis**	**hayas reñido**	**hayáis reñido**
riña	**riñan**	**haya reñido**	**hayan reñido**
7 imperfecto de subjuntivo		14 pluscuamperfecto de subjuntivo	
riñera	**riñéramos**	**hubiera reñido**	**hubiéramos reñido**
riñeras	**riñerais**	**hubieras reñido**	**hubierais reñido**
riñera	**riñeran**	**hubiera reñido**	**hubieran reñido**
OR		OR	
riñese	**riñésemos**	**hubiese reñido**	**hubiésemos reñido**
riñeses	**riñeseis**	**hubieses reñido**	**hubieseis reñido**
riñese	**riñesen**	**hubiese reñido**	**hubiesen reñido**

imperativo	
—	**riñamos**
riñe; no riñas	**reñid; no riñáis**
riña	**riñan**

Words related to this verb
reñidor, reñidora quarreller   **la reñidura**   reprimand, scolding
reñidamente stubbornly

repetir Gerundio **repitiendo** Part. pas. **repetido**

to repeat

The Seven Simple Tenses		The Seven Compound Tenses	
Singular	Plural	Singular	Plural
1 presente de indicativo		8 perfecto de indicativo	
repito	**repetimos**	**he repetido**	**hemos repetido**
repites	**repetís**	**has repetido**	**habéis repetido**
repite	**repiten**	**ha repetido**	**han repetido**
2 imperfecto de indicativo		9 pluscuamperfecto de indicativo	
repetía	**repetíamos**	**había repetido**	**habíamos repetido**
repetías	**repetíais**	**habías repetido**	**habíais repetido**
repetía	**repetían**	**había repetido**	**habían repetido**
3 pretérito		10 pretérito anterior	
repetí	**repetimos**	**hube repetido**	**hubimos repetido**
repetiste	**repetisteis**	**hubiste repetido**	**hubisteis repetido**
repitió	**repitieron**	**hubo repetido**	**hubieron repetido**
4 futuro		11 futuro perfecto	
repetiré	**repetiremos**	**habré repetido**	**habremos repetido**
repetirás	**repetiréis**	**habrás repetido**	**habréis repetido**
repetirá	**repetirán**	**habrá repetido**	**habrán repetido**
5 potencial simple		12 potencial compuesto	
repetiría	**repetiríamos**	**habría repetido**	**habríamos repetido**
repetirías	**repetiríais**	**habrías repetido**	**habríais repetido**
repetiría	**repetirían**	**habría repetido**	**habrían repetido**
6 presente de subjuntivo		13 perfecto de subjuntivo	
repita	**repitamos**	**haya repetido**	**hayamos repetido**
repitas	**repitáis**	**hayas repetido**	**hayáis repetido**
repita	**repitan**	**haya repetido**	**hayan repetido**
7 imperfecto de subjuntivo		14 pluscuamperfecto de subjuntivo	
repitiera	**repitiéramos**	**hubiera repetido**	**hubiéramos repetido**
repitieras	**repitierais**	**hubieras repetido**	**hubierais repetido**
repitiera	**repitieran**	**hubiera repetido**	**hubieran repetido**
OR		OR	
repitiese	**repitiésemos**	**hubiese repetido**	**hubiésemos repetido**
repitieses	**repitieseis**	**hubieses repetido**	**hubieseis repetido**
repitiese	**repitiesen**	**hubiese repetido**	**hubiesen repetido**

imperativo	
—	**repitamos**
repite; no repitas	**repetid; no repitáis**
repita	**repitan**

Words related to this verb
la repetición repetition
repetidamente repeatedly

repitiente *(adj.)* repeating
repetirse to repeat to oneself

to answer, to reply, to respond

The Seven Simple Tenses		The Seven Compound Tenses	
Singular	Plural	Singular	Plural
1 presente de indicativo		8 perfecto de indicativo	
respondo	**respondemos**	**he respondido**	**hemos respondido**
respondes	**respondéis**	**has respondido**	**habéis respondido**
responde	**responden**	**ha respondido**	**han respondido**
2 imperfecto de indicativo		9 pluscuamperfecto de indicativo	
respondía	**respondíamos**	**había respondido**	**habíamos respondido**
respondías	**respondíais**	**habías respondido**	**habíais respondido**
respondía	**respondían**	**había respondido**	**habían respondido**
3 pretérito		10 pretérito anterior	
respondí	**respondimos**	**hube respondido**	**hubimos respondido**
respondiste	**respondisteis**	**hubiste respondido**	**hubisteis respondido**
respondió	**respondieron**	**hubo respondido**	**hubieron respondido**
4 futuro		11 futuro perfecto	
responderé	**responderemos**	**habré respondido**	**habremos respondido**
responderás	**responderéis**	**habrás respondido**	**habréis respondido**
responderá	**responderán**	**habrá respondido**	**habrán respondido**
5 potencial simple		12 potencial compuesto	
respondería	**responderíamos**	**habría respondido**	**habríamos respondido**
responderías	**responderíais**	**habrías respondido**	**habríais respondido**
respondería	**responderían**	**habría respondido**	**habrían respondido**
6 presente de subjuntivo		13 perfecto de subjuntivo	
responda	**respondamos**	**haya respondido**	**hayamos respondido**
respondas	**respondáis**	**hayas respondido**	**hayáis respondido**
responda	**respondan**	**haya respondido**	**hayan respondido**
7 imperfecto de subjuntivo		14 pluscuamperfecto de subjuntivo	
respondiera	**respondiéramos**	**hubiera respondido**	**hubiéramos respondido**
respondieras	**respondierais**	**hubieras respondido**	**hubierais respondido**
respondiera	**respondieran**	**hubiera respondido**	**hubieran respondido**
OR		OR	
respondiese	**respondiésemos**	**hubiese respondido**	**hubiésemos respondido**
respondieses	**respondieseis**	**hubieses respondido**	**hubieseis respondido**
respondiese	**respondiesen**	**hubiese respondido**	**hubiesen respondido**

imperativo	
—	**respondamos**
responde; no respondas	**responded; no respondáis**
responda	**respondan**

Words related to this verb
una respuesta answer, reply, response
respondiente respondent
la correspondencia correspondence
correspondientemente correspondingly

responsivo, responsiva responsive
corresponder to correspond
corresponder a to reciprocate

to revolve, to turn around, to turn over, to turn upside down

The Seven Simple Tenses		The Seven Compound Tenses	
Singular	Plural	Singular	Plural
1 presente de indicativo		8 perfecto de indicativo	
revuelvo	revolvemos	he revuelto	hemos revuelto
revuelves	revolvéis	has revuelto	habéis revuelto
revuelve	revuelven	ha revuelto	han revuelto
2 imperfecto de indicativo		9 pluscuamperfecto de indicativo	
revolvía	revolvíamos	había revuelto	habíamos revuelto
revolvías	revolvíais	habías revuelto	habíais revuelto
revolvía	revolvían	había revuelto	habían revuelto
3 pretérito		10 pretérito anterior	
revolví	revolvimos	hube revuelto	hubimos revuelto
revolviste	revolvisteis	hubiste revuelto	hubisteis revuelto
revolvió	revolvieron	hubo revuelto	hubieron revuelto
4 futuro		11 futuro perfecto	
revolveré	revolveremos	habré revuelto	habremos revuelto
revolverás	revolveréis	habrás revuelto	habréis revuelto
revolverá	revolverán	habrá revuelto	habrán revuelto
5 potencial simple		12 potencial compuesto	
revolvería	revolveríamos	habría revuelto	habríamos revuelto
revolverías	revolveríais	habrías revuelto	habríais revuelto
revolvería	revolverían	habría revuelto	habrían revuelto
6 presente de subjuntivo		13 perfecto de subjuntivo	
revuelva	revolvamos	haya revuelto	hayamos revuelto
revuelvas	revolváis	hayas revuelto	hayáis revuelto
revuelva	revuelvan	haya revuelto	hayan revuelto
7 imperfecto de subjuntivo		14 pluscuamperfecto de subjuntivo	
revolviera	revolviéramos	hubiera revuelto	hubiéramos revuelto
revolvieras	revolvierais	hubieras revuelto	hubierais revuelto
revolviera	revolvieran	hubiera revuelto	hubieran revuelto
OR		OR	
revolviese	revolviésemos	hubiese revuelto	hubiésemos revuelto
revolvieses	revolvieseis	hubieses revuelto	hubieseis revuelto
revolviese	revolviesen	hubiese revuelto	hubiesen revuelto

	imperativo
—	revolvamos
revuelve; no revuelvas	revolved; no revolváis
revuelva	revuelvan

Words and expressions related to this verb
huevos revueltos   scrambled eggs   **el revolvimiento**   revolving, revolution
la revolución   revolution   **revueltamente**   upside down
For other words and expressions related to this verb, see **volver.**

Gerundio **rogando**   Part. pas. **rogado**   **rogar**

to supplicate, to ask, to ask for, to request, to beg, to pray

The Seven Simple Tenses		The Seven Compound Tenses	
Singular	Plural	Singular	Plural
1 presente de indicativo		8 perfecto de indicativo	
ruego	rogamos	he rogado	hemos rogado
ruegas	rogáis	has rogado	habéis rogado
ruega	ruegan	ha rogado	han rogado
2 imperfecto de indicativo		9 pluscuamperfecto de indicativo	
rogaba	rogábamos	había rogado	habíamos rogado
rogabas	rogabais	habías rogado	habíais rogado
rogaba	rogaban	había rogado	habían rogado
3 pretérito		10 pretérito anterior	
rogué	rogamos	hube rogado	hubimos rogado
rogaste	rogasteis	hubiste rogado	hubisteis rogado
rogó	rogaron	hubo rogado	hubieron rogado
4 futuro		11 futuro perfecto	
rogaré	rogaremos	habré rogado	habremos rogado
rogarás	rogaréis	habrás rogado	habréis rogado
rogará	rogarán	habrá rogado	habrán rogado
5 potencial simple		12 potencial compuesto	
rogaría	rogaríamos	habría rogado	habríamos rogado
rogarías	rogaríais	habrías rogado	habríais rogado
rogaría	rogarían	habría rogado	habrían rogado
6 presente de subjuntivo		13 perfecto de subjuntivo	
ruegue	roguemos	haya rogado	hayamos rogado
ruegues	roguéis	hayas rogado	hayáis rogado
ruegue	rueguen	haya rogado	hayan rogado
7 imperfecto de subjuntivo		14 pluscuamperfecto de subjuntivo	
rogara	rogáramos	hubiera rogado	hubiéramos rogado
rogaras	rogarais	hubieras rogado	hubierais rogado
rogara	rogaran	hubiera rogado	hubieran rogado
OR		OR	
rogase	rogásemos	hubiese rogado	hubiésemos rogado
rogases	rogaseis	hubieses rogado	hubieseis rogado
rogase	rogasen	hubiese rogado	hubiesen rogado

imperativo	
—	roguemos
ruega; no ruegues	rogad; no roguéis
ruegue	rueguen

Sentence using this verb and words related to it

A Dios rogando y con el mazo dando.   Put your faith in God and keep
your powder dry.

rogador, rogadora supplicant   **rogar por** to plead for
rogativo, rogativa supplicatory

romper — Gerundio **rompiendo** — Part. pas. **roto**

to break, to shatter, to tear

The Seven Simple Tenses		The Seven Compound Tenses	
Singular	Plural	Singular	Plural
1 presente de indicativo		8 perfecto de indicativo	
rompo	rompemos	he roto	hemos roto
rompes	rompéis	has roto	habéis roto
rompe	rompen	ha roto	han roto
2 imperfecto de indicativo		9 pluscuamperfecto de indicativo	
rompía	rompíamos	había roto	habíamos roto
rompías	rompíais	habías roto	habíais roto
rompía	rompían	había roto	habían roto
3 pretérito		10 pretérito anterior	
rompí	rompimos	hube roto	hubimos roto
rompiste	rompisteis	hubiste roto	hubisteis roto
rompió	rompieron	hubo roto	hubieron roto
4 futuro		11 futuro perfecto	
romperé	romperemos	habré roto	habremos roto
romperás	romperéis	habrás roto	habréis roto
romperá	romperán	habrá roto	habrán roto
5 potencial simple		12 potencial compuesto	
rompería	romperíamos	habría roto	habríamos roto
romperías	romperíais	habrías roto	habríais roto
rompería	romperían	habría roto	habrían roto
6 presente de subjuntivo		13 perfecto de subjuntivo	
rompa	rompamos	haya roto	hayamos roto
rompas	rompáis	hayas roto	hayáis roto
rompa	rompan	haya roto	hayan roto
7 imperfecto de subjuntivo		14 pluscuamperfecto de subjuntivo	
rompiera	rompiéramos	hubiera roto	hubiéramos roto
rompieras	rompierais	hubieras roto	hubierais roto
rompiera	rompieran	hubiera roto	hubieran roto
OR		OR	
rompiese	rompiésemos	hubiese roto	hubiésemos roto
rompieses	rompieseis	hubieses roto	hubieseis roto
rompiese	rompiesen	hubiese roto	hubiesen roto

imperativo	
—	rompamos
rompe; no rompas	romped; no rompáis
rompa	rompan

Words and expressions related to this verb

un rompenueces nutcracker
una rompedura breakage, rupture
romper la cabeza to rack one's brains
romper con to break relations with

romper a + inf. to start suddenly + inf.
romper a llorar to break into tears
romper las relaciones to break off relations, an engagement

Gerundio **sabiendo**   Part. pas. **sabido**   **saber**

to know, to know how

The Seven Simple Tenses		The Seven Compound Tenses	
Singular	Plural	Singular	Plural
1 presente de indicativo		**8 perfecto de indicativo**	
sé	sabemos	he sabido	hemos sabido
sabes	sabéis	has sabido	habéis sabido
sabe	saben	ha sabido	han sabido
2 imperfecto de indicativo		**9 pluscuamperfecto de indicativo**	
sabía	sabíamos	había sabido	habíamos sabido
sabías	sabíais	habías sabido	habíais sabido
sabía	sabían	había sabido	habían sabido
3 pretérito		**10 pretérito anterior**	
supe	supimos	hube sabido	hubimos sabido
supiste	supisteis	hubiste sabido	hubisteis sabido
supo	supieron	hubo sabido	hubieron sabido
4 futuro		**11 futuro perfecto**	
sabré	sabremos	habré sabido	habremos sabido
sabrás	sabréis	habrás sabido	habréis sabido
sabrá	sabrán	habrá sabido	habrán sabido
5 potencial simple		**12 potencial compuesto**	
sabría	sabríamos	habría sabido	habríamos sabido
sabrías	sabríais	habrías sabido	habríais sabido
sabría	sabrían	habría sabido	habrían sabido
6 presente de subjuntivo		**13 perfecto de subjuntivo**	
sepa	sepamos	haya sabido	hayamos sabido
sepas	sepáis	hayas sabido	hayáis sabido
sepa	sepan	haya sabido	hayan sabido
7 imperfecto de subjuntivo		**14 pluscuamperfecto de subjuntivo**	
supiera	supiéramos	hubiera sabido	hubiéramos sabido
supieras	supierais	hubieras sabido	hubierais sabido
supiera	supieran	hubiera sabido	hubieran sabido
OR		OR	
supiese	supiésemos	hubiese sabido	hubiésemos sabido
supieses	supieseis	hubieses sabido	hubieseis sabido
supiese	supiesen	hubiese sabido	hubiesen sabido

imperativo	
—	sepamos
sabe; no sepas	sabed; no sepáis
sepa	sepan

Words and expressions related to this verb
sabio, sabia   wise, learned   **Que yo sepa . . .**   As far as I know . . .
un sabidillo, una sabidilla   a know-it-all individual
la sabiduría   knowledge, learning, wisdom
¿Sabe Ud. nadar?   Do you know how to swim?

sacar	Gerundio **sacando**	Part. pas. **sacado**

to take out, to get

The Seven Simple Tenses		The Seven Compound Tenses	
Singular	Plural	Singular	Plural
1 presente de indicativo		**8 perfecto de indicativo**	
saco	sacamos	he sacado	hemos sacado
sacas	sacáis	has sacado	habéis sacado
saca	sacan	ha sacado	han sacado
2 imperfecto de indicativo		**9 pluscuamperfecto de indicativo**	
sacaba	sacábamos	había sacado	habíamos sacado
sacabas	sacabais	habías sacado	habíais sacado
sacaba	sacaban	había sacado	habían sacado
3 pretérito		**10 pretérito anterior**	
saqué	sacamos	hube sacado	hubimos sacado
sacaste	sacasteis	hubiste sacado	hubisteis sacado
sacó	sacaron	hubo sacado	hubieron sacado
4 futuro		**11 futuro perfecto**	
sacaré	sacaremos	habré sacado	habremos sacado
sacarás	sacaréis	habrás sacado	habréis sacado
sacará	sacarán	habrá sacado	habrán sacado
5 potencial simple		**12 potencial compuesto**	
sacaría	sacaríamos	habría sacado	habríamos sacado
sacarías	sacaríais	habrías sacado	habríais sacado
sacaría	sacarían	habría sacado	habrían sacado
6 presente de subjuntivo		**13 perfecto de subjuntivo**	
saque	saquemos	haya sacado	hayamos sacado
saques	saquéis	hayas sacado	hayáis sacado
saque	saquen	haya sacado	hayan sacado
7 imperfecto de subjuntivo		**14 pluscuamperfecto de subjuntivo**	
sacara	sacáramos	hubiera sacado	hubiéramos sacado
sacaras	sacarais	hubieras sacado	hubierais sacado
sacara	sacaran	hubiera sacado	hubieran sacado
OR		OR	
sacase	sacásemos	hubiese sacado	hubiésemos sacado
sacases	sacaseis	hubieses sacado	hubieseis sacado
sacase	sacasen	hubiese sacado	hubiesen sacado

imperative	
—	saquemos
saca; no saques	sacad; no saquéis
saque	saquen

Words and expressions related to this verb

sacar agua to draw water   **sacar fotos** to take pictures
sacar a paseo to take out for a walk; **ensacar** to put in a bag, to bag
un saco bag, sack; **saco de noche** overnight bag
un sacapuntas pencil sharpener (**un afilalápices**)

to go out, to leave

The Seven Simple Tenses		The Seven Compound Tenses	
Singular	Plural	Singular	Plural
1 presente de indicativo		8 perfecto de indicativo	
salgo	**salimos**	**he salido**	**hemos salido**
sales	**salís**	**has salido**	**habéis salido**
sale	**salen**	**ha salido**	**han salido**
2 imperfecto de indicativo		9 pluscuamperfecto de indicativo	
salía	**salíamos**	**había salido**	**habíamos salido**
salías	**salíais**	**habías salido**	**habíais salido**
salía	**salían**	**había salido**	**habían salido**
3 pretérito		10 pretérito anterior	
salí	**salimos**	**hube salido**	**hubimos salido**
saliste	**salisteis**	**hubiste salido**	**hubisteis salido**
salió	**salieron**	**hubo salido**	**hubieron salido**
4 futuro		11 futuro perfecto	
saldré	**saldremos**	**habré salido**	**habremos salido**
saldrás	**saldréis**	**habrás salido**	**habréis salido**
saldrá	**saldrán**	**habrá salido**	**habrán salido**
5 potencial simple		12 potencial compuesto	
saldría	**saldríamos**	**habría salido**	**habríamos salido**
saldrías	**saldríais**	**habrías salido**	**habríais salido**
saldría	**saldrían**	**habría salido**	**habrían salido**
6 presente de subjuntivo		13 perfecto de subjuntivo	
salga	**salgamos**	**haya salido**	**hayamos salido**
salgas	**salgáis**	**hayas salido**	**hayáis salido**
salga	**salgan**	**haya salido**	**hayan salido**
7 imperfecto de subjuntivo		14 pluscuamperfecto de subjuntivo	
saliera	**saliéramos**	**hubiera salido**	**hubiéramos salido**
salieras	**salierais**	**hubieras salido**	**hubierais salido**
saliera	**salieran**	**hubiera salido**	**hubieran salido**
OR		OR	
saliese	**saliésemos**	**hubiese salido**	**hubiésemos salido**
salieses	**salieseis**	**hubieses salido**	**hubieseis salido**
saliese	**saliesen**	**hubiese salido**	**hubiesen salido**

imperativo	
—	**salgamos**
sal; no salgas	**salid; no salgáis**
salga	**salgan**

Words and expressions related to this verb

la salida   exit
sin salida   no exit, dead-end street
salir de compras   to go out shopping
salir mal   to go wrong, to do badly

salir a   to resemble, to look like
salir al encuentro de   to go to meet
salir de   to leave from, to get out of

secar	Gerundio **secando**	Part. pas. **secado**

to dry, to wipe dry

The Seven Simple Tenses		The Seven Compound Tenses	
Singular	Plural	Singular	Plural
1 presente de indicativo		**8 perfecto de indicativo**	
seco	secamos	he secado	hemos secado
secas	secáis	has secado	habéis secado
seca	secan	ha secado	han secado
2 imperfecto de indicativo		**9 pluscuamperfecto de indicativo**	
secaba	secábamos	había secado	habíamos secado
secabas	secabais	habías secado	habíais secado
secaba	secaban	había secado	habían secado
3 pretérito		**10 pretérito anterior**	
sequé	secamos	hube secado	hubimos secado
secaste	secasteis	hubiste secado	hubisteis secado
secó	secaron	hubo secado	hubieron secado
4 futuro		**11 futuro perfecto**	
secaré	secaremos	habré secado	habremos secado
secarás	secaréis	habrás secado	habréis secado
secará	secarán	habrá secado	habrán secado
5 potencial simple		**12 potencial compuesto**	
secaría	secaríamos	habría secado	habríamos secado
secarías	secaríais	habrías secado	habríais secado
secaría	secarían	habría secado	habrían secado
6 presente de subjuntivo		**13 perfecto de subjuntivo**	
seque	sequemos	haya secado	hayamos secado
seques	sequéis	hayas secado	hayáis secado
seque	sequen	haya secado	hayan secado
7 imperfecto de subjuntivo		**14 pluscuamperfecto de subjuntivo**	
secara	secáramos	hubiera secado	hubiéramos secado
secaras	secarais	hubieras secado	hubierais secado
secara	secaran	hubiera secado	hubieran secado
OR		OR	
secase	secásemos	hubiese secado	hubiésemos secado
secases	secaseis	hubieses secado	hubieseis secado
secase	secasen	hubiese secado	hubiesen secado

	imperativo	
—	sequemos	
seca; no seques	secad; no sequéis	
seque	sequen	

Words and expressions related to this verb

seco, seca dry, dried up   **limpiar en seco** to dry-clean
la seca drought   **en seco** high and dry
secado al sol sun dried   **la secadora** dryer, clothes dryer
   máquina para secar la ropa machine to dry the clothes

268

Gerundio **siguiendo**   Part. pas. **seguido**   **seguir**

to follow, to pursue, to continue

The Seven Simple Tenses		The Seven Compound Tenses	
Singular	Plural	Singular	Plural
1 presente de indicativo		8 perfecto de indicativo	
sigo	seguimos	he seguido	hemos seguido
sigues	seguís	has seguido	habéis seguido
sigue	siguen	ha seguido	han seguido
2 imperfecto de indicativo		9 pluscuamperfecto de indicativo	
seguía	seguíamos	había seguido	habíamos seguido
seguías	seguíais	habías seguido	habíais seguido
seguía	seguían	había seguido	habían seguido
3 pretérito		10 pretérito anterior	
seguí	seguimos	hube seguido	hubimos seguido
seguiste	seguisteis	hubiste seguido	hubisteis seguido
siguió	siguieron	hubo seguido	hubieron seguido
4 futuro		11 futuro perfecto	
seguiré	seguiremos	habré seguido	habremos seguido
seguirás	seguiréis	habrás seguido	habréis seguido
seguirá	seguirán	habrá seguido	habrán seguido
5 potencial simple		12 potencial compuesto	
seguiría	seguiríamos	habría seguido	habríamos seguido
seguirías	seguiríais	habrías seguido	habríais seguido
seguiría	seguirían	habría seguido	habrían seguido
6 presente de subjuntivo		13 perfecto de subjuntivo	
siga	sigamos	haya seguido	hayamos seguido
sigas	sigáis	hayas seguido	hayáis seguido
siga	sigan	haya seguido	hayan seguido
7 imperfecto de subjuntivo		14 pluscuamperfecto de subjuntivo	
siguiera	siguiéramos	hubiera seguido	hubiéramos seguido
siguieras	siguierais	hubieras seguido	hubierais seguido
siguiera	siguieran	hubiera seguido	hubieran seguido
OR		OR	
siguiese	siguiésemos	hubiese seguido	hubiésemos seguido
siguieses	siguieseis	hubieses seguido	hubieseis seguido
siguiese	siguiesen	hubiese seguido	hubiesen seguido

imperativo	
—	sigamos
sigue; no sigas	seguid; no sigáis
siga	sigan

Words and expressions related to this verb
según according to
al día siguiente on the following day
las frases siguientes the following sentences
seguir + pres. part. to keep on + pres. part.;
  Siga leyendo Keep on reading.

proseguir to continue, proceed
perseguir to pursue
seguirle los pasos a uno to keep
  one's eye on someone

269

to sit down

The Seven Simple Tenses		The Seven Compound Tenses	
Singular	Plural	Singular	Plural
1 presente de indicativo		8 perfecto de indicativo	
me siento	nos sentamos	me he sentado	nos hemos sentado
te sientas	os sentáis	te has sentado	os habéis sentado
se sienta	se sientan	se ha sentado	se han sentado
2 imperfecto de indicativo		9 pluscuamperfecto de indicativo	
me sentaba	nos sentábamos	me había sentado	nos habíamos sentado
te sentabas	os sentabais	te habías sentado	os habíais sentado
se sentaba	se sentaban	se había sentado	se habían sentado
3 pretérito		10 pretérito anterior	
me senté	nos sentamos	me hube sentado	nos hubimos sentado
te sentaste	os sentasteis	te hubiste sentado	os hubisteis sentado
se sentó	se sentaron	se hubo sentado	se hubieron sentado
4 futuro		11 futuro perfecto	
me sentaré	nos sentaremos	me habré sentado	nos habremos sentado
te sentarás	os sentaréis	te habrás sentado	os habréis sentado
se sentará	se sentarán	se habrá sentado	se habrán sentado
5 potencial simple		12 potencial compuesto	
me sentaría	nos sentaríamos	me habría sentado	nos habríamos sentado
te sentarías	os sentaríais	te habrías sentado	os habríais sentado
se sentaría	se sentarían	se habría sentado	se habrían sentado
6 presente de subjuntivo		13 perfecto de subjuntivo	
me siente	nos sentemos	me haya sentado	nos hayamos sentado
te sientes	os sentéis	te hayas sentado	os hayáis sentado
se siente	se sienten	se haya sentado	se hayan sentado
7 imperfecto de subjuntivo		14 pluscuamperfecto de subjuntivo	
me sentara	nos sentáramos	me hubiera sentado	nos hubiéramos sentado
te sentaras	os sentarais	te hubieras sentado	os hubierais sentado
se sentara	se sentaran	se hubiera sentado	se hubieran sentado
OR		OR	
me sentase	nos sentásemos	me hubiese sentado	nos hubiésemos sentado
te sentases	os sentaseis	te hubieses sentado	os hubieseis sentado
se sentase	se sentasen	se hubiese sentado	se hubiesen sentado

imperativo	
—	sentémonos; no nos sentemos
siéntate; no te sientes	sentaos; no os sentéis
siéntese; no se siente	siéntense; no se sienten

Words and expressions related to this verb

un asiento a seat
sentado, sentada seated
¡Siéntese Ud.! Sit down!
¡Vamos a sentarnos! Let's sit down!

sentar, asentar to seat
una sentada a sitting; **de una sentada**
  in one sitting

to feel sorry, to regret, to feel

The Seven Simple Tenses		The Seven Compound Tenses	
Singular	Plural	Singular	Plural
1 presente de indicativo		**8 perfecto de indicativo**	
siento	**sentimos**	**he sentido**	**hemos sentido**
sientes	**sentís**	**has sentido**	**habéis sentido**
siente	**sienten**	**ha sentido**	**han sentido**
2 imperfecto de indicativo		**9 pluscuamperfecto de indicativo**	
sentía	**sentíamos**	**había sentido**	**habíamos sentido**
sentías	**sentíais**	**habías sentido**	**habíais sentido**
sentía	**sentían**	**había sentido**	**habían sentido**
3 pretérito		**10 pretérito anterior**	
sentí	**sentimos**	**hube sentido**	**hubimos sentido**
sentiste	**sentisteis**	**hubiste sentido**	**hubisteis sentido**
sintió	**sintieron**	**hubo sentido**	**hubieron sentido**
4 futuro		**11 futuro perfecto**	
sentiré	**sentiremos**	**habré sentido**	**habremos sentido**
sentirás	**sentiréis**	**habrás sentido**	**habréis sentido**
sentirá	**sentirán**	**habrá sentido**	**habrán sentido**
5 potencial simple		**12 potencial compuesto**	
sentiría	**sentiríamos**	**habría sentido**	**habríamos sentido**
sentirías	**sentiríais**	**habrías sentido**	**habríais sentido**
sentiría	**sentirían**	**habría sentido**	**habrían sentido**
6 presente de subjuntivo		**13 perfecto de subjuntivo**	
sienta	**sintamos**	**haya sentido**	**hayamos sentido**
sientas	**sintáis**	**hayas sentido**	**hayáis sentido**
sienta	**sientan**	**haya sentido**	**hayan sentido**
7 imperfecto de subjuntivo		**14 pluscuamperfecto de subjuntivo**	
sintiera	**sintiéramos**	**hubiera sentido**	**hubiéramos sentido**
sintieras	**sintierais**	**hubieras sentido**	**hubierais sentido**
sintiera	**sintieran**	**hubiera sentido**	**hubieran sentido**
OR		OR	
sintiese	**sintiésemos**	**hubiese sentido**	**hubiésemos sentido**
sintieses	**sintieseis**	**hubieses sentido**	**hubieseis sentido**
sintiese	**sintiesen**	**hubiese sentido**	**hubiesen sentido**

imperativo	
—	**sintamos**
siente; no sientas	**sentid; no sintáis**
sienta	**sientan**

Words and expressions related to this verb
Lo siento. I regret it; I'm sorry.
el sentimiento feeling, sentiment
sentimentalmente sentimentally
el sentir feeling; judgment
un, una sentimental sentimentalist
For additional words and expressions related to this verb, see **sentirse**.

271

sentirse   Gerundio **sintiéndose**   Part. pas. **sentido**

to feel (well, ill)

The Seven Simple Tenses		The Seven Compound Tenses	
Singular	Plural	Singular	Plural
1 presente de indicativo		8 perfecto de indicativo	
me siento	nos sentimos	me he sentido	nos hemos sentido
te sientes	os sentís	te has sentido	os habéis sentido
se siente	se sienten	se ha sentido	se han sentido
2 imperfecto de indicativo		9 pluscuamperfecto de indicativo	
me sentía	nos sentíamos	me había sentido	nos habíamos sentido
te sentías	os sentíais	te habías sentido	os habíais sentido
se sentía	se sentían	se había sentido	se habían sentido
3 pretérito		10 pretérito anterior	
me sentí	nos sentimos	me hube sentido	nos hubimos sentido
te sentiste	os sentisteis	te hubiste sentido	os hubisteis sentido
se sintió	se sintieron	se hubo sentido	se hubieron sentido
4 futuro		11 futuro perfecto	
me sentiré	nos sentiremos	me habré sentido	nos habremos sentido
te sentirás	os sentiréis	te habrás sentido	os habréis sentido
se sentirá	se sentirán	se habrá sentido	se habrán sentido
5 potencial simple		12 potencial compuesto	
me sentiría	nos sentiríamos	me habría sentido	nos habríamos sentido
te sentirías	os sentiríais	te habrías sentido	os habríais sentido
se sentiría	se sentirían	se habría sentido	se habrían sentido
6 presente de subjuntivo		13 perfecto de subjuntivo	
me sienta	nos sintamos	me haya sentido	nos hayamos sentido
te sientas	os sintáis	te hayas sentido	os hayáis sentido
se sienta	se sientan	se haya sentido	se hayan sentido
7 imperfecto de subjuntivo		14 pluscuamperfecto de subjuntivo	
me sintiera	nos sintiéramos	me hubiera sentido	nos hubiéramos sentido
te sintieras	os sintierais	te hubieras sentido	os hubierais sentido
se sintiera	se sintieran	se hubiera sentido	se hubieran sentido
OR		OR	
me sintiese	nos sintiésemos	me hubiese sentido	nos hubiésemos sentido
te sintieses	os sintieseis	te hubieses sentido	os hubieseis sentido
se sintiese	se sintiesen	se hubiese sentido	se hubiesen sentido

imperativo	
—	sintámonos; no nos sintamos
siéntete; no te sientas	sentíos; no os sintáis
siéntase; no se sienta	siéntanse; no se sientan

Words and expressions related to this verb

¿**Cómo se siente Ud.?** How do you feel?   **Me siento mal.** I feel sick.
el sentido sense; **los sentidos** the senses
For additional words and expressions related to this verb, see **sentir.**

The Seven Simple Tenses		The Seven Compound Tenses	
Singular	Plural	Singular	Plural
1 presente de indicativo		**8 perfecto de indicativo**	
soy	somos	he sido	hemos sido
eres	sois	has sido	habéis sido
es	son	ha sido	han sido
2 imperfecto de indicativo		**9 pluscuamperfecto de indicativo**	
era	éramos	había sido	habíamos sido
eras	erais	habías sido	habíais sido
era	eran	había sido	habían sido
3 pretérito		**10 pretérito anterior**	
fui	fuimos	hube sido	hubimos sido
fuiste	fuisteis	hubiste sido	hubisteis sido
fue	fueron	hubo sido	hubieron sido
4 futuro		**11 futuro perfecto**	
seré	seremos	habré sido	habremos sido
serás	seréis	habrás sido	habréis sido
será	serán	habrá sido	habrán sido
5 potencial simple		**12 potencial compuesto**	
sería	seríamos	habría sido	habríamos sido
serías	seríais	habrías sido	habríais sido
sería	serían	habría sido	habrían sido
6 presente de subjuntivo		**13 perfecto de subjuntivo**	
sea	seamos	haya sido	hayamos sido
seas	seáis	hayas sido	hayáis sido
sea	sean	haya sido	hayan sido
7 imperfecto de subjuntivo		**14 pluscuamperfecto de subjuntivo**	
fuera	fuéramos	hubiera sido	hubiéramos sido
fueras	fuerais	hubieras sido	hubierais sido
fuera	fueran	hubiera sido	hubieran sido
OR		OR	
fuese	fuésemos	hubiese sido	hubiésemos sido
fueses	fueseis	hubieses sido	hubieseis sido
fuese	fuesen	hubiese sido	hubiesen sido

	imperativo
—	seamos
sé; no seas	sed; no seáis
sea	sean

Common idiomatic expressions using this verb

Dime con quien andas y te diré quien eres.   Tell me who your friends are and I will tell you who you are.

es decir   that is, that is to say; **Si yo fuera usted . . .**   If I were you . . .

¿Qué hora es?   What time is it?   **Es la una.**   It is one o'clock.   **Son las dos.** It is two o'clock.

servir	Gerundio **sirviendo**	Part. pas. **servido**

to serve

The Seven Simple Tenses		The Seven Compound Tenses	
Singular	Plural	Singular	Plural
1 presente de indicativo		8 perfecto de indicativo	
sirvo	**servimos**	he servido	hemos servido
sirves	**servís**	has servido	habéis servido
sirve	**sirven**	ha servido	han servido
2 imperfecto de indicativo		9 pluscuamperfecto de indicativo	
servía	**servíamos**	había servido	habíamos servido
servías	**servíais**	habías servido	habíais servido
servía	**servían**	había servido	habían servido
3 pretérito		10 pretérito anterior	
serví	**servimos**	hube servido	hubimos servido
serviste	**servisteis**	hubiste servido	hubisteis servido
sirvió	**sirvieron**	hubo servido	hubieron servido
4 futuro		11 futuro perfecto	
serviré	**serviremos**	habré servido	habremos servido
servirás	**serviréis**	habrás servido	habréis servido
servirá	**servirán**	habrá servido	habrán servido
5 potencial simple		12 potencial compuesto	
serviría	**serviríamos**	habría servido	habríamos servido
servirías	**serviríais**	habrías servido	habríais servido
serviría	**servirían**	habría servido	habrían servido
6 presente de subjuntivo		13 perfecto de subjuntivo	
sirva	**sirvamos**	haya servido	hayamos servido
sirvas	**sirváis**	hayas servido	hayáis servido
sirva	**sirvan**	haya servido	hayan servido
7 imperfecto de subjuntivo		14 pluscuamperfecto de subjuntivo	
sirviera	**sirviéramos**	hubiera servido	hubiéramos servido
sirvieras	**sirvieras**	hubieras servido	hubierais servido
sirviera	**sirvieran**	hubiera servido	hubieran servido
OR		OR	
sirviese	**sirviésemos**	hubiese servido	hubiésemos servido
sirvieses	**sirvieseis**	hubieses servido	hubieseis servido
sirviese	**sirviesen**	hubiese servido	hubiesen servido

imperativo	
—	sirvamos
sirve; no sirvas	servid; no sirváis
sirva	sirvan

Words and expressions related to this verb
servidor, servidora servant, waiter, waitress
el servicio service
una servilleta table napkin
servirse to serve oneself

¡Sírvase usted! Help yourself!
Esto no sirve para nada This serves no purpose.
servir para to be good for

to be accustomed to, to be in the habit of, to have the custom of

The Seven Simple Tenses		The Seven Compound Tenses	
Singular	Plural	Singular	Plural
1 presente de indicativo		8 perfecto de indicativo	
suelo	**solemos**	**he solido**	**hemos solido**
sueles	**soléis**	**has solido**	**habéis solido**
suele	**suelen**	**ha solido**	**han solido**
2 imperfecto de indicativo			
solía	**solíamos**		
solías	**solíais**		
solía	**solían**		
6 presente de subjuntivo			
suela	**solamos**		
suelas	**soláis**		
suela	**suelan**		

This verb is defective and it is, therefore, used primarily in the tenses given above. When used, it is always followed by an infinitive.
Example:
Suelo acostarme a las diez.   I am in the habit of going to bed at ten.

soñar	Gerundio **soñando**	Part. pas. **soñado**

to dream

The Seven Simple Tenses	The Seven Compound Tenses

Singular	Plural	Singular	Plural
1 presente de indicativo		8 perfecto de indicativo	
sueño	soñamos	he soñado	hemos soñado
sueñas	soñáis	has soñado	habéis soñado
sueña	sueñan	ha soñado	han soñado
2 imperfecto de indicativo		9 pluscuamperfecto de indicativo	
soñaba	soñábamos	había soñado	habíamos soñado
soñabas	soñabais	habías soñado	habíais soñado
soñaba	soñaban	había soñado	habían soñado
3 pretérito		10 pretérito anterior	
soñé	soñamos	hube soñado	hubimos soñado
soñaste	soñasteis	hubiste soñado	hubisteis soñado
soñó	soñaron	hubo soñado	hubieron soñado
4 futuro		11 futuro perfecto	
soñaré	soñaremos	habré soñado	habremos soñado
soñarás	soñaréis	habrás soñado	habréis soñado
soñará	soñarán	habrá soñado	habrán soñado
5 potencial simple		12 potencial compuesto	
soñaría	soñaríamos	habría soñado	habríamos soñado
soñarías	soñaríais	habrías soñado	habríais soñado
soñaría	soñarían	habría soñado	habrían soñado
6 presente de subjuntivo		13 perfecto de subjuntivo	
sueñe	soñemos	haya soñado	hayamos soñado
sueñes	soñéis	hayas soñado	hayáis soñado
sueñe	sueñen	haya soñado	hayan soñado
7 imperfecto de subjuntivo		14 pluscuamperfecto de subjuntivo	
soñara	soñáramos	hubiera soñado	hubiéramos soñado
soñaras	soñarais	hubieras soñado	hubierais soñado
soñara	soñaran	hubiera soñado	hubieran soñado
OR		OR	
soñase	soñásemos	hubiese soñado	hubiésemos soñado
soñases	soñaseis	hubieses soñado	hubieseis soñado
soñase	soñasen	hubiese soñado	hubiesen soñado

	imperativo	
—	soñemos
sueña; no sueñes	soñad; no soñéis
sueñe	sueñen

Words and expressions related to this verb

soñar con, soñar en   to dream of
soñar despierto   to daydream
soñador, soñadora   dreamer
el sueño   sleep, dream
tener sueño   to be sleepy

un sueño hecho realidad   a dream come true
sueño pesado   sound sleep
echar un sueño   to take a nap

to smile

The Seven Simple Tenses		The Seven Compound Tenses	
Singular	Plural	Singular	Plural
1 presente de indicativo		8 perfecto de indicativo	
sonrío	sonreímos	he sonreído	hemos sonreído
sonríes	sonreís	has sonreído	habéis sonreído
sonríe	sonríen	ha sonreído	han sonreído
2 imperfecto de indicativo		9 pluscuamperfecto de indicativo	
sonreía	sonreíamos	había sonreído	habíamos sonreído
sonreías	sonreíais	habías sonreído	habíais sonreído
sonreía	sonreían	había sonreído	habían sonreído
3 pretérito		10 pretérito anterior	
sonreí	sonreímos	hube sonreído	hubimos sonreído
sonreíste	sonreísteis	hubiste sonreído	hubisteis sonreído
sonrió	sonrieron	hubo sonreído	hubieron sonreído
4 futuro		11 futuro perfecto	
sonreiré	sonreiremos	habré sonreído	habremos sonreído
sonreirás	sonreiréis	habrás sonreído	habréis sonreído
sonreirá	sonreirán	habrá sonreído	habrán sonreído
5 potencial simple		12 potencial compuesto	
sonreiría	sonreiríamos	habría sonreído	habríamos sonreído
sonreirías	sonreiríais	habrías sonreído	habríais sonreído
sonreiría	sonreirían	habría sonreído	habrían sonreído
6 presente de subjuntivo		13 perfecto de subjuntivo	
sonría	sonriamos	haya sonreído	hayamos sonreído
sonrías	sonriáis	hayas sonreído	hayáis sonreído
sonría	sonrían	haya sonreído	hayan sonreído
7 imperfecto de subjuntivo		14 pluscuamperfecto de subjuntivo	
sonriera	sonriéramos	hubiera sonreído	hubiéramos sonreído
sonrieras	sonrierais	hubieras sonreído	hubierais sonreído
sonriera	sonrieran	hubiera sonreído	hubieran sonreído
OR		OR	
sonriese	sonriésemos	hubiese sonreído	hubiésemos sonreído
sonrieses	sonrieseis	hubieses sonreído	hubieseis sonreído
sonriese	sonriesen	hubiese sonreído	hubiesen sonreído

imperativo	
—	sonriamos
sonríe; no sonrías	sonreíd; no sonriáis
sonría	sonrían

Words related to this verb
la sonrisa, el sonriso smile   **un, una sonriente** smiling person
For additional words and expressions related to this verb, see **reír.**

telefonear	Gerundio **telefoneando**	Part. pas. **telefoneado**

to telephone

The Seven Simple Tenses		The Seven Compound Tenses	
Singular	Plural	Singular	Plural

1 presente de indicativo		8 perfecto de indicativo	
telefoneo	**telefoneamos**	**he telefoneado**	**hemos telefoneado**
telefoneas	**telefoneáis**	**has telefoneado**	**habéis telefoneado**
telefonea	**telefonean**	**ha telefoneado**	**han telefoneado**

2 imperfecto de indicativo		9 pluscuamperfecto de indicativo	
telefoneaba	**telefoneábamos**	**había telefoneado**	**habíamos telefoneado**
telefoneabas	**telefoneabais**	**habías telefoneado**	**habíais telefoneado**
telefoneaba	**telefoneaban**	**había telefoneado**	**habían telefoneado**

3 pretérito		10 pretérito anterior	
telefoneé	**telefoneamos**	**hube telefoneado**	**hubimos telefoneado**
telefoneaste	**telefoneasteis**	**hubiste telefoneado**	**hubisteis telefoneado**
telefoneó	**telefonearon**	**hubo telefoneado**	**hubieron telefoneado**

4 futuro		11 futuro perfecto	
telefonearé	**telefonearemos**	**habré telefoneado**	**habremos telefoneado**
telefonearás	**telefonearéis**	**habrás telefoneado**	**habréis telefoneado**
telefoneará	**telefonearán**	**habrá telefoneado**	**habrán telefoneado**

5 potencial simple		12 potencial compuesto	
telefonearía	**telefonearíamos**	**habría telefoneado**	**habríamos telefoneado**
telefonearías	**telefonearíais**	**habrías telefoneado**	**habríais telefoneado**
telefonearía	**telefonearían**	**habría telefoneado**	**habrían telefoneado**

6 presente de subjuntivo		13 perfecto de subjuntivo	
telefonee	**telefoneemos**	**haya telefoneado**	**hayamos telefoneado**
telefonees	**telefoneéis**	**hayas telefoneado**	**hayáis telefoneado**
telefonee	**telefoneen**	**haya telefoneado**	**hayan telefoneado**

7 imperfecto de subjuntivo		14 pluscuamperfecto de subjuntivo	
telefoneara	**telefoneáramos**	**hubiera telefoneado**	**hubiéramos telefoneado**
telefonearas	**telefonearais**	**hubieras telefoneado**	**hubierais telefoneado**
telefoneara	**telefonearan**	**hubiera telefoneado**	**hubieran telefoneado**
OR		OR	
telefonease	**telefoneásemos**	**hubiese telefoneado**	**hubiésemos telefoneado**
telefoneases	**telefoneaseis**	**hubieses telefoneado**	**hubieseis telefoneado**
telefonease	**telefoneasen**	**hubiese telefoneado**	**hubiesen telefoneado**

	imperativo	
—	**telefoneemos**	
telefonea; no telefonees	**telefonead; no telefoneéis**	
telefonee	**telefoneen**	

Words and expressions related to this verb

el teléfono   telephone
telefonista   telephone operator
telefónico, telefónica   telephonic
la guía telefónica   telephone book

la cabina telefónica   telephone booth
el número de teléfono   telephone number
por teléfono   by telephone

Gerundio **telegrafiando**   Part. pas. **telegrafiado**   **telegrafiar**

to telegraph, to cable

The Seven Simple Tenses		The Seven Compound Tenses	
Singular	Plural	Singular	Plural
1 presente de indicativo		8 perfecto de indicativo	
telegrafío	telegrafiamos	he telegrafiado	hemos telegrafiado
telegrafías	telegrafiáis	has telegrafiado	habéis telegrafiado
telegrafía	telegrafían	ha telegrafiado	han telegrafiado
2 imperfecto de indicativo		9 pluscuamperfecto de indicativo	
telegrafiaba	telegrafiábamos	había telegrafiado	habíamos telegrafiado
telegrafiabas	telegrafiabais	habías telegrafiado	habíais telegrafiado
telegrafiaba	telegrafiaban	había telegrafiado	habían telegrafiado
3 pretérito		10 pretérito anterior	
telegrafié	telegrafiamos	hube telegrafiado	hubimos telegrafiado
telegrafiaste	telegrafiasteis	hubiste telegrafiado	hubisteis telegrafiado
telegrafió	telegrafiaron	hubo telegrafiado	hubieron telegrafiado
4 futuro		11 futuro perfecto	
telegrafiaré	telegrafiaremos	habré telegrafiado	habremos telegrafiado
telegrafiarás	telegrafiaréis	habrás telegrafiado	habréis telegrafiado
telegrafiará	telegrafiarán	habrá telegrafiado	habrán telegrafiado
5 potencial simple		12 potencial compuesto	
telegrafiaría	telegrafiaríamos	habría telegrafiado	habríamos telegrafiado
telegrafiarías	telegrafiaríais	habrías telegrafiado	habríais telegrafiado
telegrafiaría	telegrafiarían	habría telegrafiado	habrían telegrafiado
6 presente de subjuntivo		13 perfecto de subjuntivo	
telegrafíe	telegrafiemos	haya telegrafiado	hayamos telegrafiado
telegrafíes	telegrafiéis	hayas telegrafiado	hayáis telegrafiado
telegrafíe	telegrafíen	haya telegrafiado	hayan telegrafiado
7 imperfecto de subjuntivo		14 pluscuamperfecto de subjuntivo	
telegrafiara	telegrafiáramos	hubiera telegrafiado	hubiéramos telegrafiado
telegrafiaras	telegrafiarais	hubieras telegrafiado	hubierais telegrafiado
telegrafiara	telegrafiaran	hubiera telegrafiado'	hubieran telegrafiado
OR		OR	
telegrafiase	telegrafiásemos	hubiese telegrafiado	hubiésemos telegrafiado
telegrafiases	telegrafiaseis	hubieses telegrafiado	hubieseis telegrafiado
telegrafiase	telegrafiasen	hubiese telegrafiado	hubiesen telegrafiado

imperativo	
—	telegrafiemos
telegrafía; no telegrafíes	telegrafiad; no telegrafiéis
telegrafíe	telegrafíen

Words and expressions related to this verb
el telégrafo   telegraph
el telegrama   telegram, cablegram
telegrafista   telegraph operator
la telegrafía   telegraphy
el telégrafo sin hilos   wireless telegraph

tener	Gerundio **teniendo**	Part. pas. **tenido**

to have, to hold

The Seven Simple Tenses		The Seven Compound Tenses	
Singular	Plural	Singular	Plural
1 presente de indicativo		8 perfecto de indicativo	
tengo	tenemos	he tenido	hemos tenido
tienes	tenéis	has tenido	habéis tenido
tiene	tienen	ha tenido	han tenido
2 imperfecto de indicativo		9 pluscuamperfecto de indicativo	
tenía	teníamos	había tenido	habíamos tenido
tenías	teníais	habías tenido	habíais tenido
tenía	tenían	había tenido	habían tenido
3 pretérito		10 pretérito anterior	
tuve	tuvimos	hube tenido	hubimos tenido
tuviste	tuvisteis	hubiste tenido	hubisteis tenido
tuvo	tuvieron	hubo tenido	hubieron tenido
4 futuro		11 futuro perfecto	
tendré	tendremos	habré tenido	habremos tenido
tendrás	tendréis	habrás tenido	habréis tenido
tendrá	tendrán	habrá tenido	habrán tenido
5 potencial simple		12 potencial compuesto	
tendría	tendríamos	habría tenido	habríamos tenido
tendrías	tendríais	habrías tenido	habríais tenido
tendría	tendrían	habría tenido	habrían tenido
6 presente de subjuntivo		13 perfecto de subjuntivo	
tenga	tengamos	haya tenido	hayamos tenido
tengas	tengáis	hayas tenido	hayáis tenido
tenga	tengan	haya tenido	hayan tenido
7 imperfecto de subjuntivo		14 pluscuamperfecto de subjuntivo	
tuviera	tuviéramos	hubiera tenido	hubiéramos tenido
tuvieras	tuvierais	hubieras tenido	hubierais tenido
tuviera	tuvieran	hubiera tenido	hubieran tenido
OR		OR	
tuviese	tuviésemos	hubiese tenido	hubiésemos tenido
tuvieses	tuvieseis	hubieses tenido	hubieseis tenido
tuviese	tuviesen	hubiese tenido	hubiesen tenido

imperativo	
—	tengamos
ten; no tengas	tened; no tengáis
tenga	tengan

Common idiomatic expressions using this verb
Anda despacio que tengo prisa.   Make haste slowly.

tener prisa	to be in a hurry	**tener frío**	to be (feel) cold (persons)
tener hambre	to be hungry	**tener calor**	to be (feel) warm (persons)
tener sed	to be thirsty	**retener**	to retain

Gerundio **terminando**   Part. pas. **terminado**   **terminar**

to end, to terminate, to finish

The Seven Simple Tenses		The Seven Compound Tenses	
Singular	Plural	Singular	Plural
1 presente de indicativo		**8 perfecto de indicativo**	
termino	**terminamos**	**he terminado**	**hemos terminado**
terminas	**termináis**	**has terminado**	**habéis terminado**
termina	**terminan**	**ha terminado**	**han terminado**
2 imperfecto de indicativo		**9 pluscuamperfecto de indicativo**	
terminaba	**terminábamos**	**había terminado**	**habíamos terminado**
terminabas	**terminabais**	**habías terminado**	**habíais terminado**
terminaba	**terminaban**	**había terminado**	**habían terminado**
3 pretérito		**10 pretérito anterior**	
terminé	**terminamos**	**hube terminado**	**hubimos terminado**
terminaste	**terminasteis**	**hubiste terminado**	**hubisteis terminado**
terminó	**terminaron**	**hubo terminado**	**hubieron terminado**
4 futuro		**11 futuro perfecto**	
terminaré	**terminaremos**	**habré terminado**	**habremos terminado**
terminarás	**terminaréis**	**habrás terminado**	**habréis terminado**
terminará	**terminarán**	**habrá terminado**	**habrán terminado**
5 potencial simple		**12 potencial compuesto**	
terminaría	**terminaríamos**	**habría terminado**	**habríamos terminado**
terminarías	**terminaríais**	**habrías terminado**	**habríais terminado**
terminaría	**terminarían**	**habría terminado**	**habrían terminado**
6 presente de subjuntivo		**13 perfecto de subjuntivo**	
termine	**terminemos**	**haya terminado**	**hayamos terminado**
termines	**terminéis**	**hayas terminado**	**hayáis terminado**
termine	**terminen**	**haya terminado**	**hayan terminado**
7 imperfecto de subjuntivo		**14 pluscuamperfecto de subjuntivo**	
terminara	**termináramos**	**hubiera terminado**	**hubiéramos terminado**
terminaras	**terminarais**	**hubieras terminado**	**hubierais terminado**
terminara	**terminaran**	**hubiera terminado**	**hubieran terminado**
OR		OR	
terminase	**terminásemos**	**hubiese terminado**	**hubiésemos terminado**
terminases	**terminaseis**	**hubieses terminado**	**hubieseis terminado**
terminase	**terminasen**	**hubiese terminado**	**hubiesen terminado**

imperativo	
—	**terminemos**
termina; no termines	**terminad; no terminéis**
termine	**terminen**

Words and expressions related to this verb
la terminación   termination, ending, completion   **terminante**   conclusive
el término   end, ending; term   **determinar**   to determine
en otros términos   in other terms, in other words
estar en buenos términos con   to be on good terms with

| tirar | Gerundio **tirando** | Part. pas. **tirado** |

to pull, to draw, to pitch (a ball), to shoot (a gun), to throw, to fling

The Seven Simple Tenses		The Seven Compound Tenses	
Singular	Plural	Singular	Plural
1 presente de indicativo		8 perfecto de indicativo	
tiro	tiramos	he tirado	hemos tirado
tiras	tiráis	has tirado	habéis tirado
tira	tiran	ha tirado	han tirado
2 imperfecto de indicativo		9 pluscuamperfecto de indicativo	
tiraba	tirábamos	había tirado	habíamos tirado
tirabas	tirabais	habías tirado	habíais tirado
tiraba	tiraban	había tirado	habían tirado
3 pretérito		10 pretérito anterior	
tiré	tiramos	hube tirado	hubimos tirado
tiraste	tirasteis	hubiste tirado	hubisteis tirado
tiró	tiraron	hubo tirado	hubieron tirado
4 futuro		11 futuro perfecto	
tiraré	tiraremos	habré tirado	habremos tirado
tirarás	tiraréis	habrás tirado	habréis tirado
tirará	tirarán	habrá tirado	habrán tirado
5 potencial simple		12 potencial compuesto	
tiraría	tiraríamos	habría tirado	habríamos tirado
tirarías	tiraríais	habrías tirado	habríais tirado
tiraría	tirarían	habría tirado	habrían tirado
6 presente de subjuntivo		13 perfecto de subjuntivo	
tire	tiremos	haya tirado	hayamos tirado
tires	tiréis	hayas tirado	hayáis tirado
tire	tiren	haya tirado	hayan tirado
7 imperfecto de subjuntivo		14 pluscuamperfecto de subjuntivo	
tirara	tiráramos	hubiera tirado	hubiéramos tirado
tiraras	tirarais	hubieras tirado	hubierais tirado
tirara	tiraran	hubiera tirado	hubieran tirado
OR		OR	
tirase	tirásemos	hubiese tirado	hubiésemos tirado
tirases	tiraseis	hubieses tirado	hubieseis tirado
tirase	tirasen	hubiese tirado	hubiesen tirado

imperativo	
—	tiremos
tira; no tires	tirad; no tiréis
tire	tiren

Words and expressions related to this verb

tirar a to shoot at
tirar una línea to draw a line
a tiro within reach; **a tiro de piedra** within a stone's throw; **ni a tiros** not for love nor money; **al tiro** right away

Gerundio **tocando**	Part. pas. **tocado**	**tocar**

to play (music or a musical instrument), to touch

The Seven Simple Tenses		The Seven Compound Tenses	
Singular	Plural	Singular	Plural
1 presente de indicativo		8 perfecto de indicativo	
toco	tocamos	he tocado	hemos tocado
tocas	tocáis	has tocado	habéis tocado
toca	tocan	ha tocado	han tocado
2 imperfecto de indicativo		9 pluscuamperfecto de indicativo	
tocaba	tocábamos	había tocado	habíamos tocado
tocabas	tocabais	habías tocado	habíais tocado
tocaba	tocaban	había tocado	habían tocado
3 pretérito		10 pretérito anterior	
toqué	tocamos	hube tocado	hubimos tocado
tocaste	tocasteis	hubiste tocado	hubisteis tocado
tocó	tocaron	hubo tocado	hubieron tocado
4 futuro		11 futuro perfecto	
tocaré	tocaremos	habré tocado	habremos tocado
tocarás	tocaréis	habrás tocado	habréis tocado
tocará	tocarán	habrá tocado	habrán tocado
5 potencial simple		12 potencial compuesto	
tocaría	tocaríamos	habría tocado	habríamos tocado
tocarías	tocaríais	habrías tocado	habríais tocado
tocaría	tocarían	habría tocado	habrían tocado
6 presente de subjuntivo		13 perfecto de subjuntivo	
toque	toquemos	haya tocado	hayamos tocado
toques	toquéis	hayas tocado	hayáis tocado
toque	toquen	haya tocado	hayan tocado
7 imperfecto de subjuntivo		14 pluscuamperfecto de subjuntivo	
tocara	tocáramos	hubiera tocado	hubiéramos tocado
tocaras	tocarais	hubieras tocado	hubierais tocado
tocara	tocaran	hubiera tocado	hubieran tocado
OR		OR	
tocase	tocásemos	hubiese tocado	hubiésemos tocado
tocases	tocaseis	hubieses tocado	hubieseis tocado
tocase	tocasen	hubiese tocado	hubiesen tocado

	imperativo	
—	toquemos	
toca; no toques	tocad; no toquéis	
toque	toquen	

Common idiomatic expressions using this verb

¿Sabe Ud. tocar el piano?   Do you know how to play the piano?
Sí, yo sé tocar el piano   Yes, I know how to play the piano.
tocar a la puerta   to knock on the door
el tocadiscos   record player
tocar a uno   to be someone's turn; **Le toca a Juan.**   It's John's turn.

tomar   Gerundio **tomando**   Part. pas. **tomado**

to take, to have (something to eat or drink)

The Seven Simple Tenses		The Seven Compound Tenses	
Singular	Plural	Singular	Plural
1 presente de indicativo		8 perfecto de indicativo	
tomo	tomamos	he tomado	hemos tomado
tomas	tomáis	has tomado	habéis tomado
toma	toman	ha tomado	han tomado
2 imperfecto de indicativo		9 pluscuamperfecto de indicativo	
tomaba	tomábamos	había tomado	habíamos tomado
tomabas	tomabais	habías tomado	habíais tomado
tomaba	tomaban	había tomado	habían tomado
3 pretérito		10 pretérito anterior	
tomé	tomamos	hube tomado	hubimos tomado
tomaste	tomasteis	hubiste tomado	hubisteis tomado
tomó	tomaron	hubo tomado	hubieron tomado
4 futuro		11 futuro perfecto	
tomaré	tomaremos	habré tomado	habremos tomado
tomarás	tomaréis	habrás tomado	habréis tomado
tomará	tomarán	habrá tomado	habrán tomado
5 potencial simple		12 potencial compuesto	
tomaría	tomaríamos	habría tomado	habríamos tomado
tomarías	tomaríais	habrías tomado	habríais tomado
tomaría	tomarían	habría tomado	habrían tomado
6 presente de subjuntivo		13 perfecto de subjuntivo	
tome	tomemos	haya tomado	hayamos tomado
tomes	toméis	hayas tomado	hayáis tomado
tome	tomen	haya tomado	hayan tomado
7 imperfecto de subjuntivo		14 pluscuamperfecto de subjuntivo	
tomara	tomáramos	hubiera tomado	hubiéramos tomado
tomaras	tomarais	hubieras tomado	hubierais tomado
tomara	tomaran	hubiera tomado	hubieran tomado
OR		OR	
tomase	tomásemos	hubiese tomado	hubiésemos tomado
tomases	tomaseis	hubieses tomado	hubieseis tomado
tomase	tomasen	hubiese tomado	hubiesen tomado

imperativo	
—	tomemos
toma; no tomes	tomad; no toméis
tome	tomen

Sentences and expressions using this verb and words related to it

¿**A qué hora toma Ud. el desayuno?**   At what time do you have breakfast?
Tomo el desayuno a las siete y media.   I have breakfast at seven thirty.
¿**Qué toma Ud. en el desayuno?**   What do you have for breakfast?
tomar el sol   to take a sun bath   **tomar en cuenta**   to consider
                                                    tomar parte en   to take part in

Gerundio **trabajando**   Part. pas. **trabajado**   **trabajar**

The Seven Simple Tenses		The Seven Compound Tenses	
Singular	Plural	Singular	Plural

1   presente de indicativo

		8 perfecto de indicativo	
trabajo	trabajamos	he trabajado	hemos trabajado
trabajas	trabajáis	has trabajado	habéis trabajado
trabaja	trabajan	ha trabajado	han trabajado

2   imperfecto de indicativo

		9 pluscuamperfecto de indicativo	
trabajaba	trabajábamos	había trabajado	habíamos trabajado
trabajabas	trabajabais	habías trabajado	habíais trabajado
trabajaba	trabajaban	había trabajado	habían trabajado

3   pretérito

		10 pretérito anterior	
trabajé	trabajamos	hube trabajado	hubimos trabajado
trabajaste	trabajasteis	hubiste trabajado	hubisteis trabajado
trabajó	trabajaron	hubo trabajado	hubieron trabajado

4   futuro

		11 futuro perfecto	
trabajaré	trabajaremos	habré trabajado	habremos trabajado
trabajarás	trabajaréis	habrás trabajado	habréis trabajado
trabajará	trabajarán	habrá trabajado	habrán trabajado

5   potencial simple

		12 potencial compuesto	
trabajaría	trabajaríamos	habría trabajado	habríamos trabajado
trabajarías	trabajaríais	habrías trabajado	habríais trabajado
trabajaría	trabajarían	habría trabajado	habrían trabajado

6   presente de subjuntivo

		13 perfecto de subjuntivo	
trabaje	trabajemos	haya trabajado	hayamos trabajado
trabajes	trabajéis	hayas trabajado	hayáis trabajado
trabaje	trabajen	haya trabajado	hayan trabajado

7   imperfecto de subjuntivo

		14 pluscuamperfecto de subjuntivo	
trabajara	trabajáramos	hubiera trabajado	hubiéramos trabajado
trabajaras	trabajarais	hubieras trabajado	hubierais trabajado
trabajara	trabajaran	hubiera trabajado	hubieran trabajado
OR		OR	
trabajase	trabajásemos	hubiese trabajado	hubiésemos trabajado
trabajases	trabajaseis	hubieses trabajado	hubieseis trabajado
trabajase	trabajasen	hubiese trabajado	hubiesen trabajado

imperativo	
—	trabajemos
trabaja; no trabajes	trabajad; no trabajéis
trabaje	trabajen

Words and expressions related to this verb
el trabajo   work
trabajador, trabajadora   worker
trabajar de manos   to do manual work
trabajar en + inf.   to strive + inf.
tener trabajo que hacer   to have work to do

| **traducir** | Gerundio **traduciendo** | Part. pas. **traducido** |

to translate

The Seven Simple Tenses		The Seven Compound Tenses	
Singular	Plural	Singular	Plural
1 presente de indicativo		8 perfecto de indicativo	
traduzco	traducimos	he traducido	hemos traducido
traduces	traducís	has traducido	habéis traducido
traduce	traducen	ha traducido	han traducido
2 imperfecto de indicativo		9 pluscuamperfecto de indicativo	
traducía	traducíamos	había traducido	habíamos traducido
traducías	traducíais	habías traducido	habíais traducido
traducía	traducían	había traducido	habían traducido
3 pretérito		10 pretérito anterior	
traduje	tradujimos	hube traducido	hubimos traducido
tradujiste	tradujisteis	hubiste traducido	hubisteis traducido
tradujo	tradujeron	hubo traducido	hubieron traducido
4 futuro		11 futuro perfecto	
traduciré	traduciremos	habré traducido	habremos traducido
traducirás	traduciréis	habrás traducido	habréis traducido
traducirá	traducirán	habrá traducido	habrán traducido
5 potencial simple		12 potencial compuesto	
traduciría	traduciríamos	habría traducido	habríamos traducido
traducirías	traduciríais	habrías traducido	habríais traducido
traduciría	traducirían	habría traducido	habrían traducido
6 presente de subjuntivo		13 perfecto de subjuntivo	
traduzca	traduzcamos	haya traducido	hayamos traducido
traduzcas	traduzcáis	hayas traducido	hayáis traducido
traduzca	traduzcan	haya traducido	hayan traducido
7 imperfecto de subjuntivo		14 pluscuamperfecto de subjuntivo	
tradujera	tradujéramos	hubiera traducido	hubiéramos traducido
tradujeras	tradujerais	hubieras traducido	hubierais traducido
tradujera	tradujeran	hubiera traducido	hubieran traducido
OR		OR	
tradujese	tradujésemos	hubiese traducido	hubiésemos traducido
tradujeses	tradujeseis	hubieses traducido	hubieseis traducido
tradujese	tradujesen	hubiese traducido	hubiesen traducido

	imperativo	
—	traduzcamos	
traduce; no traduzcas	traducid; no traduzcáis	
traduzca	traduzcan	

Words related to this verb
la traducción translation
traducible translatable
traductor, traductora translator

Gerundio **trayendo**   Part. pas. **traído**   **traer**

The Seven Simple Tenses		The Seven Compound Tenses	
Singular	Plural	Singular	Plural
1 presente de indicativo		8 perfecto de indicativo	
traigo	traemos	he traído	hemos traído
traes	traéis	has traído	habéis traído
trae	traen	ha traído	han traído
2 imperfecto de indicativo		9 pluscuamperfecto de indicativo	
traía	traíamos	había traído	habíamos traído
traías	traíais	habías traído	habíais traído
traía	traían	había traído	habían traído
3 pretérito		10 pretérito anterior	
traje	trajimos	hube traído	hubimos traído
trajiste	trajisteis	hubiste traído	hubisteis traído
trajo	trajeron	hubo traído	hubieron traído
4 futuro		11 futuro perfecto	
traeré	traeremos	habré traído	habremos traído
traerás	traeréis	habrás traído	habréis traído
traerá	traerán	habrá traído	habrán traído
5 potencial simple		12 potencial compuesto	
traería	traeríamos	habría traído	habríamos traído
traerías	traeríais	habrías traído	habríais traído
traería	traerían	habría traído	habrían traído
6 presente de subjuntivo		13 perfecto de subjuntivo	
traiga	traigamos	haya traído	hayamos traído
traigas	traigáis	hayas traído	hayáis traído
traiga	traigan	haya traído	hayan traído
7 imperfecto de subjuntivo		14 pluscuamperfecto de subjuntivo	
trajera	trajéramos	hubiera traído	hubiéramos traído
trajeras	trajerais	hubieras traído	hubierais traído
trajera	trajeran	hubiera traído	hubieran traído
OR		OR	
trajese	trajésemos	hubiese traído	hubiésemos traído
trajeses	trajeseis	hubieses traído	hubieseis traído
trajese	trajesen	hubiese traído	hubiesen traído

	imperativo	
—	traigamos
trae; no traigas	traed; no traigáis
traiga	traigan

Words and expressions related to this verb
el traje   costume, dress, suit
el traje de baño   bathing suit
el traje hecho   ready-made suit

traer entre ojos   to hate
contraer   to contract

tropezar	Gerundio **tropezando**	Part. pas. **tropezado**

to stumble, to blunder

The Seven Simple Tenses		The Seven Compound Tenses	

Singular	Plural	Singular	Plural
1 presente de indicativo		8 perfecto de indicativo	
tropiezo	**tropezamos**	**he tropezado**	**hemos tropezado**
tropiezas	**tropezáis**	**has tropezado**	**habéis tropezado**
tropieza	**tropiezan**	**ha tropezado**	**han tropezado**
2 imperfecto de indicativo		9 pluscuamperfecto de indicativo	
tropezaba	**tropezábamos**	**había tropezado**	**habíamos tropezado**
tropezabas	**tropezabais**	**habías tropezado**	**habíais tropezado**
tropezaba	**tropezaban**	**había tropezado**	**habían tropezado**
3 pretérito		10 pretérito anterior	
tropecé	**tropezamos**	**hube tropezado**	**hubimos tropezado**
tropezaste	**tropezasteis**	**hubiste tropezado**	**hubisteis tropezado**
tropezó	**tropezaron**	**hubo tropezado**	**hubieron tropezado**
4 futuro		11 futuro perfecto	
tropezaré	**tropezaremos**	**habré tropezado**	**habremos tropezado**
tropezarás	**tropezaréis**	**habrás tropezado**	**habréis tropezado**
tropezará	**tropezarán**	**habrá tropezado**	**habrán tropezado**
5 potencial simple		12 potencial compuesto	
tropezaría	**tropezaríamos**	**habría tropezado**	**habríamos tropezado**
tropezarías	**tropezaríais**	**habrías tropezado**	**habríais tropezado**
tropezaría	**tropezarían**	**habría tropezado**	**habrían tropezado**
6 presente de subjuntivo		13 perfecto de subjuntivo	
tropiece	**tropecemos**	**haya tropezado**	**hayamos tropezado**
tropieces	**tropecéis**	**hayas tropezado**	**hayáis tropezado**
tropiece	**tropiecen**	**haya tropezado**	**hayan tropezado**
7 imperfecto de subjuntivo		14 pluscuamperfecto de subjuntivo	
tropezara	**tropezáramos**	**hubiera tropezado**	**hubiéramos tropezado**
tropezaras	**tropezarais**	**hubieras tropezado**	**hubierais tropezado**
tropezara	**tropezaran**	**hubiera tropezado**	**hubieran tropezado**
OR		OR	
tropezase	**tropezásemos**	**hubiese tropezado**	**hubiésemos tropezado**
tropezases	**tropezaseis**	**hubieses tropezado**	**hubieseis tropezado**
tropezase	**tropezasen**	**hubiese tropezado**	**hubiesen tropezado**

	imperativo	
—	**tropecemos**	
tropieza; no tropieces	**tropezad; no tropecéis**	
tropiece	**tropiecen**	

Words and expressions related to this verb
tropezar con alguien to run across someone, to meet someone unexpectedly
la tropezadura stumbling
tropezador, tropezadora tripper, stumbler
dar un tropezón to trip, to stumble

Gerundio **uniendo**	Part. pas. **unido**	**unir**

to connect, to unite, to join, to bind, to attach

The Seven Simple Tenses		The Seven Compound Tenses	
Singular	Plural	Singular	Plural
1 presente de indicativo		**8 perfecto de indicativo**	
uno	unimos	he unido	hemos unido
unes	unís	has unido	habéis unido
une	unen	ha unido	han unido
2 imperfecto de indicativo		**9 pluscuamperfecto de indicativo**	
unía	uníamos	había unido	habíamos unido
unías	uníais	habías unido	habíais unido
unía	unían	había unido	habían unido
3 pretérito		**10 pretérito anterior**	
uní	unimos	hube unido	hubimos unido
uniste	unisteis	hubiste unido	hubisteis unido
unió	unieron	hubo unido	hubieron unido
4 futuro		**11 futuro perfecto**	
uniré	uniremos	habré unido	habremos unido
unirás	uniréis	habrás unido	habréis unido
unirá	unirán	habrá unido	habrán unido
5 potencial simple		**12 potencial compuesto**	
uniría	uniríamos	habría unido	habríamos unido
unirías	uniríais	habrías unido	habríais unido
uniría	unirían	habría unido	habrían unido
6 presente de subjuntivo		**13 perfecto de subjuntivo**	
una	unamos	haya unido	hayamos unido
unas	unáis	hayas unido	hayáis unido
una	unan	haya unido	hayan unido
7 imperfecto de subjuntivo		**14 pluscuamperfecto de subjuntivo**	
uniera	uniéramos	hubiera unido	hubiéramos unido
unieras	unierais	hubieras unido	hubierais unido
uniera	unieran	hubiera unido	hubieran unido
OR		OR	
uniese	uniésemos	hubiese unido	hubiésemos unido
unieses	unieseis	hubieses unido	hubieseis unido
uniese	uniesen	hubiese unido	hubiesen unido

imperativo	
—	unamos
une; no unas	unid; no unáis
una	unan

Words and expressions related to this verb
unido, unida united
los Estados Unidos the United States
la unión union, agreement, harmony

unirse to be united; to get married
La unión hace la fuerza There is strength in unity.

usar	Gerundio **usando**	Part. pas. **usado**

to use, to employ, to wear

The Seven Simple Tenses		The Seven Compound Tenses	
Singular	Plural	Singular	Plural
1 presente de indicativo		**8 perfecto de indicativo**	
uso	usamos	he usado	hemos usado
usas	usáis	has usado	habéis usado
usa	usan	ha usado	han usado
2 imperfecto de indicativo		**9 pluscuamperfecto de indicativo**	
usaba	usábamos	había usado	habíamos usado
usabas	usabais	habías usado	habíais usado
usaba	usaban	había usado	habían usado
3 pretérito		**10 pretérito anterior**	
usé	usamos	hube usado	hubimos usado
usaste	usasteis	hubiste usado	hubisteis usado
usó	usaron	hubo usado	hubieron usado
4 futuro		**11 futuro perfecto**	
usaré	usaremos	habré usado	habremos usado
usarás	usaréis	habrás usado	habréis usado
usará	usarán	habrá usado	habrán usado
5 potencial simple		**12 potencial compuesto**	
usaría	usaríamos	habría usado	habríamos usado
usarías	usaríais	habrías usado	habríais usado
usaría	usarían	habría usado	habrían usado
6 presente de subjuntivo		**13 perfecto de subjuntivo**	
use	usemos	haya usado	hayamos usado
uses	uséis	hayas usado	hayáis usado
use	usen	haya usado	hayan usado
7 imperfecto de subjuntivo		**14 pluscuamperfecto de subjuntivo**	
usara	usáramos	hubiera usado	hubiéramos usado
usaras	usarais	hubieras usado	hubierais usado
usara	usaran	hubiera usado	hubieran usado
OR		OR	
usase	usásemos	hubiese usado	hubiésemos usado
usases	usaseis	hubieses usado	hubieseis usado
usase	usasen	hubiese usado	hubiesen usado

imperativo	
—	usemos
usa; no uses	usad; no uséis
use	usen

Words and expressions related to this verb

¿**Usa usted guantes?** Do you wear gloves?
el uso use, usage
usado, usada used
desusar to disuse

en buen uso in good condition
en uso in use, in service
usar + inf. to be used + inf.

Gerundio **valiendo**   Part. pas. **valido**   **valer**

The Seven Simple Tenses		The Seven Compound Tenses	
Singular	Plural	Singular	Plural
1 presente de indicativo		8 perfecto de indicativo	
valgo	valemos	he valido	hemos valido
vales	valéis	has valido	habéis valido
vale	valen	ha valido	han valido
2 imperfecto de indicativo		9 pluscuamperfecto de indicativo	
valía	valíamos	había valido	habíamos valido
valías	valíais	habías valido	habíais valido
valía	valían	había valido	habían valido
3 pretérito		10 pretérito anterior	
valí	valimos	hube valido	hubimos valido
valiste	valisteis	hubiste valido	hubisteis valido
valió	valieron	hubo valido	hubieron valido
4 futuro		11 futuro perfecto	
valdré	valdremos	habré valido	habremos valido
valdrás	valdréis	habrás valido	habréis valido
valdrá	valdrán	habrá valido	habrán valido
5 potencial simple		12 potencial compuesto	
valdría	valdríamos	habría valido	habríamos valido
valdrías	valdríais	habrías valido	habríais valido
valdría	valdrían	habría valido	habrían valido
6 presente de subjuntivo		13 perfecto de subjuntivo	
valga	valgamos	haya valido	hayamos valido
valgas	valgáis	hayas valido	hayáis valido
valga	valgan	haya valido	hayan valido
7 imperfecto de subjuntivo		14 pluscuamperfecto de subjuntivo	
valiera	valiéramos	hubiera valido	hubiéramos valido
valieras	valierais	hubieras valido	hubierais valido
valiera	valieran	hubiera valido	hubieran valido
OR		OR	
valiese	valiésemos	hubiese valido	hubiésemos valido
valieses	valieseis	hubieses valido	hubieseis valido
valiese	valiesen	hubiese valido	hubiesen valido

	imperativo
—	valgamos
val *or* vale; no valgas	valed; no valgáis
valga	valgan

Sentences using this verb and words related to it
Más vale pájaro en mano que ciento volando.   A bird in the hand is worth two
 in the bush.
Más vale tarde que nunca.   Better late than never.
el valor   value, price, valor   **valorar**   to appraise, to increase the value

vencer	Gerundio **venciendo**	Part. pas. **vencido**

to conquer, to overcome, to defeat

The Seven Simple Tenses		The Seven Compound Tenses	
Singular	Plural	Singular	Plural
1 presente de indicativo		8 perfecto de indicativo	
venzo	vencemos	he vencido	hemos vencido
vences	vencéis	has vencido	habéis vencido
vence	vencen	ha vencido	han vencido
2 imperfecto de indicativo		9 pluscuamperfecto de indicativo	
vencía	vencíamos	había vencido	habíamos vencido
vencías	vencíais	habías vencido	habíais vencido
vencía	vencían	había vencido	habían vencido
3 pretérito		10 pretérito anterior	
vencí	vencimos	hube vencido	hubimos vencido
venciste	vencisteis	hubiste vencido	hubisteis vencido
venció	vencieron	hubo vencido	hubieron vencido
4 futuro		11 futuro perfecto	
venceré	venceremos	habré vencido	habremos vencido
vencerás	venceréis	habrás vencido	habréis vencido
vencerá	vencerán	habrá vencido	habrán vencido
5 potencial simple		12 potencial compuesto	
vencería	venceríamos	habría vencido	habríamos vencido
vencerías	venceríais	habrías vencido	habríais vencido
vencería	vencerían	habría vencido	habrían vencido
6 presente de subjuntivo		13 perfecto de subjuntivo	
venza	venzamos	haya vencido	hayamos vencido
venzas	venzáis	hayas vencido	hayáis vencido
venza	venzan	haya vencido	hayan vencido
7 imperfecto de subjuntivo		14 pluscuamperfecto de subjuntivo	
venciera	venciéramos	hubiera vencido	hubiéramos vencido
vencieras	vencierais	hubieras vencido	hubierais vencido
venciera	vencieran	hubiera vencido	hubieran vencido
OR		OR	
venciese	venciésemos	hubiese vencido	hubiésemos vencido
vencieses	vencieseis	hubieses vencido	hubieseis vencido
venciese	venciesen	hubiese vencido	hubiesen vencido

imperativo	
—	venzamos
vence; no venzas	venced; no venzáis
venza	venzan

Words and expressions related to this verb
vencedor, vencedora victor
vencible conquerable

darse por vencido to give in
vencerse to control oneself

The Seven Simple Tenses		The Seven Compound Tenses	
Singular	Plural	Singular	Plural
1 presente de indicativo		**8 perfecto de indicativo**	
vendo	vendemos	he vendido	hemos vendido
vendes	vendéis	has vendido	habéis vendido
vende	venden	ha vendido	han vendido
2 imperfecto de indicativo		**9 pluscuamperfecto de indicativo**	
vendía	vendíamos	había vendido	habíamos vendido
vendías	vendíais	habías vendido	habíais vendido
vendía	vendían	había vendido	habían vendido
3 pretérito		**10 pretérito anterior**	
vendí	vendimos	hube vendido	hubimos vendido
vendiste	vendisteis	hubiste vendido	hubisteis vendido
vendió	vendieron	hubo vendido	hubieron vendido
4 futuro		**11 futuro perfecto**	
venderé	venderemos	habré vendido	habremos vendido
venderás	venderéis	habrás vendido	habréis vendido
venderá	venderán	habrá vendido	habrán vendido
5 potencial simple		**12 potencial compuesto**	
vendería	venderíamos	habría vendido	habríamos vendido
venderías	venderíais	habrías vendido	habríais vendido
vendería	venderían	habría vendido	habrían vendido
6 presente de subjuntivo		**13 perfecto de subjuntivo**	
venda	vendamos	haya vendido	hayamos vendido
vendas	vendáis	hayas vendido	hayáis vendido
venda	vendan	haya vendido	hayan vendido
7 imperfecto de subjuntivo		**14 pluscuamperfecto de subjuntivo**	
vendiera	vendiéramos	hubiera vendido	hubiéramos vendido
vendieras	vendierais	hubieras vendido	hubierais vendido
vendiera	vendieran	hubiera vendido	hubieran vendido
OR		OR	
vendiese	vendiésemos	hubiese vendido	hubiésemos vendido
vendieses	vendieseis	hubieses vendido	hubieseis vendido
vendiese	vendiesen	hubiese vendido	hubiesen vendido

imperativo	
—	vendamos
vende; no vendas	vended; no vendáis
venda	vendan

Words and expressions related to this verb

vendedor, vendedora   seller, sales person
la venta   sale
venta al mayor, venta por mayor   wholesale
venta al menor, venta por menor   retail sale

vender a comisión   to sell on commission
vender al peso   to sell by weight
revender   to resell

venir   Gerundio **viniendo**   Part. pas. **venido**

to come

The Seven Simple Tenses		The Seven Compound Tenses	
Singular	Plural	Singular	Plural
1 presente de indicativo		8 perfecto de indicativo	
vengo	venimos	he venido	hemos venido
vienes	venís	has venido	habéis venido
viene	vienen	ha venido	han venido
2 imperfecto de indicativo		9 pluscuamperfecto de indicativo	
venía	veníamos	había venido	habíamos venido
venías	veníais	habías venido	habíais venido
venía	venían	había venido	habían venido
3 pretérito		10 pretérito anterior	
vine	vinimos	hube venido	hubimos venido
viniste	vinisteis	hubiste venido	hubisteis venido
vino	vinieron	hubo venido	hubieron venido
4 futuro		11 futuro perfecto	
vendré	vendremos	habré venido	habremos venido
vendrás	vendréis	habrás venido	habréis venido
vendrá	vendrán	habrá venido	habrán venido
5 potencial simple		12 potencial compuesto	
vendría	vendríamos	habría venido	habríamos venido
vendrías	vendríais	habrías venido	habríais venido
vendría	vendrían	habría venido	habrían venido
6 presente de subjuntivo		13 perfecto de subjuntivo	
venga	vengamos	haya venido	hayamos venido
vengas	vengáis	hayas venido	hayáis venido
venga	vengan	haya venido	hayan venido
7 imperfecto de subjuntivo		14 pluscuamperfecto de subjuntivo	
viniera	viniéramos	hubiera venido	hubiéramos venido
vinieras	vinierais	hubieras venido	hubierais venido
viniera	vinieran	hubiera venido	hubieran venido
OR		OR	
viniese	viniésemos	hubiese venido	hubiésemos venido
vinieses	vinieseis	hubieses venido	hubieseis venido
viniese	viniesen	hubiese venido	hubiesen venido

imperativo	
—	vengamos
ven; no vengas	venid; no vengáis
venga	vengan

Common idiomatic expressions using this verb

la semana que viene next week
el mes que viene next month
el porvenir the future
Venga lo que venga Come what may.

venir a las manos to come to blows
venir a buscar to come for, to get
en el *or* **en lo porvenir** hereafter

to see

The Seven Simple Tenses		The Seven Compound Tenses	
Singular	Plural	Singular	Plural
1 presente de indicativo		8 perfecto de indicativo	
veo	**vemos**	**he visto**	**hemos visto**
ves	**veis**	**has visto**	**habéis visto**
ve	**ven**	**ha visto**	**han visto**
2 imperfecto de indicativo		9 pluscuamperfecto de indicativo	
veía	**veíamos**	**había visto**	**habíamos visto**
veías	**veíais**	**habías visto**	**habíais visto**
veía	**veían**	**había visto**	**habían visto**
3 pretérito		10 pretérito anterior	
vi	**vimos**	**hube visto**	**hubimos visto**
viste	**visteis**	**hubiste visto**	**hubisteis visto**
vio	**vieron**	**hubo visto**	**hubieron visto**
4 futuro		11 futuro perfecto	
veré	**veremos**	**habré visto**	**habremos visto**
verás	**veréis**	**habrás visto**	**habréis visto**
verá	**verán**	**habrá visto**	**habrán visto**
5 potencial simple		12 potencial compuesto	
vería	**veríamos**	**habría visto**	**habríamos visto**
verías	**veríais**	**habrías visto**	**habríais visto**
vería	**verían**	**habría visto**	**habrían visto**
6 presente de subjuntivo		13 perfecto de subjuntivo	
vea	**veamos**	**haya visto**	**hayamos visto**
veas	**veáis**	**hayas visto**	**hayáis visto**
vea	**vean**	**haya visto**	**hayan visto**
7 imperfecto de subjuntivo		14 pluscuamperfecto de subjuntivo	
viera	**viéramos**	**hubiera visto**	**hubiéramos visto**
vieras	**vierais**	**hubieras visto**	**hubierais visto**
viera	**vieran**	**hubiera visto**	**hubieran visto**
OR		OR	
viese	**viésemos**	**hubiese visto**	**hubiésemos visto**
vieses	**vieseis**	**hubieses visto**	**hubieseis visto**
viese	**viesen**	**hubiese visto**	**hubiesen visto**

imperativo	
—	**veamos**
ve; no veas	**ved; no veáis**
vea	**vean**

Words and expressions related to this verb

¡**Vamos a ver!** Let's see
¡**A ver!** Let's see!
Ver es creer.   Seeing is believing.
la vista sight, seeing, view, vision

Está por ver It remains to be seen.
Es de ver It is worth seeing.
ver claro to see clearly
¡**Ya se ve!** Of course! Certainly!

vestirse   Gerundio **vistiéndose**   Part. pas. **vestido**

to dress oneself, to get dressed

The Seven Simple Tenses		The Seven Compound Tenses	
Singular	Plural	Singular	Plural
1 presente de indicativo		**8 perfecto de indicativo**	
me visto	nos vestimos	me he vestido	nos hemos vestido
te vistes	os vestís	te has vestido	os habéis vestido
se viste	se visten	se ha vestido	se han vestido
2 imperfecto de indicativo		**9 pluscuamperfecto de indicativo**	
me vestía	nos vestíamos	me había vestido	nos habíamos vestido
te vestías	os vestíais	te habías vestido	os habíais vestido
se vestía	se vestían	se había vestido	se habían vestido
3 pretérito		**10 pretérito anterior**	
me vestí	nos vestimos	me hube vestido	nos hubimos vestido
te vestiste	os vestisteis	te hubiste vestido	os hubisteis vestido
se vistió	se vistieron	se hubo vestido	se hubieron vestido
4 futuro		**11 futuro perfecto**	
me vestiré	nos vestiremos	me habré vestido	nos habremos vestido
te vestirás	os vestiréis	te habrás vestido	os habréis vestido
se vestirá	se vestirán	se habrá vestido	se habrán vestido
5 potencial simple		**12 potencial compuesto**	
me vestiría	nos vestiríamos	me habría vestido	nos habríamos vestido
te vestirías	os vestiríais	te habrías vestido	os habríais vestido
se vestiría	se vestirían	se habría vestido	se habrían vestido
6 presente de subjuntivo		**13 perfecto de subjuntivo**	
me vista	nos vistamos	me haya vestido	nos hayamos vestido
te vistas	os vistáis	te hayas vestido	os hayáis vestido
se vista	se vistan	se haya vestido	se hayan vestido
7 imperfecto de subjuntivo		**14 pluscuamperfecto de subjuntivo**	
me vistiera	nos vistiéramos	me hubiera vestido	nos hubiéramos vestido
te vistieras	os vistierais	te hubieras vestido	os hubierais vestido
se vistiera	se vistieran	se hubiera vestido	se hubieran vestido
OR		OR	
me vistiese	nos vistiésemos	me hubiese vestido	nos hubiésemos vestido
te vistieses	os vistieseis	te hubieses vestido	os hubieseis vestido
se vistiese	se vistiesen	se hubiese vestido	se hubiesen vestido

imperativo	
—	vistámonos; no nos vistamos
vístete; no te vistas	vestíos; no os vistáis
vístase; no se vista	vístanse; no se vistan

Words and expressions related to this verb

vestir to clothe, to dress
desvestirse to undress oneself,
    to get undressed
el vestido clothing, clothes, dress

bien vestido well dressed
vestir de uniforme to dress in uniform
vestir de blanco to dress in white
vestidos usados secondhand clothing

Gerundio **viajando**   Part. pas. **viajado**   **viajar**

to travel

The Seven Simple Tenses		The Seven Compound Tenses	
Singular	Plural	Singular	Plural
1 presente de indicativo		8 perfecto de indicativo	
viajo	viajamos	he viajado	hemos viajado
viajas	viajáis	has viajado	habéis viajado
viaja	viajan	ha viajado	han viajado
2 imperfecto de indicativo		9 pluscuamperfecto de indicativo	
viajaba	viajábamos	había viajado	habíamos viajado
viajabas	viajabais	habías viajado	habíais viajado
viajaba	viajaban	había viajado	habían viajado
3 pretérito		10 pretérito anterior	
viajé	viajamos	hube viajado	hubimos viajado
viajaste	viajasteis	hubiste viajado	hubisteis viajado
viajó	viajaron	hubo viajado	hubieron viajado
4 futuro		11 futuro perfecto	
viajaré	viajaremos	habré viajado	habremos viajado
viajarás	viajaréis	habrás viajado	habréis viajado
viajará	viajarán	habrá viajado	habrán viajado
5 potencial simple		12 potencial compuesto	
viajaría	viajaríamos	habría viajado	habríamos viajado
viajarías	viajaríais	habrías viajado	habríais viajado
viajaría	viajarían	habría viajado	habrían viajado
6 presente de subjuntivo		13 perfecto de subjuntivo	
viaje	viajemos	haya viajado	hayamos viajado
viajes	viajéis	hayas viajado	hayáis viajado
viaje	viajen	haya viajado	hayan viajado
7 imperfecto de subjuntivo		14 pluscuamperfecto de subjuntivo	
viajara	viajáramos	hubiera viajado	hubiéramos viajado
viajaras	viajarais	hubieras viajado	hubierais viajado
viajara	viajaran	hubiera viajado	hubieran viajado
OR		OR	
viajase	viajásemos	hubiese viajado	hubiésemos viajado
viajases	viajaseis	hubieses viajado	hubieseis viajado
viajase	viajasen	hubiese viajado	hubiesen viajado

imperativo		
—	viajemos	
viaja; no viajes	viajad; no viajéis	
viaje	viajen	

Words and expressions related to this verb

el viaje   trip
hacer un viaje   to take a trip
un viaje de ida y vuelta   round trip
viajero, viajera   traveler

¡Buen viaje!   Have a good trip!
un viaje de negocios   business trip
un viaje redondo   round trip
viajes espaciales   space travel

297

visitar Gerundio **visitando** Part. pas. **visitado**

to visit

The Seven Simple Tenses		The Seven Compound Tenses	
Singular	Plural	Singular	Plural
1 presente de indicativo		8 perfecto de indicativo	
visito	**visitamos**	**he visitado**	**hemos visitado**
visitas	**visitáis**	**has visitado**	**habéis visitado**
visita	**visitan**	**ha visitado**	**han visitado**
2 imperfecto de indicativo		9 pluscuamperfecto de indicativo	
visitaba	**visitábamos**	**había visitado**	**habíamos visitado**
visitabas	**visitabais**	**habías visitado**	**habíais visitado**
visitaba	**visitaban**	**había visitado**	**habían visitado**
3 pretérito		10 pretérito anterior	
visité	**visitamos**	**hube visitado**	**hubimos visitado**
visitaste	**visitasteis**	**hubiste visitado**	**hubisteis visitado**
visitó	**visitaron**	**hubo visitado**	**hubieron visitado**
4 futuro		11 futuro perfecto	
visitaré	**visitaremos**	**habré visitado**	**habremos visitado**
visitarás	**visitaréis**	**habrás visitado**	**habréis visitado**
visitará	**visitarán**	**habrá visitado**	**habrán visitado**
5 potencial simple		12 potencial compuesto	
visitaría	**visitaríamos**	**habría visitado**	**habríamos visitado**
visitarías	**visitaríais**	**habrías visitado**	**habríais visitado**
visitaría	**visitarían**	**habría visitado**	**habrían visitado**
6 presente de subjuntivo		13 perfecto de subjuntivo	
visite	**visitemos**	**haya visitado**	**hayamos visitado**
visites	**visitéis**	**hayas visitado**	**hayáis visitado**
visite	**visiten**	**haya visitado**	**hayan visitado**
7 imperfecto de subjuntivo		14 pluscuamperfecto de subjuntivo	
visitara	**visitáramos**	**hubiera visitado**	**hubiéramos visitado**
visitaras	**visitarais**	**hubieras visitado**	**hubierais visitado**
visitara	**visitaran**	**hubiera visitado**	**hubieran visitado**
OR		OR	
visitase	**visitásemos**	**hubiese visitado**	**hubiésemos visitado**
visitases	**visitaseis**	**hubieses visitado**	**hubieseis visitado**
visitase	**visitasen**	**hubiese visitado**	**hubiesen visitado**

imperativo	
—	**visitemos**
visita; no visites	**visitad; no visitéis**
visite	**visiten**

Words and expressions related to this verb
una visita visit
visitante visitor
visitarse to visit one another
hacer una visita to pay a call, a visit

una visitación visitation
pagar la visita to return a visit
tener visita to have company

The Seven Simple Tenses		The Seven Compound Tenses	
Singular	Plural	Singular	Plural

1   presente de indicativo

		8 perfecto de indicativo	
vivo	vivimos	he vivido	hemos vivido
vives	vivís	has vivido	habéis vivido
vive	viven	ha vivido	han vivido

2   imperfecto de indicativo

		9 pluscuamperfecto de indicativo	
vivía	vivíamos	había vivido	habíamos vivido
vivías	vivíais	habías vivido	habíais vivido
vivía	vivían	había vivido	habían vivido

3   pretérito

		10 pretérito anterior	
viví	vivimos	hube vivido	hubimos vivido
viviste	vivisteis	hubiste vivido	hubisteis vivido
vivió	vivieron	hubo vivido	hubieron vivido

4   futuro

		11 futuro perfecto	
viviré	viviremos	habré vivido	habremos vivido
vivirás	viviréis	habrás vivido	habréis vivido
vivirá	vivirán	habrá vivido	habrán vivido

5   potencial simple

		12 potencial compuesto	
viviría	viviríamos	habría vivido	habríamos vivido
vivirías	viviríais	habrías vivido	habríais vivido
viviría	vivirían	habría vivido	habrían vivido

6   presente de subjuntivo

		13 perfecto de subjuntivo	
viva	vivamos	haya vivido	hayamos vivido
vivas	viváis	hayas vivido	hayáis vivido
viva	vivan	haya vivido	hayan vivido

7   imperfecto de subjuntivo

		14 pluscuamperfecto de subjuntivo	
viviera	viviéramos	hubiera vivido	hubiéramos vivido
vivieras	vivierais	hubieras vivido	hubierais vivido
viviera	vivieran	hubiera vivido	hubieran vivido
OR		OR	
viviese	viviésemos	hubiese vivido	hubiésemos vivido
vivieses	vivieseis	hubieses vivido	hubieseis vivido
viviese	viviesen	hubiese vivido	hubiesen vivido

imperativo	
—	vivamos
vive; no vivas	vivid; no viváis
viva	vivan

Words and expressions related to this verb

vivir de to live on	**vivir del aire** to live on thin air
la vida life	**vivir para ver** to live and learn
en vida while living, while alive	**vivir a oscuras** to live in ignorance
ganarse la vida to earn one's living	**revivir** to revive

299

volar	Gerundio **volando**	Part. pas. **volado**

to fly

The Seven Simple Tenses		The Seven Compound Tenses	
Singular	Plural	Singular	Plural
1 presente de indicativo		8 perfecto de indicativo	
vuelo	volamos	he volado	hemos volado
vuelas	voláis	has volado	habéis volado
vuela	vuelan	ha volado	han volado
2 imperfecto de indicativo		9 pluscuamperfecto de indicativo	
volaba	volábamos	había volado	habíamos volado
volabas	volabais	habías volado	habíais volado
volaba	volaban	había volado	habían volado
3 pretérito		10 pretérito anterior	
volé	volamos	hube volado	hubimos volado
volaste	volasteis	hubiste volado	hubisteis volado
voló	volaron	hubo volado	hubieron volado
4 futuro		11 futuro perfecto	
volaré	volaremos	habré volado	habremos volado
volarás	volaréis	habrás volado	habréis volado
volará	volarán	habrá volado	habrán volado
5 potencial simple		12 potencial compuesto	
volaría	volaríamos	habría volado	habríamos volado
volarías	volaríais	habrías volado	habríais volado
volaría	volarían	habría volado	habrían volado
6 presente de subjuntivo		13 perfecto de subjuntivo	
vuele	volemos	haya volado	hayamos volado
vueles	voléis	hayas volado	hayáis volado
vuele	vuelen	haya volado	hayan volado
7 imperfecto de subjuntivo		14 pluscuamperfecto de subjuntivo	
volara	voláramos	hubiera volado	hubiéramos volado
volaras	volarais	hubieras volado	hubierais volado
volara	volaran	hubiera volado	hubieran volado
OR		OR	
volase	volásemos	hubiese volado	hubiésemos volado
volases	volaseis	hubieses volado	hubieseis volado
volase	volasen	hubiese volado	hubiesen volado

imperativo	
—	volemos
vuela; no vueles	volad; no voléis
vuele	vuelen

Words and expressions related to this verb
Más vale pájaro en mano que ciento volando.　A bird in the hand is worth two in the bush.
el vuelo　flight
el volante　steering wheel

Las horas vuelan.　The hours go flying by.
volear　to volley (a ball); **el voleo**　volley

to return, to go back

The Seven Simple Tenses		The Seven Compound Tenses	
Singular	Plural	Singular	Plural
1 presente de indicativo		8 perfecto de indicativo	
vuelvo	**volvemos**	**he vuelto**	**hemos vuelto**
vuelves	**volvéis**	**has vuelto**	**habéis vuelto**
vuelve	**vuelven**	**ha vuelto**	**han vuelto**
2 imperfecto de indicativo		9 pluscuamperfecto de indicativo	
volvía	**volvíamos**	**había vuelto**	**habíamos vuelto**
volvías	**volvíais**	**habías vuelto**	**habíais vuelto**
volvía	**volvían**	**había vuelto**	**habían vuelto**
3 pretérito		10 pretérito anterior	
volví	**volvimos**	**hube vuelto**	**hubimos vuelto**
volviste	**volvisteis**	**hubiste vuelto**	**hubisteis vuelto**
volvió	**volvieron**	**hubo vuelto**	**hubieron vuelto**
4 futuro		11 futuro perfecto	
volveré	**volveremos**	**habré vuelto**	**habremos vuelto**
volverás	**volveréis**	**habrás vuelto**	**habréis vuelto**
volverá	**volverán**	**habrá vuelto**	**habrán vuelto**
5 potencial simple		12 potencial compuesto	
volvería	**volveríamos**	**habría vuelto**	**habríamos vuelto**
volverías	**volveríais**	**habrías vuelto**	**habríais vuelto**
volvería	**volverían**	**habría vuelto**	**habrían vuelto**
6 presente de subjuntivo		13 perfecto de subjuntivo	
vuelva	**volvamos**	**haya vuelto**	**hayamos vuelto**
vuelvas	**volváis**	**hayas vuelto**	**hayáis vuelto**
vuelva	**vuelvan**	**haya vuelto**	**hayan vuelto**
7 imperfecto de subjuntivo		14 pluscuamperfecto de subjuntivo	
volviera	**volviéramos**	**hubiera vuelto**	**hubiéramos vuelto**
volvieras	**volvierais**	**hubieras vuelto**	**hubierais vuelto**
volviera	**volvieran**	**hubiera vuelto**	**hubieran vuelto**
OR		OR	
volviese	**volviésemos**	**hubiese vuelto**	**hubiésemos vuelto**
volvieses	**volvieseis**	**hubieses vuelto**	**hubieseis vuelto**
volviese	**volviesen**	**hubiese vuelto**	**hubiesen vuelto**

imperativo

—	**volvamos**
vuelve; no vuelvas	**volved; no volváis**
vuelva	**vuelvan**

Common idiomatic expressions using this verb
volver en sí   to regain consciousness, to come to
volver sobre sus pasos   to retrace one's steps
una vuelta   turn, revolution, turning
dar una vuelta   to take a stroll
See also **devolver** and **revolver.**

un revólver   revolver, pistol
revolver   to revolve, to shake (up), to turn around
revolverse   to turn around (oneself)

Index of English-Spanish verbs

The purpose of this index is to give you instantly the Spanish verb for the English verb you have in mind to use. This saves you time if you do not have a standard English-Spanish word dictionary at your fingertips.

When you find the Spanish verb you need through the English verb, look up its verb forms in this book where all verbs are listed alphabetically at the top of each page. If it is not listed among the 301 verbs in this book, consult the list of over 1,000 Spanish verbs conjugated like model verbs among the 301 which begins on p. 310. If it is not listed there, consult my more comprehensive book, *501 Spanish verbs fully conjugated in all the tenses,* 4th edition.

A

able, to be **poder,** 240
absolve **absolver,** 2
abstain **abstenerse,** 3
accept **aceptar,** 7
accompany **acompañar,** 11
accuse **acusar,** 17
acquainted with, to be **conocer,** 89
acquire **adquirir,** 21
acquit **absolver,** 2
add **añadir,** 32
admire **admirar,** 18
admit **admitir,** 19; **permitir,** 239
adore **adorar,** 20
advance **avanzar,** 49
advantage, to take
  aprovecharse, 39
advise **aconsejar,** 12; **advertir,** 22
affirm **asegurar,** 41
agree upon **acordar,** 13
aid **ayudar,** 51
allow **dejar,** 112; **permitir,** 239
angry, to become **enfadarse,** 142;
  enojarse, 143
annoy **aburrir,** 4
answer **contestar,** 94;
  responder, 261
appear **aparecer,** 34
appear (seem) **parecer,** 230
applaud **aplaudir,** 35
approach **acercarse,** 9
arrange **ordenar,** 225;
  organizar, 226
arrive **llegar,** 199
ask **preguntar,** 245; **rogar,** 263
ask for **pedir,** 235; **rogar,** 263
assert **asegurar,** 41

assist **ayudar,** 51
assure **asegurar,** 41
attach **unir,** 289
attack **atacar,** 46
attain **conseguir,** 90
attend **asistir,** 43
attest **certificar,** 76
avail oneself **aprovecharse,** 39
awaken **despertar,** 122

B

bake **cocer,** 77
baptize **bautizar,** 56
bath, to take a **bañarse** 54
bathe oneself **bañarse,** 54
be **estar,** 156; **ser,** 273
be able **poder,** 240
be accustomed **acostumbrar,** 16;
  soler, 275
be acquainted with **conocer,** 89
be bored **aburrirse,** 5
be born **nacer,** 212
be called **llamarse,** 198
be contained in **caber,** 63
be enough **bastar,** 55
be frightened **asustarse,** 45
be glad **alegrarse,** 28
be important **importar,** 181
be in the habit of **acostumbrar,** 16;
  soler, 275
be lacking **faltar,** 161
be mistaken **equivocarse,** 149
be named **llamarse,** 198
be pleasing **agradar,** 24
be pleasing to **gustar,** 173

dispense **dispensar,** 129
distinguish **distinguir,** 130
distribute **dispensar,** 129
divide **partir,** 232
do **hacer,** 177
do (something) right **acertar,** 10
doubt **dudar,** 134
draw near **acercarse,** 9
draw (pull) **tirar,** 282
dream **soñar,** 276
dress oneself **vestirse,** 296
drink **beber,** 57
drive (a car) **conducir,** 87
dry **secar,** 268
dwell **habitar,** 175

E

earn **ganar,** 167
eat **comer,** 83
eat breakfast **desayunarse,** 115
eat lunch **almorzar,** 29
eat supper **cenar,** 74
elect **elegir,** 137
employ **emplear,** 139; **usar,** 290
enclose **incluir,** 182
encounter **encontrar,** 140
end **acabar,** 6; **terminar,** 281
enjoy **gozar,** 169
enjoy oneself **divertirse,** 131
enliven **despertar,** 122
enter **entrar,** 146
enunciate **enunciar,** 147
erase **borrar,** 59
err **errar,** 150
escape **huir,** 180
escort **acompañar,** 11
excuse **dispensar,** 129
exempt **dispensar,** 129
exercise **ejercer,** 136
exert **ejercer,** 136
expect **aguardar,** 26; **esperar,** 155
explain **explicar,** 159
express **expresar,** 160

F

fall **caer,** 64
fall asleep **dormirse,** 133
fasten **fijar,** 164
fatigue **cansar,** 68
feel **sentir(se),** 271-2
feel sorry **sentir,** 271

felicitate **felicitar,** 162
fill **llenar,** 200
find **encontrar(se),** 140-1;
    hallar, 178
find out **averiguar,** 50
finish **acabar,** 6
fit (into) **caber,** 63
fix (fasten) **fijar,** 164
flee **huir,** 180
fling **arrojar,** 40; **echar,** 135;
    lanzar, 191; **tirar,** 282
flow **correr,** 99
fly **volar,** 300
follow **seguir,** 269
forbid **defender,** 111
forget **olvidar,** 224
frighten **asustar,** 44
fry **freír,** 166
fulfill **cumplir,** 106
fun of, to make **burlarse,** 61
function (machine) **marchar,** 204

G

gain **ganar,** 167
get **adquirir,** 21; **conseguir,** 90;
    obtener, 218; **recibir,** 255;
    sacar, 266
get angry **enojarse,** 143
get cross **enojarse,** 143
get dressed **vestirse,** 296
get married **casarse,** 72
get tired **cansarse,** 72
get undressed **desvestirse,** 125
get up **levantarse,** 196
get weary **cansarse,** 69
give **dar,** 107
give back (an object) **devolver,** 127
give notice **advertir,** 22
give warning **advertir,** 22
go **ir,** 188
go away **irse,** 189;
    marcharse, 205
go back **volver,** 301
go down **bajar,** 53
go in **entrar,** 146
go out **salir,** 267
go through **atravesar,** 47
go to bed **acostarse,** 15
go with **acompañar,** 11
good-by, to say **despedirse,** 121
good time, to have a **divertirse,** 131
grab **coger,** 78
grant **admitir,** 19; **permitir,** 239

grasp **asir,** 42; **coger,** 78
grieve **gemir,** 168
groan **gemir,** 168
grow **crecer,** 101
grow tired **aburrirse,** 5
grow weary **aburrirse,** 5
growl **gruñir,** 171
grumble **gruñir,** 171
grunt **gruñir,** 171
guide **guiar,** 172

H

habit, to be in the **soler,** 275
hang up **colgar,** 80
happen **pasar,** 233
harm **herir,** 179
hasten **apresurarse,** 38
have (as an auxiliary verb)
  haber, 174
have (hold) **tener,** 280
have a good time **divertirse,** 131
have breakfast **desayunarse,** 115
have lunch **almorzar,** 29
have supper **cenar,** 74
have the custom of **soler,** 275
have to **deber,** 108
hear **oír,** 222
heave **alzar,** 30
help **ayudar,** 51
hit the mark **acertar,** 10
hit upon **acertar,** 10
hold **tener,** 280
hope **esperar,** 155
hurl **arrojar,** 40; **echar,** 135;
  lanzar, 191
hurry **apresurarse,** 38
hurt **herir,** 179
hustle **bullir,** 60

I

include **incluir,** 182
indicate **indicar,** 183
induce **inducir,** 184
influence **inducir,** 184; **influir,** 185
inhabit **habitar,** 175
inquire **averiguar,** 50;
  preguntar, 245
insist **insistir,** 186
insure **asegurar,** 41
introduce **introducir,** 187
investigate **averiguar,** 50

J

join **unir,** 289

K

keep (a promise) **cumplir,** 106
keep quiet **callarse,** 65
keep still **callarse,** 65
kill **matar,** 206
know **conocer,** 89; **saber,** 265
know how **saber,** 265

L

labor **trabajar,** 285
lack **faltar,** 161
lacking, to be **faltar,** 161
laugh **reír,** 258
launch **lanzar,** 191
lead **conducir,** 87; **guiar,** 172
learn **aprender,** 37
leave **dejar,** 112; **marcharse,** 205;
  partir, 232; **salir,** 267
leave (go out) **salir,** 267
lend **prestar,** 247
let **dejar,** 112
let go **dejar,** 112
lie down **acostarse,** 15
lie (tell a lie) **mentir,** 207
lift **alzar,** 30; **levantar,** 195
like (be pleasing to) **gustar,** 173
listen (to) **escuchar,** 153
live **vivir,** 299
live in (reside) **habitar,** 175
load **cargar,** 71
look **mirar,** 208
look alike **parecerse,** 231
look at **mirar,** 208
look for **buscar,** 62
lose **perder,** 238
love **amar,** 31
lunch **almorzar,** 29

M

make **hacer,** 177
make fun of **burlarse,** 61
make up (constitute) **constituir,** 91
march **marchar,** 204
marry **casarse,** 72
matter **importar,** 181

meet **encontrar(se)**, 140-1
miss **errar**, 150; **faltar**, 161
mistaken, to be **equivocarse**, 149
moan **gemir**, 168
move along **caminar**, 67
must **deber**, 108

N

name **llamar**, 197
named, to be **llamarse**, 198
need **faltar**, 161; **necesitar**, 214

O

obey **obedecer**, 217
obtain **adquirir**, 21; **conseguir**, 90;
    obtener, 218; **recibir**, 255
occupy **ocupar**, 219
occur **ocurrir**, 220
offer **ofrecer**, 221
open **abrir**, 1
order **ordenar**, 225
organize **organizar**, 226
overcome **vencer**, 292
overtake **alcanzar**, 27
owe **deber**, 108

P

parade **pasearse**, 234
pass (by) **pasar**, 233
pay **pagar**, 228
pay attention **fijarse**, 165
permit **dejar**, 112; **permitir**, 239
persist **insistir**, 186
persuade **inducir**, 184
pick up **alzar**, 30
pitch **echar**, 135
pitch (a ball) **tirar**, 282
place **colocar**, 81; **poner**, 241
place near **acercar**, 8
play (a game) **jugar**, 190
play (music or a musical instrument)
    tocar, 283
play (a sport) **jugar**, 190
please **agradar**, 24
point out **enseñar**, 144; **indicar**,
    183; **mostrar**, 211
poke fun at **burlarse**, 61
possession, to take **apoderarse**, 36
power, to take **apoderarse**, 36

practice **practicar**, 243
prefer **preferir**, 244
prepare **preparar**, 246
prohibit **defender**, 111
pronounce **pronunciar**, 250
protect **proteger**, 251
prove **demostrar**, 114; **probar**, 248
pull **tirar**, 282
purchase **comprar**, 85
pursue **seguir**, 269
put **colocar**, 81; **poner**, 241
put in order **ordenar**, 225
put on **ponerse**, 242

Q

quarrel **reñir**, 259
question **preguntar**, 245
quiet, to keep **callarse**, 65

R

race **correr**, 99
rain **llover**, 203
raise (breed) **criar**, 103
raise (lift) **levantar**, 195
raise (prices) **alzar**, 30
reach one's birthday **cumplir**, 106
read **leer**, 194
rear (bring up, breed) **criar**, 103
recall **recordar**, 256
receive **recibir**, 255
refer **referir**, 257
refund **devolver**, 127
register (a letter) **certificar**, 76
regret **sentir**, 271
rejoice **alegrarse**, 28
relate **contar**, 93; **referir**, 257
remain **quedarse**, 252
remember **acordarse**, 14;
    recordar, 256
remove (oneself) **quitarse**, 254
repeat **repetir**, 260
reply **contestar**, 94; **responder**, 261
request **pedir**, 235; **rogar**, 263
require **exigir**, 158
resemble each other **parecerse**, 231
reside **habitar**, 175
respond **responder**, 261
rest **descansar**, 116
return (an object) **devolver**, 127
return (go back) **volver**, 301
revolve **revolver**, 262

ridicule **burlarse,** 61
rise (get up) **levantarse,** 196
roam **errar,** 150
run **correr,** 99
run away **huir,** 180
run (machine) **marchar,** 204
run through **atravesar,** 47
rush **apresurarse,** 38

S

say **decir,** 110
say good-by to **despedirse,** 121
scare **asustar,** 44
scatter **esparcir,** 154
scent **oler,** 223
scold **reñir,** 259
scream **gritar,** 170
see **ver,** 295
seek **buscar,** 62
seem **parecer,** 230
seize **asir,** 42; **coger,** 78
select **escoger,** 151; **elegir,** 137
sell **vender,** 293
send **enviar,** 148
serve **servir,** 274
set (of sun) **ponerse,** 242
set up (organize) **organizar,** 226
settle in **fijarse,** 165
shatter **romper,** 264
shave oneself **afeitarse,** 23
shoot (a gun) **tirar,** 282
shout **gritar,** 170
show **enseñar,** 144; **mostrar,** 211
show up **aparecer,** 34
shriek **gritar,** 170
sing **cantar,** 70
sit down **sentarse,** 270
sketch **describir,** 117
sleep **dormir,** 132
slip away **huir,** 180
smell **oler,** 223
smile **sonreír,** 277
snow **nevar,** 216
speak **hablar,** 176
spend (time) **pasar,** 233
split **partir,** 232
spread (scatter) **esparcir,** 154
start **comenzar,** 82; **empezar,** 138
state **enunciar,** 147
stay **quedarse,** 252
still, to keep **callarse,** 65
stop (oneself) **detenerse,** 126;
  pararse, 229

study **estudiar,** 157
stumble **tropezar,** 288
succeed (in) **acertar,** 10
suffice **bastar,** 55
supplicate **rogar,** 263
swim **nadar,** 213

T

take **coger,** 78; **tomar,** 284
take a bath **bañarse,** 54
take a walk **pasearse,** 234
take advantage **aprovecharse,** 39
take away **llevar,** 201
take leave of **despedirse,** 121
take notice (of) **advertir,** 22;
  fijarse, 165
take off (clothing) **quitarse,** 254
take out (something) **sacar,** 266
take possession **apoderarse,** 36
take power **apoderarse,** 36
talk **hablar,** 176
teach **enseñar,** 144
tear (break) **romper,** 264
telegraph **telegrafiar,** 279
telephone **telfonear,** 278
tell **contar,** 93; **decir,** 110
tell a lie **mentir,** 207
terminate **terminar,** 281
test **probar,** 248
thank **agradecer,** 25
think **pensar,** 237
throw **arrojar,** 40; **echar,** 135;
  lanzar, 191; **tirar,** 282
tire **cansar,** 68
touch **tocar,** 283
translate **traducir,** 286
travel **viajar,** 297
try **probar,** 248
try on **probar(se),** 248-9
turn around (revolve)
  revolver, 262
turn over **revolver,** 262
turn upside down **revolver,** 262

U

understand **comprender,** 86;
  entender, 145
undress (oneself) **desvestirse,** 125
unite **unir,** 289
urge **exigir,** 158
use **usar,** 290; **emplear,** 139

V

venture **osar,** 227; **atreverse,** 48
vex **aburrir,** 4
visit **visitar,** 298

W

wait for **aguardar,** 26;
 esperar, 155
wake up (oneself) **despertarse,** 123
walk **andar,** 33; **caminar,** 67;
 marchar, 204
walk, to take a **pasearse,** 234
wander **errar,** 150
want **desear,** 119; **querer,** 253

wanting, to be **faltar,** 161
warn **advertir,** 22
wash oneself **lavarse,** 193
watch **mirar,** 208
wear **llevar,** 201; **usar,** 290
weary **cansar,** 68
weep **llorar,** 202
whine **llorar,** 202
win **ganar,** 167
wipe dry **secar,** 268
wish **desear,** 119; **querer,** 253
withdraw **quitarse,** 254
work **trabajar,** 285
worship **adorar,** 20
worth, to be **valer,** 291
wound **herir,** 179
write **escribir,** 152

Index of common irregular Spanish verb forms identified by infinitive

The purpose of this index is to help you identify those verb forms that cannot be readily identified because they are irregular in some way. For example, if you come across the verb form *fui* (which is very common) in your Spanish readings, this index will tell you that *fui* is a form of *ir* or *ser.* Then you look up *ir* and *ser* in this book and you will find that verb form on the page where all the forms of *ir* and *ser* are given.

Verb forms whose first three or four letters are the same as the infinitive have not been included because they can easily be identified by referring to the alphabetical listing of the 301 verbs in this book.

A

abierto **abrir**
acierto, *etc.* **acertar**
acuerdo, *etc.* **acordar**
acuesto, *etc.*
 acostarse
alce, *etc.* **alzar**
ase, *etc.* **asir**
asgo, *etc.* **asir**
ate, *etc.* **atar**

C

caí, *etc.* **caer**
caía, *etc.* **caer**
caigo, *etc.* **caer**
cayera, *etc.* **caer**
cierro, *etc.* **cerrar**

cojo, *etc.* **coger**
cuece, *etc.* **cocer**
cuelgo, *etc.* **colgar**
cuento, *etc.* **contar**
cuesta, *etc.* **costar**
cuezo, *etc.* **cocer**
cupiera, *etc.* **caber**

D

da, *etc.* **dar**
dad **dar**
dé **dar**
demos **dar**
des **dar**
di, *etc.* **dar, decir**
dice, *etc.* **decir**
dicho **decir**
diciendo **decir**

diera, *etc.* **dar**
diese, *etc.* **dar**
digo, *etc.* **decir**
dije, *etc.* **decir**
dimos, *etc.* **dar**
dio **dar**
diré, *etc.* **decir**
diría, *etc.* **decir**
doy **dar**
duermo, *etc.* **dormir**
durmamos **dormir**
durmiendo **dormir**

E

eliges, *etc.* **elegir**
eligiendo **elegir**
eligiera, *etc.* **elegir**
elijo, *etc.* **elegir**

era, *etc.* **ser**
eres **ser**
es **ser**

F

fíe, *etc.* **fiar**
fío, *etc.* **fiar**
friendo **freír**
friera, *etc.* **freír**
frío, *etc.* **freír**
frito **freír**
fue, *etc.* **ir, ser**
fuera, *etc.* **ir, ser**
fuese, *etc.* **ir, ser**
fui, *etc.* **ir, ser**

G

gima, *etc.* **gemir**
gimiendo **gemir**
gimiera, *etc.* **gemir**
gimiese, *etc.* **gemir**
gimo, *etc.* **gemir**
goce, *etc.* **gozar**
gocé **gozar**

H

ha **haber**
habré, *etc.* **haber**
haga, *etc.* **hacer**
hago, *etc.* **hacer**
han **haber**
haría, *etc.* **hacer**
has **haber**
haya, *etc.* **haber**
haz **hacer**
he **haber**
hé **haber**
hecho **hacer**
hemos **haber**
hice, *etc.* **hacer**
hiciera, *etc.* **hacer**
hiciese, *etc.* **hacer**
hiera, *etc.* **herir**
hiero, *etc.* **herir**
hiramos **herir**
hiriendo **herir**
hiriera, *etc.* **herir**
hiriese, *etc.* **herir**
hizo **hacer**
hube, *etc.* **haber**
hubiera, *etc.* **haber**

hubiese, *etc.* **haber**
huela, *etc.* **oler**
huelo, *etc.* **oler**
huya, *etc.* **huir**
huyendo **huir**
huyera, *etc.* **huir**
huyese, *etc.* **huir**
huyo, *etc.* **huir**

I

iba, *etc.* **ir**
id **ir**
ido **ir**
idos **irse**

J

juego, *etc.* **jugar**
juegue, *etc.* **jugar**

L

lea, *etc.* **leer**
leído **leer**
leo, *etc.* **leer**
leyendo **leer**
leyera, *etc.* **leer**
leyese, *etc.* **leer**
llueva **llover**
llueve **llover**

M

mienta, *etc.* **mentir**
miento, *etc.* **mentir**
mintiendo **mentir**
mintiera, *etc.* **mentir**
mintiese, *etc.* **mentir**
muerda, *etc.* **morder**
muerdo, *etc.* **morder**
muero, *etc.* **morir**
muerto **morir**
muestre, *etc.* **mostrar**
muestro, *etc.* **mostrar**
muramos **morir**
muriendo **morir**
muriera, *etc.* **morir**
muriese, *etc.* **morir**

N

nazca, *etc.* **nacer**
nazco, *etc.* **nacer**

niego, *etc.* **negar**
niegue, *etc.* **negar**
nieva **nevar**
nieve **nevar**

O

oíd, *etc.* **oír**
oiga, *etc.* **oír**
oigo, *etc.* **oír**
oliendo **oler**
oliera, *etc.* **oler**
oliese, *etc.* **oler**
oye, *etc.* **oír**
oyendo **oír**
oyera, *etc.* **oír**
oyese, *etc.* **oír**

P

pida, *etc.* **pedir**
pidamos **pedir**
pidiendo **pedir**
pidiera, *etc.* **pedir**
pidiese, *etc.* **pedir**
pidiese, *etc.* **pedir**
pido, *etc.* **pedir**
pienso, *etc.* **pensar**
pierda, *etc.* **perder**
pierdo, *etc.* **perder**
ponga, *etc.* **poner**
pongámonos
    ponerse
ponte **ponerse**
pruebe, *etc.* **probar**
pruebo, *etc.* **probar**
pude, *etc.* **poder**
pudiendo **poder**
pudiera, *etc.* **poder**
pudiese, *etc.* **poder**
puedo, *etc.* **poder**
puesto **poner**
puse, *etc.* **poner**
pusiera, *etc.* **poner**
pusiese, *etc.* **poner**

Q

quepo, *etc.* **caber**
quiero, *etc.* **querer**
quise, *etc.* **querer**
quisiera, *etc.* **querer**
quisiese, *etc.* **querer**

R

ría, *etc*. **reír**
raimos **reír**
riendo **reír**
riera, *etc*. **reír**
riese, *etc*. **reír**
riña, *etc*. **reñir**
riñendo **reñir**
riñera, *etc*. **reñir**
riñese, *etc*. **reñir**
riño, *etc*. **reñir**
río, *etc*. **reír**
roto **romper**
ruego, *etc*. **rogar**
ruegue, *etc*. **rogar**

S

saque, *etc*. **sacar**
sé **saber, ser**
sea, *etc*. **ser**
sed **ser**
sepa, *etc*. **saber**
seque, *etc*. **secar**
sido **ser**
siendo **ser**
siento, *etc*. **sentar,
  sentir**
sigo, *etc*. **seguir**
siguiendo **seguir**
siguira, *etc*. **seguir**
siguiese, *etc*. **segur**

sintiendo **sentir**
sintiera, *etc*. **sentir**
sintiese, *etc*. **sentir**
sintió **sentir**
sirviendo **servir**
sirvo, *etc*. **servir**
sois **ser**
somos **ser**
son **ser**
soy **ser**
suela, *etc*. **soler**
suelo, *etc*. **soler**
sueño, *etc*. **soñar**
supe, *etc*. **saber**
supiera, *etc*. **saber**
supiese, *etc*. **saber**

T

tienes, *etc*. **tener**
toque, *etc*. **tocar**
traigo, *etc*. **traer**
traje, *etc*. **traer**
tuve, *etc*. **tener**

U

uno, *etc*. **unir**

V

va **ir**
vais **ir**

vámonos **irse**
vamos **ir**
van **ir**
vas **ir**
vaya, *etc*. **ir**
ve **ir, ver**
vea, *etc*. **ver**
ved **ver**
vendré, *etc*. **venir**
venga, vengo **venir**
veo, *etc*. **ver**
ves, *etc*. **ver**
vete, *etc*. **irse**
vi, *etc*. **ver**
viendo, *etc*. **ver**
viene, *etc*. **venir**
viera, *etc*. **ver**
viese, *etc*. **ver**
vimos, *etc*. **ver**
vine, *etc*. **venir**
vio **ver**
viste **ver, vestir**
vistiendo **vestir**
vistiese **vestir(se)**
visto **ver, vestir**
voy **ir**
vuelo, *etc*. **volar**
vuelto **volver**
vuelvo, *etc*. **volver**

Y

yendo **ir**
yerro, *etc*. **errar**

Over 1,000 Spanish verbs conjugated like model verbs among the 301

The number after each verb is the page number in this book where a model verb is shown fully conjugated.

enojar 143
enrollar 178
ensañar 144
ensayar 51
ensayer 51
ensillar 178
ensuciar 250
entablar 176
entablillar 178
enterar 146
enterrar 237
entramar 31
entregar 228
entretener 280
entrever 295
entristecer 101
envestir 296
envolver 301
equipar 219
equiparar 219
equivaler 291
equivocar 149
escapar 219
escarpar 219
esforzar 29
espantar 7
especificar 76
esposar 17
establecer 101
estatuir 91
estimar 31
estrechar 135
evitar 170
evocar 283
exagerar 176
examinar 67
exceptuar 95
excitar 170
exclamar 31
excluir 182
excusar 17
exhalar 178
existir 299
expedir 235
explorar 202
exponer 241
exprimir 299
extender 111
extinguir 130
extraer 287

F

fabricar 62
facilitar 162
facturar 73
falsear 139
falsificar 76
fallar 178

fallecer 89
familiarizar 226
fanatizar 226
fatigar 228
favorecer 101
festejar 53
fingir 158
firmar 31
flechar 135
florecer 101
fluir 185
formar 31
formular 176
fornicar 76
forzar 29
fotografiar 279
frisar 160
fruir 180
fumar 31
funcionar 67

G

galantear 139
galibar 6
gallear 139
gandujar 285
gandulear 139
gañir 171
garabatear 278
garlar 176
gastar 176
generar 20
germinar 67
gobernar 237
golpear 119
golpetear 119
gormar 31
graduar 95
granar 167
gratar 206
guardar 176
guisar 17

H

habituar 95
hacinar 67
hadar 213
halagar 228
hambrear 139
haraganear 278
hastiar 103
heñir 259
heredar 176
holgar 80
honrar 20
hurtar 7

I

identificar 76
ignorar 20
igualar 176
iludir 35
iluminar 67
ilusionar 225
ilustrar 146
imaginar 67
imbuir 97
imbursar 17
imitar 170
impedir 235
implicar 62
implorar 202
imponer 241
impresionar 67
incendiar 66
incitar 175
inclinar 67
inducir 87
inferir 257
influenciar 250
informar 31
iniciar 250
inocular 176
inscribir 152
inscribirse 152, 296
insinuar 95
inspirar 18
instituir 91
instruir 92
interpretar 247
inventar 7
investigar 228
investir 296
invitar 170
invocar 283
irritar 170

J

jabonar 284
jacarear 139
jactarse 28
jalar 176
jamar 31
jarapotear 139
jetar 206
juntar 245
jurar 176

L

ladrar 85
lagrimar 67
lamentar 7

313

AT A GLANCE Series

Barron's new series gives travelers instant access to the most common idiomatic expressions used during a trip—the kind one needs to know instantly, like "Where can I find a taxi?" and "How much does this cost?"

Organized by situation (arrival, customs, hotel, health, etc.) and containing additional information about pronunciation, grammar, shopping plus special facts about the country, these most convenient, pocket-size reference books will be the tourist's most helpful guides.

Special features include a bilingual dictionary section with over 2000 key words, maps of each country and major cities, and helpful phonetic spellings throughout.

Each book paperback, 256 pp., 3 3/4" x 6"

ARABIC AT A GLANCE, Wise (0-7641-1248-1) $8.95, Can. $12.50
CHINESE AT A GLANCE, Seligman & Chen (0-7641-1250-3) $8.95, Can. $12.50
FRENCH AT A GLANCE, 4th, Stein & Wald (0-7641-2512-5) $6.95, Can. $9.95
GERMAN AT A GLANCE, 4th, Strutz (0-7641-2516-8) $6.95, Can. $9.95
ITALIAN AT A GLANCE, 4th, Costantino (0-7641-2513-3) $6.95, Can. $9.95
JAPANESE AT A GLANCE, 3rd, Akiyama (0-7641-0320-2) $8.95, Can. $11.95
KOREAN AT A GLANCE, Holt (0-8120-3998-X) $8.95, Can. $11.95
RUSSIAN AT A GLANCE, Beyer (0-7641-1251-1) $8.95, Can. $12.50
SPANISH AT A GLANCE, 4th, Wald (0-7641-2514-1) $6.95, Can. $9.95

Barron's Educational Series, Inc.
250 Wireless Blvd., Hauppauge, NY 11788
Call toll-free: 1-800-645-3476
In Canada: Georgetown Book Warehouse, 34 Armstrong Ave.
Georgetown, Ont. L7G 4R9, Call toll-free: 1-800-247-7160
Visit our website at: www.barronseduc.com

Books may be purchased at your bookstore, or by mail from Barron's. Enclose check or money order for total amount plus sales tax where applicable and 18% for postage and handling (minimum charge $5.95). Prices subject to change without notice.

Can. $ = Canadian dollars

(#25) R 6/03

3 Foreign Language Series From Barron's!

The **VERB SERIES** offers more than 300 of the most frequently used verbs. The **GRAMMAR SERIES** provides complete coverage of the elements of grammar. The **VOCABULARY SERIES** offers more than 3500 words and phrases with their foreign language translations. Each book: paperback.

FRENCH GRAMMAR
ISBN: 0-7641-1351-8
$5.95, Can. $8.50

GERMAN GRAMMAR
ISBN: 0-8120-4296-4
$6.95, Can. $8.95

ITALIAN GRAMMAR
ISBN: 0-8120-4311-1
$6.95, Can. $8.95

JAPANESE GRAMMAR
ISBN: 0-7641-2061-1
$6.95, Can. $9.95

RUSSIAN GRAMMAR
ISBN: 0-8120-4902-0
$6.95, Can. $8.95

SPANISH GRAMMAR
ISBN: 0-7641-1615-0
$5.95, Can. $8.50

FRENCH VERBS
ISBN: 0-7641-1356-9
$5.95, Can. $8.50

GERMAN VERBS
ISBN: 0-8120-4310-3
$7.95, Can. $11.50

ITALIAN VERBS
ISBN: 0-7641-2063-8
$5.95, Can. $8.50

SPANISH VERBS
ISBN: 0-7641-1357-7
$5.95, Can. $8.50

FRENCH VOCABULARY
ISBN: 0-7641-1999-0
$6.95, Can. $9.95

GERMAN VOCABULARY
ISBN: 0-8120-4497-5
$6.95, Can. $8.95

ITALIAN VOCABULARY
ISBN: 0-7641-2190-0
$6.95, Can. $9.95

JAPANESE VOCABULARY
ISBN: 0-8120-4743-5
$6.95, Can. $8.95

RUSSIAN VOCABULARY
ISBN: 0-8120-1554-1
$6.95, Can. $8.95

SPANISH VOCABULARY
ISBN: 0-7641-1985-3
$6.95, Can. $9.95

Barron's Educational Series, Inc.
250 Wireless Blvd., Hauppauge, NY 11788 • Call toll-free: 1-800-645-3476
In Canada: Georgetown Book Warehouse
34 Armstrong Ave., Georgetown, Ontario L7G 4R9 • Call toll-free: 1-800-247-7160
www.barronseduc.com
Can. $ = Canadian dollars